Collins

Your

THE COMPLETE
PSHE PROGRAMME

CHOICE

Key Stage 4

KATE DANIELS & SIMON FOSTER

William Collins's dream of knowledge for all began with the publication of his first book in 1819.
A self-educated mill worker, he not only enriched millions of lives, but also founded a flourishing publishing house. Today, staying true to this spirit, Collins books are packed with inspiration, innovation and practical expertise. They place you at the centre of a world of possibility and give you exactly what you need to explore it.

Collins. Freedom to teach.

Published by Collins

An imprint of HarperCollins*Publishers*
The News Building, 1 London Bridge Street,
London SE1 9GF, UK

HarperCollins*Publishers*
1st Floor, Watermarque Building,
Ringsend Road, Dublin 4, Ireland

Browse the complete Collins catalogue at
www.collins.co.uk

© HarperCollins*Publishers* Limited 2021

10 9 8 7 6 5 4 3 2

ISBN 978-0-00-843401-4

British Library Cataloguing-in-Publication Data

A catalogue record for this publication is available from the British Library.

Authors: Kate Daniels and Simon Foster
Publisher: Katie Sergeant
Product manager: Catherine Martin
Development and copy editor: Jo Kemp
Proofreader: Sonya Newland
Cover designer: Amparo Barrera, Kneath Associates and Ken Vail Graphic Design
Internal designer: Hugh Hillyard-Parker
Production controller: Katharine Willard
Printed and bound by Ashford Colour Press Ltd.

MIX
Paper from
responsible sources
FSC www.fsc.org **FSC™ C007454**

This book is produced from independently certified FSC™ paper to ensure responsible forest management.

For more information visit:
www.harpercollins.co.uk/green

Contents

Introduction: How to use this resource

The *Your Choice Complete PSHE Programme for KS4* provides ready-made, editable teaching resources to help you to deliver effective lessons in relationships and sex education (RSE), health education and PSHE.

This introduction explains how the lesson plans are structured so they can be adapted to fit a school's own curriculum for RSHE/PHSE. Lessons have been designed to offer a flexible approach to learning, which can be tailored to the needs of your students and your school's timetable.

How the *Your Choice* resources meet the requirements for RSHE and PSHE

The *Your Choice Complete PSHE Programme for KS4* and *Your Choice Books One*, *Two* and *Three* for KS3 together cover all the statutory requirements for RSHE and PSHE for secondary schools. The unit overviews on pages vii–xv demonstrate how the *Your Choice* resources meet the requirements of the statutory RSHE curriculum and cover objectives from the PSHE Association's Programme of Study, providing a coherent programme of lessons for Years 10 and 11. The curriculum coverage map, included as part of the download that supports the printed pack, shows where each statutory objective has been covered across the series as a whole.

Planning your KS4 curriculum

This resource has been written to support students in Years 10 and 11. Schools should decide which topics are taught in each year and in which order, according to the particular needs of their context, cohort and the individuals within each cohort, and following the RSHE policies agreed with parents and governors. Whatever approach a school adopts, there is enough material to provide a full two-year course.

In planning the course for their school, senior managers and/or the PSHE coordinator can follow the ten steps set out in the 'Roadmap to statutory RSE' prepared by the Sex Education Forum and the PSHE Association. To help guide planning, it can be useful for the PSHE coordinator to talk to local organisations or public service providers such as the police, to gather information on the particular issues that may affect young people in your area.

Each unit in this pack focuses on a specific topic and is divided into a series of lessons. The lessons are planned so that there is a clear progression to develop the students' knowledge and understanding of the topic, building on the knowledge already developed through *Your Choice* at KS3.

Each lesson plan is presented on a single sheet, so that it can be duplicated and given to all the teachers in the team responsible for delivering RSHE and PSHE. Coordinators can decide whether to do this as part of a planning meeting with team members or whether to distribute them to individual teachers. Either way, it is important that both coordinators and teachers familiarise themselves with all the topics, resources and links to be used, and to make sure they are teaching to the specific needs of each class/individual. It is also important to discuss and adapt each lesson where needed to accommodate these needs and to make each lesson fully inclusive. Prior to teaching these lessons, we advise teachers to discuss individuals in each class with their Senior Leadership Team and/or safeguarding lead to fully understand students' requirements, including any emotional/physical health issues, child protection issues, vulnerabilities or special educational needs.

Assessment throughout is crucial to track each student's progress. A baseline needs assessment will inform you of what students know or do not know about a topic, continuous assessment during lessons will enable you to follow students' understanding, and assessment at the end of a lesson or unit will inform your next steps in teaching.

Most of the lessons are supported with a photocopiable worksheet or worksheets, and all lessons are supported with a PowerPoint to help teachers present key information to the class and to share scenarios, images and questions for discussion.

Setting guidelines for PSHE lessons

The course is designed to give students opportunities to explore a range of topics in depth, providing them with essential information to enable them to have informed and frank discussions, and to share their views. Students are encouraged to use exploratory talk to help them to formulate their own opinions. In this way, they will be empowered to make their own choices in real life.

Because many of the topics are sensitive, it is essential that discussion of these areas be controlled to safeguard students who might otherwise find them upsetting. Students have the right not to reveal anything that they do not want to reveal and should not be pressurised to talk about things they do not want to talk about. When group or paired discussions are being set up, teachers need to think carefully about which students will be working together, in which lessons they will allow students to choose their own groups and in which lessons they will decide the groups.

Since so many of the activities involve discussion, it is vital to make students aware of how they are expected to behave across all lessons and discussions. This is covered in Worksheet 1.1a, a 'working agreement' for PSHE lessons. It is recommended that this worksheet is used at the beginning of Year 10 to establish rules for students to follow, and that it should be referred back to regularly.

Teachers and support staff should carefully monitor paired work, group discussions and role-plays to ensure these guidelines and ground rules are being followed and to notice any children who may need further support or who may present concerns that need flagging to the Senior Leadership Team and safeguarding lead. It is important for teachers to signpost within each lesson where students can go for further information or support, both within the school and outside school via websites, helplines, supporting organisations or relevant public services.

Using the lesson plans, worksheets and PowerPoints

The lessons are divided into sections to offer you the flexibility to fit the learning into your timetable in a way that suits you – so each one could be taught as a complete one-hour lesson or across several shorter periods, for example in form time. Each lesson plan follows the same structure:

- The **learning objectives** are stated clearly at the top of the lesson plan, with details of any **resources** that are required for the activities. (Note some research tasks require internet access.) **Key vocabulary** is also listed.

- A **Get them thinking!** starter is provided to stimulate discussion and allow baseline assessments.

- The **Core learning** section is 25 minutes long. This main part of the lesson offers a range of suggested activities, with guidance on when and how to use the supporting PowerPoints and worksheet(s). The overall aim of the worksheets is to increase students' understanding of a topic. The worksheets often provide scaffolding for students' thinking and the PowerPoints support and extend the learning using a mix of information, scenarios and images.

- The **Additional learning** section offers an extra 15 minutes of learning and activities.

- The five-minute **plenary** is a chance to reflect and pull learning together, and the additional **extension** and **home learning** activities can further enrich and extend the learning.

- Finally, an **assessment opportunity** has been included within each lesson in order that each student's understanding and progress can be checked and recorded throughout.

- Often the lesson plan includes **useful links** to organisations offering further support, to websites or articles, and sometimes to short videos. (Please note, these links are live at the time of going to press. If a link to specific content has expired when you come to use the lesson plan, please try searching on the main website using relevant search terms. Teachers should review each of the recommendations to determine whether they are appropriate to use or pass on to their students.)

Knowing each individual's needs prior to the lesson will allow you to differentiate so that each lesson can be fully inclusive for all. As noted above, extra challenge and support has been built into the lesson plans and worksheets to help you support the full range of learners.

The *Your Choice* course is designed to prepare students for life in contemporary society, presenting them with information on key issues that will enable them to develop not only their understanding, but also the skills necessary to make informed choices and thus to lead safe and healthy lives. We hope that the resources will lead to lessons involving a lively exchange of views that both teachers and students will enjoy and find rewarding.

Simon Foster and Kate Daniels

Unit overviews

Lesson title	Learning objectives	Curriculum objectives
Unit 1 You and your life		
Lesson 1: Knowing ourselves	• To understand the concept of emotional intelligence • To learn how to become more self-aware • To recognise emotions in ourselves and others	**Mental wellbeing (HE)** • how to talk about their emotions accurately and sensitively, using appropriate vocabulary • how to recognise the early signs of mental wellbeing concerns • how to critically evaluate when something they do or are involved in has a positive or negative effect on their own or others' mental health
Lesson 2: Families	• To learn about what makes a healthy family and how dynamics change over time • To understand when a relationship in a family might be unsafe or unhealthy and how to seek advice and support for yourself or others	**Families (RSE)** • that there are different types of committed, stable relationships • how these relationships might contribute to human happiness and their importance for bringing up children • the roles and responsibilities of parents with respect to raising of children, including the characteristics of successful parenting • how to: determine whether other children, adults or sources of information are trustworthy; judge when a family, friend, intimate or other relationship is unsafe (and to recognise in others' relationships); and, how to seek help or advice, including reporting concerns about others, if needed.
Unit 2: You and your relationships		
Lesson 1: Respecting others	• To consider the importance of respect • To understand how respect can be shown • To learn to recognise disrespectful habits or behaviours and how to change them	**Respectful relationships, including friendships (RSE)** • the characteristics of positive and healthy friendships (in all contexts, including online) including: trust, respect, honesty, kindness, generosity, boundaries, privacy, consent and the management of conflict, reconciliation and ending relationships. This includes different (non-sexual) types of relationship. • practical steps they can take in a range of different contexts to improve or support respectful relationships • that some types of behaviour within relationships are criminal, including violent behaviour and coercive control **Being safe (RSE)** • the concepts of, and laws relating to, sexual consent, sexual exploitation, abuse, grooming, coercion, harassment, rape, domestic abuse, forced marriage, honour-based violence and FGM, and how these can affect current and future relationships • how people can actively communicate and recognise consent from others, including sexual consent, and how and when consent can be withdrawn (in all contexts, including online)
Lesson 2: Healthy relationships and dating	• To understand that there are different types of intimate, consensual relationships • To understand the realities of romantic relationships • To consider how to use online dating apps or social media sites safely	**Respectful relationships, including friendships (RSE)** • the characteristics of positive and healthy friendships (in all contexts, including online) including: trust, respect, honesty, kindness, generosity, boundaries, privacy, consent and the management of conflict, reconciliation and ending relationships. This includes different (non-sexual) types of relationship. • practical steps they can take in a range of different contexts to improve or support respectful relationships **Intimate and sexual relationships, including sexual health (RSE)** • how to recognise the characteristics and positive aspects of healthy one-to-one intimate relationships, which include mutual respect, consent, loyalty, trust, shared interests and outlook, sex and friendship **Being safe (RSE)** • how people can actively communicate and recognise consent from others, including sexual consent, and how and when consent can be withdrawn (in all contexts, including online)

Lesson title	Learning objectives	Curriculum objectives
Lesson 3: Unhealthy relationships	• To recognise the 'red flags' in a relationship online or offline • To understand what domestic abuse is and what help is available • To spot the signs of sexual exploitation and grooming	**Respectful relationships, including friendships (RSE)** • that some types of behaviour within relationships are criminal, including violent behaviour and coercive control • what constitutes sexual harrassment and sexual violence and why these are always unacceptable

Unit 3: You and society

Lesson title	Learning objectives	Curriculum objectives
Lesson 1: Equality	• To understand what equality is • To learn about the nine protected characteristics • To understand discrimination and stereotyping	**Respectful relationships, including friendships (RSE)** • how stereotypes, in particular stereotypes based on sex, gender, race, religion, sexual orientation or disability, can cause damage (e.g. how they might normalise non-consensual behaviour or encourage prejudice) • that in school and in wider society they can expect to be treated with respect by others, and that in turn they should show due respect to others, including people in positions of authority and due tolerance of other people's beliefs • the legal rights and responsibilities regarding equality (particularly with reference to the protected characteristics as defined in the Equality Act 2010) and that everyone is unique and equal.
Lesson 2: Social injustice	• To understand what social injustice means • To learn about unconscious bias • To learn about the Black Lives Matter movement	**Respectful relationships, including friendships (RSE)** • how stereotypes, in particular stereotypes based on sex, gender, race, religion, sexual orientation or disability, can cause damage (e.g. how they might normalise non-consensual behaviour or encourage prejudice) • that in school or wider society they can expect to be treated with respect by others, and that in turn they should show due respect to others, including people in positions of authority and due tolerance of other people's beliefs

Unit 4: You and your values

Lesson title	Learning objectives	Curriculum objectives
Lesson 1: Voting systems and elections	• To understand the voting process • To understand how we elect an MP at a general election. • To understand different voting systems	No relevant objectives
Lesson 2: Pressure groups	• To understand what a pressure group is • To understand the four different types of pressure group • To understand what a new social movement is	No relevant objectives

Unit 5: You and your future

Lesson title	Learning objectives	Curriculum objectives
Lesson 1: You and your career	• To learn what a career is • To understand how skills, interests and knowledge contribute to careers	**Learning skills (PSHE Association Living in the Wider World)** • L3. how their strengths, interests, skills and qualities are changing and how these relate to future career choices **Choices and pathways (PSHE Association Living in the Wider World)** • L6. about the information, advice and guidance available to them on next steps and careers; how to access appropriate support and opportunities employability **Work and career (PSHE Association Living in the Wider World)** • L10. to develop their career identity, including values in relation to work, and how to maximise their chances when applying for education or employment opportunities

Lesson title	Learning objectives	Curriculum objectives
Lesson 2: You and your options	• To understand the differences between the options available after 16 for education and training for students in England, Wales, Northern Ireland and Scotland	**Choices and pathways (PSHE Association Living in the Wider World)** • L4. about the range of opportunities available to them for career progression, including in education, training and employment • L6. about the information, advice and guidance available to them on next steps and careers; how to access appropriate support and opportunities
Lesson 3: You, work and technology	• To learn how labour markets have changed over the last 100 years and how they may change in the future • To look at the effects of automation and AI • To examine how the manufacturing sector is declining and the service sector is growing	**Choices and pathways (PSHE Association Living in the Wider World)** • L5. about the need to challenge stereotypes about particular career pathways, maintain high aspirations for their future and embrace new opportunities **Work and career (PSHE Association Living in the Wider World)** • L7. about the labour market, local, national and international employment opportunities • L8. about employment sectors and types, and changing patterns of employment
Lesson 4: You and your workplace skills	• To identify acceptable and unacceptable behaviour at work • To distinguish between workplace bullying and harassment, with examples	**Learning skills (PSHE Association Living in the Wider World)** • L1. to evaluate and further develop their study and employability skills **Work and career (PSHE Association Living in the Wider World)** • L7. about the labour market, local, national and international employment opportunities • L9. to research, secure and take full advantage of any opportunities for work experience that are available **Employment rights and responsibilities (PSHE Association Living in the Wider World)** • L13. the skills and attributes to manage rights and responsibilities at work including health and safety procedures • L15. about the unacceptability and illegality of discrimination and harassment in the workplace, and how to challenge it

Unit 6: Your healthy body

Lesson title	Learning objectives	Curriculum objectives
Lesson 1: Keeping physically healthy	• To understand the different elements required to keep ourselves physically fit and healthy • To understand the importance of personal hygiene and self-examination	**Physical health and fitness (HE)** • the positive associations between physical activity and promotion of mental wellbeing, including as an approach to combat stress • the characteristics and evidence of what constitutes a healthy lifestyle, maintaining a healthy weight, including the links between an inactive lifestyle and ill health, including cancer and cardiovascular ill-health **Healthy eating (HE)** • how to maintain healthy eating and the links between a poor diet and health risks, including tooth decay and cancer **Health and prevention (HE)** • (late secondary) the benefits of regular self-examination and screening • the importance of sufficient good quality sleep for good health and how a lack of sleep can affect weight, mood and ability to learn
Lesson 2: Your self-image	• To consider what is a healthy and unhealthy self-image • To evaluate our own self-image and where we can go for help • To consider the concept of a 'perfect' body	**Internet safety and harms (HE)** • the similarities and differences between the online world and the physical world, including: the impact of unhealthy or obsessive comparison with others online (including through setting unrealistic expectations for body image) **Changing adolescent body (HE)** • the main changes which take place in males and females, and the implications for emotional and physical health
Lesson 3: First aid	• To learn basic life support first aid skills	**Basic first aid (HE)** • life-saving skills [...]

Lesson title	Learning objectives	Curriculum objectives
Unit 7: Your healthy mind		
Lesson 1: Mental health	• To understand what mental health is • To learn how to recognise the early signs of mental health concerns • To know what to do to help ourselves and others	**Mental wellbeing (HE)** • that happiness is linked to being connected to others • how to recognise the early signs of mental wellbeing concerns • how to critically evaluate when something they do or are involved in has a positive or negative effect on their own or others' mental health • the benefits and importance of physical exercise, time outdoors, community participation and voluntary and service-based activities on mental wellbeing and happiness
Lesson 2: Exam stress	• To understand stress and how to deal with it • To consider a range of different studying techniques • To learn some simple mindfulness and meditation techniques	**Mental wellbeing (HE)** • how to talk about their emotions accurately and sensitively, using appropriate vocabulary • that happiness is linked to being connected to others • how to critically evaluate when something they do or are involved in has a positive or negative effect on their own or others' mental health • the benefits and importance of physical exercise, time outdoors, community participation and voluntary and service-based activities on mental wellbeing and happiness **Physical health and fitness (HE)** • the positive associations between physical activity and promotion of mental wellbeing, including as an approach to combat stress
Unit 8: You and your money		
Lesson 1: Getting paid	• To understand that there are different types of job contract • To understand payslips • To know what income tax and National Insurance are, and the difference between net and gross pay	**Financial choices (PSHE Association Living in the Wider World)** • L21. to evaluate the financial advantages, disadvantages and risks of different models of contractual terms, including self-employment full-time, part-time and zero-hours contracts
Lesson 2: Becoming financially independent	• To distinguish between the short run and the long run, and between variable and fixed costs • To understand what fraud and phishing are and to discuss the best fraud prevention measures • To plan a budget for independent financial living	**Financial choices (PSHE Association Living in the Wider World)** • L16. how to effectively budget, including the benefits of saving • L17. how to effectively make financial decisions, including recognising the opportunities and challenges involved in taking financial risks • L18. to recognise and manage the range of influences on their financial decisions
Unit 9: Sexual relationships		
Lesson 1: Sex and relationship responsibilities	• To be able to explain the laws around sex • To learn about LGBTQI+ rights • To explore the characteristics and qualities needed for healthy intimate relationships	**Being safe (RSE)** • the concepts of, and laws relating to, sexual consent, sexual exploitation, abuse, grooming, coercion, harassment, rape, domestic abuse, forced marriage, honour-based violence and FGM, and how these can affect current and future relationships **Intimate and sexual relationships, including sexual health (RSE)** • how to recognise the characteristics and positive aspects of healthy one-to-one intimate relationships, which include mutual respect, consent, loyalty, trust, shared interests and outlook, sex and friendship • how to get further advice, including how and where to access confidential sexual and reproductive health advice and treatment

Lesson title	Learning objectives	Curriculum objectives
Lesson 2: Keeping sexually healthy	• To learn which contraception methods prevent STIs • To learn about the full range of contraception available and show their understanding • To begin to make responsible choices for their ongoing sexual health	**Intimate and sexual relationships, including sexual health (RSE)** • the facts about the full range of contraceptive choices, efficacy and options available • how the different sexually transmitted infections (STIs), including HIV/AIDS, are transmitted, how risk can be reduced through safer sex (including through condom use) and the importance of and facts about testing • how to get further advice, including how and where to access confidential sexual and reproductive health advice and treatment **Changing adolescent body (HE)** • key facts about [...] menstrual wellbeing
Lesson 3: Understanding fertility, infertility and different routes to parenthood	• To understand the terms fertility, infertility and miscarriage • To understand the different options for starting a family • To learn where to get reproductive health advice and treatment	**Intimate and sexual relationships, including sexual health (RSE)** • the facts about reproductive health, including fertility, and the potential impact of lifestyle on fertility for men and women and menopause • the facts around pregnancy including miscarriage • how to get further advice, including how and where to access confidential sexual and reproductive health advice and treatment
Unit 10: Sexually explicit content online		
Lesson 1: Sexual content online	• To know what indecent content online is and what the laws around these are for young people • To know where to report anything indecent online • To understand the laws around youth produced sexual imagery	**Internet safety and harms (HE)** • how to identify harmful behaviours online (including bullying, abuse or harassment) and how to report, or find support, if they have been affected by those behaviours **Online and media (RSE)** • about online risks, including that any material someone provides to another has the potential to be shared online and the difficulty of removing potentially compromising material placed online • that sharing and viewing indecent images of children (including those created by children) is a criminal offence which carries severe penalties including jail • what to do and where to get support to report material or manage issues online
Lesson 2: Pornography	• To understand the laws around pornography • To learn about the impacts and dangers of viewing pornography	**Online and media (RSE)** • the impact of viewing harmful content • that specifically sexually explicit material, e.g. pornography presents a distorted picture of sexual behaviours, can damage the way people see themselves in relation to others and negatively affect how they behave towards sexual partners • that sharing and viewing indecent images of children (including those created by children) is a criminal offence which carries severe penalties including jail **Internet safety and harms (HE)** • how to identify harmful behaviours online (including bullying, abuse or harassment) and how to report, or find support, if they have been affected by those behaviours

Lesson title	Learning objectives	Curriculum objectives
Unit 11: Sexuality and gender identity		
Lesson 1: Gender	• To understand the difference between sex, gender and gender identity • To learn what intersex means • To consider how gender stereotypes affect us all	**Respectful relationships, including friendships (RSE)** • how stereotypes, in particular stereotypes based on sex, gender, race, religion, sexual orientation or disability, can cause damage (e.g. how they might normalise non-consensual behaviour or encourage prejudice). • that in school and in wider society they can expect to be treated with respect by others, and that in turn they should show due respect to others, including people in positions of authority and due tolerance of other people's beliefs • the legal rights and responsibilities regarding equality (particularly with reference to the protected characteristics as defined in the Equality Act 2010) and that everyone is unique and equal.
Lesson 2: Sexuality	• To understand what sexuality is • To learn about different sexual identities • To consider how a young person can prepare to come out safely when they feel ready	**Respectful relationships, including friendships (RSE)** • how stereotypes, in particular stereotypes based on sex, gender, race, religion, sexual orientation or disability, can cause damage (e.g. how they might normalise non-consensual behaviour or encourage prejudice) • that in school and in wider society they can expect to be treated with respect by others, and that in turn they should show due respect to others, including people in positions of authority, and due tolerance of people's beliefs • the legal rights and responsibilities regarding equality (particularly with reference to the protected characteristics as defined in the Equality Act 2010) and that everyone is unique and equal.
Unit 12: You and your choices		
Lesson 1: Addiction	• To understand why people might take drugs and drink alcohol • To understand the wider impacts of taking drugs • To learn about addictions and recovery	**Drugs, alcohol and tobacco (HE)** • the facts about legal and illegal drugs and their associated risks, including the link between drug use, and the associated risks, including the link to the serious mental health conditions • the physical and psychological risks associated with alcohol consumption and what constitutes low risk alcohol consumption in adulthood • the physical and psychological consequences of addiction, including alcohol dependency • awareness of the dangers of drugs which are prescribed but still present serious health risks
Lesson 2: Alcohol, drugs, tobacco and the law	• To learn about the laws around smoking tobacco • To learn about the laws around alcohol • To learn about the laws around illegal drugs	**Drugs, alcohol and tobacco (HE)** • the law relating to the supply and possession of illegal substances • the physical and psychological consequences of addiction, including alcohol dependency • the facts about the harms from smoking tobacco (particularly the link to lung cancer), the benefits of quitting and how to access support to do so.
Lesson 3: Illegal drugs and crime	• To learn that drug-taking can be linked to criminal activities • To learn to recognise the signs of criminal exploitation	**Drugs, alcohol and tobacco (HE)** • the law relating to the supply and possession of illegal substances • the physical and psychological consequences of addiction, including alcohol dependency **Social influences (PSHE Association Relationships)** • R37. to recognise situations where they are being adversely influenced, or are at risk, due to being part of a particular group or gang; strategies to access appropriate help • R38. factors which contribute to young people becoming involved in serious organised crime, including cybercrime

Lesson title	Learning objectives	Curriculum objectives
Unit 13: You online		
Lesson 1: Our online lives	• To understand what your digital footprint is • To understand the right to privacy and its limits • To know what the right to be forgotten is	**Internet safety and harms (HE)** • the similarities and differences between the online world and the physical world, including: [...] how advertising and information is targeted at them and how to be a discerning consumer of information online **Online and media (RSE)** • their rights, responsibilities and opportunities online, including that the same expectations of behaviour apply in all contexts, including online • what to do and where to get support to report material or manage issues online • the impact of viewing harmful content • how information and data is generated, collected, shared and used online • not to provide material to others that they would not want shared further and not to share personal material which is sent to them **Media literacy and digital resilience (PSHE Association Living in the Wider World)** • L12. strategies to manage their online presence and its impact on career opportunities
Lesson 2: Online bullying	• To understand what online bullying is • To understand the laws on online bullying • To consider the effects of online bullying	**Respectful relationships, including friendships (RSE)** • about different types of bullying (including cyberbullying), the impact of bullying, responsibilities of bystanders to report bullying and how and where to get help **Online and media (RSE)** • their rights, responsibilities and opportunities online, including that the same expectations of behaviour apply in all contexts, including online • not to provide material to others that they would not want shared further and not to share personal material which is sent to them **Internet safety and harms (HE)** • how to identify harmful behaviours online (including bullying, abuse or harassment) and how to report, or find support, if they have been affected by those behaviours
Unit 14: You as a consumer		
Lesson 1: Consumer rights, advice and awareness	• To understand what a nudge is and why shops use it • To know what consumers' rights are, and to be aware of the main three rights • To understand how goods can be returned and in what condition and circumstances	No relevant objectives

Lesson title	Learning objectives	Curriculum objectives
Lesson 2: Advertising, data and consumer ethics	• To think about the different ways organisations collect digital data • To understand what GDPR is and how it limits the collection and use of data within the UK	**Online and media (RSE)** • how information and data is generated, collected, shared and used online. **Financial choices (PSHE Association Living in the Wider World)** • L20. the skills to challenge or seek support for financial exploitation in different contexts including online **Media literacy and digital resilience (PSHE Association Living in the Wider World)** • L22. that there are positive and safe ways to create and share content online and the opportunities this offers • L23. strategies for protecting and enhancing their personal and professional reputation online • L24. that social media may disproportionately feature exaggerated or inaccurate information about situations, or extreme viewpoints; to recognise why and how this may influence opinions and perceptions of people and events • L25. how personal data is generated, collected and shared, including by individuals, and the consequences of this
Unit 15: You and the future of our planet		
Lesson 1: You and the environment	• To understand what an ecosystem is • To understand what biodiversity is • To know what ecologism is and examine the difference between shallow and deep ecologists	No relevant objectives
Lesson 2: Power and pollution	• To distinguish between the different types of pollution • To examine the relative merits of nuclear power and renewable energy • To look at the work of Extinction Rebellion	No relevant objectives
Unit 16: Fake news and disinformation		
Lesson 1: Fake news	• To define what fake news is • To discuss whether social media companies should be responsible for the content they publish • To identify common flaws in critical thinking	**Media literacy and digital resilience (PSHE Association Living in the Wider World)** • L27. strategies to critically assess bias, reliability and accuracy in digital content • L29. to recognise the shared responsibility to challenge extreme viewpoints that incite violence or hate and ways to respond to anything that causes anxiety or concern
Lesson 2: The news agenda, censorship and free speech	• To understand what bias is • To understand how the news agenda is shaped • To understand what censorship is and discuss when it is and is not appropriate	No relevant objectives

Lesson title	Learning objectives	Curriculum objectives
Unit 17: You and the law		
Lesson 1: How laws affect your life	• To understand the different ages at which different laws apply to children in the UK • To understand what the age of criminal responsibility is in the UK • To understand what a youth court is and where you can get legal advice in the UK	No relevant objectives
Lesson 2: You and the police	• To understand the age of criminality • To understand what a police caution is and an ABSO are • To understand how a youth detention centre is an alternative to prison for those aged 17 or below	No relevant objectives
Unit 18: You and the world		
Lesson 1: Local, regional and national government	• To understand the three main types of local council • To examine devolution and regional government in the UK • To understand the role of the civil service	No relevant objectives
Lesson 2: International organisations	• To recognise that international organisations have a profound influence on many areas of our lives • To learn about the aims, objectives and membership of four international organisations	No relevant objectives
Unit 19: You and the global economy		
Lesson 1: You and economic issues	• To distinguish between a free market, a mixed economy and a command economy • To understand what economic growth is • To examine other ways of measuring economic progress	No relevant objectives
Lesson 2: The World Trade Organization	• To understand what trade is • To learn about the WTO, its role and objectives • To evaluate whether free trade is good or bad in the UK	No relevant objectives
Unit 20: Reflecting on your choices		
Lesson 1: Reflection and feedback	• To understand how reflection helps us to improve • To recall three positive experiences and identify what these memories have in common • To understand how to give feedback effectively	**Learning skills (PSHE Association Living in the Wider World)** • L2. to evaluate their own personal strengths and areas for development and use this to inform goal setting
Lesson 2: Your choices	• To learn how to balance breathing • To learn how to set SMART targets • To learn how to set PURE targets	**Learning skills (PSHE Association Living in the Wider World)** • L2. to evaluate their own personal strengths and areas for development and use this to inform goal setting

Learning objectives:

- To understand the concept of emotional intelligence
- To learn how to become more self-aware
- To recognise emotions in ourselves and others

Resources:

- PowerPoint 1.1
- Worksheets 1.1a, 1.1b (plus a copy enlarged for you) and 1.1c
- Link to KS3: Book 3, Units 1.2 and 13.4

Key vocabulary:

physical, emotional, spiritual, IQ (Intelligence Quotient), EQ (Emotional Quotient), EI (Emotional Intelligence), self-awareness

Get them thinking! (5 mins)

- Ask students: 'Who are you?' Encourage them to think in terms of who they are physically, emotionally and perhaps spiritually. Ask them to share their ideas if they feel comfortable doing so.

Core learning (25 mins)

- Create a working agreement with your class, using **Worksheet 1.1a** as a template if you wish.

- Ask: 'What was the aspect of ourselves we felt most comfortable talking about?' *(Usually basic physical appearance; less for spiritual and even less for our emotional selves.)* 'Why do you think this is?'

- Show **Slide 1** about IQ and EQ. Go through it with the class and then ask what they think is more important for success – emotional or academic intelligence. Let them explore this through discussion.

- Show **Slide 2** and then allow students time, working in pairs, to go through the examples of emotional intelligence on **Slide 3**. *(Statements 2, 3 and 5 show emotional intelligence.)*

- Hand out **Worksheet 1.1b**. Use an enlarged copy to model how to complete it, being as honest as you can while remaining professional. Then allow time for students to complete it independently.

- Put students into pairs to share their work and then collect in the worksheets for further assessment.

Additional learning (15 mins)

- Ask: 'What are the hardest emotions to share with others and why?' Lead a class discussion and then show **Slide 4,** or show it earlier if they need prompts. Explain that often we don't share honestly how we feel because we worry what people will think. Add that no emotion is 'bad', but some might feel harder to deal with or share than others.

- Hand out **Worksheet 1.1c** and ask students to complete it. *(They should consider body language, facial expressions and what they are, or are not, saying.)*

- Ask: 'What can we do to support one another to be more open about our feelings?' *(Examples might include noticing, trusting our gut instincts, choosing good moments to ask if someone is OK, telling a trusted adult if you are worried about someone.)* Now ask: 'What can we do to help ourselves?' *(Notice things about ourselves, be honest, trust our gut instincts, tell a trusted friend or adult if we are worried.)*

Plenary (5 mins)

- Get students into a circle. Encourage them to offer positive affirmations/things they like about the more emotionally intelligent aspects of people in the group (preferably not always their best friends!). Work around the circle, but allow students to opt out if they wish.

- Use **Slide 5** to remind students that emotions are normal but that if they are worried, talking to someone is both valuable and important.

Assessment

- Use **Worksheet 1.1c** to assess students' understanding. It is important to note any students who may reveal areas of concern – you may wish to discuss this further with your SLT.

Extension or home learning

- Home learning: Ask students to research emotional intelligence further, looking at Daniel Goleman's five main areas of emotional intelligence on **Slide 2**.

- Extension: Using this research, ask students to consider their personal skills in these areas – what they are good at, what they need to develop further and how they can do this. *(e.g. I need to understand myself more, so I am going to keep a diary about my feelings for a week, and then review it.)*

Worksheet 1.1a Our working agreement

1. We understand that we all come to these lessons with different knowledge and understanding.

2. We will respect each other even if or when we don't agree.

3. We will listen attentively and kindly to one another and remain open-minded.

4. We will make sure that anything confidential or controversial that is shared in these lessons is kept private – we will not talk about people outside the classroom.

5. We will not use real names or examples.

6. We have the right to opt out of discussions or activities if we feel uncomfortable.

7. We will consider the language we use and sensitively consider those around us.

8. We will make the space safe for everyone to learn and to ask any questions they need answered without feeling judged.

9. We understand that getting things wrong can be an important part of the learning process and will support each other with this.

10. We will talk to an adult we trust if anything in these lessons makes us feel uncomfortable, worried or upset.

Signed: .... **Date:** ....

Suggestions for additional rules:

....

....

....

....

....

....

....

....

Worksheet 1.1b Knowing ourselves

Understanding ourselves – building our emotional intelligence

Complete each section as honestly as you can.

What do you do well? (What are your strengths, skills and things you are proud of? For example, do you admit when you make mistakes? Are you someone who does not give up?)

1. ....

2. ....

3. ....

4. ....

What do you feel are areas that you could improve in? (This could be emotionally, socially and in terms of reaching your goals. For example, are you a perfectionist? Do you judge easily, either yourself or others?)

1. ....

2. ....

3. ....

4. ....

What sort of a friend are you? (Both socially and emotionally: for example, do you notice when friends need support? Do you notice their emotional needs?)

1. ....

2. ....

3. ....

4. ....

Who will you go to for help if you struggle with your emotional or mental wellbeing, now or in the future?

1. ....

2. ....

3. ....

> **Childline** is available 24/7 to anyone up to the age of 19 to discuss any worries. You can contact them via online chat or email at www.childline.org.uk, or by free call or text on 0800 1111.

Unit 1 You and your life, Lesson 1

Worksheet 1.1c Knowing ourselves

How can we spot when someone is feeling down or hiding something?

Look at this picture of a group of friends. Consider their body language, facial expressions and how they are interacting with the group.

Can you tell how someone is feeling (even if they are trying to hide it)? If so, what tells you this?

Study each person carefully and add labels around the picture of anyone you think might be feeling down or hiding something. Write down what you have noticed and give reasons why you think this shows they are a friend who might need some support.

Remember that sometimes people who look like they don't need help can be the ones who need it most.

4   Unit 1 You and your life, Lesson 1

Learning objectives:

- To learn about what makes a healthy family and how dynamics change over time
- To understand when a relationship in a family might be unsafe or unhealthy, and how to seek advice and support for yourself or others

Resources:

- PowerPoint 1.2
- Worksheets 1.2a and 1.2b
- Access to the internet
- Sticky notes
- Link to KS3: Book 1, Unit 5.1; Book 2, Unit 5.1; Book 3, Units 8.1 and 8.2

Key vocabulary:

guardian, carer, adopted, biological, abuse: emotional, physical and sexual

- See KS3 links above for previous lessons on families, child abuse, partnerships and relationships.

Get them thinking! (5 mins)

- Ask: 'What does a healthy, happy family look like to you?' *(e.g. a safe environment, love and support for each other, help with worries/problems, enjoying time spent together).* Encourage students to think of all the different types of family *(e.g. same-sex parents, single parents, blended families, extended families).* Get students to think quietly or work in pairs before sharing ideas as a whole class.

Core learning (25 mins)

- Show **Slide 1**. Go through the pictures, making it clear that families come in lots of different shapes and sizes and clarifying any misconceptions if required. See the notes on the slide. Explain that the most important thing about a family isn't who it is made up of, but what it provides to those in the home.

- Hand out copies of **Worksheet 1.2a** for students to work through, ranking each statement in order of importance. Discuss these rankings as a class. Then encourage students to feed ideas from the second question into the discussion where relevant, noting any standouts for assessment.

- Show **Slide 2**. Ask small groups to discuss the different ways in which we need our families at different ages and then feed back to you. Alternatively, give each group a different stage to focus on. Discuss these, pulling out any key threads that stay the same or change, and then use **Slide 3** to reinforce these changing family dynamics.

Additional learning (15 mins)

- Read through the instructions on **Slide 4** and then guide students on a visualisation. Encourage them to relax and really explore their imagination. Ask: 'Where will you be living? Who will you be living with? What sort of family unit will you have? Would you like to be a parent? What sort of a parent will you be?'

- Ask students to discuss their visualisations briefly in pairs or as a whole class and then complete **Worksheet 1.2b** using their visualisation.

Plenary (5 mins)

- Use **Slides 5** and **6** to discuss things that can go wrong in families. Ask: 'How might we judge if a family relationship is unsafe?' *(e.g. If someone felt anxious, scared, unsupported, uncared for, bullied or abused within a family environment.)* You could go to www.childline.org.uk/info-advice/bullying-abuse-safety/abuse-safety/ to explain the different types of abuse. Discuss asking for help and talking to someone, and remind students about the Childline information on their worksheet.

Assessment

- Give the class sticky notes on which to write two things they have learned in this lesson and one thing they would like to know more about (you could use these to explore this subject further). The worksheets are also useful for assessment.

Extension or home learning

- Extension: Looking back at **Worksheet 1.2a**, ask students to imagine they are parents. Ask: 'How do parents learn to do these things?' *(From their families if they have them, by reading books, parenting classes, trial and error!)* Then ask: 'If you were a first-time parent, would you find the worksheet useful? Why?' They could create a poster on how to raise (or not raise) a child, like this one from the NSPCC: https://learning.nspcc.org.uk/media/1195/positive-parenting.pdf.

- Home learning: Ask students to visit the Childline website and to find out what sort of information it includes and the support available. They could create an advertisement for it, based on what they found, and put these up around school.

Look at the following list. Decide which of these is important in a family. Then rate the statement according to how important you think it is, on a scale of 1 to 5, where 1 is not important and 5 is the most important. Give reasons for your views.

Situation	Important? (yes/no)	How important? (1 to 5)	Reason
1. Having love and affection.			
2. Having lots of nice things bought for you.			
3. Having a safe space to live.			
4. Having people around you who support you and 'have your back'.			
5. Having people to teach and guide you, and to push you to be the best you can be.			
6. Having fun and enjoying each other's company.			
7. Having people to talk to about things that worry you or that you need help with.			
8. Having someone who cleans your clothes and feeds you.			

What other aspects of family life are important to you? Why do you feel they are important?

....

....

....

....

> If you feel unsafe or worried about your family or home life, or need to talk to someone about your family or anything else that is worrying you, **Childline** is available on the phone (0800 1111) or online chat (www.childline.org.uk/get-support/1-2-1-counsellor-chat/) 24/7 to everyone up to the age of 19. Calls are free and nothing shows up on your bill.

Worksheet 1.2b Visualising your family life

You have done a visualisation where you zoomed 10 years into the future. Now, use these questions to write down how you think your family life might look 10 years from now. Remember, this might not happen, but you are using your imagination to try and guess!

1. Where will you be living?

   ....

   ....

   ....

2. Who will you be living with?

   ....

   ....

   ....

3. Will you be a parent? If so, what sort of parent will you be and why?

   ....

   ....

   ....

4. What sort of a family unit will you have and why?

   ....

   ....

   ....

5. Use this space to add anything else you 'saw' in your family life visualisation.

   ....

   ....

   ....

   ....

   ....

2.1 Respecting others

Learning objectives:
- To consider the importance of respect
- To understand how respect can be shown
- To learn to recognise disrespectful habits or behaviours and how to change them

Resources:
- PowerPoint 2.1
- Worksheet 2.1
- Link to KS3: Book 1, Unit 5.2

Key vocabulary:
respect, self-respect, communities, disrespect

Get them thinking! (5 mins)
- Ask students: 'What does the word respect mean to you?' Ask them to discuss this in pairs and then share as a class. Write their ideas on the board. *(Respect: to have or show consideration for something or someone.)*

Core learning (25 mins)
- This section needs to be kept pacey and punchy. Give students two minutes for each question, working as a pair or team, to come up with as many thoughts and ideas on this as possible. Then collate their ideas through quick-fire feedback.
- Ask students: 'What would self-respect (respect for ourselves) look like?' Take suggestions, and then go through **Slide 1** and discuss any ideas not included previously by students.
- Ask students: 'What would respect for our families look like?' Take suggestions, and then go through **Slide 2**, discussing any ideas not included previously by students.
- Ask students: 'What would respect for our communities (schools, local neighbourhoods) look like?' Take suggestions, and then go through **Slide 3**, discussing any ideas not included previously by students.

Additional learning (15 mins)
- Ask students: 'What would respecting our friends look like?' Discuss as a class and write their ideas on the board. Then consider when we might accidentally disrespect our friends. Get students to write down examples or share them as a class. *(These might include taking control, not allowing them to hang out with other people, telling them what to wear/do/say, punching them (for a laugh), not noticing when they are unhappy, laughing at them/making jokes or talking about them behind their backs, online or offline.)*
- Ask: 'How can we recognise when we are being disrespectful to others?' *(e.g. from the other person's body language, avoidance by not looking at them or avoiding them altogether, quietness).*
- Go through the scenario **Slide 4**, and then ask: 'What would be the right thing to do?' *(apologise, recognise our mistake, change our behaviour)* Discuss how this would be hard for this person as they don't like looking weak, but what might be the consequences if they don't? See the extension activity for further work on this.

Plenary (5 mins)
- Look back at the 'Get them thinking!' question. Have students' answers to this changed? If so, why, and how? Is there anything they need to change from what they have learned?
- Go to **Slide 5** to reflect on how we can behave if we have disrespected someone or been disrespected.

Assessment
- Ask students to complete **Worksheet 2.1**.

Extension or home learning
- Extension: Get students into small groups and set up a 'freeze frame' activity. Groups act out and then freeze frame a scenario where one friend (or several) is disrespecting another and show the (often subtle) reaction to this. Allow students to practise. Then watch each group and get the class to tell you how each 'character' feels while they are frozen. Tell the class to instruct the group how to correct it with an apology, or by recognition and a change of behaviour.
- Home learning: Ask students to create a poem or set of song lyrics on the consequences of disrespect in our society (**Slide 3** may inspire some ideas for this).

Worksheet 2.1 Respecting others: What have you learned?

1. How can you show respect to yourself?

....

....

....

2. How can you show respect to your family?

....

....

....

3. How can you show respect to your community?

....

....

....

4. How could you accidentally be disrespectful to your friends?

....

....

....

5. What can you do if you notice you are being or have been disrespectful to someone?

....

....

....

6. What can you do if you feel someone is disrespecting you?

....

....

....

2.2   Healthy relationships and dating

Learning objectives:
- To understand that there are different types of intimate, consensual relationships
- To understand the realities of romantic relationships
- To consider how to use online dating apps and social media sites safely

Resources:
- PowerPoint 2.2
- Worksheet 2.2 (plus a copy enlarged for you)
- Large paper and pens
- Link to KS3: Book 2, Units 2.2 and 3.1; Book 3, Unit 8.2

Key vocabulary:
intimate, age of consent, asexual, sexual attraction, faithful, insecure, dating, online dating

- See KS3 links above for previous lessons on relationships and consent.

Get them thinking! (5 mins)

- Ask: 'Is a healthy romantic/intimate relationship always long term? Why?' Students think quietly or work in pairs before explaining their answer *(e.g. a holiday romance and a one-night stand are not long term)*.

Core learning (25 mins)

- Ask students what a 'relationship' is and how people know when they are in one. Explain that while many romantic relationships are sexual, some may not be. Ask them to think of examples *(e.g. because of religious or moral beliefs; because one or both partners is/are under the age of consent (in the UK, this is at 16 years old); because someone is asexual, so they do not feel sexual attraction towards anyone, but may still have relationships and enjoy romantic attraction)*.

- Divide the class into groups and ask them to write down all the different types of intimate relationships they have heard of – allow them 2 minutes to write down as many as they can think of *(e.g. girlfriend/boyfriend, seeing one another, long distance, casual, married, partners, living together)*. Do not give them any guidance as you will use this as an assessment.

- Tell students that whether sex is involved or not, people have expectations of intimate relationships. Show **Slide 1**. Discuss each quotation, asking: 'What's the story here?' (see the notes on the slide). Encourage students to think about how each person might have got to this point and what the statement tells us about how they are feeling now/how things have changed. Note the fact that often reality doesn't live up to expectations. Discuss that this may be due to the way relationships are portrayed in the media.

- Show **Slide 2**. Discuss each statement briefly and hand out **Worksheet 2.2**. Model writing an email using the template, including giving some practical advice (see the notes on the slide).

Additional learning (15 mins)

- Write these questions on the board: 1. 'How can you tell if someone is interested in you?'; 2. 'How do you ask someone out?'; 3. 'What happens if they say no?'; 4. 'Is it easier to do this face to face or online? Why?'; 5. 'What are the advantages and disadvantages of each approach?' Divide the class into small groups to consider these questions, writing their ideas on a large sheet of paper and then feeding back. *(Face to face: you can choose a good moment, see their reaction and don't have to wait for the reply; online: it's less embarrassing, it allows for thinking time as you can write it and then send it later.)*

- Introduce the idea of online dating and tell students that this has become an accepted way for adults to meet someone, regardless of sexuality or gender identity. Read through **Slide 3** and explain that although this can be a good way for adults to meet new people, it does come with risks.

- Go through **Slide 4** with the class, discussing and clarifying as you go. (See also the note on the slide.) Then go through **Slide 5** to clarify the importance of safety online, again looking at the notes.

Plenary (5 mins)

- Recap relationships, discussing how they are all unique and rarely perfect, but they should never be scary, worrying or harmful – these emotions suggest an unhealthy relationship. (See Lesson 2.3.)

Assessment

- Ask students to think again about the question in 'Get them thinking!' and then do a quick-fire session, where students shout out anything new they have learned during the lesson.

Extension or home learning

- Extension: Ask students to write a series of interview questions to ask adults who are in healthy, happy relationships, to get a better understanding of the ingredients of a good relationship.

Worksheet 2.2 Difficult emotions in relationships

Choose a quotation on the slide from someone whom you think you can help. Write this person an email, using the template below. You can imagine that they are a friend or that they are a stranger who has written to you as an expert in this field for some relationship advice. Try to offer some good practical advice that will really help them.

To:	
Cc:	
Subject	
From:	

....

....

....

....

....

....

....

....

....

....

....

....

....

Learning objectives:

- To recognise the 'red flags' in a relationship online or offline
- To understand what domestic abuse is and what help is available.
- To spot the signs of sexual exploitation and grooming

Resources:

- PowerPoint 2.3
- Worksheets 2.3a and 2.3b
- Question box
- Link to KS3: Book 2, Unit 2.3; Book 3, Unit 3.2

Key vocabulary:

domestic abuse/violence, controlling, coercive, grooming, sexual exploitation, trafficked, CEOP

Get them thinking! (5 mins)

- Ask students to discuss in pairs: 'What have we learned about healthy relationships?' Then discuss as a class. If students don't raise this themselves, remind them that healthy relationships allow each person to remain an individual, having different interests, other friends, time apart as well as together, and so on.

Core learning (25 mins)

- Tell students there is an anonymous question box for them to put questions in at the end of this lesson.

- Hand out **Worksheet 2.3a** and go through the instructions with the class. Allow students time to complete this individually or in pairs, and then discuss. *(Answers: 1. unhealthy, 2. unhealthy, 3. healthy, 4. healthy, 5. healthy, 6. unhealthy, 7. healthy, 8. unhealthy, 9. unhealthy, 10. healthy.)*

- Ask: 'How might we know when a healthy relationship is becoming unhealthy?' Draw out that most relationships start well, and that everyone has their issues to deal with, but if a relationship is becoming unhealthy, there will signs that things are not going so well. Sometimes these signs are so small or build over such a long period of time that they might not be easy to spot. Unhealthy relationships can become serious and develop into controlling, bullying, violent and harassing relationships.

- Show **Slide 1** and discuss what controlling behaviour is, and then look at the examples on **Slide 2**. Finally, read through the definition of domestic abuse on **Slide 3**.

- Ask: 'What signs might you spot in yourself or others of being subject to domestic abuse?' Get students to discuss this in pairs and feed back their ideas *(e.g. changes in behaviour, not going out or seeing friends so much, needing permission to do things, having to check in a lot, being anxious or nervous)*.

- Ask: 'What could you do to help yourself or others?' Ask students to discuss this in pairs and feed back their ideas *(e.g. tell someone you trust, or contact Childline or a domestic abuse charity helpline, call the police in an emergency, get out of the house/away from them if you can)*.

- Tell students to work in pairs to create a short drama involving people of any gender where a relationship starts off really well, but subtle 'red flags' gradually appear. Give students time to develop these before performing them for the class. The rest of the class must try to spot the red flags.

Additional learning (15 mins)

- As a class, discuss how you can spot an unhealthy relationship building online. Go through **Slides 4** and **5**. Tell students that, as with domestic abuse, while the relationship might begin well, there may be red flags that can warn us that things aren't right.

- Ask pairs to discuss what signs they might spot in themselves or others that they are being groomed. Ask them to feed back to the class *(e.g. initially it will feel 'too good to be true', then it might involve missing school, not wanting to hang out with friends, being picked up by older strangers, having more money than usual, having injuries, behaving differently)*.

- Discuss with the class what someone in this situation could do *(tell someone they trust, report anything suspicious online to CEOP – see below, call a charity such as Childline, call the police in an emergency)*.

Plenary (5 mins)

- Invite students to ask questions about what they have learned, or to write them and put them in the question box to keep them anonymous. Go through these and answer students' queries.

Assessment

- Hand out copies of **Worksheet 2.3b** for students to complete. Then take them in to use for assessment.

Extension or home learning

- Home learning: Ask students to visit the CEOP (Child Exploitation and Online Protection) website and look at the process of reporting abuse: https://www.ceop.police.uk/ceop-reporting/

Worksheet 2.3a Healthy or unhealthy?

Go through these statements and complete the sheet, considering whether each is healthy (add a tick) or unhealthy (add a cross). If you are not sure, add a question mark. Then explain why you think this in the final column.

Statement	Healthy or unhealthy?	Why do you think this?
1. They want to spend every minute of every day with you.		
2. They pinch you under the table if you say something silly in public.		
3. They want to go the gym alone every morning.		
4. They like you to hang out with your mates and do your own thing whenever you want to, and they do the same.		
5. After an argument has died down, they talk to you and work as a team to find solutions.		
6. They like to choose your outfits for you every day. They point out what you should buy when you go shopping.		
7. They are a good friend.		
8. They tell you that you are the reason they are angry or sad all the time.		
9. They only shout at you, they never hit you.		
10. They believe in you and support you and your dreams.		

Worksheet 2.3b Unhealthy relationships: What have you learned?

1. What might be the red flags that suggest a relationship is becoming unhealthy?

....

....

....

2. What could you do to help yourself or others in this situation?

....

....

....

3. What might be the red flags that you or someone you know is being groomed or sexually exploited?

....

....

....

4. What could you do to help yourself or others?

....

....

....

5. Do you remember what consent is? Explain below.

....

....

....

Is there anything else you would like to learn about relationships?

....

....

....

If you feel unsafe or worried about how someone is treating you on or offline, or you need to talk to someone about anything else that is worrying you, **Childline** is available on the phone (0800 1111) or online (www.childline.org.uk/get-support/1-2-1-counsellor-chat/) 24/7 to everyone up to the age of 19. Calls are free and nothing shows up on your bill. You can also contact **CEOP** if you are worried about online sexual abuse or the way someone has been communicating with you online: www.ceop.police.uk/ceop-reporting/

3.1 Equality

Learning objectives:
- To understand what equality is
- To learn about the nine protected characteristics
- To understand discrimination and stereotyping

Resources:
- PowerPoint 3.1
- Worksheets 3.1a and 3.1b
- Laptops and search terms or websites
- Link to KS3: Book 2, Units 6.2 and 15.2; Book 3, Unit 3.4

Key vocabulary:
equality, discrimination protected characteristics, hate crimes, stereotyping

Get them thinking! (5 mins)
- Ask students: 'What does equality mean to you?' Allow time for students to discuss in pairs or as a class as you feel appropriate and then to feed back their thoughts and ideas.

Core learning (25 mins)
- Explain that equality is all about people being equal to each other in all aspects of life, including having equal rights under the law.
- Ask students what discrimination is. Explain that it is when someone is treated unfairly/unequally because of a certain characteristic they have. Display **Slide 1** and go through the nine protected characteristics briefly. *(Examples include: age, e.g. an older person with great qualifications and experience who can't get a job because of their age; sex, e.g. a woman being paid less than a man for the same job.)* Ask students if they can think of any examples from real life, books, films or on TV.
- Show **Slide 2** and go through the information about the Equality Act that protects these characteristics.
- Ask students: 'What different types of discrimination are there?' Discuss as a class and then hand out **Worksheet 3.1a**. Allow time for students to work through this alone or in pairs. Then go through it with them, checking their answers. *(Answers: 1. Religion or belief; 2. Pregnancy and maternity; 3. Sexual orientation; 4. Race; 5. Disability; 6. Gender reassignment.)*
- Show **Slide 3** and read through it to clarify the locations and situations where people are protected.
- Show **Slide 4** and read out the definition of a hate crime and the note about this. If there is time, discuss some of the current hate crimes in the news (you could print some off to explore this further as an extension) or refer to well-known examples, such as the murder of Stephen Lawrence in 1993.

Additional learning (15 mins)
- Show **Slide 5** and read out the definition of stereotyping and the examples. Ask students to brainstorm other examples of stereotyping *(e.g. gender stereotyping – women are not good at science; racial stereotyping – all Black people are amazing dancers; ageist stereotyping – all old people are weak).*
- Ask: 'What effects do these stereotypes have in our society?' Write students' ideas on the board.
- Hand out **Worksheet 3.1b** about the ways in which teenagers can be stereotyped. Students should complete it individually or in pairs. Allow time afterwards to discuss their thoughts as a class.

Plenary (5 mins)
- End with a discussion about why stereotypes can be damaging and how they can contribute to hate crimes.

Assessment
- Use students' responses to the worksheets and discussions to assess their understanding.

Extension or home learning
- Extension: Divide the class into nine groups and give each group a different protected characteristic. Encourage them to work as a team to consider all the ways that people with this characteristic could be discriminated against. You could give them laptops so they can research and find out more online. (Research ahead of the lesson and provide a list of quality websites for them to use, e.g. Citizens Advice, GOV.UK.) Ask the class to collate their team learning and create a display or a class book looking at the Equality Act and how it can help to end discrimination for each protected characteristic.
- Home learning: Ask students to create a piece of art to highlight a chosen protected characteristic and the beauty of the people in this group. Create a mosaic of the final artworks to display in class or online.

Look at the list of situations in the table. Decide which of the protected characteristics is being discriminated against in each situation and write this into column 2.

Then, in column 3, add why you think this is discrimination.

Add your own situations for numbers 7 and 8 and complete as above.

Remember, discrimination means when someone is treated unfairly or unequally because of a certain characteristic they have.

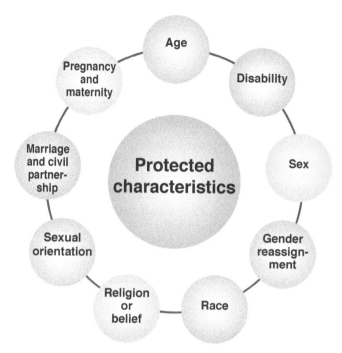

Situation	Protected characteristic	Why do you think this is discrimination?
1. Someone consistently makes offensive jokes about your religion.		
2. In a job interview, an employer asks you if you plan to have children.		
3. You're asked to leave a restaurant because you are cuddling your same-sex partner.		
4. You are stopped by police and searched because of the colour of your skin.		
5. People ignore you because you are in a wheelchair.		
6. You identify as female, using gender neutral pronouns, but people continue to refer to you as 'he'.		
7.		
8.		

Worksheet 3.1b Stereotyping: teenagers

Consider how teenagers are stereotyped in the UK. Use the table below to write a common stereotype and then write what you think about this and why in the second column. One example has been given.

Stereotype	Why is this stereotype incorrect?
Teenagers in hoodies are always up to no good.	A hoodie is an item of clothing that lots of people like the style of, and the hoods are often worn to keep warm or dry. There is no way that every person who wears a hoodie is 'up to something' and this statement assumes all teenagers are the same, which they are not!
1.	
2.	
3.	
4.	

Choose another protected characteristic and consider how you feel about a common stereotype for this group of people. Write your thoughts below.

Protected characteristic: ....

A common stereotype: ....

How I feel about it: ....

....

....

....

....

....

....

....

....

3.2 Social injustice

Learning objectives:
- To understand what social injustice means
- To learn about unconscious bias
- To learn about the Black Lives Matter movement

Resources:
- PowerPoint 3.2
- Worksheet 3.2
- Art materials
- Access to the internet
- Link to KS3: Book 3, Units 4.1 and 4.2; Book 2, Unit 6.1

Key vocabulary:
social injustice, Black Lives Matter (BLM), white privilege, systemic racism, ally

Get them thinking! (5 mins)
- Ask students to discuss in pairs and then feed back to the class their answers to the question: 'What do you think the impact of racism is in the UK today? Why? Can you give some examples?' Use students' responses as an assessment of their understanding.

Core learning (25 mins)
- Ask students if they know of any people or events in the past that highlight the history of racial injustice (e.g. Rosa Parks, Martin Luther King Jr, Nelson Mandela, the Windrush scandal, slavery, the civil rights movement). Show **Slide 1**. Introduce the Black Lives Matter movement (see also the link in the notes).

- Show **Slide 2** and discuss George Floyd's story with the class. Explain that these are examples of social injustice, which is when people (individuals or groups) are not treated fairly in society and are discriminated against because of one or more of their characteristics. Remind students of the protected characteristics listed in the Equality Act and the harmful effects of stereotyping from the previous lesson.

- Read **Slide 3**, taking ideas and then giving some examples (see the notes on the slide). Explain that unconscious bias can become very toxic when embedded in institutions.

- Show **Slide 4** and then go to the Barnardo's blog entry 'How systemic racism affects young people in the UK' (https://www.barnardos.org.uk/blog/how-systemic-racism-affects-young-people-uk) to learn more about this issue and how it can affect people's lives. Use the whiteboard to do this as a whole class.

- Hand out **Worksheet 3.2**. Allow time for students to read the questions and reflect on them individually. If appropriate to your cohort, they could discuss the questions and their reflections in pairs or groups. Then bring the class back together to discuss the questions.

- Introduce the concept of privilege by showing the film 'Life of Privilege Explained in a $100 Race' (this can be found online, for example on YouTube). Discuss the film as a class. Ask: 'Are we always conscious of the privileges we might have compared to other people?'

- If students have heard the term 'white privilege' and have questions about it, the information and resources on the Newsround website may be useful (https://www.bbc.co.uk/newsround/52937905).

- Show **Slide 5**. Ask students to begin to create a piece of writing or art (sketching if you only have a short lesson) to express their feelings about the issues they have explored today. They could focus on a specific area, such as the Black Lives Matter movement, systemic racism and its effect on different people, or on something else related that they feel moved to explore.

Additional learning (15 mins)
- Ask students to complete their writing/artwork and then share it with the class.

Plenary (5 mins)
- Encourage students to discuss each other's work and to express their feelings about their learning today.

Assessment
- Use students' work to assess their level of understanding and to see where further teaching is needed.

Extension or home learning
- Extension: Ask students to extend and build on their artwork to create a more detailed piece and to set up an art exhibition from the pieces they have created for the same purpose.

Worksheet 3.2 Social injustice

To understand social injustice related to race on a personal level, read the questionnaire below.

Consider these statements.

1. I always see films where the main characters have my colour skin.

2. I get treated differently from other people by the police.

3. I have had racist remarks and/or insults made towards me.

4. I see/read books where the main characters are people of colour.

5. I notice that most of my teachers are the same colour as me.

6. I feel like I have to represent all people like me.

7. I am asked where I am from, or where my family is from, a lot.

8. I find that hair products often don't work in my hair.

9. I get treated with suspicion in public places.

10. I see lots of people like me in high-paying jobs in society.

11. I think life would be easier for me if my skin were a different colour.

12. I have been taught about my ancestors' history.

13. I often feel like I stand out in crowds because of the colour of my skin.

Add your own examples here:

14. ....

15. ....

When you have finished, discuss the questions with a partner.

What do these questions tell you about social injustice?

....

....

....

....

....

....

....

NB: Remember that social injustice can also be apparent in people's lives because of other characteristics, such as class/socioeconomic background, sexual orientation, gender, age, disability, and so on (see others in the Equality Act).

Learning objectives:

- To understand the voting process
- To understand how we elect an MP at a general election
- To understand different voting systems

Resources:

- PowerPoint 4.1
- Worksheets 4.1a and 4.1b
- Access to the internet
- Printouts of the full results of the 2019 UK general election downloaded from: https://commonslibrary.parliament.uk
- Link to KS3: Book 2, Unit 15.1

Key vocabulary:

general election, ballot, vote, constituency, returning officer, first past the post

Get them thinking! (5 mins)

- Ask students what political parties they have heard of, and if they know how to vote in an election.

Core learning (25 mins)

- Go through **Slide 1** with the class and explain what a general election is. Then go through **Slide 2** and ask students to find out who their MP is, using the website or modelling the process yourself.

- Explain how a general election works using **Slide 3** (see the notes on the slide for an explanation of the first past the post system) and declaring the winner on **Slide 4**. You could use the internet to play a clip from a previous general election to illustrate what happens on election night.

- Ask students to complete **Worksheet 4.1a**. *(Answers: 1. F); 2. D); 3. G); 4. E); 5. I); 6. J); 7. H); 8. C); 9. B); 10. A).).*

Additional learning (15 mins)

- Go through **Slide 5** but don't get the students to do the activity yet. Instead, ask them to look at the results for the last general election in **Worksheet 4.1b** and calculate what the number of seats would be for each party if the seats had matched the percentage of votes cast for each party. Discuss the differences and whether students think the current system is fair. *(Answers for final column: Conservatives 283 seats (−82); Labour 209 seats (+7); SNP 25 seats (−23); Lib Dems 75 seats (+64); Plaid Cymru 3 seats (-1); Greens 18 seats (+17); Brexit Party 13 seats (+13); Northern Ireland 18 seats (this has to stay the same because of the constituency boundaries in Northern Ireland); others (includes speaker) 6 seats (+5).)*

- The results above follow the national list system. The advantage of this system is that it is completely proportional. The disadvantage of this system is that it can give too much power to smaller parties: if a party gets 0.6% of the vote by advocating extremist policies, an extremist will be elected as an MP.

- Ask students to complete the quick activity on **Slide 5** by looking at the results for four constituencies in a city or local area. *(Totals for each party are Conservatives 77k, Lib Dem 74k, Labour 96k and Green 64k – see the notes on the slide for more information.)* Discuss whether students think the results are fair, or if we should change to a different system, such as a form of proportional representation, which means the total number of votes more fairly matches the number of seats. Note that this would mean that each party gets one seat in this example.

Plenary (5 mins)

- Ask students to discuss as a class whether our election system needs to change and why.

Assessment

- Check that all students have completed **Worksheets 4.1a** and **Worksheet 4.1b**. Take in the worksheets and use these for assessment.

Extension or home learning

- Home learning: The elections to the Scottish Parliament, the Welsh Assembly, the Northern Ireland Assembly and the London Mayor use a different voting system. Ask students to research each of these voting systems. Further information about STV (the single transferrable vote) can be found here: https://www.electoral-reform.org.uk/voting-systems/types-of-voting-system/single-transferable-vote/

- Extension: Divide the class into groups. Ask them to research what each of the main political parties stands for, who their leader is, and how many MPs each party has (e.g. Conservatives, Labour, etc.).

Worksheet 4.1a How does a general election work?

Look at the table below. Match each stage in the first column with an action to be taken in the third column. An explanation is provided in the second column to help. The first one has been done for you.

Stage	Explanation	Action to be taken	Match?
1. Making sure everyone is on the electoral register.	Many people are missing from the register. Why do you think this is?	A) Seeing which party has the most MPs and who becomes the government.	1. F)
2. Requesting a postal or proxy vote.	This is done for people who can't travel to the polling station, who are away on holiday or now live abroad but have lived in the UK in the last 20 years.	B) Getting results around the country to see who has got the most MPs.	
3. Being sent a polling card.	You don't need your polling card to vote.	C) Declaring the winner for a constituency.	
4. Going to the polling station.	Voting is done by marking an X in a box for one candidate in a general election.	D) Checking to see if you can't get to the polling station and therefore need another way to vote.	
5. Transporting the ballot boxes.	There is a race each year to see which constituency can be fastest to declare a result.	E) They check your name and address and give you a ballot paper	
6. First part of the count (when votes are counted): to check that all the ballot papers are legal and correct.	Officials and parties are at the count to make sure it is done fairly.	F) Checking that everyone over 18 (or over 16 in Scotland and Wales for their national elections) is registered to vote.	
7. Second part of the count: to determine which candidate got the most votes.	There may be a recount if the result is close.	G) Telling you when the election is and where your polling station is.	
8. The declaration at the end of the count, one per constituency.	Once made, a declaration can only be overturned by a court if there is a problem.	H) Finding out who has the most votes and therefore has become an MP.	
9. Getting results in from constituency declarations around the country.	This often goes on through the night and into the next day.	I) Getting all the votes in one place.	
10. Which party has the most MPs, and has won the general election?	There are 650 MPs, so you need at least 325 MPs to have a majority that forms the Government.	J) Checking to see that all the ballot papers have an official mark on them.	

Worksheet 4.1b Parties and voting

Look at the results of the 2019 UK general election in the first four columns of the table below.

Using these figures, work the number of seats each party would have received, if the system of proportional representation had been used. Under proportional representation the number of seats per party roughly equals the percentage of votes received.

What happens? Do the Conservatives still have a majority? Which parties gain seats and which parties lose seats?

Party	2019 MPs/seats	% of vote in 2019	% of MPs/seats in 2019	Number of MPs/ seats under PR
Conservative	365	43.6%	56.15%	283
Labour	202	32.2%	31.07%	
SNP	48	3.9%	7.38%	
Liberal Democrat	11	11.5%	1.79%	
Plaid Cymru	4	0.5%	0.61%	
Green	1	2.7%	0.15%	
Brexit Party	0	2.0%	0	
Northern Ireland	18	2.5%	2.7%	
Other	1	1.1%	0.15%	
Total	650	100	100	650

Some countries use a national list system of proportional representation where the number of seats won by each party is almost exactly proportionate to the number of votes they received.

In Ireland and the Northern Irish Assembly, as well as in local elections in Scotland and Northern Ireland, STV is used: the single transferable vote. Here, a constituency elects several representatives and you vote for candidates in order of preference. More information about this system can be found here:

https://www.electoral-reform.org.uk/voting-systems/types-of-voting-system/single-transferable-vote/

In Scotland, Wales, and the London Assembly, they use the Additional Member system for regional government assemblies – a mixture of first past the post topped up with PR.

Learning objectives:

- To understand what a pressure group is
- To understand the four different types of pressure group
- To understand what a new social movement is

Resources:

- PowerPoint 4.2
- Worksheets 4.2a and 4.2b
- Access to the internet
- Link to KS3: Book 2, Unit 15.3

Key vocabulary:

single issue, sectional, insider, outsider, new social movement, pressure group, lobbying

Get them thinking! (5 mins)

- Ask students to name any pressure groups they have heard of. Write their answers on the board.

Core learning (25 mins)

- Using **Slide 1**, define a pressure group as a group that wants to influence a decision without taking power. Show **Slide 2** and remind students of the difference between sectional and promotional groups.

- Go through **Slide 3** to show the difference between insider and outsider groups, giving examples such as the Scottish Council for Homelessness, which has a close relationship with the Scottish government (insider group) and Fathers4Justice, which disagrees with the UK government's approach to the issue of parental access, and which engages in civil disobedience (outsider group).

- Ask students to complete **Worksheet 4.2a** in pairs. Then work through it together as a class. *(Insider and sectional groups: CBI, TaxPayers' Alliance; outsider and sectional: NEU; insider and promotional: RSPB; outsider and promotional: CND, Amnesty International.)* As a challenge activity for fast finishers, students could classify any other pressure groups they can think of.

- Ask what a new social movement is, and define it using **Slide 4**. Then look at the case study on **Slide 5** and discuss what students think of this group. Ask whether they are aware of its aims and objectives, looking together at https://blacklivesmatter.com/about/.

Additional learning (15 mins)

- Ask students to list all the campaign methods they can think of that pressure groups use. Then ask them to divide them into insider or outsider campaign methods. *(Insider methods: lobbying (meeting with a decision-maker to present a case), official reports, joint press releases with decision-makers; outsider methods: civil disobedience (breaking the law to a minimal extent), strikes, boycotts (refusing to buy goods or services or to participate in an event), marches, sit-ins.)*

Plenary (5 mins)

- Ask students to discuss and then rank the reasons why a pressure group may or may not be successful. *(Reasons include: size, money, celebrity endorsements, campaign methods, group type, existence of an opposing group, insider/outsider status, political climate and popularity.)*

Assessment

- Ask students to complete **Worksheet 4.2b**. *(Answers: 1. influence; 2. new social movement; 3. promotional group; 4. insider groups; 5. a sectional group; 6. lobbying; 7. civil disobedience; 8. a boycott; 9. outsider group; 10. new social movement; Tiebreaker: CBI.)*

Extension or home learning

- Home learning: Ask students to pick one pressure group, research it and write a short report stating what sort of group it is, what methods it uses, and whether or not it has been successful in achieving its aims.

- Extension: Invite a member of a pressure group to come and speak to the class. Students should prepare questions in advance on the type of group, membership, campaign methods and success.

- Extension: Hold a debate to discuss the question, 'Can civil disobedience and breaking the law for political aims ever be justified?'

Worksheet 4.2a Types of pressure groups

Look at the definitions below of different type of pressure group.

Definitions

Insider group: a group that has a close relationship with and access to the government.

Outsider group: a group that has a distant relationship with and often a lack of access to the government.

Sectional group: a group that represents a particular section of society, with a limited membership (e.g. the Education Union for Teachers), but which campaigns on a wide range of issues.

Promotional group: a group that promotes a single issue, but which anyone can join.

Now look at this list of organisations.

- Confederation of British Industry (CBI)
- Royal Society for the Protection of Birds (RSPB)
- The National Education Union (NEU)
- The Campaign for Nuclear Disarmament (CND)
- Amnesty International
- TaxPayers' Alliance

Work in groups to decide whether each one is an insider or outsider group, and a sectional or promotional group. Decide which group goes in which area of the diagram below. (Note that some may fit in more than one area. For example, the TaxPayers' Alliance is both an insider group and a promotional group.)

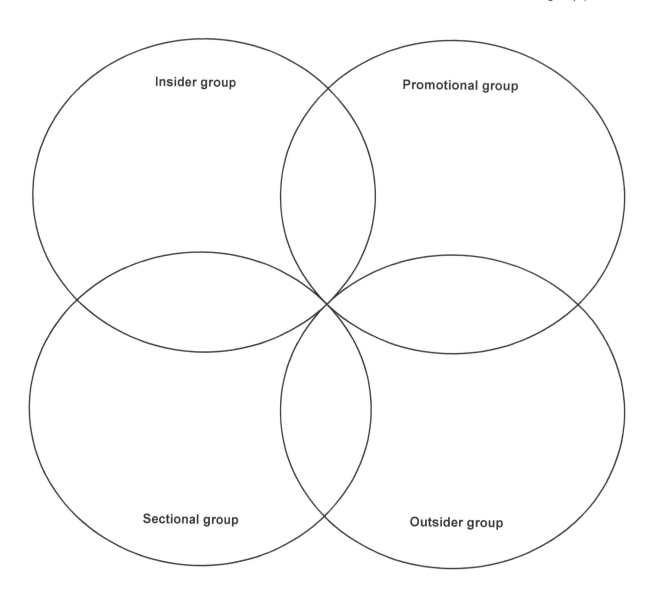

Worksheet 4.2b Pressure groups quiz

Look at the following questions and write down your answers. Then compare your answers in pairs or groups. Finally, check your answers as a class.

1. Are pressure groups interested in power or influence?

   ....

2. What sort of pressure group is Black Lives Matter?

   ....

3. Which is likely to have the biggest membership – a sectional or promotional group?

   ....

4. Groups that are close to and have good access to the government are known as what?

   ....

5. What sort of group is most likely to represent a particular profession?

   ....

6. What is meeting directly with a decision-maker to present a case known as?

   ....

7. What is breaking the law to a minimum extent in order to make a political point known as?

   ....

8. Not buying a particular brand of goods to make a political point is known as what?

   ....

9. Fathers4Justice is an example of what sort of group?

   ....

10. Which type of pressure group appears and disappears most quickly?

   ....

Tiebreaker: Which insider group describes itself as the UK's premier lobbying organisation?

   ....

5.1   You and your career

Learning objectives:
- To learn what a career is
- To understand how skills, interests and knowledge contribute to careers

Resources:
- PowerPoint 5.1
- Worksheet 5.1
- Access to the internet
- Link to KS3: Book 3, Unit 1.1

Key vocabulary:
career, skills, knowledge, opportunities, careers advisor

- Advice for teachers preparing this lesson is available here: https://www.gatsby.org.uk/education/focus-areas/good-career-guidance.

Get them thinking! (5 mins)
- Ask students to work in groups to discuss what their ideal jobs would be. Ask them to give reasons.

Core learning (25 mins)
- Elicit from the class what they think the word 'career' means and note ideas on the board. Then go through **Slide 1** and make sure everyone understands what a career is.

- Give students a copy of **Worksheet 5.1** and ask them to fill it in as you go through **Slides 2–4**. For **Slide 2**, model the process first – for example, saying that you like working with people aged 14–16 and that you enjoy finding out and sharing new knowledge. For **Slide 4**, get them to think in particular about any gaps in their skills or knowledge.

- Before you show **Slide 5**, explain what a careers advisor is, giving details of any careers advice services at your school. After you have discussed the information, ask students to work in groups to discuss what opportunities are available to them (a useful website for this is https://nationalcareers.service.gov.uk/). Also see the note on the slide.

Additional learning (15 mins)
- Ask students to work in pairs to discuss whether the skills they have and the things they enjoy doing point towards any particular careers. Then ask them to list any aptitudes or characteristics they think they have that would be useful in the world of work.

- Ask students, in groups, to discuss what their second and third choice career options would be, and to consider the skills, knowledge and experience they would need to acquire to undertake these careers.

Plenary (5 mins)
- Hold a discussion about all the 'opportunities' students wrote on their worksheets and any others they can think of. Note the answers on the board, under the headings 'local', 'regional' and 'national'. Make sure local work-experience opportunities and part-time jobs are included, along with visiting a local careers advisor. Local opportunities could be jobs in the nearest town; regional opportunities may be available in nearby big cities. National opportunities would include the armed forces and jobs in particular areas, such as the financial sector in London.

Assessment
- Ask students to check each other's worksheets and discuss if there are any particular areas they need to concentrate on, and what support they need in any particular areas for future learning. Monitor the class at this point to check that all worksheets have been completed correctly with as much detail as possible.

Extension or home learning
- Extension: Encourage as many students as possible to visit the careers advisor at your school during a PSHE lesson, to discuss what they might like to do as a career.

- Extension or home learning: Encourage students to look at and complete programs online that help them identify their interests, skills and possible future jobs. Then in groups, get them to compare these websites to see which are the most useful. Popular websites include http://www.lmiforall.org.uk/explore_lmi/ and https://nationalcareers.service.gov.uk/ and https://icould.com/ .

Worksheet 5.1 You and your career

Write your ideal career below. Then fill in the columns as instructed by your teacher. If you don't have an ideal job, think about an industry that you could work in or a job that you would like to do. It doesn't have to be forever – this is just to give you an idea about what your skills and strengths are as a person, and whether there are any particular areas that you would like to develop.

Write a job/area of work in the 'Interests' column and then think about what skills and knowledge you would need to work in that area of interest, filling in the other columns with the details. Repeat the process for other areas of interest.

Ideal career: _____

Interests	Current skills	Skills to acquire	Knowledge to acquire	Opportunities
1.				
2.				
3.				
4.				

Learning objectives:	Resources:	Key vocabulary:
• To understand the differences between the options available after 16 for education and training for students in England, Wales, Northern Ireland and Scotland	• PowerPoint 5.2 • Worksheets 5.2a and 5.2b • Link to KS3: Book 3, Unit 1	A Levels, T Levels, BTECs, SVQs, NVQs, apprenticeship, degree apprenticeship, vocational

Get them thinking! (5 mins)

• Ask students to write down what options they have at 16. Write these on the board. Elicit A Levels, T Levels, BTECs and apprenticeships.

Core learning (25 mins)

• Using **Slide 1**, explain the different options for students at the age of 16. Point out that these options are different depending on where you live in the UK (e.g. T Levels are only available in England).

• Go through **Slides 2–5** explaining to students the different options that are available.

• Then divide the class into three groups and ask them to write down the advantages and disadvantages of each option in their part of the country (e.g. T Levels for England, BTECs for Wales/Northern Ireland and SVQs for Scotland).

• Ask students to study **Worksheet 5.2a** on their own and pick their favourite option. Then ask them to work in groups of three to explain their choices. One person explains their choice, one person asks them about it and one person observes, listening for good reasoning and then feeding back. Each student takes a turn in each of these activity positions.

Additional learning (15 mins)

• Ask students to complete **Worksheet 5.2b** on their own or in pairs, and then discuss their answers in groups. At each stage of the pyramid, students should think about what they need to be doing in order to achieve the next stage, how technology will change in each stage, and how this may change what they do.

Plenary (5 mins)

• Lead a class discussion on which options on **Worksheet 5.2a** are the most popular and why, asking students for reasons for their views.

Assessment

• Take in students' completed versions of **Worksheet 5.2b** and provide any feedback or support needed in the next lesson.

Extension or home learning

• Extension: Students research in depth what particular options are available in their local area. What A Levels, BTECs, T Levels or Scottish Highers will they choose and why? Ask students to discuss this in groups of three, with one person explaining, one person asking questions and one person listening. Each person takes a turn. Here are some websites that may be of particular use (note that T Levels are only gradually being introduced):
T Levels: https://www.gov.uk/government/publications/introduction-of-t-levels/introduction-of-t-levels
A Levels: https://www.theuniguide.co.uk/advice/a-level-choices/six-things-you-need-to-know-before-making-your-a-level-choices and https://www.informedchoices.ac.uk/
BTECs: https://targetcareers.co.uk/careers-advice/a-level-choices/1033932-what-are-btecs

• Home learning: Ask students to find out what the difference is between an apprenticeship and a degree apprenticeship, which is a different option at 18: https://www.gov.uk/topic/further-education-skills/apprenticeships..

• Extension: Ask students go back and repeat the process of all the activities on this page for their third career choice. Are the courses they pick the same? Do they need to keep their options open, or are they fixed on a particular career choice? Either is OK.

Worksheet 5.2a You and your options

- Read the four case studies below. Decide which route you think would make the most sense for the potentially ideal career you identified in Lesson 5.1. Think about the advantages and disadvantages of the route you have picked

- Then pick the second-best option and decide on the advantages and disadvantages for that career route.

- Finally, compare the two. Decide which route would be your preferred option, and which your backup option. Has the order changed now you've compared them again?

Case study 1: Owen, BTECs, Animal Husbandry

I live in rural Wales, so I've always been interested in animals. I thought about being a vet, but I know it's really competitive and I'm not that academic – I really don't enjoy exams. When I saw a BTEC in Animal Husbandry I jumped at the chance. It includes coursework which I can submit a number of times, which really suits me academically. And if I do really well at the BTEC, I still have an opportunity to go to university.

Case study 2: Jess, A Levels, Photography

I've always been interested in photography and working in the media. I thought about a BTEC in photography, but couldn't find the right course. I also wanted to keep my options open, as I fancy a career working in the media as well. In the end I chose to study Photography, Media Studies and English Language at A Level. All are good because they include some coursework. English Language is important because it's a preferred subject for the course I want to do according to https://www.informedchoices.ac.uk/. This gives me the option of studying Photography or Media at a top UK university, so I can keep my options open after university.

Case study 3: Samuel, Apprenticeships, Hairdressing

There's no way I'm carrying on with A Levels or academic study. I want out of school, and I want out as quickly as possible. I've always wanted to be a hairdresser, so doing an apprenticeship with a local hairdresser makes sense for me. There's one day a week at college as part of it, so I still come out with a qualification. But it's work experience and learning on the job that's most important to me, plus a good chance of a steady job at the end of it, and a little bit of money.

Case study 4: Sasha, T Levels, Engineering

I wanted to study engineering, but the idea of doing Maths and Physics at A Level didn't appeal to me. When I saw the new T Levels that were being introduced in England, these seemed to suit me much better. Now I've got the opportunity to study Engineering from 2022 for two years, with practical experience, before I apply to university to do a degree in Engineering. I don't know which type of Engineering I will do at uni yet, which is why a general T Level in Engineering is a good option for me.

Case study 5: Hannah, A Levels, Medicine

I've always wanted to be a doctor. I looked at BTECs and quickly realised I wouldn't get into medical school with a BTEC – it has to be A Levels, with very good grades, and in specific subjects for Russell Group universities. So I decided to do Maths, Chemistry and Biology, along with the Extended Project to give me the edge on my university application. It's a lot of academic work, but I'm determined to succeed.

Case study 6: John, a mixture, Music Production

Music and dance are my life. So I've chosen to do Dance and Drama A Levels. But for music, I'm doing a BTEC in Music Production, which is the equivalent of one A Level. It's important to do a practical subject so I can do Music Technology as a degree at a university that specialises in this sort of course. It's all about practical experience on my course.

Worksheet 5.2b Your next steps

Fill in the pyramid, starting at the top with where you want to be in 10 years' time, and working backwards. At each stage, think about what you need to be doing in order to achieve the next stage.

Also think about how technology may have changed at each stage. What changes in technology may have occurred in the labour market that could affect your career choice and the skills and experience you need for each stage?

For example: *In 10 years' time I want to be a top lawyer. So, in four years' time I need to be doing a law degree at a good university and monitoring how the legal profession is changing. There's likely to be more homeworking, so I also need to be up to date on the electronic meeting platforms, in case we have more virtual trials. So, in two years' time I need to be on course to get As and Bs in my A Levels, and make sure I have good IT skills. So in two years' time I need to have at least five GCSEs at grade 4 or higher – my target will be 6s or 7s. So, in one year's time I need to have a good study plan for my GCSEs. That means in six months' time I need to have made real progress in my GCSEs.*

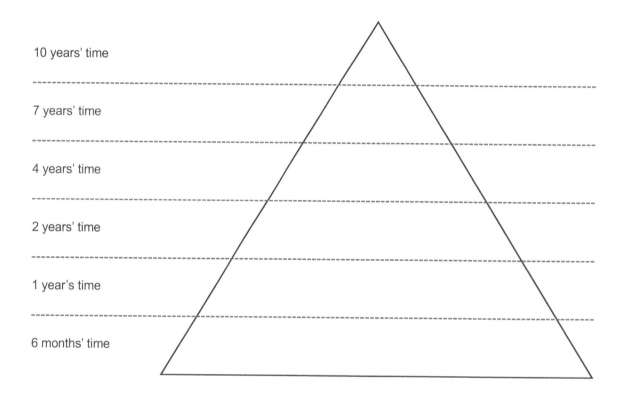

10 years' time

7 years' time

4 years' time

2 years' time

1 year's time

6 months' time

> **How long it usually takes to gain each qualification**
> A Levels – two years
> BTEC Level 3 – two years
> BTEC Level 1 or 2 – one year
> Apprenticeship – two years
> T Levels – two years
> Degree – three years
> Degree apprenticeship – three years
> Postgraduate qualification, e.g. PGCE for teacher training – one year
> Masters degree – one year
> PhD (doctorate) – three years

Note: At the end of the course, revisit this sheet and make sure that your targets are SMART and PURE, as detailed in Lesson 20.2, and that all of you is happy with this plan. (Does your heart feel it is OK? Does your head think it's a good idea? Can you gut accept what you have written?)

5.3 You, work and technology

Learning objectives:

- To know how labour markets have changed over the last 100 years and how they may change in the future
- To look at the effects of automation and AI
- To examine how the manufacturing sector is declining and the service sector is growing

Resources:

- PowerPoint 5.3
- Worksheets 5.3a and 5.3b
- Relevant resources from your history department
- Link to KS3: Book 3, Unit 5.2

Key vocabulary:

labour market, automation, artificial intelligence, structural unemployment, primary, secondary (manufacturing) and tertiary (services) sector

Get them thinking! (5 mins)

- Ask students to list how they think work has changed over the last 100 years. Ask them to share their ideas and note them on the board.

Core learning (25 mins)

- Go through **Slide 1**, showing what the UK labour market was like 100 years ago. (Use additional resources from your history department if they are available.) Point out three main differences: the lack of technology, the number of women working and how people often did the same job for life.

- Explain how the UK economy can be divided into the primary sector (which provides raw materials, e.g. the mining, fishing and agriculture industries), the manufacturing sector (making goods, e.g. car manufacturing) and the tertiary sector (providing services, e.g. a law firm or a bank). Use **Slide 2** to explore how this relates to your local area.

- Use current economic statistics from the government (such as the Office of National Statistics: https://www.ons.gov.uk/businessindustryandtrade/manufacturingandproductionindustry) to show how the manufacturing sector has declined and the service sector has grown over time (e.g. manufacturing has led to car plants now using many more robots than people to make cars; meanwhile, the UK has become a leader in services, such as the financial service sector, with many banks in London). Mention how some economists now say there is a fourth sector – providing digital information and knowledge (e.g. the growth of computer firms along the M4 corridor between London and Wales).

- Go through **Slides 3** and **4**, defining automation and artificial intelligence (AI). Ask students what other industries they think will be most affected by automation and AI. *(Examples include any industry where there are physically repetitive tasks, e.g. car manufacturing, or the same analysis of complex data, e.g. calculating insurance premiums).* Write these on the board.

- Ask students to discuss the statements on **Slide 5** in groups. Follow up with the plenary below.

Additional learning (15 mins)

- Ask students, in pairs, to complete **Worksheet 5.3a**, exploring terminology that shows how technology is transforming our working lives. *(Answers: 1H, 2E, 3D, 4G, 5I, 6C, 7J, 8B, 9F, 10A.)*

Plenary (5 mins)

- Hold a discussion on whether AI and automation are good or bad, and discuss how students think they will affect your local economy in the next 10 years.

Assessment

- Check that students have completed **Worksheet 5.3a** and then take them in to use for assessment.

Extension or home learning

- Extension: Ask students, in pairs, to complete **Worksheet 5.3b**, deciding which situations are fair or unfair. *(Answers: unfair/illegal – 3, 5 and 6; 3 and 5 are unfair/illegal for age discrimination, 6 is illegal because it is a work expense, which the company should be paying.)*

- Home learning: Ask students to pick a particular business or set of businesses in the same sector in their local area (see **Slide 2**) and write a report on how they think these businesses will change in the next 10, 50 and 100 years.

Worksheet 5.3a Technical mix-up

Look at the following table. Match the words with the definitions.

Word	Match		Definition
1. Distance learning			A. Working from home, which has become increasingly common over the last 10 years, and particularly in 2020.
2. Artificial Intelligence			B. Making a firm smaller so fewer people are working there, to save costs.
3. Breakout room			C. Having robots and machines, rather than a person, complete a job or process.
4. Technophobe			D. A room away from the main meeting room, where people discuss a particular issue. When a meeting is online, participants may move to a separate chat room to discuss an issue or question, before returning to the main discussion group.
5. Outsourcing			E. The ability of computers to think and learn on their own, without being programmed by humans.
6. Automation			F. A new part of the economy dealing with digital information and knowledge
7. Blog			G. Somebody who hates technology and doesn't like learning to use new programs or applications.
8. Downsizing			H. Learning that is done remotely via a computer, using digital resources and digital meetings via the internet such as Zoom, Google Meet or Microsoft Teams.
9. Fourth sector			I. Moving a job from being done inside a firm to an external company.
10. Homeworking			J. A regularly updated website, usually written in an informal style, sometimes using the style of a diary.

Stretch activity: What other issues can you think of that may affect how people work due to a rise in the use of technology?

....

....

....

....

....

Worksheet 5.3b Fair or unfair?

Look at the situations in the table. In pairs, decide whether you think each situation is fair or unfair, and why, giving reasons for your views. Compare your answers with those of another pair or group.

Scenario	Fair or unfair?	Why?
A car worker is made redundant after 20 years working at a factory, because their job can now be done by a robot. They are not offered alternative employment by the company.		
A teacher is told their contract is being reduced from full time to part time, because more lessons can now be delivered online. They are offered another part-time contract to teach another subject, which they do not like.		
An older worker is told they have not been successful in a job application because of the amount of data entry that is involved, even though they are highly computer literate.		
A barista is sacked from their job because they refuse to learn how the new coffee machine works, because it is too complicated and they don't like it.		
A younger worker doesn't get a part-time data-entry job because they are told, 'young people don't have the attention span' to use the new computers the company is using.		
A web designer is told they can carry on working for their company, but only if they pay for their own training to use the new software the company is converting to. The training will cost £500.		

5.4   You and your workplace skills

Learning objectives:
- To identify acceptable and unacceptable behaviour at work
- To distinguish between workplace bullying and harassment, with examples

Resources:
- PowerPoint 5.4
- Worksheets 5.4a and 5.4b
- Access to the internet
- Link to KS3: Book 3, Unit 4

Key vocabulary:
confidentiality, health and safety, punctuality, harassment, discrimination

Get them thinking! (5 mins)
- Ask students if there is anything a person has to do at work, or can't do at work, that is different from when they are not at work. Note the ideas on the board.

Core learning (25 mins)
- Ask students to read the information at https://www.reed.co.uk/career-advice/jobs-for-14-year-olds/ to see what work they can do now (this can be introduced earlier if you wish – see Slide 5 in Lesson 5.1).
- Go through **Slide 1** with students, asking the three questions and comparing these with the ideas students came up with at the beginning of the lesson. For example, 'How should you behave?' might include being punctual, reliable, friendly, at ease and trustworthy.
- Ask students to complete **Worksheet 5.4a** in pairs and then compare their answers in groups. Explain to students that they should first decide whether each situation is acceptable or not. If not, what needs to change? *(Suggested answers for unacceptable are 1, 3, 6, 8, 9 and 10. The other answers depend on the circumstance, e.g. 4 needs to occur outside in a designated smoking area; 7 may be illegal; 9 is illegal for the employer.)* As a stretch activity for fast finishers, students could rank these situations in order of importance, and then discuss their answers in groups. Monitor to make sure every student completes the worksheet.
- Show **Slide 2** and discuss what is meant by confidential information at work. Give examples, such as a customer's name, address and telephone number (mention data protection here: how this information is confidential). Make it clear that confidential information should not be shared.
- Ask students what they think health and safety at work means. Go through **Slide 3**, pointing out that workers – as well as employers – have a responsibility to keep each other safe.

Additional learning (15 mins)
- Go through **Slides 4–6**, covering the difference between discrimination (treating somebody unfairly because of one of their personal characteristics) and harassment (paying somebody undue and persistent attention) at work. Point out how both are illegal under the 2010 Equality Act, and how managers, colleagues, human resource departments (which are responsible for making sure workers are treated fairly) and trade unions (see Lesson 4.2 on pressure groups) can help resolve these issues.
- Ask students to imagine they are going to a job interview. They should come up with as many ideas as possible for what they can do to make a good impression in order to get the job.

Plenary (5 mins)
- Discuss with students what they think are the top three ways to make a good impression at a job interview *(e.g. turn up on time and well prepared, dress smartly, have two or three questions to ask)*.

Assessment
- Check that all students have completed the **Worksheet 5.4a** and then take it in to use for assessment.

Extension or home learning
- Home learning: Ask students to find a job advert they are interested in or to imagine they are going to a job interview. Then tell them to follow the advice on **Worksheet 5.4b** to prepare for an interview.
- Extension: Ask students to research what work experience they wish to undertake, linked to their targets and choices from Lessons 5.1, 5.2 and 5.3. Then get them to plan who to approach for the best work-experience opportunity and draft a letter or email to an employer, for you to check before they apply for work experience, if appropriate to your school's work-experience programme. The following website is useful: https://www.getmyfirstjob.co.uk/Choices/WorkExperience.aspx.

Worksheet 5.4a You at work

Look at the table below. For each situation, fill in whether you think it is acceptable or not, why and what needs to change. Then rank the situations in order of how acceptable they are. Finally, compare your answer with another pair or group, giving reasons for your views.

Situation	Acceptable or not?	Why and what needs to change?	Rank in order of acceptability
1. Turning up to work five minutes late.	Depends whether it's a one-off or repeated, and whether you can easily make up five minutes at the end of the day.	Punctuality!	
2. Wearing makeup at work.			
3. Swearing at work.			
4. Smoking at work.			
5. Not finishing all the jobs you had to do that day and not telling anyone.			
6. Refusing to wear a short skirt or shorts at work.			
7. Leaving work 10 mins early if you can get away with it.			
8. Refusing to work with somebody or to give them a job because of their gender, age or ethnicity.			
9. Sharing confidential information with a friend because you think it's funny.			

Worksheet 5.4b Preparing for an interview

Before the interview:

1. Research the company. Find out what exactly it does. Note down the date and time of the interview, and who will be interviewing you. Work out how long it will take you to get there. Look carefully at any job description you have been given.

2. Make a list of the key skills required in the job. Common key skills include the ability to deal with confidential information, deal with money, work on your own, work as part of a team, demonstrate good customer service and/or interpersonal skills, including the ability to listen.

3. Think about your experience, qualifications and your personality. Match up areas you can discuss on your CV and features of your personality that you think match the job description.

4. Write down a list of the top five questions you think you will be asked in the interview. Common questions include:

   a) Why do you want this job in particular?

   b) Where do you see yourself in five or 10 years' time?

   c) What is your greatest success or greatest strength?

   d) Describe something that you failed at and what you learned from the experience.

   e) What is your greatest weakness and how do you compensate for it?

5. Make sure you also have a few questions of your own to ask – this is your opportunity to find out more about the company you will be working for to see whether you feel it would be a good fit for you.

On the day of the interview:

1. Dress smartly and professionally (e.g. a suit and a tie, a smart dress and jacket).

6. Take a copy of your CV, job application, and notes that you have made, including prompts and questions from 1–5) above.

7. Make sure you arrive in plenty of time, but not too early. About 10–15 minutes early is about right, giving you a chance to look over your notes for the interview.

Right before the interview:

Practise the balanced breathing exercise on **PowerPoint 20.2 slide 1**. This will help you relax and this in turn will help you perform better in the interview.

During the interview:

1. Keep calm – remember, it is better to give a slow answer and take your time to think about what you are saying.

2. Listen carefully to what the interviewer(s) are saying and asking.

After the interview:

Always ask for feedback – this will help you learn from it for any future interview. For more details about receiving feedback, see **Unit 20.2**.

6.1 | Keeping physically healthy

Learning objectives:
- To understand the different elements required to keep ourselves physically fit and healthy
- To understand the importance of personal hygiene and self-examination

Resources:
- PowerPoint 6.1
- Worksheets 6.1a, 6.1b and 6.1c
- Working/graffiti wall and board pens
- Access to the internet
- Link to KS3: Book 1, Units 14.1 and 13.1; Book 2, Unit 9.1

Key vocabulary:
aerobic exercise, Eatwell Guide, carbohydrates/carbs, personal hygiene, self-examination

Get them thinking! (5 mins)
- Ask: 'What keeps us physically healthy?' Discuss this as a class and note ideas on the board (e.g. exercise, healthy eating, hydration and sleep).

Core learning (25 mins)
- Ask the class if they know how much exercise they should be getting each day. Then go to **Slide 1** to clarify. Are they surprised?
- With a prepared graffiti or working wall/display area, hand out bright board pens. Ask students to write all the different ways to exercise they can think of on the wall. This could be organised sports, playing with mates in the park, dancing around at home, and so on.
- After the activity, remind students of any they might have forgotten about. Explain that any exercise is better than none, whether it's 30 minutes or 10 minutes a day, and simple decisions like taking stairs rather than escalators or lifts can contribute to our fitness. Remind them that keeping physically fit also helps our mental health, e.g. reducing stress (see KS3 links).
- Show the Eatwell Guide on **Slide 2**. Hand out **Worksheet 6.1a** and tell students they are going to write questions for a partner to answer based on the Eatwell Guide. Model an example question (see the notes on the slide) and allow time for students to write their own questions.
- Go through the healthy eating tips on **Slide 3**. Ask students to work with the same partner to explain why each of these points are important for our health. Then go through them again as a class (see the notes on the slide for suggestions). Also see KS3 Book 1, Unit 13.1.

Additional learning (15 mins)
- Hand out **Worksheet 6.1b** and allow the class time to consider the importance of water and sleep for our physical health. Students can work independently or in pairs to complete the worksheet. Then work through **Slides 4** and **5** as a class to check the answers, which can be found in the notes section on the slides. (NB. The extension activity could be used here and the worksheet used as an extension instead, you can choose depending on your students' needs.)

Plenary (5 mins)
- Recap the different areas students have learned about today – exercise, healthy eating, water and sleep. Answer any questions they may have.

Assessment
- Use the worksheets and home learning activity to assess students' understanding.

Extension or home learning
- Extension: Hand out **Worksheet 6.1c** about self-examination (also see KS3, Book 2, Unit 9.1). Give students these links to find out how to do self-examinations – breast self-examination: https://www.nhs.uk/common-health-questions/womens-health/how-should-i-check-my-breasts/; testicle self examination: https://www.macmillan.org.uk/cancer-information-and-support/testicular-cancer/how-to-check
- Home learning: Ask students to create a poster, bringing together all the different areas of maintaining a healthy body they have learned about in this lesson. Use this for assessment.

Worksheet 6.1a The Eatwell Guide

Using the guide below, write some questions about healthy eating for your partner to answer.
Swap sheets and then mark your partner's work.

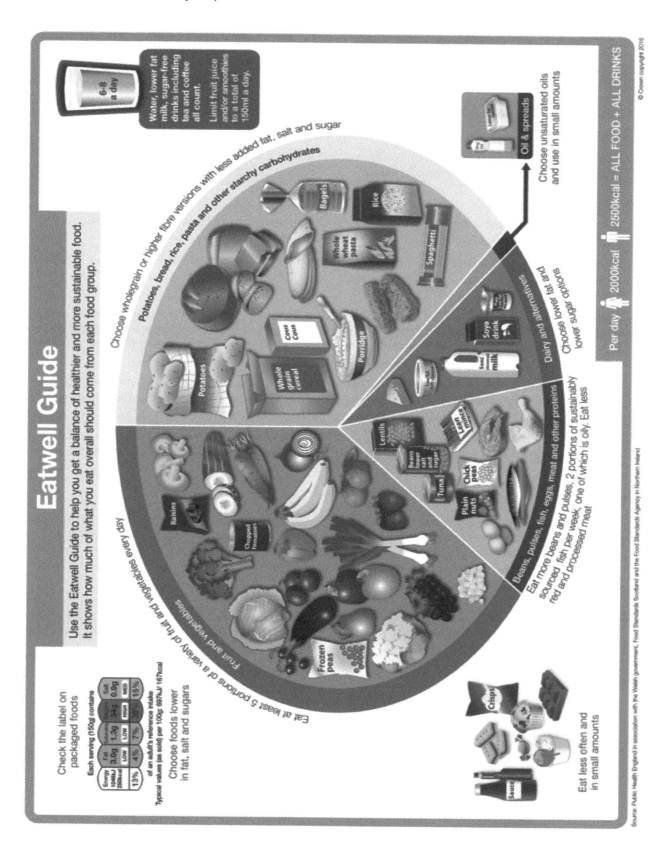

Write your questions about healthy eating here.

1. ....
....
....
....

2. ....
....
....
....

3. ....
....
....
....

4. ....
....
....
....

Worksheet 6.1b Keeping physically healthy

Read and answer the questions below. If you don't know the answer, just have a guess!

Water

1. How much of the human body is made up of water?

    ....

2. How long would you stay alive without drinking fluids?

    ....

3. How might the body use water?

    ....

4. How many glasses of water does the Eatwell Guide say our body needs each day?

    ....

5. How much water do you think you drink a day?

    ....

6. If you don't drink enough, what could you do to help you drink more?

    ....

Sleep

7. How many hours of sleep do you think 14–17-year-olds need each night?

    ....

8. How does sleep help your physical health?

    ....

9. How does sleep help your brain and mental health?

    ....

10. How many hours a night do you think you sleep?

    ....

11. If you find it hard to sleep, what helps you?

    ....

Worksheet 6.1c Self-examination

Keeping our bodies clean every day, including our private areas and armpits, is really important as we go through puberty.

As you grow older it is also important to keep an eye out for any lumps or bumps, or to see if anything looks or feels different on your body.

Self-examination needs to be done frequently, and if you find anything different or unusual, however small, anywhere on your body, it is important to go to a parent or carer and see a doctor to check it out. (Getting help quickly can be the difference between a fast cure or a longer-term health issue.)

- Breasts: You need to do regular checks every month once you reach your twenties, but it's good to keep an eye out for any lumps, bumps, soreness, discharge (or pain if it is not around your period) now.

- Testicles: It is good to start checking these monthly from the age of 14 or 15, testing for any lumps or bumps by gently rolling your fingers across them. Look out also for pain, swollen areas or changes in the look or shape of them. (Although rare in teenagers, testicular cancer is still the most common cancer for boys/men between the ages of 15 and 35.)

Read the information at the link appropriate to your body and then answer the questions below.

Breast self-examination:
https://www.nhs.uk/common-health-questions/womens-health/how-should-i-check-my-breasts/,

Testicle self-examination:
https://www.macmillan.org.uk/cancer-information-and-support/testicular-cancer/how-to-check

1. How often should you check yourself?

    ....

2. How do you do a self-examination?

    ....

    ....

    ....

    ....

    ....

3. What are you looking for?

    ....

    ....

4. Why is it important to do self-examinations?

    ....

    ....

5. What should you do if you find anything that doesn't seem right?

    ....

6.2 Your self-image

Learning objectives:

- To consider what is a healthy and unhealthy self-image
- To evaluate our own self-image and where we can go for help
- To consider the concept of a 'perfect' body

Resources:

- PowerPoint 6.2
- Worksheet 6.2
- A4 paper and pens/pencils
- Resources for projects as required
- Access to the internet
- Link to KS3: Book 1, Unit 13.2; Book 3, Unit 9.1

Key vocabulary:

self-image, self-esteem, traits, gender, trans, gender fluid, body image

Get them thinking! (5 mins)

- Ask: 'What does the term self-image mean to you?' Allow students to discuss this as a class or in pairs without directing them – use their responses as an assessment of their understanding.

Core learning (25 mins)

- Go to **Slides 1** and **2** to introduce the concept of self-image. Explain that self-image is made up of how we see ourselves and how others see us. Ask the class whether what we see in ourselves is the same as what others see in us. Encourage them to explore this a little in a class discussion.

- IMPORTANT: Make sure you revisit your working agreement for this lesson and remind students that the focus is on kindness and respect. Show **Slide 3** and read through the instructions with the class. When putting them into pairs for this activity, mixing them up so they are not with their best friends may be more impactful, but it is important that you only do this if you feel students will be kind and supportive to each other; if not, let them choose who to pair with so they feel comfortable. When they have finished, tell them to share with each other what they have written.

- Hand out **Worksheet 6.2** and allow students quiet time to complete their reflection on this activity. On completion, ask if they would like to discuss what they found; if not, leave them to process this independently if this feels more appropriate for your cohort. They can keep the worksheet if they wish.

- Ask students: 'Do you feel we are judged on our "inside" selves or our "outside" selves? Why?' Get them to share examples, perhaps from films, books or TV. If the conversation becomes about gender issues, encourage them to be inclusive and think of all genders – including pressures on those who identify as trans, gender fluid or non-binary; the same applies to issues of race and other aspects of our identities.

- Display **Slide 4** and explore the idea of social pressures with students. Ask: 'What stereotypes of body image do the media present?' (Go to the BBC Teach Film in the extension to consider this further.)

Additional learning (15 mins)

- Go to **Slide 5** to explore the concept of perfectionism further. Discuss the two questions, allowing students to mull over different ideas they may have.

- Tell students you are going to give them a project to work on in groups to explore and present however they wish. The title is 'Perfect Body'. This can be interpreted however they want; encourage them to consider a wide variety of contexts and people (e.g. different bodies, genders, cultures) and the pressures to be perfect. Tell them they will present their projects in the next or future lessons and they will begin planning it now. (Adapt to suit your cohort and timetable.)

Plenary (5 mins)

- Tell students that if they feel that pressure to be a certain way is making them struggle with their body image or general self-image, it is important that they talk to a trusted adult. Share this website and go through it with them briefly: https://youngminds.org.uk/find-help/feelings-and-symptoms/body-image/.

Assessment

- Once completed, assess projects against the learning objectives and feed back to students.

Extension or home learning

- Extension or home learning: Using this BBC PSHE KS3/GCSE clip to inspire them, ask students to explore the concept of cultural influences on body ideals and image, creating a collage to show how they view their own or another culture's ideals or the westernisation of identities: https://www.bbc.co.uk/teach/class-clips-video/pshe-ks3--ks4-cultural-influences-on-body-ideals-image/zkxhy9q (You might need to explain that PNG stands for Papua New Guinea.)

Worksheet 6.2 Self-image

Activity reflection

You have just done an activity to consider whether your self-image is the same as the image others have of you. Using what your partner has written, answer the questions below independently, spending some time to reflect quietly on this experience and what you can take from it.

1. What did your partner say about you?

    ....

    ....

    ....

    ....

2. Were you surprised about what your partner saw in you? Why?

    ....

    ....

    ....

    ....

3. Has it made you question anything you thought about yourself? Explain.

    ....

    ....

    ....

    ....

4. How can you build on this experience to re-evaluate your self-image and self-awareness?

    ....

    ....

    ....

    ....

5. Is there anything else you want to note or to explore further regarding self-image?

    ....

    ....

    ....

    ....

6.3 First aid

Learning objectives:

- To learn basic life support first aid skills

Note: We think further lifesaving skills are better taught by an expert in person so please arrange for further support on topics such as CPR and defibrillation.

Resources:

- PowerPoint 6.3
- Worksheet 6.3
- Art materials
- Link to KS3: Book 1, Unit 20.1

Key vocabulary:

primary survey, acronym – DRABC (or DRSABC where S = shout), conscious, semiconscious unconscious

Get them thinking! (5 mins)

- Ask: 'What are your reactions like in an emergency? How is it best to react in an emergency?' Discuss with the class and assess their understanding of what skills are required in an emergency situation, e.g. calmness and decisiveness.

Core learning (25 mins)

- Display **Slide 1**. Discuss what could have happened and what students would do in this situation *(e.g. he could have had a heart attack, fainted or knocked his head)*. Explain that being calm but acting quickly are the best ways to help in an emergency.

- Show the St John Ambulance video on how to do a primary survey of a casualty at https://www.sja.org.uk/get-advice/first-aid-advice/how-to/how-to-do-the-primary-survey/. Then go through the steps with students in more detail to make sure they understand exactly what is involved.

- Show **Slide 2** and go through the acronym a few times: DRABC or DRSABC.

- If this is a short lesson, ask students to design a poster for the acronym or practise how they would make an emergency call, including what information they would need to give to be of use. They could do this as a role-play. If this is a longer lesson, ask them to plan and create a comic strip – see additional learning below.

Additional learning (15 mins)

- Hand out copies of **Worksheet 6.3** and ask students to use it to plan and create a comic strip. It should show an emergency scenario, with them in the pictures, coming to assist someone who is lying on the floor conscious, semiconscious or unconscious, following the primary survey steps. Go through the instructions with them, making sure they use the acronym D – danger, R – response, S – shout/call 999, A – airways and B – breathing, as outlined on the worksheet.

Plenary (5 mins)

- Allow time for students to share their work and go through any misconceptions or questions.

Assessment

- Use the comic strip activity to assess their understanding.

Extension or home learning

- Extension: Get the class to research when the recovery position is useful and when it is not useful. As an extra extension, ask them to learn how to put somebody into the recovery position.

- Extension: Invite an expert to the school to teach first aid, including CPR and defibrillation (methods used to resuscitate someone), and to cover the circulation aspect of the acronym DRSABC. Alternatively, this BBC Teach video could be used to introduce the class to CPR and defibrillation: https://www.bbc.co.uk/teach/class-clips-video/pshe-ks3-how-to-administer-cpr/zrkgydm.

Comic strip

Complete this comic strip to show what you have learned about the first vital stages needed in a primary survey when there is an emergency. Use the boxes in the strip to show you finding someone at the beginning, and then following each step of the acronym DRSAB:

- Check for Danger (D)
- Check for Response (R)
- (Also Shout and call 999) (S)
- Check/Open Airway (A)
- Check Breathing (B)
- and finally, you staying with the patient at the end.

Note: The last letter of the acronym is C for circulation. You will learn about this and how to resuscitate (to revive someone when they are unconscious or not breathing) at a later date.

Learning objectives:

- To understand what mental health is
- To learn how to recognise the early signs of mental health concerns
- To know what to do to help ourselves and others

Resources:

- PowerPoint 7.1
- Worksheet 7.1
- A4 paper or books
- Access to the internet
- Link to KS3: Book 3, Units 13.1, 13.3 and 13.4

Key vocabulary:

mental health, emotional health, wellbeing, common mental health problems, psychotic symptoms

Get them thinking! (5 mins)

- Ask students to discuss in pairs: 'Why, as a society, do we find it easier to talk about our physical ill health than our mental ill health?' Invite students to feed back to the class.

Core learning (25 mins)

- Discuss how the class would define mental health, and then show **Slide 1**. Reinforce that often people think of mental health just in terms of *poor* mental health but, like physical health, it refers to the full spectrum, from good mental health through to seriously poor mental health and everything in between.

- Show **Slide 2**. Explain that poor mental health doesn't necessarily mean that someone has a serious mental health condition – there is a wide range of mental illnesses, from mild to serious: see **Slide 3**.

- Ask students to think about what can affect day-to-day mental health both positively and negatively. Discuss as a class, and then hand out **Worksheet 7.1** for students to complete individually, in pairs or in small groups, depending on what is best for your class.

- Go through the sheet with them and discuss their ideas at the end. *(Answers: P = Positive, N = Negative: 1. P; 2. P; 3. N; 4. P; 5. N; 6. N; 7. P; 8. P; 9. N; 10. P; 11. P; 12. N; 13. P; 14. N; 15. P. Note that some students may feel some of these are not black and white, that they might be positive in some instances and negative in others, e.g. fine occasionally but less good if they were daily habits.)*

- Watch the Childline film 'Asking an adult for help', which can be found in the 'Ways to feel confident' section at https://www.childline.org.uk/info-advice/bullying-abuse-safety/getting-help/asking-adult-help/

- Go through **Slide 4** and reinforce to students how important it is to seek help for themselves, their friends or family members if they feel they are not coping well or are behaving in a different or out-of-character way. Then go through **Slide 5**.

Additional learning (15 mins)

- Using the Childline video from the core learning, ask students to note down all the ways to talk to someone that have been recommended and then add any further ideas they have. Then tell them to use these notes to write simple instructions (or a poem) called 'How to talk to someone about how you feel'.

Plenary (5 mins)

- Listen to students' instructions/poems and feed back. These could be designed as posters to encourage a school ethos of talking to others about feelings.

Assessment

- Work with the class to complete a spider diagram on the board that includes everything they have learned about mental health today and what they would like to learn more about.

Extension or home learning

- Homework: Set homework to investigate different types of mental health using charities such as Childline: https://www.childline.org.uk/info-advice/your-feelings/mental-health/ or Young Minds: www.youngminds.org.uk/find-help/feelings-and-symptoms/ to support their learning. They could then create a PowerPoint or an information booklet.

- Extension: Go to the 'Types of mental health problems' page of the Mind website for more information: www.mind.org.uk/information-support/types-of-mental-health-problems/. Ask students to explore the individual symptoms further in pairs or groups of three.

Worksheet 7.1 What can affect day-to-day mental health both online and offline?

Go through some of the things we do and decide if they are good for our mental health or not so good. Explain why you think this.

Things we do	Positive or negative?	Why do you think this?
1. Getting out of the house/outside		
2. Going to a doctor with worries		
3. Comparing ourselves with others		
4. Calling up helplines for support		
5. Working hard with no breaks		
6. Scrolling social media for hours		
7. Keeping fit		
8. Having fun with mates		
9. Isolating ourselves in our rooms		
10. Going to see a counsellor		
11. Eating healthily and sleeping well		
12. Not being honest with family/carers		
13. Taking time to relax and be mindful		
14. Saying we're 'fine' to our friends when we're not		
15. Finding gratitude for small things		

What do you think works best in helping positive mental health and wellbeing? Share your tips below.

....

....

....

Learning objectives:
- To understand stress and how to deal with it
- To consider a range of different studying techniques
- To learn some simple mindfulness and meditation techniques

Resources:
- PowerPoint 7.2
- Worksheets 7.2a and 7.2b
- Sticky notes
- Link to KS3: Book 2, Units 12.1 and 12.3; Book 3, Unit 1.3

Key vocabulary:
stress, stressors, stress response, exams, revision

Get them thinking! (5 mins)

- Ask students: 'What happens to your body and your mind when you feel stressed?' Encourage them to think quietly and then discuss their ideas with them briefly (e.g. muscles feel tense, emotionally irritable, anxious, find it hard to sleep).

Core learning (25 mins)

- Ask the class what makes them stressed. Give them a few minutes to jot down as many stressful things as they can think of as a small group. Then go through this all together and do a quick tally of the most common on the board as they feed back.

- Go through **Slides 1** and **2** with students. Then show **Slide 3** and read it as a class. Work with students to consider what a balanced revision/study day might look like.

- Read through **Slide 4**. Then get the class in a circle and ask students to share: 1. How they notice they are getting stressed; 2. What they do to destress. Do a full circle around the class for each new question, allowing students to 'pass' if they wish – this is a good way for those who are struggling with stress to get new ideas.

- Once back at their tables, ask students if anyone has any really good revision or exam tips (such as the value of timetabling with regular breaks, eating healthily, exercise, doing practice exams, asking a family member or carer to ask them questions, writing notes, recording information, watching revision films online, making up songs/poems, acronyms). Tell them it's worth trying out different methods in order to find the one that best suits their learning style.

- Hand out **Worksheet 7.2a** and go through the revision and studying techniques together. Then allow time for students to work through this alone and make 'promises to themselves'. Listen to a few of their promises. Once you have marked these, return them so students can refer back to them.

Additional learning (15 mins)

- Display **Slide 5** and read through it with the class. However, caution them that if they are in a very challenging or distressing situation it might be better to seek professional support from a GP or school counsellor before doing mindfulness or meditation.

- Lead students through the two examples on **Worksheet 7.2b** so they do the exercises while you instruct them. Explain that these can be done anywhere and at any time and as often as they wish.

- After they have done the two exercises, allow time for them to share their experiences. Hand out copies of the worksheets for students to take home so they can use the guidance to relax in their own time.

Plenary (5 mins)

- Revisit what the students have learned, taking any questions. Remind them that it is really important that they talk to an adult they trust if they feel they can't cope with their stress or any other feelings around exams. Ask them how you and your colleagues can support them further with this. (Be sure to pass this on to colleagues and plan in lessons following this.)

Assessment

- The circle activity and **Worksheet 7.2a** can be used for assessment.

Extension or home learning

- Extension or home learning: Ask students to explore and plan their revision further, incorporating their learning styles and trying a range of different techniques and methods to see which suits them best.

Worksheet 7.2a Revision and exam strategies

Mark Roberts, in his book called *You Can't Revise for GCSE English* (Collins, 2020), suggests that there are six steps that will help you with revision and preparing for your exams.

Go through these six steps and make a commitment to yourself, thinking of a change or a new action for each that you will commit to do in order to help yourself.

1. Get organised

Look at the time you have before your exam and create a timetable/plan and then stick to it (you might need to review and adapt it though).

I will ....

....

2. Study in the right environment

Studies have shown that noise, music and smartphones reduce your focus and will be a disadvantage.

I will ....

....

3. Cope with exam worries

Don't put off studying or avoid the tricky stuff – focus on what you can change, not what you can't. Breathe deeply and practise relaxation techniques when you feel worried (see **Worksheet 7.2b**).

I will ....

....

4. Exercise regularly

Studies show that exercise is really good for the brain as well as the body. Remember, 60 minutes a day is advised but you don't have to do this all in one go – you can plan little exercise/desk breaks. And if you can't manage 60 minutes, any exercise is better than none.

I will ....

....

5. Take breaks and get enough sleep

Studies have shown that people who allow themselves breaks in their study days, e.g. to have some fun, do better as our brains need a break to absorb new information. Sleep is also really important; 8–10 hours is perfect, give yourself time to relax for an hour before bed.

I will ....

....

6. Stay motivated and show resilience

Recognise how much more you know now compared with a younger you – and don't give up! Having small 'tickable' targets will keep you focused on what you are doing well.

I will ....

....

Worksheet 7.2b Mindfulness and meditation

1. Mindfulness

Coming into the moment

Often when we are stressed, we are not 'in the moment'. Our heads might be thinking about something in the past or we may be worrying about something in the future. Or our brains could be on 'standby', staring at a computer or mobile phone. We are often unaware of our surroundings and of this moment. Simply bringing our attention back into the moment can calm us down.

You could do this anywhere and at any time you start to feel stressed, such as when you need a break from studying, when you are queuing in a shop or before you go into an exam.

> **Instructions:**
> * Stop what you are doing and quieten down your thinking.
> * Without moving your head, look at what is in front of you – notice colours and textures – really look.
> * Then look to your left and then to your right, very slowly, looking at everything in detail.
> * Don't judge anything, just look.
> * Now open up your ears and listen to the sounds around you.
> * Now open up your other senses and become aware of what you feel on your skin, what you smell.
> * This moment is unique, it will never come again – enjoy it.
> * When you are ready, carry on with what you were doing.

2. Meditation

Body scan

When we are stressed, we can hold a lot of tension in our thoughts but also in our bodies, often without realising. This simple meditation gives us a chance to become aware of this, to release tension and to relax more deeply. This can be done anywhere and as often as is required.

> **Instructions:**
> * Stop what you are doing and freeze your body. Close your eyes and don't move a muscle.
> * Using your mind, scan your body slowly from the tips of your toes to the top of your head.
> * Notice any areas of pain or tension.
> * Notice how you are breathing.
> * Once you have done this, go back to the tips of your toes again and rescan.
> * This time stop at each part: your feet, your lower legs, your knees and so on, all the way up to the top of your head.
> * As you focus on each part of your body, imagine a warm light soothing and relaxing each spot, let your muscles relax and sink into the chair or floor as you relax further and further.
> * Once you have scanned all the way to the top of your head, notice your breathing.
> * If you are not breathing calmly and deeply already, do this now, taking three long deep breaths in and out.
> * When you are ready, open your eyes and have a good stretch.

Learning objectives:

- To understand that there are different types of job contract
- To understand payslips
- To know what income tax and National Insurance are, and the difference between net and gross pay

Resources:

- PowerPoint 8.1
- Worksheets 8.1a and 8.1b
- Link to KS3: Book 3, Unit 15.1

Key vocabulary:

job contract, part time, full time, zero hours, maternity cover, verbal contract, basic pay, commission, income tax, National Insurance, net, gross

Get them thinking! (5 mins)

- Ask students if they know what a contract is. Elicit some ideas and then write the following definition on the board: 'A contract is a spoken or written agreement which has a legal status – it can be enforced by law. Examples of contracts include work contracts and mobile phone contracts.' Ask students if anyone in the class works at all and, if so, what sort of contract or agreement they have (e.g. a verbal contract with another family member to help with their business, or a paper round).

Core learning (25 mins)

- Display **Slide 1** and explain the difference between a temporary contract and a permanent contract. Then talk through other contracts as shown on **Slide 2**. Explain how, even if there isn't a written contract between you and an employer, a verbal contract still exists.
- Ask students how they get paid. Then show **Slide 3** and talk through the different ways in which people can be paid. Distinguish between a basic rate of pay, commission and bonuses, as shown on the slide.
- Ask students if they know what the laws are for employing young people below the age of 18. Listen to their suggestions and then go through the information about this on **Slides 4** and **5**.
- Hand out **Worksheet 8.1a** and discuss the example payslip with students, making sure they understand the difference between gross pay and net pay. Then go through the rest of the information on the sheet, explaining what overtime is and what the different tax rates are. Ask students to work in pairs to calculate how much tax a person pays if they earn £20,000 *(£1500)*, £50,000 *(£7500)*, £100,000 *(£27,500,)* and £500,000 *(£205,000)*. Explain that the UK has a progressive income tax system: the more you earn, the more you pay.
- Tell students that everyone is given a National Insurance number on a card when they turn 16. Use the information on the worksheet to explain what National Insurance is used for, and how much National Insurance you must pay from what you earn.

Additional learning (15 mins)

- Define what arrears are (money that is outstanding or owed; many jobs pay wages or salary in arrears) and what compensation is (something, usually money, paid to a person or company in recognition of suffering, injury or loss that has been caused). Ask students to complete **Worksheet 8.1b** in pairs or groups, and then compare their answers as a group or class, talking through the correct answers where necessary. *(Legal: A, D, H, I; illegal: B (without notice depends how long you've worked there and on your contract, e.g. a notice period will be specified there; if you are on probation at the start of a contract, you can be dismissed without notice), C, E, F, G, J.)*

Plenary (5 mins)

- Ask students what sort of jobs they would be willing to do at different times in their lives, and what sort of contract they would agree to for each, giving reasons for their views. For example, when you are at college or university you might take a temporary job or a zero hours contract; when you are older and have a family you might take a full-time job with a steady income.

Assessment

- Use students' responses to **Worksheet 8.1b** to assess their understanding.

Extension or home learning

- Extension: Ask students to design a poster summarising what they have learned from this lesson.
- Home learning: Students use the following websites to access the latest rates for National Insurance and then find out how much National Insurance a person must pay if they are earning £20,000, £50,000, £100,000 and £500,000. https://www.gov.uk/national-insurance-rates-letters; for the different categories of National Insurance use https://www.gov.uk/national-insurance-rates-letters/category-letters.

Worksheet 8.1a Payslips

This is what a payslip looks like.

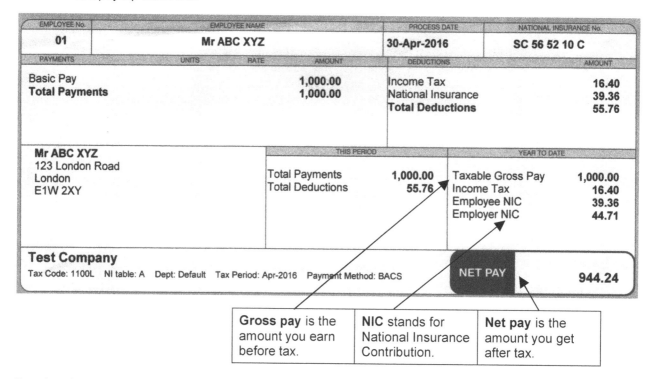

EMPLOYEE No.	EMPLOYEE NAME	PROCESS DATE	NATIONAL INSURANCE No.
01	Mr ABC XYZ	30-Apr-2016	SC 56 52 10 C

PAYMENTS	UNITS	RATE	AMOUNT	DEDUCTIONS	AMOUNT
Basic Pay			1,000.00	Income Tax	16.40
Total Payments			1,000.00	National Insurance	39.36
				Total Deductions	55.76

Mr ABC XYZ
123 London Road
London
E1W 2XY

	THIS PERIOD		YEAR TO DATE	
Total Payments	1,000.00	Taxable Gross Pay	1,000.00
Total Deductions	55.76	Income Tax	16.40
		Employee NIC	39.36
		Employer NIC	44.71

Test Company
Tax Code: 1100L   NI table: A   Dept: Default   Tax Period: Apr-2016   Payment Method: BACS

NET PAY   944.24

Gross pay is the amount you earn before tax.	**NIC** stands for National Insurance Contribution.	**Net pay** is the amount you get after tax.

Overtime is any extra work that you have done. For example, if your contract says that you work 37.5 hours per week, but you worked 40 hours that week, you would be paid 2.5 hours' overtime if your contract allows for that.

Tax is the amount of money you pay to the government. In return, the government provides services, like the National Health Service. Income tax is the amount of money you pay on your earnings. The amount you pay depends on how much you earn per annum (each year). This is called a tax band.

- For earnings up to £12,500 you pay 0%.
- For earnings from £12,501 to £50,000 you pay 20%.
- For earnings from £50,000 to £150,000 you pay 40%.
- The additional rate for those earning over £150,000 is 45%.

Everyone pays all these different tax rates, no matter how much they earn. So, a person earning £1 million will pay nothing on the first £12,500, 20% on the next £37,500 (£7500), 40% on the next £100,000 (£40,000) and then 45% on the next £850,000 (£382,500). This means that their total tax bill would be £430,000, so their actual tax bill would equate to 43% of their total earning, not 45%, because of the lower tax rates on the first part of their income.

The amount of National Insurance you have paid will be shown on your payslip. National Insurance is a tax. Everyone over 16 pays National Insurance if they earn more than £183 per week or over around £6000 per year. It goes towards your state pension, towards a maternity allowance if you have children, and towards a bereavement allowance so your partner and/or children have some money if you die.

Working in pairs and using the information on tax bands above, calculate how much tax each person in the list below pays. Then check the correct answers with your teacher. What do you notice about how much tax you actually pay on what you earn?

- someone who earns £20,000
- someone who earns £50,000
- someone who earns £100,000
- someone who earns £500,000

Worksheet 8.1b Work contracts: What's legal and what's not?

Look at the table below. In groups, decide whether you think each situation is legal or illegal. For any situation that you think is illegal, note down what you think the employer should do to remedy the situation. Then compare your answers as a class.

Situation	Legal or illegal	What do you think the employer should do to remedy the situation?
A. An employer doesn't pay you for an hour because you turned up late by one hour every day for an entire week.		
B. An employer sacks you without notice, doesn't give you a reason and doesn't give you any compensation.		
C. An employer decides without warning to pay you two months in arrears, but your contract says one month.		
D. Your employer makes you redundant due to a pandemic crisis, and gives you two months' pay as compensation.		
E. Your employer keeps making you work Sunday overtime but only pays you the same rate as a weekday.		
F. Your employer wants you to work extra hours but refuses to pay you extra.		
G. Your employer says you have to do the extra shifts before Christmas, even though your college work may suffer.		
H. Your employer says you must wear a uniform at work and this is in your contract.		
I. Your employer says you must wear a hair net if you are operating machinery.		
J. Your employer pays women less than men at the company.		

8.2 Becoming financially independent

Learning objectives:

- To distinguish between the short run and the long run, and between variable and fixed costs
- To understand what fraud and phishing are and to discuss the best fraud prevention measures
- To plan a budget for independent financial living

Resources:

- PowerPoint 8.2
- Worksheets 8.2a and 8.2b
- Link to KS3: Book 1, Unit 16.2

Key vocabulary:

financial independence, fraud, phishing, short run versus long run, fixed costs, variable costs

Get them thinking! (5 mins)

- Ask students to imagine that they are living independently when they are 16 at college or 18 after leaving home or going to university. What would they have to pay for? List their suggestions on the board.

Core learning (25 mins)

- Go through **Slide 1** with the class. Ask students what they think the difference is between fixed costs and variable costs. Explain, using **Slide 2**, that fixed costs can't be changed in the short run, whereas variable costs (**Slide 3**) can; all costs can be changed in the long run (see slides for examples).

- Use the list from the 'Get them thinking!' section to ask students which costs they think are fixed costs and which are variable costs. Then check their answers with them using **Slides 2** and **3**.

- Hand out copies of **Worksheet 8.2a**. Read through the example budget with the class. Ask students to imagine they are financially independent and to plan their own financial budget by filling in the empty columns in the table. Then get them to compare their budgets with a partner, checking whether they think they are realistic, before answering the questions. (*Answers: 1. 90 hours; 2. 20 hours.*)

Additional learning (15 mins)

- Ask the class to name all the types of fraud they know of, and then go through **Slide 4**. Emphasise the importance of keeping personal data safe and not giving away information unnecessarily when filling in forms online.

- Read through **Slide 5** with students and emphasise that phishing is just one type of fraud. (A list of common frauds aimed at teenagers can be found at https://www.investopedia.com/financial-edge/1012/common-scams-targeted-at-teens.aspx if you think it will be useful.) Then ask students to complete **Worksheet 8.2b**.

Plenary (5 mins)

- Ask students to discuss what should be done to help combat fraud against young people in their local area.

Assessment

- Use students' responses to **Worksheets 8.2a** and **8.2b** to assess their understanding.

Extension or home learning

- Extension: Ask students to make a list of all the different ways they could keep their data safe (e.g. not filling out online questionnaires with personal details, having a variety of passwords, checking who they are giving their data to). Then get them to work in pairs to rank these in order of the ways they think are the best to keep their data safe. They ask them to compare their answers first in groups and finally as a class, giving reasons for their views.

- Extension: Ask students to discuss how useful parental cards schemes are in getting young people used to shopping with cards (e.g. https://www.gohenry.com/uk).

- Home learning: Ask students to contact trading standards in your local district council, unitary authority or metropolitan borough and ask them for details of the latest frauds they have detected in your local area. What measures are they taking to combat these frauds?

Worksheet 8.2a Independent living

Imagine you are financially independent. How much do you think it would cost to live independently? Look at one young person's budget below. Then work out how much you think it would cost you to live independently by filling in the column 'Your expenditure' with what you think your own costs might be. If you are unsure of any answers, you can discuss this with your teacher. Then compare your answers with a partner.

Expenditure: fixed costs	Amount (£)	Your expenditure	Notes
Monthly rent	300		
Council tax	100		
Electricity	15		
Gas	15		
Water	10		
TV licence	10		
Phone contract	20		
Total fixed costs	**470**		
Expenditure: variable costs			
Food and drink	220		
Toiletries/make up	20		
Extra data for the phone	10		
Cinema tickets	25		
Clothes	25		
Gym membership	30		
Savings	10		
Other (please specify)			
Total variable costs	**340**		
Total cost (fixed costs plus variable costs)	**810**		

1. Now imagine you have a job that pays £9 per hour. How many hours would you have to work each month in order to make sure you had enough money to live on?

    ....

2. Now imagine each month has 4.5 weeks. How many hours would you have to work each week?

    ....

Worksheet 8.2b Other tricks fraudsters use

Look at the following tricks that fraudsters use to gain your money or your data. Which do you think are the biggest threat to young people? Work in pairs to rank them, where 1 is the highest threat and 10 is the lowest threat. Then discuss your answers in groups, giving reasons for your views.

Fraudulent behaviour	Ranking
A. Calling people and offering to upgrade their phone contract using the SIM swap service. The fake SIM swap is then used to gather people's personal data without their knowledge.	
B. Contacting people who wish to cash in their pension in order to get the best deal, then taking all their bank details and stealing all the money they have saved in their pension.	
C. A holiday scam, where people are offered a discounted holiday provided they pay a significant amount as a deposit in advance. Of course, the holiday never appears.	
D. A get-rich-quick scheme on the internet, where people are offered the chance to make a lot of money quickly just by filling in financial forms for a company and transferring money between accounts. In reality, they laundering money for criminals such as drugs gangs (moving illegally gained money into legitimate businesses). People are often not paid the full amount for their work either.	
E. A company offering the chance of modelling work, but the person has to pay first for photographs and the creation of a modelling CV. The person is overcharged for the photographs and gets little or no modelling work.	
F. A romance fraud known as catfishing, where a person pretends to be someone else on the internet. They seem the perfect partner for you and seek first to gain your trust; they then gradually ask you for small amounts of money, for what sound like really good reasons (e.g. 'my grandmother is sick and I want to get her some extra medicine and will pay you back next week'). The amount of money increases, but you never manage to arrange to meet the person in real life. If you insist, they suddenly disappear with your money.	
G. Searching through people's rubbish to find out if they have thrown out any bank or credit card statements. These are then used to steal as much personal information as possible to commit fraud in the future.	
H. Being offered money by a gang to move drugs from a city to a small town. The first time a person does this, they are usually mugged by gang members they don't know. From that moment on, the person is in debt to the gang for not delivering the drugs, and they force the person to work for them. This kind of drugs operation is known as county lines.	
I. The chance to download a computer modification to help you cheat in an online game. Instead, your computer gets locked by the program that a fraudster has written, and you are blackmailed to pay them money, or lose all the information on your computer, usually in a short time frame.	

Sex and relationship responsibilities

Learning objectives:

- To be able to explain the laws around sex
- To learn about LGBTQI+ rights
- To explore the characteristics and qualities needed for healthy intimate relationships

Resources:

- PowerPoint 9.1
- Worksheet 9.1
- Art materials of your choosing
- Cameras if available
- Link to KS3: Book 1, Units 6.2, 7.2; Book 2, Units 2.2 and 2.3

Key vocabulary:

age of consent, Sexual Offences Act, Equalities Act, LGBTQI, bisexual, gay (homosexual), lesbian, straight (heterosexual), characteristics

Get them thinking! (5 mins)

- As a whole class discuss: 'What is the age of consent and what does that mean?' (See **Slide 1**.)

Core learning (25 mins)

- Explain that this lesson revisits the legal framework that protects young people in relationships, before exploring how we can treat our friends and partners with respect. Display **Slide 1** to revisit the age of consent law. Make sure students understand how it is designed to protect them from abuse or from having sex before they are ready. See the notes on the slide.

- Show the class the 'Cup of Tea' video about consent (https://sexualrespect.columbia.edu/tea-and-consent-video). Discuss with the class for 5 minutes how consent must always be given for any sexual activity, and what they have learned from the video about consent.

- Then talk through **Slides 2** and **3** together. These explain the laws around sexual activity that is not consensual. See the notes on the slide for links should you wish to explore further. Finally, read through **Slide 4**, which references the Equality Act in regards to gender and sexual orientation.

Additional learning (15 mins)

- Tell students they are going to explore the values and ingredients that characterise healthy intimate relationships. Discuss some ideas but don't give too much away – listen rather than lead and use this as an assessment of students' initial understanding (building on the work from KS3 and Unit 2).

- Organise the class into teams of four and hand out **Worksheet 9.1**. Ask teams to think about what makes a respectful relationship (of any sexuality, between people of any gender). What values do they have in common? What qualities do people need to show? How should partners treat each other? Encourage students to list as many ideas as they can. Then, considering actions, thoughts and emotions, they should write these on the labels, using as many worksheets as they need.

- Place all the labels the class have made on a display to use as a resource in the future. For example, if somebody is not being respectful to a peer in a lesson, they can go to the display and remind the class of the definition of respect. Suggested values might include tolerance, flexibility, patience, loyalty, trust, kindness, listening, giving each other space and, of course, consent.

Plenary (5 mins)

- Recap on what students have learned and revisit **Slide 3** to signpost where they can go for support if anything covered today is worrying them and needs to be discussed further. Also highlight who they can talk to in school if they need further support, clarifying where that person can be found.

Assessment

- Use the introduction and activity discussions for assessment, along with the images of the worksheet activity to see how well they have understood the concept of a healthy relationship.

Extension or home learning

- Extension: Display **Slide 5** and read through the instructions with the class. In their same teams of four, students should plan a sketch and act it out. They could first come up with the names, ages and gender(s) of their couple. Members of the team who are not doing the acting or writing should feed back to those who are, commenting on whether their 'healthy' approach is effective.

- Extension: Ask students to revisit https://www.themix.org.uk/crime-and-safety/personal-safety/sexual-offences-explained-9112.html to learn more about sexual offences and consent. Ask them to follow the links in the 'next steps' section and check out Survivors UK and Rape Crisis using the links. They could produce a signposting/support guide for those who may have been victims of sexual abuse.

Worksheet 9.1 Respectful relationships

On a separate piece of paper, write the characteristics and behaviour you and your team think each person needs to demonstrate in order to be a good partner in a relationship. Once you have agreed, write the things from your list on these tags (one on each).

Consensual – always asking permission

58

Unit 9 Sexual relationships, Lesson 1

Learning objectives:

- To learn which contraception methods prevent STIs
- To learn about the full range of contraception available and show their understanding
- To make responsible choices for their ongoing sexual health

Resources:

- PowerPoint 9.2
- Worksheet 9.2a and 9.2b
- A4 paper and pens
- Link to KS3: Book 1, Unit 6.3, Book 2, Units 4.3, 4.1 and 4.2

Key vocabulary:

STIs (sexually transmitted infections), condoms, dental dam, birth control, sexual health services, confidential, emergency contraception

- This lesson builds on from KS3 lessons, so please see the links above to make sure all students understand the previous learning on this topic, including symptoms of STIs.

Get them thinking! (5 mins)

- Ask students as a class: 'Which contraceptives prevent people from catching STIs?' *(Only barrier methods: condoms, external or internal, or a dental dam – see **Slide 2** for further information.)*

Core learning (25 mins)

- Ask the class what advice they would give to someone who wants to keep sexually healthy. Explain the WHO definition of sexual health is not just the absence of disease but the ability to enjoy sex without harm. Show **Slide 1** and go through the points with them. Next, go through **Slides 2** and **3** and make sure everyone understands that only barrier methods help to protect against STIs.

- Move on to **Slide 4** and make it clear that even though the age of consent is 16, sexual health advice and contraception are available for people under 16 from a GP or sexual health clinic. Does this surprise them? Why do they think this is? *(To protect young people from harm, unwanted pregnancies and STIs.)*

- Ask students how many different contraceptive options they know or have heard of and write these on the board. Show **Slides 5** and **6** and briefly go through the different options with them.

- Hand out **Worksheet 9.2a** and leave students to go through the information about each method, either alone or in pairs. Encourage them to really explore and learn about these different options, regardless of gender. Make sure they understand that it is important for everyone to be responsible for their contraception choices – it will be their STI or baby if they don't! Share responses about the best options for each young person or couple on the worksheet. (Suggested answers could include: *1. Contraceptive implant or injection, 2. Combined pill, patch or IUS, 3. IUD/IUS, implant or injection, 4. External condoms and dams, 5. Pill, implant or injection and condoms/dams. Emphasise the need for sexual health screening of both partners before couples stop using barrier methods to protect against STIs.)*

- Finally go to **Slide 7** to consider emergency contraception. (See the link in the slide notes.)

Additional learning (15 mins)

- Tell students they are going to explore real-life situations now and see if they can be good agony aunts/uncles/people. Ask them, in pairs, to discuss and then write a reply to support someone who has asked one of the questions on **Slide 8** (or they can make up their own scenario if they prefer).

- Tell pairs to brainstorm the best advice and write their answers on an A4 sheet, considering all they know about consent (e.g. the right to say no), healthy relationships (e.g. importance of good communication, respect and support), and sexual health (e.g. the implications of STIs and pregnancy).

Plenary (5 mins)

- Ask a few members of the class to feed back their advice and discuss the responses as a class. Then hand out **Worksheet 9.2b** and ask students to complete it.

Assessment

- Assess students' understanding using their responses to **Worksheet 9.2b**.

Extension or home learning

- Extension or home learning: https://www.nhs.uk/conditions/contraception/emergency-contraception/ Ask learners to visit this website to learn more about when a person might need emergency contraception, how it works, side effects, facts and other useful information.

- Extension: Ask students to create an information flyer/leaflet, simplifying all the information they have learned about contraception.

Worksheet 9.2a Keeping sexually healthy

Take your time to look through and familiarise yourself with the different contraceptive methods below.

sexwise.org.uk/contraception

fpa — the sexual health charity

Contraceptive methods that don't depend on you remembering to take or use them:

— 40mm —

	Contraceptive implant	Intrauterine device (IUD)	Intrauterine system (IUS)	Contraceptive injection
What is it?	A small, flexible rod put under the skin of the upper arm releases progestogen.	A small plastic and copper device is put into the uterus (womb).	A small, T-shaped progestogen-releasing plastic device is put into the uterus (womb).	An injection of progestogen.
Effectiveness	Perfect use: over 99% Typical use: over 99%	Perfect use: over 99% Typical use: over 99%	Perfect use: over 99% Typical use: over 99%	Perfect use: over 99% Typical use: around 94%
Advantage(s)	Works for 3 years but can be taken out sooner if you choose.	Works for 5 or 10 years depending on the type but can be taken out sooner if you choose.	Works for 3 or 5 years but can be taken out sooner if you choose. Periods often become lighter, shorter and less painful.	Works for either 8 or 13 weeks – you don't have to think about contraception during this time.
Disadvantage(s)	It requires a small procedure to fit and remove it.	Periods may be heavier, longer or more painful.	Irregular bleeding or spotting is common in the first 6 months.	Can't be removed from the body so any side effects may continue while it works and for some time afterwards.

Contraceptive methods that you have to use and think about regularly or each time you have sex:

	Contraceptive patch	Contraceptive vaginal ring	Combined pill (COC)	Progestogen-only pill (POP)	External condom	Internal condom	Diaphragm/cap with spermicide
What is it?	A small patch stuck to the skin releases estrogen and progestogen.	A small, flexible plastic ring put into the vagina releases estrogen and progestogen.	A pill containing estrogen and progestogen, taken orally.	A pill containing progestogen, taken orally.	A very thin latex (rubber) polyurethane (plastic) or synthetic sheath, put over the erect penis.	Soft, thin polyurethane sheath that loosely lines the vagina and covers the area just outside.	A flexible latex (rubber) or silicone device, used with spermicide, is put into the vagina to cover the cervix.
	PERFECT USE MEANS USING THE METHOD CORRECTLY EVERY TIME. TYPICAL USE IS WHEN YOU DON'T ALWAYS USE THE METHOD CORRECTLY.						
Effectiveness	Perfect use: over 99% Typical use: around 91%	Perfect use: over 99% Typical use: around 91%	Perfect use: around 99% Typical use: around 91%	Perfect use: over 99% Typical use: around 91%	Perfect use: 98% Typical use: around 82%	Perfect use: 95% Typical use: around 79%	Perfect use: 92–96% Typical use: 71–88%
Advantage(s)	Can make bleeds regular, lighter and less painful.	One ring stays in for 3 weeks. It usually makes bleeding regular, lighter and less painful.	Often reduces bleeding and period pain, and may help with premenstrual symptoms.	Can be used if you smoke and are over 35 or if you can't use estrogen.	Condoms are the best way to help protect yourself from sexually transmitted infections		Can be put in before sex.
Disadvantage(s)	May be seen and can cause skin irritation.	You must be comfortable with inserting and removing it.	Missing pills, vomiting or severe diarrhoea can make it less effective.	Late pills, vomiting or severe diarrhoea can make it less effective.	May slip off or split if not used correctly or if the wrong size or shape.	Not as widely available as external condoms.	You need to use the right size. If you have sex again extra spermicide is needed.

Unit 9 Sexual relationships, Lesson 2

Decide which options you think would be best for each young person or couple below and why you think this. Look at the possible advantages and disadvantages of each method to make your choices. Don't forget to consider **dental dams** (not shown in the table) to help protect against STIs. They are a latex or polyurethane square which can be placed over the genital area (female) or anus during oral sex.

1. Tom and Ayanna are considering their options for contraception. They have been using condoms for a year but want to try something else now. They are both forgetful though! Which options do you think would be best for them and why?

....

....

....

2. Sam is considering their contraceptive options with their partner. They have really painful and heavy periods. Which options do you think would be best for them and why?

....

....

....

3. Payal is a firefighter who works shifts so she doesn't get up at the same time every day. She is looking for a reliable, long-term contraception to prevent pregnancy. Which options would be best for her and why?

....

....

....

4. Mikey has recently started seeing Sean, with whom he would like to have a relationship. Which option(s) would be best for them and why?

....

....

....

5. Kaley has both male and female partners. She is looking for a long-term contraception to prevent pregnancy and wants to protect herself against STIs. Which options would be best for her and why?

....

....

....

Which contraceptive method/methods do you feel would be best for a person like you if they had to use them and why do you think this?

....

....

....

Worksheet 9.2b What have you learned?

1. How often should you get a sexual health check at a sexual health clinic?

....

....

2. What is the best thing to do before you have sex with a new partner? Why?

....

....

....

3. Which contraception methods prevent the spread of STIs (sexually transmitted infections)?

....

....

....

4. Can you go to a sexual health clinic if you are under 16?

....

5. Which contraceptive methods do you think are best and why?

....

....

....

6. Where can you get emergency contraception?

....

....

....

Is there anything else you would like to learn about STIs or contraception?

....

....

....

Understanding fertility, infertility and different routes to parenthood

Learning objectives:

- To understand the terms fertility, infertility and miscarriage
- To understand the different options for starting a family
- To learn where to get reproductive health advice and treatment

Resources:

- PowerPoint 9.3
- Worksheets 9.3a and 9.3b
- Laptops or tablets and access to the internet
- Link to KS3: Book 1, Units 2.1 and 2.2; Book 3, Unit 7.1

Key vocabulary:

conception, fertilisation, fertility, infertility, miscarriage, in vitro fertilisation (IVF), intrauterine insemination (IUI), egg/sperm donation, co-parenting, donor insemination, surrogacy, adoption, fostering

---

- Prior to teaching this you may wish to revisit previous lessons on periods in KS3 Your Choice, Book 1, Unit 2.2 and Book 3, Unit 7.1, to remind students of the details of the menstrual cycle and ovulation.

Get them thinking! (5 mins)

- Ask: 'What do you know about fertility and infertility?' Invite suggestions (and also questions) from students. At this stage just listen to their ideas, as this will be useful assessment.

Core learning (25 mins)

- Show **Slide 1** and go through it with the class, explaining that they will learn about insemination, co-parenting, surrogacy and more later on in the lesson (see the definitions in the slide notes).

- Ask students what they remember about 'how babies are made'. Work through **Slide 2** to refresh students' understanding of the process of conception. (Also see the notes on the slide.)

- Move on to **Slide 3**. Work through this and ask questions after each point – ask them to guess their best answers in pairs or small teams. (See the notes on the slide for example questions and answers.)

- Hand out **Worksheet 9.3a** and go through it with students. If classroom technology permits, explain that they will be going online and visiting the NHS web page 'LGBT paths to parenthood' (www.nhs.uk/live-well/healthy-body/gay-health-having-children/) to find the answers to the true or false questions. Alternatively, students can answer the questions themselves before you go through the answers with the class and allow them time to mark their work. Discuss their thoughts on these briefly, along with what they learned. *(1. False; 2. False; 3. True; 4. True; 5. True; 6. False; 7. True; 8. False; 9. False; 10. True)*

- Display **Slide 4**. If laptops or tablets are available, students can work in pairs to investigate each method, using the NHS web pages on infertility: https://www.nhs.uk/conditions/infertility/treatment/. Ask them to write notes and then focus on one or two treatments to use for home learning (see below). Alternatively, ask them to tell you what they know about each method and discuss using webpage on the whiteboard.

Additional learning (15 mins)

- Show **Slide 5** and to through where a couple/person would go for support if they are having problems conceiving or are worried about infertility, and what kind of support is available.

- Hand out **Worksheet 9.3b**. Tell students to read the three stories and write how they would feel if they were each person. Give them time to complete the worksheet, then go through this with them. If time allows, students could think about how they could, as a friend or family member, support each of the people on the worksheet – Jonny, Sam and Amy – using what they have learned in this lesson.

Plenary (5 mins)

- Create a learning wall using a large piece of paper or a display. Ask students to jot down their thoughts on 'What I have learned that I didn't know before'. Answer any unanswered questions from the start.

Assessment

- Compare students' ideas from the beginning of the lesson with the learning wall at the end of the lesson to monitor understanding and highlight any gaps.

Extension or home learning

- Home learning: Ask students to create a leaflet about fertility using their notes from this lesson or using the link: https://www.nhs.uk/conditions/infertility/treatment/. They should add diagrams and design features to complete their work. These can then be displayed alongside the learning wall.

Worksheet 9.3a Different routes to parenthood

Go to the NHS website (www.nhs.uk/live-well/healthy-body/gay-health-having-children/) and search 'LGBT paths to parenthood'. Read through all the information carefully, then answer the true or false questions below.

If a statement is false, add the real facts into the comments column. If the statement is true, make a note of your thoughts about it. If you are not sure, write what you think.

Statement	True or false?	Comments
1. Co-parenting is when one person has a baby.		
2. Surrogacy is illegal in the UK.		
3. Donor insemination is available to both single people and those in a relationship.		
4. LGBTQI+ couples in the UK are legally permitted to adopt or foster a child together.		
5. Trans people have exactly the same rights as anyone else who wants to be a parent.		
6. The number of LGBTQI+ people who become parents is decreasing.		
7. When looking for donor insemination, it is best to go to a licensed clinic where they can make sure the sperm is healthy.		
8. Co-parenting doesn't need much thought.		
9. When adopting or fostering, an LGBTQI+ couple can only apply to the local authority they live in.		
10. If you are trans and are going through or planning to go through treatment to alter your body, you can preserve your fertility.		

Worksheet 9.3b What's it like to have fertility problems?

Read these three stories and write how you would feel if you were each person.

Jonny's story: 'I'm 28 and my partner and I have been trying for a baby with no luck yet. I had some tests and I've just found out I have a low sperm count. Now I have to go and tell my partner. We've been hoping to have children, and I've been the one pushing it as I've always wanted them. I come from a large family. Everyone's always said to me, "You'll make a brilliant dad". Well, now I probably won't!'

How would you feel if you were Jonny and why?

....

....

....

....

Sam's story: 'When I came out to my parents, the first thing my mum said was, "How will you have children?" I looked into it and realised there were lots of ways, so I was really relieved as I'd love to have a child (just the one will do – I'm not greedy!). I may not have met the right person yet, but I wasn't worried as I know I could cope as a single parent and there are lots of options for LGBTQI+ people like me. Then I went along to the clinic to discuss my options last week and after running some tests they have told me I am infertile.'

How would you feel if you were Sam and why?

....

....

....

....

Amy's story: 'I always thought I'd have kids. You know, it's just something you expect. I met someone lovely and we got married. My husband and I decided to focus on our careers before trying, so we did that, bought a house and so on. When I was 34 years old, we thought, "Right, let's do this!" We stopped using contraception and thought it was going to just happen straight away, "Boom!", but it didn't. We tried and tried and still I couldn't get pregnant. We've been trying for about a year and decided to find out if one of us has a problem and see what we can do about it. We're going to the GP tomorrow. Wish us luck!'

How would you feel if you were Amy and why?

....

....

....

....

Learning objectives:

- To learn what indecent content online is and to demonstrate understanding of the laws around it
- To learn how to report indecent content online
- To understand the laws around youth-produced sexual imagery

Resources:

- PowerPoint 10.1
- Worksheet 10.1a (cut up and put into sets or envelopes),10.1b and 10.1c
- Link to KS3: Book 2, Units 5.2 and 5.3

Key vocabulary:

indecent, youth-produced sexual imagery, parasite porn websites, sexting

---

- It might be useful to revisit Unit 2 to recap on grooming and sexual exploitation if this was taught some time ago. You may also wish to revisit Unit 5 in KS3 Book 2 too.

Get them thinking! (5 mins)

- Ask: 'What might be examples of offensive online content?' Take ideas from the class.

Core learning (25 mins)

- Go to **Slide 1** to look at the list of offensive online content. (Pornography is covered in Lesson 10.2.)
- Display **Slide 2** and remind students that sexual images or videos of people under 18 are against the law, even clothed pictures of a suggestive nature and even when they are 'youth-produced'. (See notes.)
- Hand out the cut-up copies of **Worksheet 10.1a** and ask students to complete the card sort activity in pairs or alone. Go through their answers when they have finished, discussing why each is a good or bad idea, and which would be illegal. *(Answers: 1. No (illegal if the person in the photo was under 18); 2. No; 3. Yes; 4. No (illegal if boy in the photo is under 18); 5. Yes; 6. No (illegal if the young people in the video are under 18); 7. No; 8. Yes (illegal if young person being sent the image is under 18); 9. No.)* Draw out which scenarios seem dangerous and should ring alarm bells for young people.
- Hand out **Worksheet 10.1b**, outlining the laws around youth-produced sexual imagery. Make sure students understand all the terms, and then allow them time to complete their reflections on the sheet. Collect the completed worksheets so you can answer any questions at the end of the lesson.

Additional learning (15 mins)

- Show **Slide 3** and ask students to discuss the scenario in pairs and then as a class. (See slide notes.)
- Go through **Slide 4** with the class, taking ideas for what students advise the person to do. (See notes.)
- Then show **Slide 5** and discuss how to report an indecent image online. Childline has set up a 'Report, Remove' service linked to the Internet Watch Foundation. Visit the Childline website and go through this with the class (https://www.childline.org.uk/info-advice/bullying-abuse-safety/online-mobile-safety/sexting/report-nude-image-online/). (See the notes on the slide for more information.)
- Show **Slide 6** and explain the risks of photos or videos being hacked and placed on a 'parasite porn' website. Ask students for their reactions. Were they aware of this risk? Discuss what this could mean for someone now and in the future. How might it affect their lives?

Plenary (5 mins)

- Revisit all that students have learned today, answering any questions submitted via **Worksheet 10.1b** and checking for any misunderstandings. (Students could submit questions anonymously through an 'ask it' basket, alternatively.)

Assessment

- Use the card-sorting activity and scenario discussions to assess students' understanding of this lesson.

Extension or home learning

- Extension: Show **Slide 7** and hand out **Worksheet 10.1c** for more about the legal aspects of youth-produced imagery – in this case, police procedures. Allow students time to complete the reflection activity, then discuss this as a class and collect the worksheets for further assessment.
- Extension: Ask students to explore places to go for further support and information online regarding sexting, such as 'So you got naked online...', a resource provided by the South West Grid for Learning: https://swgfl.org.uk/resources/so-you-got-naked-online/ and Childline's webpage on 'Sexting and sending nudes': https://www.childline.org.uk/info-advice/bullying-abuse-safety/online-mobile-safety/sexting/.

Worksheet 10.1a Relationships, sex and dating online

Cut out the cards, then read each card, looking carefully at who sent it and why. Sort them into two piles: yes/good idea or no/bad idea. Finally, decide in which of the situations somebody would be at risk of breaking the law.

1. 'Can you please send me a nude photo? I promise I won't show it to anyone.' (a long-term girlfriend)	**2.** 'The app states you have to be 18 to join, so I'll just put that.' (a 16-year-old on a dating app)	**3.** 'I can't meet you alone because I don't know you, but I can come with my mum/dad/ carer.' (a new chat on a dating app)
4. 'This really hot boy sent me a picture of him in his boxers last night. I'll send it to you.' (friend to another friend)	**5.** 'It feels weird going on an app to find a girlfriend. I'd rather meet someone I know in real life.' (a 19-year-old talking to a friend)	**6.** 'I want to see that video of us making out last night. Can you send it to me?' (a boy you are seeing)
7. 'Hey, yeah, I live on that street!' (a new chat on social media)	**8.** 'This man sent me an indecent image last night. I'm going to report him.' (a young person on social media)	**9.** 'This girl who friended me online says she is coming to our school next term and she wants to meet me tomorrow.' (a 14-year-old)

Worksheet 10.1b Sexual imagery and the law

The law on indecent imagery of under-18s

- Possessing and distributing any picture of someone who is under 18 which is 'indecent' is illegal. (This could be an image of yourself if you are under 18.)

- It is an offence to possess, distribute, show and make indecent images of children. (Here, for the purposes of indecent images, a child is anyone under the age of 18.)

- When cases are prosecuted, the question of whether any photograph of a child is indecent is for a jury, magistrate or District Judge to decide based on what is the recognised standard.

- For most purposes, if images contain a naked young person, a topless girl, and/or displays genitals or sex acts alone or with someone else, then it will be considered indecent. These may also include obviously sexual images of young people in their underwear.

[UK Council for Child Internet Safety (UKCCIS)]

Working alone or with a partner, read the text above and answer the following questions.

1. In the law on indecent images, what age is a child? ....

    ....

2. What is it illegal to do with indecent images of children? Try to explain each term.

    a. ....

    b. ....

    c. ....

    d. ....

3. Is it illegal to possess an indecent picture of yourself if you are under 18? ....

4. Is it illegal to distribute an indecent picture of yourself if you are under 18? ....

5. What else have you learned about sexual imagery and the law? ....

    ....

    ....

6. Do you have any questions about sexual imagery and the law? ....

    ....

    ....

    ....

    ....

    ....

    ....

Worksheet 10.1c Sexual imagery and the police

What will the police do?

- The National Police Chiefs Council (NPCC) has made clear that incidents involving youth-produced sexual imagery should primarily be treated as safeguarding issues.

- The police may need to be involved in cases to ensure thorough investigation, including collection of all evidence.

- Even when the police are involved, however, a criminal justice response and formal sanction against a young person would only be considered likely in certain circumstances.

- Where the police are notified of incidents of youth-produced sexual imagery they are obliged, under the law, to record the incident on their crime systems.

- The incident will be listed as a 'crime' and the young person involved will be listed as a 'suspect'. This is not the same as having a criminal record.

[UK Council for Child Internet Safety (UKCCIS)]

Read the information above and explain what you have learned in your own words. Write down any further thoughts or questions you might have about the information.

....
....
....
....
....
....
....
....
....
....
....
....
....

10.2 Pornography

Learning objectives:

- To understand the laws around pornography
- To learn about the impacts and dangers of viewing pornography

Resources:

- PowerPoint
- Worksheet 10.2a & 10.2b
- Large paper and pens
- Link to KS3: Book 3, Unit 2.2

Key vocabulary:

pornography, neurological, addiction, consent, objectification, desensitisation, objectified

- Make sure you have refreshed your working agreement with your students, so they understand the expectations for discussions and that this is a safe, respectful environment. If questions arise that you don't feel comfortable answering, tell the class you will need to discuss them with your SLT first.

Get them thinking! (5 mins)

- Ask: 'What is pornography?' Discuss as a class.

Core learning (25 mins)

- Go to **Slide 1** to clarify what pornography is. Read the definition, explaining that it can be any media, including video, photography or writing.

- Show **Slide 2** and go through the laws on watching pornography. (The slide notes on extreme pornography can be shared at your discretion.) Ask students, 'Why do you think the legal age for watching pornography is 18 years old?' Discuss as a class.

- Show students a BBC Teach film to support these ideas: https://www.bbc.co.uk/teach/class-clips-video/pshe-computing-gcse-pornography/zh76xyc. (Please check the film is suitable for your class first.) Discuss any issues or questions that arise from the film.

- Ask: 'What do you think the harms of pornography might be?' Hand out large sheets of paper and pens to write down their ideas and either in the same pairs or in small groups, get them to work together to think of all the different reasons why pornography might be harmful.

- Show **Slide 3** and allow them time to go through this question now using the statements on this slide to focus their thinking further. On completion take feedback and discuss as a class and then use the slide notes to add information, according to what you feel is appropriate for your class.

- Hand out **Worksheet 10.2a** 'What would you advise?' Tell them they are going to read about three young people's experiences of pornography and write down what you would advise each of them to do. Allow them time to complete this and then go through these together, taking some examples from a few students and considering as a class.

Additional learning (15 mins)

- Tell students that in addition to these harms, pornography, just like alcohol, drugs or gambling, can be addictive. Display and read through **Slide 4**. Then show the film 'The Science of Pornography Addiction' (3.06 mins, available on YouTube and from the ASAP Science website https://www.asapscience.com/).

- You may want to show the film again, this time asking the students to write notes to consolidate the key points. They can then discuss what stood out for them, in pairs and then as a class.

- Hand out **Worksheet 10.2b** and allow students time to complete this and use this an assessment. (Answers: 1. *False*, 2. *True*, 3. *True*, 4. *False*, 5. *True*, 6. *False*, 7. *True*, 7. *True*.)

Plenary (5 mins)

- Recap what students have learned and remind them of the importance of talking to someone they trust if they are worried about anything. They can also visit Childline, Brook and Thinkuknow for further support and information about pornography. Ask them what else they would like to know in future lessons and to write this at the bottom of **Worksheet 10.2b** – tell them know their questions will be kept anonymous.

Assessment

- Use **Worksheet 10.2b** for assessment.

Extension or home learning

- Extension: Students could visit the ChildLine, Thinkuknow and Brook websites to see what information about, and support with, issues around pornography is available.

Worksheet 10.2a What would you advise?

Read about these young people's experiences of pornography and write down what you would advise each of them to do.

'I am 13 years old. I found my big sister's laptop open the other day. I know I shouldn't have, but I looked at it. I wish I hadn't. I found pornography on it and some of it really worried me. It's made me feel sick and I can't stop it going through my mind. I don't know who to talk to or where to go. I can't ask my sister or my carers about it as they will go crazy at me.'

If you were this person's friend what would you advise them to do?

....

....

....

....

....

'I am 16 years old. I'm a virgin and feel really unsure about how to be good at sex. I haven't really been told anything about how people "do" sex. I have heard about porn so I think I'll watch that to learn about what my sexual partners would like and how to do stuff.'

If you were this person's friend what would you advise them to do?

....

....

....

....

....

'I am 21 years old. My boyfriend and I have a good, loving relationship but every time we have sex he asks if we can have a porn video on. It started as just an occasional thing, but now it happens all the time and he wants to try out more and more stuff that they do and sometimes it can hurt me. I don't really like it, but I go along with it as I can see he loves it.'

If you were this person's friend what would you advise them to do?

....

....

....

....

....

Go through the statements below and decide if they are true or false. If a statement is false, add the real facts into the comments column. If the statement is true, make a note of your thoughts about it. If you are not sure, just have a go and write what you think.

Statement	True or false?	Comments
1. Pornography is the name for sexual videos.		
2. You can watch pornography if you are 18 years old or over.		
3. Pornography often does not address the important issues around consent.		
4. Pornography shows exactly what real sex is like.		
5. Pornography can often be violent and abusive.		
6. Only men watch pornography.		
7. Pornography can 'rewire' our brains.		
8. Pornography can be as addictive as drugs.		

Do you have any other questions about this topic that you would like your teacher to answer or teach you about in further lessons? If so write them here. (Your questions will be kept confidential and answered anonymously.)

Learning objectives:

- To understand the difference between sex, gender and gender identity
- To learn what intersex means
- To consider how gender stereotypes affect us all

Resources:

- PowerPoint 11.1
- Worksheets 11.1a and 11.1b
- Laptops
- Large paper and pens
- Links to KS3: Book 1, Unit 1.4; Book 3, Units 2.2 and 2.3.

Key vocabulary:

sex, sexuality, gender, gender identity, gender binary, non-binary, genderfluid, transgender, intersex, gender stereotypes

Get them thinking! (5 mins)

- Ask students: 'What is the difference between sex and sexuality?' *(sex = the biology of being female or male; sexuality = someone's sexual orientation)*

Core learning (25 mins)

- Ask: 'What is the difference between gender and gender identity?' Go to **Slide 1** to clarify what sex, gender and gender identity mean.
- Ask students if they know what intersex means. Show students **Slide 2** and talk through the definition.
- Watch the short film 'Being intersex: I'm genetically male, physically female' on the BBC News website https://www.bbc.co.uk/news/av/world-africa-48031130. After viewing, ask students what they have learned about being intersex from this clip. What issues and concerns do the young people in the clip raise? What advice do they give?
- Then show **Slide 3** to explore some commonly used terminology to describe different gender identities.
- Show **Slide 4** and go through the slide to refresh students' understanding of what it means to be trans. (For more information see KS3, Book 3, Unit 2.3.)
- Hand out **Worksheet 11.1a** and laptops, then go to **Slide 5**. Students should use the websites provided on the worksheet to research and explore different gender identities. When they have finished, discuss as a class what they have learned and the reasons why people may choose to use these different terms.

Additional learning (15 mins)

- Show the Always advert 'Like a Girl' (available on YouTube). Ask, how did the adults in this advert interpret the phrase 'like a girl'? How did the children? What did this make students think and feel?
- Alternatively, watch the clip 'Redraw the balance' https://www.inspiringthefuture.org/redraw-the-balance/. Ask, 'Were you surprised by the children's assumptions in their drawings? How did you feel watching the children's reactions to the visitors? What might this suggest about gender stereotypes in our society?'
- Divide the class into groups of six and give each group large sheets of paper and pens. Then give them time to complete the titles, 'Girls/women are like...', 'Boys/men are like...', writing as many gendered expectations and stereotypes as they can think of. Come together as a class to discuss how these stereotypes and expectations can negatively affect us as individuals and as a society.

Plenary (5 mins)

- Hand out **Worksheet 11.1b** and read through the instructions together. Remind students that if they are worried about anything in this lesson or want more information on these topics there is support out there, for example from the NHS and Childline. They can also submit questions to you anonymously.

Assessment

- Use **Worksheet 11.1b** to assess students' understanding of this topic.

Extension or home learning

- Home learning: Students could research the athlete Caster Semenya, finding out who she is and why her sporting career has been subject to controversy. They could write up their findings as a short report.
- Extension: Students could research the campaign to have 'X' included as a third gender-marker on UK passports, looking at what Canada have done and the pros and cons of this approach via this article: https://www.theguardian.com/world/2017/aug/31/canada-introduces-gender-neutral-x-option-on-passports

Worksheet 11.1a Gender identities

Working in pairs, investigate different gender identities using these websites.

www.amnesty.org.uk/LGBTQ-equality/gender-identity-beginners-guide-trans-allies
https://www.brook.org.uk/your-life/gender-a-few-definitions/

See what different gender identities you can find, and write them with their definitions in the table below. (Use the back of the sheet if you need more room.)

You will need to work fast... this is a timed activity!

Gender identity	Definition

Worksheet 11.1b What have you learned about sex, gender identity and gender stereotyping?

Using the space below, you are going to show everything you have learned about sex, gender, gender identity and gender stereotyping.

You can design this page however you wish. For example, you could create a mind-map, a bullet-point list or a series of thought bubbles.

You need to add everything you have learned and what each new idea has made you think about.

When you have finished, feel free to add any questions you would like to ask about any aspect of the lesson. You can also submit your questions anonymously to your teacher, if you would prefer.

Learning objectives:

- To understand what sexuality is
- To learn about different sexual identities
- To consider how a young person can prepare to come out safely when they feel ready

Resources:

- PowerPoint 11.2
- Worksheets 11.2a, 11.2b, 11.2c
- Link to KS3: Book 1, Unit 7.1; Book 3, Units 2.1, 3.4 and 8.1

Key vocabulary:

sexuality, sexual attraction, romantic, homosexual, heterosexual, bisexual, pansexual, polysexual, asexual, LGBTQI+

Get them thinking! (5 mins)

- Ask: 'What is sexual attraction?' *(When you really like someone and are attracted to them in a sexual way.)* Discuss students' thoughts as a class and then go to **Slide 1** to explore this further.

Core learning (25 mins)

- Then ask, 'What is sexuality?' Briefly listen to students' thoughts on this – this will be a good assessment of their understanding. *(Sexuality describes someone's sexual feelings and preferences: their sexual orientation and/or sexual activity.)*

- Hand out **Worksheet 11.2a** and ask students to read through it independently. Tell them this is a chance to assess their level of understanding and to ask any questions privately.

- Go through the answers as a class, and then collect in the sheets so you can answer any questions anonymously in the next lesson. *(1. False, sexuality can be seen as a scale and there are many different sexualities; 2. True, asexual people are not sexually attracted to others; sometimes people want a break from sexual relationships or wish to be celibate; 3. True; 4. True; 5. True, sexuality can be fluid or someone may identify or express their sexuality differently at different times in their life; 6. True, under the Equality Act (2010); 7. True, someone can be sexually attracted to someone they aren't romantically attracted to.)*

- To consider sexuality in more depth, go to **Slide 2** and introduce the idea of sexuality as a scale rather than a binary, using the Kinsey model from the 1940s, contextualised with the notes provided. Then present the Genderbread person on **Slide 3**, using the notes to discuss how this incorporates different gender expressions/identities as well.

- Show **Slide 4** and ask students if they know the meaning of each of the terms used to describe different sexualities. Use the slide notes to consolidate understanding and to explain any unfamiliar terms.

- Ask students if they know what 'coming out' means *(when someone decides to tell others about their sexuality)*. Show **Slide 5** and talk through. Ask: 'What issues might come up when telling friends and family about your sexuality?' Ask students: 'Do you think it is easy to be LGBQ+ these days as a teen? What can be the challenges?' Give time for them briefly to share their thoughts.

Additional learning (15 mins)

- Read through **Slide 5**, then hand out **Worksheets 11.2b** and **11.2c**. Ask students to read the real-life coming out stories on **Worksheet 11.2c**. Alternatively, show Connor Franta's coming out video (on YouTube or via https://www.independent.co.uk/news/people/connor-franta-youtube-national-coming-out-day-2016-gay-sexuality-a7354601.html).

- Show **Slide 6**. Ask the class to work in pairs to think about what advice would support a young person who wants to come out. Point out the link to further support on **Slide 5** and let students know where they can find support within your school.

Plenary (5 mins)

- Explain that you will answer their anonymous questions from **Worksheet 11.2a** in the next lesson. To close this lesson, ask students to tell a partner three new things they have learned.

Assessment

- Use the worksheets and 'what have you learned' discussion in the plenary to assess their understanding.

Extension or home learning

- Extension: Ask students to go to https://www.youngstonewall.org.uk/system/files/coming_out.pdf for 'Coming Out! Answers to some of the questions you may have' to consolidate their understanding.

Worksheet 11.2a Sexuality

True or false?

How much do you know about sexuality? Complete this worksheet to find out.

Statement	True or False?
1. There are only two different sexualities: straight (heterosexual) or gay (homosexual/lesbian).	
2. Not everyone is interested in sex and sexual relationships.	
3. 'Coming out' is a term used for when someone tells other people about their sexuality.	
4. Although there are labels, everyone's sexuality is unique and natural, and not everyone wants their sexuality to be defined by a label.	
5. People's sexuality can change at different times in their life.	
6. Discrimination towards someone because of their sexuality is an offence and is against the law.	
7. Romantic attraction and sexual attraction are not always the same.	

Any questions?

Do you have any questions about sexuality that you would like your teacher to address?
(Your teacher will answer the question in class anonymously – your name will be kept private.)

....

....

....

....

....

....

....

....

Worksheet 11.2b Coming out

Imagine a young person wants to come out and tell other people about their sexuality, but they don't know how to go about it. Using the questions below, can you advise them on how to prepare?

1. Where could they go for support or advice?

    ....

    ....

2. How will they decide who to tell, and why is this important to consider?

    ....

    ....

    ....

    ....

    ....

3. How do they want to tell people? Face to face? On a phone call or a video chat? In a group situation or individually? What are the pros and cons of each option?

    ....

    ....

    ....

    ....

    ....

4. When would be a good time to do this and when would be most comfortable for them?

    ....

    ....

    ....

    ....

5. Where would be the best place to do this? What are their best options and why?

    ....

    ....

    ....

    ....

Worksheet 11.2c Coming out stories

Read the following articles written about people's experiences of coming out.

National Coming Out Day: Connor Franta explains what revealing your sexuality to millions of people on YouTube is like

The YouTuber tells the Independent how life has changed since his coming out video went viral and why every coming out story is helpful

[…] Franta, a prominent vlogger with 3.6million subscribers, was primarily known for his comedy videos.

Then he shared a six-minute video where he spoke honestly, 'with no script, plan or fancy editing', and discussed his sexuality, introducing the world to a more three-dimensional figure.

'Coming out was by far the best thing I've ever done. It's funny because the thing that made me so uncomfortable for years and years, has now become one of the most comforting aspects of my life. I'm proud to be gay and I wouldn't have it any other way.'

[...] 'I didn't come out until I was 21-years-old because I grew up in a place where it appeared to be less common. I didn't really know any people in the LGBTQ+ community growing up, so it made me feel…abnormal. It made me repress my thoughts and feelings and hide who I truly was for such a long time.

It wasn't until I moved to California that I became friends with a lot of people in the community. That helped me beyond words and truly fast-forwarded my own process of acceptance to see others living openly and honestly.'

[...] 'People will always have to come out in some manner, but I know it will slowly become less of a big, emotional deal. I see a world, not too far off, where difference doesn't shock, surprise or scare people. You are who you are and you simply exist as that person. Imagine how beautiful that time is going to be. In the meantime, every coming out story helps get us there. The more we talk about it and become present across the world, the better. If you're struggling with your sexuality, take your time. Everyone's coming out journey is unique to them and them alone. Make sure you're in a safe environment and know that it will get better. One day, you will wholeheartedly be yourself and you'll go nowhere but forward.'

From *The Independent*, Wednesday 12 October 2016

Being a gay rugby referee has been tough, but coming out was like being born again

By Nigel Owens

When I became a referee, it became clear that there was nobody in the sport who was gay. The rugby world is very heterosexual and masculine, and this made things difficult. Although that's not to say that the sport is openly homophobic. It was just never an environment where I felt like I could be myself.

I was 18 when I started realising something was different about me. In school I had girlfriends; when I was in my early twenties I had a girlfriend for a year. But I always knew something wasn't right. I thought, 'I will make myself fall in love with this girl', but that never happened and never would. Eventually I thought, 'I can't do this anymore.'

For the next nine years I tried to hide it away […]. But again it was too much. I wasn't able to carry on with my refereeing because I wasn't happy with who I was.

It got to the point where I thought: do I carry on with my life, or do I try and hide it and continue with refereeing? Or do I come out and risk my career? There was no one who was openly gay in the world of rugby then.

In 2005, I told my mum and then my friends. Two years later, I discussed it with the Press. I was so worried but I actually got a lot of support, especially from the players and the Welsh Rugby Union.

It's impossible to try and describe how this felt. It was great to realise it made no difference to your family and friends and the people in rugby. It was like being born again.

[…] There are always going to be a small number of bullies out there. They're in the minority, yet they have a huge impact on people's lives, and they shouldn't. What people need to know is that they shouldn't be afraid.

So if I could speak to anyone in the same position I was when I was younger, I'd say, 'Trust me, everything will be OK. There might be a friend or family member who won't accept it, but things will be OK as long as you have some people around you who support you.'

From *The Independent*, Tuesday 31 March 2015

12.1 Addiction

Learning objectives:

- To understand why people might take drugs and drink alcohol
- To understand the wider impacts of taking drugs
- To learn about addictions and recovery

Resources:

- PowerPoint 12.1
- Worksheets 12.1a and 12.1b
- Links to KS3: Book 1, Unit 11.1; Book 2, Units 7.1, 7.2 and 8.3; Book 3, Unit 6.1

Key vocabulary:

tobacco, nicotine, addiction, dependency, alcoholic, addict, narcotics, recovery

- See KS3 lesson links above for further information and background, including facts on different drugs, tobacco, alcohol and alcoholism.

Get them thinking! (5 mins)

- Ask students: 'What is the biggest risk factor for death, disability and illness in the UK for people between the ages of 15 and 49?' *(Alcohol, according to Burton, R. et al., 2016)* Why do they think this is?

Core learning (25 mins)

- Ask students: 'What is addiction?' Listen to some of their ideas and then look at the definition on **Slide 1**.

- Hand out **Worksheet 12.1a** and go through it with students. Ask them why they think people might choose to take drugs and drink alcohol. Brainstorm their ideas and write these on the board as you discuss *(e.g. for fun, to escape their problems, curiosity, peers are doing it)*. Then allow the students time to complete the worksheet before listening to their ideas.

- Move on to **Slide 2**. Go through this with the students and ask them what they think might be the red flags to warn of addiction *(e.g. thinking about it more and more, being the one to drink or do more drugs than other people you know, not remembering what you did, losing friends)*. See the notes on the slide.

- Go to **Slides 3 and 4**. Discuss briefly how people can get addicted to different drugs, including street and prescription drugs. Note that some pain relief and anxiety reducing drugs can be highly addictive.

- Go through **Slide 5** with the class, explaining that it is possible to recover from addiction – though it may be a lifelong effort. Then go back to **Worksheet 12.1a** and ask students to look at what they wrote. Do they want to add or change anything? If they do, ask them to do this in another colour so you can see what they have learned, adding a key to say which colour was their first comments and which their second.

Additional learning (15 mins)

- Hand out **Worksheet 12.1b**. Read through it with students and then allow time for them to complete the bubbles. Discuss their thoughts at the end of this activity and ask what they have learned. Draw out ideas about the individual's physical and mental health, finances, their career, their personal safety, their relationships, debt; their family's anger, neglect, worry, powerlessness; the effects on the local area of crime, disturbance, drug paraphernalia (needles, etc.) in public spaces; the effects on society of public service demands on the NHS, police, prisons and the costs of recovery and support.

Plenary (5 mins)

- Refer back to **Slide 5** and remind students that there is lots of support for people who need help with alcohol or drug use, including those who are worried about family or friends. The most important thing to do is to talk to someone they trust and ask for help. (See notes on the slide for links to support.)

Assessment

- Use students' completed worksheets to assess their understanding.

Extension or home learning

- Extension: Discuss what someone might do to get help if they were slipping into alcoholism or addiction *(e.g. talking to friends and family/carers, going to the doctor, going to a counsellor, talking to a teacher, contacting Childline and looking online for support)*. Ask students to write a short story about this, focusing on the consequences. They could research recovery support available as a follow-on from this.

- Home learning: Ask students to research the lucrative drinks industry and create a project around the question: 'Why is alcohol legally sold to adults if it is harmful?'

Fill in the thought bubbles with a range of thoughts that someone might have when trying to make decisions on the risky situation of drinking alcohol and/or using drugs.

Consider the consequences of substance misuse and addiction for this individual, the people who care about them or whom they care for, and the wider community and society around them. Explain how you think each issue will affect these different people/groups – you can use the back of the sheet if you need more room.

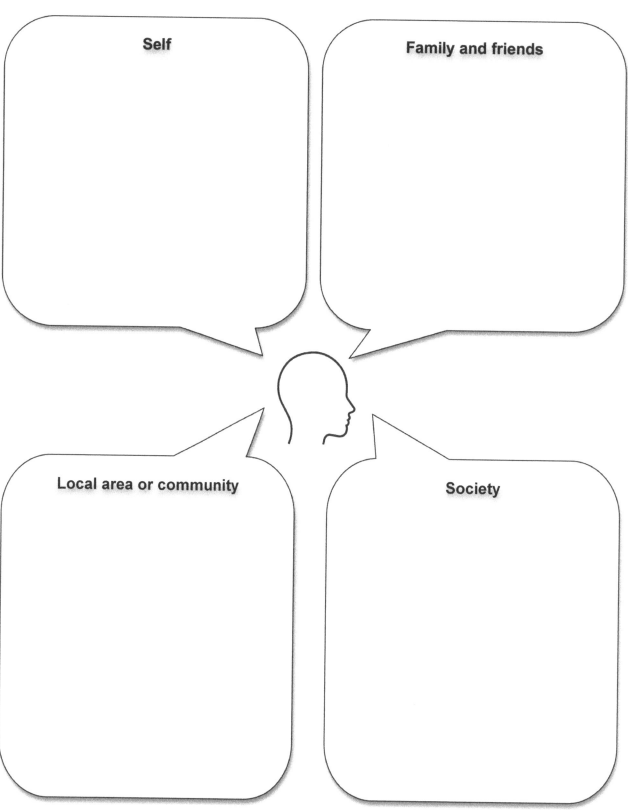

Self

Family and friends

Local area or community

Society

12.2 Alcohol, drugs, tobacco and the law

Learning objectives:

- To learn about the laws around smoking tobacco
- To learn about the laws around alcohol
- To learn about the laws around illegal drugs

Resources:

- PowerPoint 12.2
- Worksheets 12.2a and 12.2b
- Access to the internet
- Link to KS3: Book 2, Units 7.2 and 8.1; Book 3, Unit 6.1

Key vocabulary:

tobacco, cigarettes, alcohol, illegal drugs, Class A drugs, Class B drugs, Class C drugs, possession, production, supply, drug offences, penalties, sentences

Get them thinking! (5 mins)

- Ask students: 'What do you know about the laws regarding smoking, alcohol and drugs?' Let them share their ideas without contributing and use this as an initial assessment.

Core learning (25 mins)

- Go to **Slide 1** to look at the main laws around smoking tobacco. Discuss these, and ask students why they think these laws are in place. (See slide notes for information on nicotine addiction and links for quitting).
- Next, go to **Slide 2** and look at the main laws around drinking alcohol. Discuss each of these in turn – students may be surprised by some of them. For more information, go to www.drinkaware.co.uk.
- Show **Slide 3** to consider the effects of weekend drinking on UK society. Discuss as a whole class.
- Move on to **Slide 4** to consider the main laws on illegal drugs. Read through the slide. Then tell students they are going to learn more about Class A, B and C drugs and the penalties for breaking these laws.
- Hand out **Worksheet 12.2a** and go through the drug penalties with students. Then go to https://www.talktofrank.com/ and look at the website as a class before students complete the worksheet.
- Hand out **Worksheet 12.2b**. Ask students to reference **Worksheet 12.2a** and the Talk to Frank website to help them complete **Worksheet 12.2b**, finding out more about the laws relating to individual drugs and the class they have been put into. Students can research the different classes of illegal drugs alone or in pairs. They must choose drugs from all three of the classes and start with 'The Law' section of the website before researching the drugs further.

Additional learning (15 mins)

- Divide the class into three groups and give each group a class (A, B or C). Tell them to look at their research and consider the drugs in this class. Why do they think they are in that class? Do they agree that this is the correct class for these drugs, or should they be in a higher or lower class? Why? Encourage discussion, using the website if students need more information to make each decision.
- Ask each team to choose two or three key observations from their discussion of their class of drug to share with the class in the plenary.

Plenary (5 mins)

- Invite each group in turn to feed back their two or three key observations on the class of illegal drugs they considered. They should refer to the drugs and the penalties within their chosen class, and explain how they feel about this classification as a group.

Assessment

- Assessment can be made from the initial discussion at the beginning of the lesson and on marking the two worksheets.

Extension or home learning

- Extension or home learning: Students could research another country's laws on illegal drugs and compare them with the UK's, or with another country that has very different laws (e.g. Norway, Iran, Jamaica, China, Germany, Sweden). Students should bring this research back for class discussion and a reflection on UK laws.

Worksheet 12.2a Drugs penalties

Look at the penalties for the possession, supply and production of the different classes of drugs.

Class	Drug	Possession	Supply and production
A	crack cocaine, cocaine, ecstasy (MDMA), heroin, LSD, magic mushrooms, methadone, methamphetamine (crystal meth)	Up to seven years in prison, an unlimited fine, or both.	Up to life in prison, an unlimited fine, or both.
B	amphetamines, barbiturates, cannabis, codeine, ketamine, methylphenidate (Ritalin), synthetic cannabinoids, synthetic cathinones (e.g. mephedrone, methoxetamine)	Up to five years in prison, an unlimited fine, or both.	Up to 14 years in prison, an unlimited fine, or both.
C	anabolic steroids, benzodiazepines (diazepam), gamma hydroxybutyrate (GHB), gamma-butyrolactone (GBL), piperazines (BZP), khat	Up to two years in prison, an unlimited fine, or both (except anabolic steroids – it's not an offence to possess them for personal use).	Up to 14 years in prison, an unlimited fine, or both.

[Gov.UK]

Do you have any questions or thoughts about drugs and the law?

Is there anything else you would like to add or know, or that you don't understand?

1. ....

....

....

2. ....

....

....

3. ....

....

....

4. ....

....

....

Worksheet 12.2b Understanding illegal drugs and the law

Visit the website 'Talk to Frank' https://www.talktofrank.com/. Using **Worksheet 12.2a**, choose three or more drugs from each class and research these. On each drugs page there is a section called 'The Law'. Read it and note anything of interest from this section first, then research other aspects on the page. Make sure you choose drugs from all three of the classes. (If you need more room, use the back of this sheet.)

Class A

1. ....
....

2. ....
....

3. ....
....

Class B

1. ....
....

2. ....
....

3. ....
....

Class C

1. ....
....

2. ....
....

3. ....
....

12.3 Illegal drugs and crime

Learning objectives:
- To learn that drug-taking can be linked to criminal activities
- To learn to recognise the signs of criminal exploitation

Resources:
- PowerPoint 12.3
- Worksheet 12.3
- Large paper and pens
- Camera
- Link to KS3: Book 3, Unit 6.2

Key vocabulary:
crimes, criminal gangs, criminal exploitation, abuse, coerced, manipulation, resilience

Get them thinking! (5 mins)

- Ask students: 'Why might drug use lead to crimes?' Discuss this as a class and use as an assessment.

Core learning (25 mins)

- Go to **Slide 1** to consider why drugs are linked to crimes. Discuss the answers students gave to the starter question and then go through the slide with them, including the notes.

- Next, go through **Slide 2** with the class, using the definitions in the notes. Read and discuss the extract about child criminal exploitation from the government website on **Slide 3**. Ask: 'What crimes might teenagers who get into drug-taking get involved in?' *(e.g. possession, supplying, drug-running/county lines, stealing, violence with rival gangs).*

- Go to **Slide 4** to look specifically at county lines. Tell students that often people do not notice that they are being exploited because they get sucked in by manipulation or by promises of e.g. wealth or belonging/being looked after. Explain that we can all look out for our friends and they can look out for us.

- Ask: 'What signs do you think we might see if a friend was being criminally exploited?' Put the class into groups and hand out large sheets of paper and pens. Ask them to work as a team to write down all their ideas, and then feed back and discuss as a class. (See Slide 5 below for examples.)

Additional learning (15 mins)

- Go through **Slide 5** as a class, considering what each sign may 'look like'. Then ask students to create freeze frames using the list of potential signs. They have 30 seconds, working in their groups from earlier, to create a freeze frame demonstrating a concerning sign. You can either call out, giving them a minute to plan and then shouting 'freeze!', or allow them more time to explore this in their groups. (Rules: total silence while they're in the freeze frame, no props, no touching. Using a camera to photograph these will be useful for assessment.)

Plenary (5 mins)

- Recap everything students have learned this lesson. Remind them that they can always talk to you or your colleagues (name them) in the school, or contact Childline to talk to someone anonymously, if they are worried about anything or anyone (including themselves) following this lesson. They can also go straight to the police if they are worried about anyone's safety or wellbeing.

Assessment

- Students complete **Worksheet 12.3**. Go through this with them, marking their work by going back through the slides (all the answers can be found there). Use this and the activities and to assess.

Extension or home learning

- Extension: Ask students to consider how to start a conversation with a friend and/or help them if they were worried about them being criminally exploited. Organise the class into two rows of chairs, face to face. Row 1 is concerned about row 2. Students in row 1 have to find a way to tell their friend (the person opposite them) that they are concerned. Their friend feeds back and suggests how they could improve their advice. They then swap roles and repeat. Once both rows have had a turn being the worried friend, repeat the activity, telling them to take on board the advice/direction given by their partner and see if they can improve. Partners feedback and then swap and repeat. Walk around and assess.

- Home learning: Ask students to find out about the concept of resilience and how building this can help us to make the right choices in life, to know when we are making the wrong ones, and to give us the strength to change direction.

Worksheet 12.3 Drugs and crimes: What have you learned?

Use the section below to write down everything you have learned about drugs and crimes. If you are not sure, don't worry – write what you think!

1. Why do illegal drugs and crime go hand in hand? ....

   ....

   ....

   ....

2. What is your understanding of child criminal exploitation? ....

   ....

   ....

   ....

3. What do you understand by the term 'county lines'? ....

   ....

   ....

   ....

4. List five signs that you might spot if you or someone you know was being criminally exploited.

   a. ....

   b. ....

   c. ....

   d. ....

   e. ....

5. Use this section to tell your teacher what you would like to learn more about and to ask any further questions.

   ....

   ....

   ....

   ....

   ....

Our online lives

Learning objectives:	Resources:	Key vocabulary:
• To understand what your digital footprint is • To understand the right to privacy and its limits • To know what the right to be forgotten is	• PowerPoint 13.1 • Worksheet 13.1 • Link to KS3: Book 3, Unit 12.3	digital footprint, right to privacy, the right to be forgotten

Get them thinking! (5 mins)

• Ask students is there anything they should or should not share online, particularly if it is very personal and could be used to identify them. Note their ideas on the board.

Core learning (25 mins)

• Define what a digital footprint using **Slides 1** and **2**. Then explain exactly what is private online using **Slide 3**. Discuss how companies can collect and use people's data, and how the government can look at the private parts of their digital footprint under certain circumstances, such as the prevention of terrorism (e.g. looking at emails that indicate terrorist activity and monitoring phone calls) or possibly as part of a criminal investigation such as drug trafficking, county lines or child exploitation.

• Go through **Slide 4** with the class and then go back to the ideas listed on the board during the starter. Make it clear that there will be some situations where they should share information with an adult even if it has been sent to them privately, e.g. if it relates to self-harm, eating disorders, radicalisation, racism or terrorism. Mention your school's Prevent strategy and safeguarding policy here, and make sure students know who to talk to at school if they have any concerns.

• Show **Slide 5**. Make it clear that none of these types of harmful material should be shared publicly or privately on any form of social media.

Additional learning (15 mins)

• Define the right to be forgotten using **Slide 6**.

• Organise students into groups and hand out **Worksheet 13.1a**. Tell students to complete the activity, and then compare answers as a class, inviting groups to share their views and give reasons for them.

• Ask students to read **Worksheet 13.1b** on digital acceptability and to complete the table in pairs. They should then discuss the answers in groups, then as a class. (*It is suggested that scenario 1 could be perceived as an invasion of privacy but is legal; scenarios 2 and 5 are acceptable as long as in scenario 5 you give your permission; scenarios 3 and 4 are against GDPR and thus against the law in the UK.*)

Plenary (5 mins)

• GDPR allows anyone to request the removal of data under the right to be forgotten. Ask students to discuss whether they think this should always be the case, or whether an employer should be able to know somebody's past (e.g. if they posted racist tweets five years ago). Should the rules be the same for adults and children?

• Point out how the right to be forgotten may be under threat as the UK leaves the EU.

Assessment

• You can use students' responses to **Worksheet 13.1a** and **13.1b** to assess their understanding.

Extension or home learning

• Extension: Ask students to use the internet to research how the right to be forgotten has been applied since the UK left the EU in January 2021 (https://gdpr.eu/right-to-be-forgotten/).

• Home learning: Get students to research the case of Edward Snowden and write two or three paragraphs on this case, summarising what governments have done in the past with mass surveillance.

• These websites may help you to support students in relation to these difficult topics:
Suicide: https://www.papyrus-uk.org/
Bullying, harassment and self-harm: https://giveusashout.org/get-help/
Self-harm: https://youngminds.org.uk/find-help/feelings-and-symptoms/self-harm/
Terrorism and radicalisation: https://www.nspcc.org.uk/keeping-children-safe/reporting-abuse/dedicated-helplines/protecting-children-from-radicalisation/

Worksheet 13.1a Our online lives

Cut out the following situation cards. In groups, discuss which you think are the worst violations of the right to privacy. Rank them in order of the worst violation of privacy (1) to the least (9). Discuss what you would do in each situation, and why. Give reasons for your views.

Your partner wants to take a sexy photo of you in your underwear. They then share it with a mutual friend.	Your parents start reading your private emails. They are worried you are spending too much time online and not enough time on your school work.	The government starts recording your phone calls because you are friends with someone who, unknown to you, is on a terrorist watch list.
Facebook says it is now going to view all your private messages after a user complained when you accidentally shared several posts by the racist campaign group Britain First.	Your school teacher calls you in for a chat because you've been looking at websites about self-harm on the school computers.	The police call. They want to check your mobile phone number so they can confirm that you weren't near the site of a robbery. A witness says you were, but you weren't.
There's been cheating online with a school exam. The school says it wants access to all your mobile phone messages and emails for the last week to prove you weren't involved.	A friend thinks you are behind the bullying anonymous emails they have received, and wants to check your phone to confirm it was not you.	Your local football club is asking for a picture of you so they can upload it to their facial recognition system, which they are using to keep racists out of football matches.

Worksheet 13.1b Digital acceptability

Digital companies may get your permission to share data in one of several ways:

1. In the terms and conditions in the small print when you sign up initially for their services.

2. Through the use of cookies, which track how you use a website, which you have to give permission for when you access the site.

3. By contacting you through email and asking your permission to share your personal information with other third-party companies, or to use your information for a different purpose from which it was originally intended.

In pairs, look at the following situations, showing how social media companies collect your data and what they might do with it. Decide which you think are acceptable and which unacceptable by writing 'yes' or 'no' in column 2. Give reasons for your views in column 3. Then compare your answers with another pair in your class. Finally, discuss this as a whole as a class with your teacher.

Situation	Acceptable?	Why do you think this?
1. A mobile phone company tracks everywhere you have been and sends you different adverts based on your movements.		
2. A social media company sends you special offers, based on the companies you have liked on its platform.		
3. A social media company sells your digital profile, including all your likes and websites you have visited through its platform, to a US sports company, which then keeps sending you adverts and emails advertising its products.		
4. A social media company sells your profile to a political party, which plans to send you election propaganda in the run-up to your 18th birthday.		
5. Your email provider wants to sell your email address to a fashion company to send you special offers, and is asking your permission to do so.		

Learning objectives:	Resources:	Key vocabulary:
• To understand what online bullying is • To understand the laws on online bullying • To consider the effects of online bullying	• PowerPoint 13.2 • Worksheets 13.2a and 13.2b • Link to KS3: Book 1, Unit 9.2	bullying, online bullying, bully, victim, discrimination, harassment, fines, imprisonment

- See the KS3 lesson linked above for further information on how to report online bullying and how to get support with internet trolling.

Get them thinking! (5 mins)

- Ask: 'How do we know if we have hurt someone with a comment or a post online?' *(We don't! Unless we ask, or they or someone else tells us or reports us.)*

Core learning (25 mins)

- Go through **Slide 1** and discuss online bullying with the class, clarifying any misconceptions if required.

- Ask the class where online bullying can take place. Write their suggestions on the board and then go to **Slide 2** to check that they have thought of all of the different online places where bullying can occur. Discuss the potential for 'accidental' bullying online, such as banter, a comment that could be read incorrectly, ganging up in online gaming.

- Next, go through **Slide 3** with the class to clarify the law regarding online bullying. See the slide notes for details of the relevant Acts.

- Ask students: 'Why do people bully online?' Discuss their ideas and write these on the board, then go to 'Help me out – being a bully' on the BBC website: www.bbc.co.uk/cbbc/findoutmore/help-me-out-being-a-bully?collection=lifebabble-guide-to-bullying. Watch the short film 'Why do people bully?' with the class. Here young people talk about some of the reasons people bully (e.g. to fit in with a group, to not be bullied themselves, to help take their mind of their own problems, to give them a sense of power, because they don't realise they are bullying, because they are or have been bullied themselves).

- Hand out **Worksheet 13.2a** and ask students, working individually or in pairs, to write a bullying scenario, deciding on the location and the comments made according to the guidance on the worksheet. Display **Slide 2** again as support. Once they have created a scenario, they should consider how both victim and bully might feel. You might like to enlarge a copy of this worksheet to model the activity before they begin, depending on your cohort.

- Allow time for students to share their scenarios in pairs on completion.

Additional learning (15 mins)

- Go back the BBC bullying page (www.bbc.co.uk/cbbc/findoutmore/help-me-out-being-a-bully?collection=lifebabble-guide-to-bullying) and show the clips 'What can you do if you think you might have been bullying someone?' and/or 'How to stop'. Discuss these after viewing as a class.

- Hand out **Worksheet 13.2b** and allow students time to go through it and then to share it with a partner. Follow this up with a class discussion on the activity.

Plenary (5 mins)

- Recap everything students have learned and answer any questions. Then go through **Slides 4** and **5** and remind students that there are many places they can get support for bullying issues. (See the notes on the slide.)

Assessment

- Use the worksheets to assess students' understanding.

Extension or home learning

- Extension: Ask students to use **Worksheet 13.2a** to create a piece of art exploring online bullying based on the activity.

- Home learning: Ask students to research how bullying affects both victims and bullies in later life, and to share all their new knowledge with the school in an assembly.

Worksheet 13.2a Online bullying

Create an online bullying situation, then think about the consequences of this action on both the victim and the bully. Use the back of the sheet if you need more room.

1. Where is this bullying taking place online?

....

2. What has been written or posted online, now and previously, by the bully to the victim?

Comment 1. Bully:

....

....

Comment 2. Bully:

....

....

Comment 3. Bully:

....

....

Victim's response, if any: (Victims often choose not to react/respond, so you might decide not to include any response)

....

....

3. How would these comments make the victim feel? (Give a detailed description and explain why.)

....

....

4. How would this make the bully feel? (Give a detailed description and explain why.)

Immediately:

....

....

Later in life:

....

....

Imagine you are a bully. Consider these statements about what to do if you think you are bullying someone. Number them in terms of how hard you think each statement would be to do. (There are no right or wrong answers – everyone will feel and respond differently.)

Give each statement a rating from 1 to 12, where 1 is really easy to do and 12 is really hard to do.

When you have finished, compare your answers with a partner's. Were any the same? Were any different? Why do you both think this is?

Rating 1–12

Admitting to yourself you have bullied someone ☐

Apologising to the person you have bullied ☐

Working out why you did it ☐

Asking for help ☐

Stopping bullying for good ☐

Talking to someone about personal problems ☐

Imagining what it would feel like if it were you being bullied ☐

Owning up to it with your friends ☐

Owning up to it with your family/carers ☐

Asking the person you have bullied how you made them feel ☐

Admitting you made a mistake ☐

Learning from your mistake and using it to help others ☐

What do you think is the most important advice to give to someone who thinks they have been or are being a bully and why?

....

....

....

....

....

....

....

Useful websites for more information and support:

Anti-bullying Alliance: www.anti-bullyingalliance.org.uk/tools-information/if-youre-being-bullied/find-help-and-support

Childline: www.childline.org.uk/info-advice/bullying-abuse-safety/types-bullying/bullying-cyberbullying/

Consumer rights, advice and awareness

Learning objectives:	Resources:	Key vocabulary:
• To understand what a nudge is and why shops use it • To know what consumers' rights are, and to be aware of the main three rights • To understand how goods can be returned and in what condition and circumstances	• PowerPoint 14.1 • Worksheets 14.1a and 14.1b • Link to KS3: Book 3, Unit 15.1	consumer rights, category managers, nudges, BOGOF (buy one, get one free)

Get them thinking! (5 mins)

• Ask students how often they like to go shopping, and what they like to buy. Elicit whether there are any particular types of shopper in the class (e.g. impulse shopper, confused shopper, frequent shopper, shopping addict). Note these answers on the board.

Core learning (25 mins)

• Go through **Slide 1**, clarifying the different types of shopper. See if students can come up with any more types, such as impulse shopper or a shopping addict.

• Go through **Slide 2** and explain what category managers are. If you are running a longer lesson, you can do the additional learning activity here, after eliciting different types of nudges from students, such as encouraging people to buy goods due to fear or missing out (such as a 'Black Friday Sale' or 'Buy one, get one free for this week only').

• Go through **Slide 3** (there is more detail on this in KS3 Book 3, Unit 15.1) and check that students understand the consumer rights outlined here.

• Go through **Slides 4** and **5**, clearly explaining to students what their rights are in relation to buying online, how and when they can return goods and services bought over the internet. Show **Slide 6** with links to organisations where they can get further advice.

• Ask students to do the first part of **Worksheet 14.1a** individually. Then ask them to compare and rank their answers in pairs or groups, giving reasons for their views.

Additional learning (15 mins)

• Go through **Worksheet 14.1b** with the class, looking at the different types of nudge and checking that students understand them. Then ask students, in groups, to think of other examples for each type of nudge (e.g. different types of product placement). Check these together as a class.

Plenary (5 mins)

• Ask students to discuss which of the three consumer rights listed on **Slide 3** they think are the most important and why, giving reasons for their views.

Assessment

• Check that students have completed **Worksheet 14.1a** and use this for assessment.

Extension or home learning

• Extension: Contact the local Trading Standards office at your district council, unitary authority or metropolitan borough council (see https://www.gov.uk/find-local-trading-standards-office). Ask them to come into the class and speak to students about what trading standards are, why they are important and how students can contact trading standards if they have a problem.

• Home learning: Ask students to create a poster, slideshow or web page summarising what consumer rights are, and where they can go for help on their consumer rights (e.g. Citizens Advice, Trading Standards, *Which?*), to share with other classes and year groups in the school, or to place on the school website.

• Extension: Ask students to visit the *Which?* website (www.which.co.uk/consumer-rights), look at the latest three campaigns under the Campaigns tab at the top of the page, and discuss which are the most effective and why, giving reasons for their views.

• Home learning: Ask students to research the latest information from Trading Standards and the government about what fake and dangerous toys are coming to the UK market in the run-up to Christmas.

Worksheet 14.1a Behavioural economics and nudges

A nudge is something that shops and websites do to encourage us to act in a certain way. This name comes from the idea of nudging us in a certain direction. There are many different types of nudges.

Look at the table of nudges below. On your own, rank each nudge from most effective to least effective (where 1 is the most effective). Explain why in the second column. Then, in pairs or groups, discuss which nudges you think are the most effective and why, giving reasons for your views. Make any adjustments to your original ranking after the discussion.

Nudge	Why have you given this nudge this rank, and how do you think it works?	Ranking
A. Buy one, get one free (BOGOF)		
B. Putting cheap impulse goods such as chocolate and sweets by the checkout till in the supermarket		
C. Three-for-two offers		
D. Putting goods in a shop window to lure you in		
E. Time-limited sales on websites		
F. Sale in a shop with 'up to 70% off' (but most goods are actually only 5–10% off)		
G. Multiple checkout stages on a supermarket website to check whether you have 'forgotten' to buy anything		
H. Meal deals		
I. Store discount cards, where you get a discount for continually shopping at one store		
J. Holiday websites offering a deal price, but when you actually check, the date you want it is more expensive		

Worksheet 14.1b Different types of nudges

In groups, look at the different sorts of nudges outlined below. What other examples can you think of for each type of nudge? Compare your answers as a class.

1. Choice architecture

   a) Changing the way shops are laid out, such as:

      * putting sweets by the checkout
      * putting popular products on shelves at eye level.

   b) Designing buildings in particular ways, such as:

      * more stairs and fewer lifts to encourage more exercise
      * promotions at the end of shopping aisles.

   c) Default choices: making salad and vegetables the default option with main meals in a restaurant, rather than fries or chips.

   ....

   ....

2. Financial inducements, such as subsidies from the government to lower the price of healthy food.

   ....

   ....

3. Financial disincentives, such as:

   * a sugar tax to raise the price of unhealthy sugary foods
   * taxes on cigarettes to reduce smoking
   * minimum prices on alcohol to discourage binge drinking.

   ....

   ....

4. Providing extra information, such as putting the calories and sugar content on food packaging.

   ....

   ....

5. Restricting choice, such as:

   * banning fast-food outlets, including sweet shops, close to schools
   * banning smoking in buildings, public spaces, taxis and private hire vehicles.

   ....

   ....

6. Social norms, such as encouraging people to wear a mask outside, even when they don't have to, to reduce the spread of a disease during a pandemic.

   ....

   ....

Advertising, data and consumer ethics

Learning objectives:

- To think about the different ways organisations collect digital data
- To understand what GDPR is and how it limits the collection and use of data within the UK

Resources:

- PowerPoint 14.2
- Worksheets 14.2a and 14.2b
- Examples of recent successful advertising campaigns
- Link to KS3: Book 3, Unit 15.1

Key vocabulary:

advertising, watershed, GDPR, data, ethics, supply chain

Get them thinking! (5 mins)

- Ask students to think of examples of good advertising campaigns they have seen recently. Be prepared with examples of successful campaigns in case students can't think of any. Is there one in particular that stands out? As a class, discuss why students think this type of advertising is effective, and who it is aimed at.

Core learning (25 mins)

- Go through **Slide 1** with the class. Ask students why they think the government decided to impose the bans described. Do they think they will make a difference? Were these bans a good idea or not? Why?

- Go through **Slide 2** on collecting data. As an optional activity, if you have time, ask students to list all the different ways they can think of for collecting data. Examples include cookies from websites, automatically through mobile phone location data, likes from social media sites and websites people have visited or who people have emailed from their internet provider. Write these on the board.

- Explain what GDPR is using **Slide 3**. Ask the class whether they can think of more examples of ways that GDPR might protect their personal data. Note that even though the UK has left the EU, it still needs to be GDPR compliant when trading with EU firms, no matter what happens in the UK.

- Display **Slide 4** and explain what ethics are, discussing the example. Ask students if they can think of other examples, such as whether companies should use your data for a different purpose from which it was originally collected *(no, it's illegal without your permission)* or releasing where you have been to the government without your permission (due to emergency powers in a pandemic, for example).

Additional learning (15 mins)

- Go through the example of fashion on **Slide 5**. (You could refer to the BBC TV show *Stacy Dooley Investigates Fashion's Dirty Secrets*, if you search for clips on YouTube.) Then ask students to work in groups to fill out **Worksheet 14.2a**, choosing a particular product to research. For homework they can write a report of two or three paragraphs summarising what they have learned, using websites such as https://www.ethicalconsumer.org/. Alternatively, they could hold a debate on the following motion: 'This house believes that businesses should be guided by ethics first and profits second.'

Plenary (5 mins)

- Ask students whether they think the 9pm advertising watershed on sugary food and drink is a good idea, and whether there should be other limits on advertising.

Assessment

- Ask students to complete **Worksheet 14.2b** in pairs or groups *(Answers: 1, 3, 4, 5 and 10 are allowed)*. Take in this and **Worksheet 14.2a** and use these to assess students' understanding.

Extension or home learning

- Extension: Ask students to create a poster about GDPR, stating what people and companies are and are not allowed to do with data, citing the seven principles of GDPR. Use the following link as a resource: https://ico.org.uk/for-organisations/guide-to-data-protection/guide-to-the-general-data-protection-regulation-gdpr/principles/.

- Home learning: Ask students to look at the following case where an image of a drunk man used to advertise a club night at bars was banned. Ask: 'Do you think the ASA (advertising standards agency) was right remove this advert? Why do you think they did so?' https://www.asa.org.uk/news/asa-orders-immediate-removal-of-irresponsible-alcohol-ad.html

Worksheet 14.2a Advertising, business ethics and data

Look at the flowchart below, which goes through the lifecycle of a cotton t-shirt in the fashion industry. Work in groups. For each stage, choose another product and research it on the internet, using the table below. Add to the final column your suggestions for how the process could be made more ethical.

Stage	Questions	How could this be made more ethical?
Stage 1 Raw materials	Where are they sourced from? How much water was used? Is this in an area of water scarcity? Were **pesticides** and **herbicides** used? Were the local farmers paid fairly for their crop? Were the workers involved in growing and harvesting the crop paid fairly and did they have good working conditions?	
Stage 2 Transport of raw materials	How far was this in terms of miles? How much energy was used in transporting these goods? Were the drivers paid fairly?	
Stage 3 Manufacturing	What are conditions like at the factory where **manufacturing** occurs? Are the workers paid fairly? What hours are worked? Are workers entitled to join a trade union? Are they paid holiday pay, sick pay and pension contributions?	
Stage 4 Transport of goods	How far was this in terms of miles? How much energy was used in transporting these goods? Were the drivers paid fairly?	
Stage 5 Goods at the shop	How are the goods displayed? How are the shop workers paid? What are their working conditions like? What hours do they work? Can they join a union? How much are the goods sold for? Who gets what share of the profits for selling the goods across the whole production process? Can ordinary people afford the goods?	
Stage 6 Usage	How long do the goods last? How often do people use them? Are the goods made from easily recyclable material? Can the goods be easily sold on as second-hand goods and used again?	
Stage 7 Recycling and disposal	Can the goods be easily recycled for their raw materials? If not, can the goods be disposed of easily?	

Key vocabulary

pesticides and herbicides: chemicals that are used to kill off insects, pests and weeds, but which harm the natural environment as a result
manufacturing: the process of creating goods for consumption

Worksheet 14.2b Data: What you can and cannot do

Look at the following scenarios. In pairs or groups, use what you have learned about data from this unit to decide whether each company would be allowed to do what it wants under GDPR and UK law. Compare your answers as a class, and ask your teacher for the correct answers.

Example	Allowed?
1. A phone company wants to use your location data from your mobile phone to improve the accuracy of its satellite navigation app. It asks your permission to do so.	
2. A company wants to exchange details of its loyalty programme with another company in the USA, so they can compare consumer data and see what trends are occurring in both markets. It does this without asking permission.	
3. Facebook uses your data to allow specific adverts to be targeted at you when you use Facebook. There is an option to switch this off so that you only see generic adverts on Facebook.	
4. Adverts start appearing on your Twitter feed based on your personal profile on Twitter.	
5. A clothes company wants to give your details to shoe company it has a partnership with for promotional purposes. It asks your permission to share data with them.	
6. A gaming website keeps sending you notifications about new games you can play, even though you only played on the site once and ticked no to all forms of advertising when asked.	
7. A company you have never heard of emails you with details of their product. You have no idea how they got your email address.	
8. An insurance company phones up asking if you have ever been in an accident. You have told them before that you do not wish them to call any more.	
9. A mobile phone provider you used to be with keeps texting you with cheap offers. You have previously asked to be deleted from their computer system.	
10. Your bank sends you details of a loan you can take out. They can see that you are running low on funds in your bank account, and you have said the bank is allowed to send you communications.	

Learning objectives:

- To understand what an ecosystem is
- To understand what biodiversity is
- To know what ecologism is and examine the difference between shallow and deep ecologists

Resources:

- PowerPoint 15.1
- Worksheets 15.1a and 15.1b
- Link to KS3: Book 3, Units 16.1 and 16.2

Key vocabulary:

climate change, ecosystem, biodiversity, ecologism, sustainability, shallow vs. deep ecologist, light vs. dark green solutions

Get them thinking! (5 mins)

- Ask students, in pairs, to list all the living things that exist in their back garden or nearest piece of green communal land. See who can list the most.

Core learning (25 mins)

- Define 'biodiversity' using **Slide 1**. Point out that it is the number *and* the range of living things in an area. Ask students to think about which area closest to them is the most biodiverse.

- Ask students what the word 'ecosystem' means. Show **Slide 2** and give an example of a local ecosystem (e.g. a river or reef) and a regional ecosystem (e.g. the Arctic Circle melting and freezing each year).

- Go through **Slide 3** and explain the difference between an environmentalist who cares for the environment for human reasons (they want their children to be able to breathe clean air) and an ecologist who believes that the environment, nature and all living things have an inherent value in their own right. Point out the difference between a 'shallow' ecologist and a 'deep' ecologist. Explain that deep ecology would involve a fundamental change in our thinking (e.g. no oil drilling in case the noise harmed any whales or fish, no longer having any zoos holding animals in captivity, stopping cutting down any rainforest for ranch land or farming in the Amazon).

- Using **Slide 4**, distinguish between weak and strong sustainability, and light green and dark green solutions. Then ask the class, in groups, to come up with as many light and dark green solutions to improve their local area as they can think of.

Additional learning (15 mins)

- Show **Slide 5** and discuss the idea of water shortages and environmental refugees. Hand out **Worksheet 15.1a** and ask students to look at the case studies on water management and to discuss the solutions for each given at the bottom of the worksheet. (They may wish to revisit the Maldives from Book 3, Unit 16.1 when reviewing these case studies.)

- Ask students to look at the case studies on **Worksheet 15.1b** and decide which of the cases would be classed as environmental refugees. *(Answers: only number 1; for 2, A and C apply; for 3, D applies; for 4 and 5, A, C and D apply; for 6, E applies.)*

Plenary (5 mins)

- Discuss with the class how the local area in which they live and study could be improved. Write the best light green and dark green solutions on the board.

Assessment

- Check that students have completed the worksheets and then use these to assess their understanding.

Extension or home learning

- Home learning: Ask students to choose another country or part of the UK where there are water issues, and write a report (at least three paragraphs) detailing what the problem is and what solutions they would use.

- Home learning: Ask students read the following webpage and then write a short summary (two paragraphs) picking out what they feel is the most important information: https://www.weforum.org/agenda/2019/06/water-scarcity-refugee-crisis-tech-solve-it/

- Extension: Get students to look at the separate issues of food security and food miles in an industrialised and a non-industrialised country. Tell them to prepare a short PowerPoint presentation (at least five minutes long and with at least 10 slides) to present to the class.

Worksheet 15.1a Water management

Look at the following case studies. Then look at the list of solutions below.

* Which country do you think has the best water supplies and sewage systems?
* Which has the worst?
* Which solution(s) (A–F) would you favour for each country?
* Working in pairs or groups, rank the solutions in order of preference for each case.
* Discuss your choices with another pair or group. Give reasons for your views.

Case studies

1. **The Netherlands:** A lot of the Netherlands is below sea level. As a result, the Netherlands has taken major steps in terms of flood prevention. This includes dykes, flood barriers and land reclamation schemes. When a new housing estate is built in the Netherlands, it has to include dry pools and drainage areas for when it rains, so excess water can collect and not flood an area.

2. **Bangladesh:** This country lies just to the east of India, in a series of complex river deltas. As a result, it is extremely low lying and prone to flooding each year in the monsoon season. In addition to this, as a less industrialised country, Bangladesh doesn't have water or sewage systems to cover the whole country, meaning people have insecure water supplies and a lack of sanitation. With climate change causing increased flooding, more people there are forced to become environmental refugees – having to leave their homes due to the effects of climate change.

3. **The United Kingdom:** Like the Netherlands, the United Kingdom is an industrialised country with a lot of infrastructure. This means that it has access to clean water through taps, and a sewage system to deal with waste. But there are at least two problems. First, much of the water and sewage system was built by the Victorians, over 100 years ago. As a result, it is very leaky – so much so that countries with hot climates, such as Egypt and Saudi Arabia, cannot understand how we waste so much water. Second, there are areas of the United Kingdom that have steep valleys, often with rivers running through them, that are now prone to flooding because of heavier rainfall due to climate change.

4. **Egypt, Sudan and Ethiopia:** With the Nile River being the main source of water for these three countries, there is increasing tension over its use. This includes whether dams in Sudan and Ethiopia are depriving people in Egypt, further downriver, of water.

5. **The Maldives:** As a series of low-lying islands, the Maldives has to important some of its water, as there is not enough land to collect water by rainfall. In addition to this, the Maldives is under threat of flooding as sea levels rise in the long run due to climate change. The highest point in the whole of the Maldives is only 5 metres above sea level.

Water solutions

A. Desalination plants to turn seawater into drinking water. Expensive but can provide secure water supplies.
B. Providing a modern sewage system to deal within any sewage, thus keeping local water supplies clean.
C. Flood defences to prevent flooding.
D. Tidal barriers to prevent flooding from the sea and also to generate electricity.
E. Working with the United Nations, an independent organisation, to ensure that water supplies are fairly distributed between minority and majority groups in the area.
F. Education to warn people of the dangers of drinking dirty water and water-borne diseases.

For further information, contact charities such as:
Water Aid (https://www.wateraid.org/uk/)
One Drop (https://www.onedrop.org/en/)
Just a Drop (https://www.justadrop.org/)
Life4Water (https://www.life4water.org/)
charity: water (https://www.charitywater.org/uk/)

Worksheet 15.1b Environmental refugees

Defining people as environmental refugees can be difficult. They do not have to flee to a foreign country, which means they are not classed as refugees, but as 'internally displaced'. If any of the statements A–D below apply, then they are not classed as environmental refugees at this time:

A. The cause of them having to move is not necessarily proven to be climate change.

B. They do not suffer the many hardships we would expect refugees to suffer, such as a lack of regular food or water, disrupted education or unemployment.

C. The problem is one in the future – which means these people haven't had to move yet, although they will probably have to move in the future.

D. The problem is manmade.

Read the following examples and decide which of the problems above mean the refugees will not be classed as environmental refugees and which mean they will be classed as environmental refugees.

E. The rains fail in Ethiopia in 2025, not for one year as frequently happens, but for several years in a row, which has happened before. As a result, farmers have to leave their homes, as they cannot grow crops in their local area. They cross the border into Eritrea, a country bordering Ethiopia, which is closer to the sea and has had some more rainfall.

F. A person living in California loses everything in a wildfire, which burns their house to the ground along with the rest of their town. The town is clearly no longer habitable, and there is the danger of further fires in the future, as they are becoming more commonplace in the United States. The fact that these fires are now occurring every year with increasing frequency in three states – California, Oregon and Washington – suggests that climate change is responsible.

G. Many people are fleeing Syria, where there is a civil war that has been going on for years. The lack of clean water supplies caused by climate change AND water networks in Syria being damaged by war may combine to force people to move.

H. A person living in the east of England loses their house to coastal erosion, along with many neighbouring properties. About 7,000 UK properties will be lost in the UK this way over the next century. These people will be forced to move as their houses are swallowed up by the sea.*

I. A person living in the Nile Delta in Egypt will have to move by 2030 as the sea level rises. They can move to another farm, but by 2040 they will have to move again. Eventually, they might seek to change profession, and move to a city like Cairo or Alexandria to retrain in another job.

J. In India, over 3,000 dams have been built since Independence in 1947, forcing many people to move, most within India, but some to other countries.

* (For further information go to https://www.theguardian.com/environment/2014/dec/28/7000-uk-properties-sacrificed-rising-seas-coastal-erosion).

Power and pollution

Learning objectives:

- To distinguish between the different types of pollution
- To examine the relative merits of nuclear power and renewable energy
- To look at the work of Extinction Rebellion

Resources:

- PowerPoint 15.2
- Worksheets 15.2a and 15.2b
- Recycling figures from your local council for your area and nationally
- Access to the internet
- Link to KS3: Book 3, Unit 16.2

Key vocabulary:

pollution, smog, thermal energy, renewable energy

Get them thinking! (5 mins)

- Ask students name all the different types of pollution they can think of. Write these on the board (*e.g. litter, water pollution, plastic pollution, air pollution, rubbish*), then go through **Slide 1** to summarise.

Core learning (25 mins)

- Ask students how they would solve the pollution problems they have listed. Recall the difference between light and dark green solutions from Unit 15.1. Point out that the way we produce power causes much of the pollution that occurs in the UK, particularly air pollution from burning fossil fuels like oil and gas (coal now having been largely phased out).

- Go through **Slides 2** and **3**. Point out that nuclear energy now provides 21% of energy in the UK, and that nuclear power stations, which need to last for 1000 years (as that is how long the waste, usually stored nearby, remains active), need to be able to survive a 1-in-1000-year event. Refer to the Chernobyl and Fukishima nuclear disasters, where accidents caused radioactive contamination that will make surrounding areas dangerous to human life for hundreds of years.

- Ask students to list all the renewable forms of energy they can think of, then go through **Slide 4**. Point out that renewables produced 35% of the UK's energy in 2020.

- Hand out copies of **Worksheet 15.2a** and ask students to read the information and then discuss the questions in pairs or groups. Listen to their responses. *(Answers: nuclear; onshore wind; onshore wind; offshore wind? This depends on your opinion; depends on the country.)*

Additional learning (15 mins)

- Show **Slide 5** and ask students to discuss what they already know about Extinction Rebellion. Use the website https://extinctionrebellion.uk/ along with **Worksheet 15.2b**. Listen to students' responses.

- Ahead of the class, contact your local district council or unitary authority, responsible for recycling, to get the recycling rates for your local area. Also get national rates of recycling. Give this information to students and ask them to compare local and national rates of recycling. Then ask them to discuss what they think can be done to improve recycling in the local area (*e.g. more recycling centres and teams of people knocking on doors of streets where recycling rates are low – the council can tell this from what rubbish people throw out – to explain the importance of recycling*).

Plenary (5 mins)

- Ask the class to discuss whether they would support Extinction Rebellion, and whether they think its tactics of civil disobedience blunt its message or are needed given the urgency of the climate crisis.

Assessment

- Use students' responses to the worksheets to assess their understanding.

Extension or home learning

- Home learning: Get students to research the amount by which air pollution dropped during the lockdowns across the world in spring 2020 due to Covid-19, and whether there are opportunities to keep pollution lower (such as more opportunities to work from home).

- Extension: Ask students, in groups, to draw up an action plan to improve the environment and reduce pollution in their local area (e.g. a litter picking day, more recycling facilities at school, a local public awareness campaign to reduce transport, increase cycling, reduce power use, increase micro generation and generally to reduce consumption, especially of plastic and to use green alternatives where possible).

Worksheet 15.2a Power and pollution

Look at the following three case studies. Discuss the following questions.

- Which is the most reliable form of energy?
- Which is the greenest form of energy?
- Which is the cheapest form of energy?
- Which is the most practical form of energy for the UK?
- In which countries around the world could each form of energy be used?

Nuclear energy, Hinkley Point C

The go-ahead to build Hinkley Point C nuclear power station was given in 2016. Hinkley Point C should start producing energy by 2025. Nuclear power is able to produce a lot of energy – Hinkley Point C will be able to produce 3260 MW of energy with a stable power supply that should last 60 years or more.

However, there are several problems with Hinkley Point C. The first is what to do with the nuclear waste it produces, which will be dangerous for hundreds of years. It is also costing £22.5 billion – £2.9 billion more than expected. Yet there is another problem connected to building the power station.

In order to build Hinkley Point C, thousands of tonnes of material are required. These are being transported from local quarries in Somerset to Hinkley Point C, through the local towns of Glastonbury and Bridgewater. As a result, Glastonbury and Bridgewater now have London levels of traffic with congestion and air pollution, with trucks passing these towns every few minutes each day to the power station. This will continue until the construction is complete in 2025.

(For further information see https://www.theguardian.com/uk-news/2019/aug/14/hinkley-point-c-london-traffic-bridgwater-somerset .)

Wind energy

Wind energy accounts for about one-sixth of UK energy production. There are two sorts of wind energy – onshore energy and offshore energy. The UK is a world leader in offshore energy. Ten per cent of the UK's energy was produced offshore in 2020, powering over 5 million homes.

However, the wind is unpredictable so cannot be relied upon. Offshore wind energy turbines will also require maintenance in the long run, as seawater will gradually erode the bases on which they rest.

Onshore wind produces another 10% of the UK's energy, and is the most cost-effective form of green energy that exists. However, in addition to the wind being unpredictable, there have been complaints by local residents in some areas that wind turbines spoil the natural view. In addition, there is the sound the turbines generate and the danger to birds from them. As a result, it can be difficult to get planning permission for wind turbines to be built in some areas.

Tidal energy

Tidal energy is energy produced from the tides. Tidal fences with turbines are constructed in an area where the tide is concentrated – where the tide goes up and down or the waves are particularly high. Tidal energy is very predictable, as it happens every day, but only for up to 10 hours. As a result, it can form part of the energy mix, but cannot be relied upon to generate electricity all of the time. Tidal energy is still in the early phase of development in the UK and around the world, but it has already produced energy in some small-scale projects, such as around the Orkney Islands in Scotland where the waves are particularly fierce.

Look at the following information about Extinction Rebellion. In groups, discuss what you think of the group's aims and tactics. What do you agree with? What do you disagree with? Give reasons for your views.

Extinction Rebellion

Extinction Rebellion is an outsider pressure group (see Unit 4.2) that does not have close links with the government. As a result, its members can use campaign methods like civil disobedience – breaking the law in a peaceful and non-violent way – to draw attention to their aims.

The group was set up in 2018 by a group of UK academics and spurred on by the example of the Swedish schoolgirl Greta Thunberg's climate strike. It is popular among young people. It has three main aims:

1. Net zero emissions by 2025

This target relates the amount of greenhouse gases produced by transport, industry and heating peoples' homes in the UK. The UK government has set a zero emissions target of 2050. Extinction Rebellion says that with climate change affecting the world climate now, we need to act much more quickly.

2. Telling the truth

Extinction Rebellion argues that the UK government has a legal and moral duty to tell the truth about the size and depth of the ecological crisis that is affecting the world by declaring a climate emergency. They argue that the UK government should work with individuals, firms, groups, institutions and other countries to tackle climate change urgently.

3. Setting up a citizens' assembly

Extinction Rebellion argues that the UK government must set up a citizens' assembly, made up of ordinary people from different parts of the UK, of different ages, who work in different jobs, and are from different backgrounds. This assembly would hear evidence from experts and look at different policy options to deal with the climate emergency. The assembly would then make recommendations to the government on how it should respond.

To date, the government has met the third objective of setting up a citizens' assembly, but not the other two objectives.

Critics of Extinction Rebellion argue that while people have a legitimate right to protest, they should not break the law. They point out that when Extinction Rebellion blocks public transport routes, they create more private transport and congestion, which causes more pollution – the exact opposite of what Extinction Rebellion wants to achieve. They also point out that emergency vehicles such as ambulances have been delayed when Extinction Rebellion has blocked roads and bridges in London.

Extinction Rebellion points out the vast numbers of people who will die and suffer if we do not deal with the climate emergency, and that their aims are largely ignored by the UK mainstream media, meaning that they are forced to adopt extreme tactics such as civil disobedience.

Learning objectives:
- To define what fake news is
- To discuss whether social media companies should be responsible for the content they publish
- To identify common flaws in critical thinking

Resources:
- PowerPoint 16.1
- Worksheets 16.1a, 16.1b and 16.1c
- Link to KS3: Book 3, Unit 12.1

Key vocabulary:
fake news, critical thinking

Get them thinking! (5 mins)

- Ask students if they know of any fake news stories. Write the best examples on the board. Use the example of 5G towers causing Covid-19 infections from **Slide 3** if they can't think of any.

Core learning (25 mins)

- Explain what fake news is. Ask students why they think people produce fake news. Then show **Slide 1**.

- Show **Slide 2** and ask students whether unemployment is going up or down. Explain why unemployment is still going up, using maths if necessary, e.g. unemployment at 100,000 goes up by 10% in year 1 to 110,000. It goes up by 5% in year 2 to 117,000. The rate of growth in unemployment has gone down from 10% to 5%, but unemployment is still going up.

- Use **Slide 3** and the news story from *The Independent* on **Worksheet 16.1a** as a case study to explore.

- Show **Slide 4** and ask students what they think. Explain how the law states that it is the author of the post, not the social media company, that is legally responsible for it. Explain how social media companies allow thousands of possibly fake news posts to circulate on their websites every day. Point out that social media companies are trying to clean up their websites, but still have a long way to go.

- Ask students if they have heard of 'critical thinking' as a subject. Show **Slide 5** and give them an example of a critical thinking flaw, such as a sweeping generalisation (e.g. 'That young boy was dropping litter. Therefore, all young boys must drop litter.'). Then go through the other flaws on **Worksheet 16.1b** with students, looking at the first two columns only. These are things they can look out for when they are assessing an argument or information put forward.

Additional learning (15 mins)

- Ask students to complete the matching exercise on **Worksheet 16.1b**. Get pairs to compare their answers by going through them with the class (*Answers: 1. D; 2. G; 3. A; 4. I; 5. B; 6. E; 7. H; 8. C; 9. F*).

- Ask students to read the news story from *Press Gazette* on **Worksheet 16.1c** as preparation for the debate task in the Plenary, discussing the questions in pairs.

Plenary (5 mins)

- Help students to debate whether social media companies should be responsible for all their content, including fake news stories posted by individuals, and whether social media companies need to do more to stop the spread of fake news on their websites.

Assessment

- Use students' responses to **Worksheet 16.1b** to assess their understanding.

Extension or home learning

- Extension: Ask students to research two or three fake news stories, using the following website and the search term 'fake news', and decide which was the most damaging and why: www.theweek.co.uk.

- Home learning: Ask students to read https://journolink.com/resource/319-fake-news-statistics-2019-uk-worldwide-data and write a two- or three-paragraph summary of the information and trends they discover.

- Home learning: Ask students to research what other critical thinking flaws exist, using the OCR A Level Critical Thinking specification as a source (https://ocr.org.uk/Images/73470-specification.pdf). They can then design a poster summarising these flaws.

Read the following news story about coronavirus conspiracy theories. Then answer the questions below.

Coronavirus: 5G conspiracy theory now most common fake news story surrounding pandemic, Ofcom finds

Half of UK adults have now come across discredited idea new mobile technology was behind the outbreak

By Adam Forest

THE CONSPIRACY THEORY connecting the coronavirus outbreak to the roll-out of the 5G network is the most common piece of fake news about the virus seen by people in the UK, new research shows.

The proportion of British adults who have viewed misinformation about the pandemic has increased from 46 per cent to 50 per cent, according to Ofcom's latest findings.

And 50 per cent of the population said they had come across "theories linking the origins or causes of Covid-19 to 5G technology".

The watchdog's latest report on information consumption during the crisis — covering week three of the lockdown — paints a worrying picture of how widespread the utterly discredited conspiracy has become.

False narratives around 5G and the virus have been shared hundreds of thousands of times on social media, with photos and videos documenting attacks on mobile phone masts often overlaid with spurious information about Covid-19.

Some 50 fires targeting masts and other equipment have been reported in Britain in recent weeks, leading to three arrests. Telecom engineers have been abused on the job 80 times over the past month, according to trade group Mobile UK.

The UK is not the only country in which the wild and baseless conspiracy theory has taken off. Some 16 masts have been torched in the Netherlands, with attacks also reported in Ireland, Cyprus, and Belgium.

Ofcom said it has issued "guidance" to ITV over "ill-judged" comments made by Eamonn Holmes about the discredited theory. [...]

"Broadcasters have editorial freedom to discuss and challenge the approach taken by public authorities to a serious public health crisis such as the coronavirus," said an Ofcom spokeswoman.

"However, discussions of unproven claims must be put fully into context — especially at a time when mobile phone masts in the UK are being attacked, risking significant harm to the public."

Culture secretary Oliver Dowden met with Facebook, Twitter and Google officials earlier this month to discuss how they could clamp down on disinformation.

The latest Ofcom report shows people said they were most likely to seek information on the pandemic from the BBC, other broadcasters or official sources like the NHS, government or World Health Organisation (WHO).

Social media and closed groups continue to be the least trusted media, with just under a quarter of respondents saying they trusted the information viewed on WhatsApp.

In an encouraging development, the proportion of respondents who say they are "finding it hard to know what's true and what's false" about the coronavirus has dropped from 40 per cent in week one of the lockdown to 32 per cent in week three.

Meanwhile the proportion of respondents using a fact-checking site has increased since the lockdown began, from 10 per cent to 15 per cent. [...]

From *The Independent*, Tuesday 21 April 2020

1. What property has been damaged as a result of these rumours?

2. Has anyone been personally threatened as a result of these rumours?

3. Do you think social media companies should be legally responsible for checking and taking down false information? Give reasons for your views.

Worksheet 16.1b Matching critical thinking flaws with examples

Working in pairs, match the flaw in the first column with the correct Example 2 in the third column (e.g. 1. D). A first example for each flaw has been shown in the second column. Check your answers with another pair, and then with your teacher and the class.

Flaw	Example 1	Example 2
1. Ad hominem – attacking the arguer	We shouldn't eat vegetables because Stacy said we should and she's stupid.	A. The EU was wrong in the past, so it must be wrong now.
2. Appeal to authority	You must do your homework because I'm your parent and I'm telling you to.	B. I've always trusted the *Sun* as a news source, so you should too.
3. Appeal to history	This worked last year so it will definitely work next year.	C. The police protect people. This person was shot in the USA. Therefore, he can't have been shot by the police, because they protect people.
4. Appeal to emotion	Just do it because you know in your heart it's the right thing to do.	D. Boris Johnson is a Tory so you can't believe anything he says.
5. Appeal to tradition	We've always done things this way so we should not change them.	E. Voting Democrat will lead to higher taxes, which will lead to a recession and everyone will end up unemployed.
6. Slippery slope	If you don't take the job, you'll have no money, so you'll become homeless and then you will die of cold.	F. This election is a choice only between Labour and the Conservatives. No other vote is worth anything or will do anything.
7. Sweeping generalisation	My gran smoked till she was 101, so smoking must be good for you.	G. It must be true because the Prime Minister said it.
8. Affirming consequences	My dog barks at burglars. My dog hasn't barked, therefore there is no burglar.	H. Lots of young people are getting Covid-19, therefore, all young people are responsible for infecting people with Covid-19.
9. False choice	Either you cheated or he did. No other choice is possible.	I. Supporters of the Democrat Joe Biden have said, 'You know in your heart that voting for Donald Trump is wrong.'

Read the following article about social media companies' efforts to control fake news on their sites, and then answer the questions below.

MPs slam tech giants for failing to 'answer basic questions' on disinformation

MPs have accused tech giants Facebook, Google and Twitter of being "unable to answer basic questions" about disinformation during appearances before a select committee today

By PA Mediapoint

REPRESENTATIVES of the firms appeared before the Digital, Culture, Media and Sport sub-committee on online harms and disinformation, with particular focus on the spread of false narratives around the coronavirus outbreak.

Committee chairman Julian Knight said MPs would be writing to each of the tech giants to voice their "displeasure" at a "lack of answers" given on content moderation on their platforms.

The appearance of the internet giants comes as they, governments and other organisations continue to attempt to stop the spread of disinformation linked to Covid-19, which has seen incidents of fake cures touted online and phone masts attacked after a debunked conspiracy theory spread which claimed 5G technology was linked to the outbreak.

Facebook's UK public policy manager Richard Earley was criticised for not being able to confirm the number of content moderators the firm currently had reviewing explicit material flagged to the platform.

[…H]e admitted some volunteers were also being used for moderation.

"We've also had a large number of employees who don't even review content in their daily roles, volunteering to step forward and help make sure we did not see significant negative impacts on that queue," he said.

But when pressed by the committee on whether Facebook had the same number of moderators working as before the pandemic, or fewer, Earley said he was unable to answer because the situation was changing each day.

Hinds urged Facebook to respond in writing on the issue, while Knight said it appeared none of the witnesses had been supplied with "genuine, hard information on how you are specifically going about tackling Covid disinformation".

Following a number of fractious exchanges between MPs on the committee and the tech firms' representatives, Knight said he had not heard "any facts" from Facebook, while Twitter's Katy Minshall was accused of using "pre-prepared" remarks rather than attempting to answer questions.

Following an exchange between Google's public policy and government relations manager, Alina Dimofte, and SNP MP John Nicolson on online gambling, Knight expressed his frustration at the number of follow-up letters the committee would need to write because the three witnesses had been "seemingly unable to answer quite basic questions".

"We will be writing to all the organisations and frankly we will be expressing our displeasure at the quality of the answers – well a lack of answers – that we've received today and will be seeking further clarity," the committee chairman said.

From _Press Gazette_, 30 April 2020

1. Do you think social media companies should have been more open about their policies for dealing with misleading and harmful information?

2. Are you surprised that Facebook was using volunteers to remove harmful content? Do you think this should have been done by trained, specialist staff? Give reasons for your views.

3. Imagine you were running a social media company. Make a list of what you would not allow to be published on your site.

16.2　The news agenda, censorship and free speech

Learning objectives:	Resources:	Key vocabulary:
• To understand what bias is • To understand how the news agenda is shaped • To understand what censorship is and discuss when it is and is not appropriate	• PowerPoint 16.2 • Worksheets 16.2a, 16.2b, and 16.2c • Link to KS3: Book 3, Unit 12	bias, news, news agenda, freedom of speech, censorship

Get them thinking! (5 mins)

• Explain what the word 'biased' means (e.g. a point of view that favours one person or group, especially if this is done unfairly). Ask students where they get their news from. Write their responses on the board. Ask students whether they think the news source is fair and truthful, or biased in any way.

Core learning (25 mins)

• Explain what the news agenda is using **Slide 1**. Show students what a press release looks like using the example at https://class-pr.com/blog/how-to-write-a-press-release/. Talk through this and then show them **Slide 2** and explain the difference between a slow news day and a fast news day.

• Ask students what they think freedom of speech is (the right to express your opinion without limits, including being censored or the threat of legal action). Then explain what censorship is, using **Slide 3** and giving an example (e.g. North Korea only allowing its citizens to access one state TV channel).

• Use **Slide 4** to explain what cancel culture is. Point out that cancel culture is not the same as censorship – the latter involves a person not being able to express their opinion, with their freedom of expression being limited, usually by the authorities. Then go into further detail using the article and questions on **Worksheet 16.2a**.

• Ask students to complete **Worksheet 16.2b** in pairs, and then to discuss reasons for their answers in groups, and finally as a class. Discuss the cases on the worksheet further, concentrating on what students think is fair, and the difference between freedom of speech and not having to listen to somebody's views that you find offensive. For example, individuals may choose not to follow a celebrity on social media while still respecting their right to free speech.

Additional learning (15 mins)

• Ask students to read through and discuss **Worksheet 16.2c** in pairs, and decide which method they think is most effective in challenging a person's actions or behaviour they disagree with, giving reasons for their views. You can then discuss this as a class.

Plenary (5 mins)

• Discuss with students why people engage in cancel culture – does it change people's minds? *(There is little evidence that it does)*. Is it done to make an example of someone, or to act as a deterrent? *(Yes and yes, but it is uncertain how effective a deterrent it might be.)* What sort of effect might it have on a person if they are cancelled by a large number of people? *(There could be a negative effect on a person's mental health if done in a collective manner where large numbers of people show support for a cause.)*

Assessment

• Use students' responses to **Worksheet 16.2b** to assess their understanding of the issues discussed.

Extension or home learning

• Extension: Ask students to use the following website and try writing their own press release about a story in their local area for the local newspaper or a school magazine or website: https://www.theguardian.com/small-business-network/2014/jul/14/how-to-write-press-release

• Home learning: Ask students to choose one of the following organisations and write a short report on what it does to protect free speech: https://www.indexoncensorship.org/what-we-do/ or https://www.amnesty.org.uk/. Tell them to look on the websites for material about 'what we do' and 'freedom of speech'.

Worksheet 16.2a Cancel culture

Read the following article about cancel culture. Then answer the questions below.

What is cancel culture? By Caroline Westbrook

So-called 'cancel culture' has become a common part of popular culture, with many celebrities having spoken out against it

RICKY GERVAIS has recently voiced his gripes with cancel culture, and JK Rowling and Margaret Atwood were among 150 writers who signed an open letter calling for free speech and denouncing 'the restriction of debate' as well as cancel culture. So just what exactly is cancel culture? According to Ricky: 'Everyone's got a different definition'[…].

What does it mean to 'cancel' someone?

Cancel culture is a form of online boycott in which a person who has shared a controversial viewpoint, or is in the past found to have behaved in a way which is perceived to be offensive, is called out for that behaviour – leading to them being 'cancelled'.

This can lead to them being ostracized or shunned by fans, friends and supporters and having their work boycotted – which can potentially prove damaging to their career or reputation.

Ricky Gervais defined cancel culture by saying: 'When people are trying to get someone fired because they don't like their opinion about something that's nothing to do with their job, that's what I call cancel culture and that's not cool.'

Meanwhile, Metro.co.uk's own Emma Kelly describes cancel culture as: 'That wonderful phrase that actually had roots in a real issue that has come to mean "grown men and women crying over the consequences of their own actions coming to fruition".'

She adds: 'Like a massive, swelling tumour, the phrase has grown out of control to encompass all criticism of any person's opinions and behaviour, even if that behaviour involves racism, transphobia or even federal crimes.'

The idea of 'cancelling' someone – and 'cancel culture' as a whole – became popular in recent years after movements such as #MeToo began

calling for greater accountability from those in the public eye, and troubling behaviour of some formerly popular celebrities gradually came to light.

While cancel culture is seen by many as a popular form of protest, some celebrities have spoken out against it in the past due to the devastating impact that it can have on people's mental health.

Taylor Swift is among those who have spoken out about it, saying in Vogue last year: 'A mass public shaming, with millions of people saying you are quote-unquote cancelled, is a very isolating experience. When you say someone is canceled, it's not a TV show. It's a human being. You're sending mass amounts of messaging to this person to either shut up, disappear, or it could also be perceived as, "Kill yourself".'

Demi Lovato, meanwhile, has also said of the phenomenon: 'Where is the forgiveness culture? There are some people, if you have used up your second and third chances with a certain topic, you're cancelled and you should stay cancelled. But if you mess up and you apologise and come forward and say I've learned from this, then let that be an example for other people so they can change too.'

JK Rowling found herself at the centre of a social media storm after controversial tweets led her to be faced with accusations of transphobia – leading to several Harry Potter cast members speaking in support of transgender people as well as four authors leaving her literary agency in protest.

A letter was later signed by 150 people – and as well as Rowling and Atwood those who signed included author Salman Rushdie, writer Khalid Khalifa, feminist Gloria Steinem, journalist Anne Applebaum, chess grandmaster Garry Kasparov and US intellectual Noam Chomsky.

From *The Metro*, Saturday 8 August 2020

1. What is cancel culture?

2. Why do Ricky Gervais and Taylor Swift dislike cancel culture?

3. What does Emma Kelly think is valuable about cancel culture?

4. What does Demi Lovato say about cancel culture?

Worksheet 16.2b The news agenda, censorship and free speech

Look at the following situations. Decide which ones you think are fair and which unfair. In the final column, give reasons for your views. Why do you think the action described was taken against the person? Do you think the action was effective or not, or fair or not?

Situation	Effective or not? Fair or unfair?	Reasons for your views.
1. J.K. Rowling retweeting and writing allegedly transphobic tweets, so some of her followers start boycotting her books and blocking her on Twitter.		
2. Donald Trump continuing to issue false statements on his Twitter account while he was president, so Twitter puts up a warning saying the statements are false.		
3. Michael Gove, a member of the UK government, being criticised for having books on his bookshelf written by a Holocaust denier during a Zoom interview. (A Holocaust denier is a person who denies that the Nazi genocide of Jewish people and others occurred in the Second World War.)		
4. Thousands of people around the world leaving Twitter for 24 hours to protest against Twitter leaving up anti-Semitic tweets by the artist Wiley. Meanwhile, Facebook deleted Wiley's account.		
5. Members of the neo-fascist group National Action being declared part of a terrorist group, arrested and prosecuted for sharing violent racist material.		
6. A schoolteacher being sacked from teaching after playing a character in several comedy rap videos which featured offensive language, drugs and sexual references.		
7. A welder being fired from his job for flying a 'White lives matter' banner over a football game from an aircraft.		
8. Nigel Farage being removed from his job at LBC Radio after referring to the Black Lives Matter movement as 'a new form of the Taliban'.		

Worksheet 16.2c Techniques to challenge other people's actions and behaviour

Look at the following techniques that can be used to challenge actions and behaviour. In groups, discuss which ones you think are the most effective, giving reasons for your views.

1. Calling something out

This is when you challenge somebody's behaviour or actions in public, usually in the media or on social media. This can be done to challenge the behaviour or actions of an influential person in the media. It can also be used when 'calling something in' (see below) hasn't worked. Calling something out has become increasingly popular by activists on social media in recent years.

Example: Tweets by the artist Wiley were called out for being anti-Semitic. When Twitter failed to deal with the issue, thousands of people called Twitter out on their failure to act and deal with the issue, by not tweeting anything for 48 hours, in an organised international 'Twitter blackout'.

2. Calling something in

This is when you speak to a person one to one about their behaviour or actions that you think is/are causing a problem. This gives the person the chance to change their behaviour and actions privately, without causing any conflict publicly. It allows a person to develop in a positive direction rather than causing a negative conflict.

Example: A student calls another student's behaviour 'gay' as an insult in a class WhatsApp group. A third student speaks to the first student privately, one to one, pointing out that this language is never acceptable and is against the school rules, and explaining that there may be students in the classroom who are just coming to terms with their sexuality who would find this particularly upsetting or insulting. The third student gives the first student the opportunity to change their behaviour, which is homophobic and shows an insensitivity to others' feelings, by withdrawing the comment themselves and apologising.

3. No platforming

This is when a person isn't allowed to speak or participate in a debate at an institution. A favourite of university student unions, no platforming has been used on university campuses to ensure that students have a safe space in which to study and socialise. Critics of no platforming argue that it provides an unnecessary limit on freedom of speech and stifles debate, particularly in universities.

Example: In 2007 the former British National Party leader Nick Griffin was banned from Oxide, the Oxford University student radio station which is affiliated with National Union of Students. In 2010, another BNP MEP and a BNP Councillor were banned from taking part in a student debate at Durham University, after organisers were falsely told that their appearance would be illegal.

4. Boycotting

This is when you refuse to buy goods and services from an individual or company, in order to force a change in their behaviour or actions. Once the individual or company changes its behaviour or actions, then the boycott will end. This isn't just used by individuals or groups – entire countries have been encouraged by their government to take part in a boycott.

Example: Boycotting can be considered part of the cancel culture. For example, some readers who have disagreed with J.K. Rowling's views on gender identity are now boycotting her books.

Learning objectives:

- To understand the different ages at which different laws apply to children in the UK
- To understand what the age of criminal responsibility is in the UK
- To understand what a youth court is and where you can get legal advice in the UK

Resources:

- PowerPoint 17.1
- Worksheet 17.1
- Access to the internet
- Link to KS3:
  Book 2, Unit 14.1

Key vocabulary:

laws, criminal responsibility, youth court, solicitor, barrister

Get them thinking! (5 mins)

- Ask students in which different areas they think the law most affects them *(e.g. working, drinking alcohol, getting married, having sex, what sort of work they are allowed to do at what age, and when they can leave home)*. Write these on the board.

Core learning (25 mins)

- Go through **Slide 1**. Ask students what age they think they can be held responsible for breaking the law. Then go through **Slides 2** and **3**, and define the age of criminal responsibility.

- Explain what a youth court is. Show the students a video tour of a youth court, ideally around 10 minutes long (these are available by searching for 'UK Youth Court' on the internet). Go through **Slide 4** and point out that 17-year-olds can still be tried as adults. In other words, they will face the same court as an adult, with the same assumptions about how mature they should be, and the same punishments and sentences as an adult would face (although a custodial sentence may be served in a youth detention centre rather than an adult prison).

- Go through **Slide 5** and explain the different sorts of legal advice that are available. Distinguish between a solicitor and a barrister: the former will represent you if you are arrested and get in trouble with the police, whereas a barrister will represent you in court for more serious offences that are tried in court in front of a jury. Mention other places children can get legal advice, e.g. https://childlawadvice.org.uk/.

Additional learning (15 mins)

- Ask students to complete **Worksheet 17.1** in pairs or in groups *(Answers: A, D, I, M, R, S, U at 18; C, G, P, Q at 17; E, H at 16; L, O, T at 14; V at 13; J at 10; F, K at 5; B, N at birth)*. Once they have done this, including deciding which laws are fair and unfair, and giving reasons for their views, ask them to discuss their answers in larger groups or as a class.

Plenary (5 mins)

- Ask the class to which law they would reform from those they have learned about in the lesson, giving reasons for their views.

Assessment

- Use students' responses to **Worksheet 17.1** to assess their understanding.

Extension or home learning

- Home learning: Ask students to research the role of youth courts in detail by visiting https://www.gov.uk/courts/youth-courts, and then to write a short report (two or three paragraphs) about them, detailing the work they do.

- Extension: Ask students to choose one of the following areas of the law: at what age you can work; at what age you can get married and/or leave home; the age of criminal responsibility. They should produce a poster summarising what the laws are in relation to their area of choice.

- Extension: Ask students to look at the laws on the worksheet and, in groups, discuss whether there are any other laws they think should be added here at a certain age. If so, what are they? They should give reasons for their views.

Worksheet 17.1 At what age does the law apply?

Look at the following table.

- In pairs, use the internet to help you fill in at what age you think you are able to do each of the activities in the table. Then check your answers with another group, or as a class with your teacher.
- Next, still in your pairs, write down whether you think each of these age limits is fair or unfair, with any reasons for your views in the last column.
- Finally, discuss the age limits as a group or as a class, giving reasons for your views.

Law	What age?	Fair or unfair?	Why do you think this?
A. Able to leave school			
B. Have a bank account in your name			
C. Have sex			
D. Serve on a jury			
E. Drive a car			
F. Start going to school full-time			
G. Get married with a parent's consent			
H. Be sent to prison			
I. Sign a legal contract			
J. Be convicted of a criminal offence if it can be proved you knew you were doing something wrong			
K. Drink alcohol in private			

Law	What age?	Fair or unfair?	Why do you think this?
L. Be held fully responsible for a crime that you commit			
M. Buy alcohol or cigarettes			
N. Have your own passport			
O. Go into a bar			
P. Choose your own doctor			
Q. Have a drink in a pub with a meal			
R. Leave school and education to get a full-time job			
S. Legally become an adult			
T. The police can take your fingerprints			
U. View pornography on the internet			
V. Do a part-time job but only for up to two hours on a school day			

17.2 You and the police

Learning objectives:

- To understand the age of criminality
- To understand what a police caution and an ABSO are
- To understand how a youth detention centre is an alternative to prison for those aged 17 or below

Resources:

- PowerPoint 17.2
- Worksheets 17.2a and 17.2b
- Examples of crimes in a neighbouring town/city where under 18s have been punished; example of youth detention centre
- Access to the internet
- Links to KS3: Book 2, Unit 14; Book 3, Unit 11

Key vocabulary:

age of criminality, community service, fine, ABSO, suspended sentence, police caution, youth detention, jail

Get them thinking! (5 mins)

- Ask students what different punishments are available to a court if you break the law. Elicit community service, fine, ASBO, suspended sentence, police caution, jail in a youth detention centre and prison. Write these on the board.

Core learning (25 mins)

- Add to the list anything that students did not come up with in the starter. Then hand out **Worksheet 17.2a**, which lists the definitions. Go through these with the class.

- Show **Slide 1** and explain the age of criminality. Note that you can expand the lesson here by going through the whole process of being arrested, then going to court, then being sentenced. Explain what happens if you are convicted of a crime – information on the process can be found at https://www.release.org.uk/what-happens-in-court.

- Then move on so **Slide 2** and emphasise the importance of not having a criminal record.

- For each of the next three activities, use the local stories from the next town or city that you have researched ahead of the class. This will bring the lesson to life and demonstrate the consequences of specific crimes.

- Explain what a police caution is using **Slide 3**. Further information on cautions is available at https://www.cambs.police.uk/information-and-services/Cautions-warnings-penalties.

- Explain what an ASBO is and how they are intended to be a deterrent rather than a punishment, using **Slide 4** and any local examples you have found.

- Using **Slide 5**, explain what a youth detention centre is, giving an example from the internet to show students. Further information is available here at https://www.gov.uk/young-people-in-custody/what-custody-is-like-for-young-people.

Additional learning (15 mins)

- Ask students to complete **Worksheet 17.2b** in pairs or groups, and then to compare answers in groups or as a class. Note that this is a subjective activity and therefore there are no right or wrong answers; students need to be able to justify their responses and explain their reasoning.

- Ask students to use https://www.release.org.uk/what-happens-in-court to draw a flowchart of what happens from the point of being charged with a criminal offence to what happens in court.

Plenary (5 mins)

- Display **Slide 3** again and ask students to discuss to whether there is any point to police cautions.

Assessment

- Use students' responses to **Worksheet 17.2b** to assess their understanding, and test them on the definitions on **Worksheet 17.2a** – make sure they cannot see the worksheet!

Extension or home learning

- Extension: Go through the seven stages of having a criminal record with students using https://hub.unlock.org.uk/stages/.

- Home learning: Ask students to design a poster summarising what they have learned in this and the previous lesson (17.1).

Worksheet 17.2a Punishments and definitions

Community service – where you have to do a set number of voluntary hours unpaid, to help the local community, doing a task such as litter-picking.

Fine – you have to pay some money to the government for breaking the law.

ASBO (antisocial behaviour order) – you are banned from committing a form of antisocial behaviour, such as graffitiing an area or playing music loudly at night, and can receive a more serious punishment if you break the ASBO.

Police caution – the police give you a written warning for committing a crime; they do not have to prove that you did it. If you repeat the offence, the warning can be used in court and you receive a more serious sentence.

Jail in a youth detention centre or prison – you lose your freedom of movement and are held in custody for weeks, months or even years in a the most serious cases.

Suspended sentence – you don't go to jail for the full term of the sentence, but if you commit any other crime, you can go straight back to court and they can put you in jail.

Worksheet 17.2b You and the police

Look at the different crimes that have been committed by different people in different situations (A–H).
Which of the sentences (1–8) would you give in each situation? Give reasons for your views.

1. A verbal warning
2. A police caution
3. Community service
4. A fine

5. A suspended sentence
6. Custody in a youth detention centre
7. Prison
8. Other – you make up the punishment!

Case studies

A. A school chemistry lab has been set on fire. The 15-year-old who did it already has a police caution for vandalism. It's their fourth criminal offence.

Sentence: ....

Reason: ....

B. A nine-year-old is caught shoplifting for the third time.

Sentence: ....

Reason: ....

C. A 13-year-old is caught stealing money from a teacher. She says she was using it to buy food because her parents cannot afford to feed her.

Sentence: ....

Reason: ....

D. A 10-year-old is caught shoplifting for the first time.

Sentence: ....

Reason: ....

E. A 17-year-old is caught dropping objects off a motorway bridge onto passing cars. There was a threat to life because it could have caused a traffic accident.

Sentence: ....

Reason: ....

F. A 14-year-old boy is caught sharing nude pictures he tricked a girl he doesn't like into sending him.

Sentence: ....

Reason: ....

G. A 16-year-old keeps playing loud music when she gets up for college at 5.45 in the morning. She has been warned not to do this by the police.

Sentence: ....

Reason: ....

H. A 12-year-old keeps stealing food from the vending machines at the school just because they like chocolate.

Sentence: ....

Reason: ....

Learning objectives:

- To understand the three main types of local council
- To examine devolution and regional government in the UK
- To understand the role of the civil service

Resources:

- PowerPoint 18.1
- Worksheets 18.1a and 18.1b
- A map of the UK to show devolved governments
- Link to KS3: Book 2, Unit 15.1

Key vocabulary:

county council, district council, borough council, parish council, unitary authority, devolution, regional government

Get them thinking! (5 mins)

- Ask students to list everything they think could be improved in the local area in which they live. Write these ideas on the board, to refer back to in the lesson.

Core learning (25 mins)

- Go through **Slides 1** and **2** with students, then look again as a class at the problems they listed at the beginning of the lesson. Ask students to decide which problems can be dealt with by what sort of council, and why. Point out what sort of council(s) exist in your local area.

- Ask students to complete **Worksheet 18.1a** in pairs, and then compare their answers in groups or as a class. Allow students to research on the internet to clarify any areas they are unsure about, or invite them to ask you questions. *(Parish councils may be responsible for a local park, museum or the like. District councils are responsible for environmental health, planning, licensing and rubbish collection. County councils are responsible for education, libraries, social services and transport. Unitary authorities and metropolitan borough councils are responsible for the areas that both district and county councils deal with.)*

- Go through **Slides 3** and **4**, outlining the difference between the UK government, and the Welsh, Scottish and Northern Ireland governments. You could use a map of the UK to illustrate this.

Additional learning (15 mins)

- Show **Slide 5** and explain what the civil service is. Explain that the civil service is bound by two principles – to remain neutral and to remain anonymous. Also explain the idea of ministerial responsibility – that if a civil servant makes a mistake, the minister responsible for the department is responsible for the mistake and accountable to Parliament, not the civil servant. Ask students which job they would prefer and why.

Plenary (5 mins)

- Ask students to choose what they consider to be the top three problems they named at the beginning of the lesson, and to decide what action should be taken by which level of government to solve each one.

Assessment

- Use students' responses to **Worksheet 18.1a** to assess their understanding.

Extension or home learning

- Home learning: Ask students to use the internet to research one of the following organisations: one of their local councils; the UK Youth Parliament; a regional government; the national government. They should complete **Worksheet 18.1b** during this research.

- Home learning: Ask students to research and then write a full report about one of their local councils, or a regional government, or the national government and its work, and then present this to the class.

- Extension: Find out when the next Youth Parliament elections are for your area. Invite your YMP to come and speak to your class if you already have one.

- Extension: Hold a full Youth Parliament election at your school, with candidates, hustings, election materials, a campaign, and a ballot box with ballot papers to bring elections to life and teach students about the democratic process.

- Extension: At the next general or local election, invite a speaker from one of the main political parties into school to discuss the election with students.

Worksheet 18.1a Young people and local government

Look at the following areas that local councils are responsible for. Write down which council is responsible for what sort of area, and why. Then, in pairs, rank each area in order of importance. Finally, compare your answers with another pair or group, giving reasons for your views.

Area	Type of council responsible	Rank in order of importance
Education		
Rubbish collection		
Museums		
Libraries		
Maintaining a local park		
Planning		
Social services		
Licensing		
Transport		
Environmental health		

Reminder: the types of council will be either country or district councils, or a unitary authority, or a metropolitan authority, and finally, in some areas there are also parish councils.

Worksheet 18.1b Young people and local government

1. What is the name of organisation you are researching?

    ....

2. What do you think the main purpose of this organisation is?

    ....

    ....

    ....

3. If this organisation is a council, what sort of council is?

    County council   ☐

    District council   ☐

    Unitary authority or metropolitan borough council   ☐

4. Who is allowed to join this organisation?

    ....

    ....

5. What is the address of this organisation's website?

    ....

6. Add any other information about this organisation.

    ....

    ....

    ....

    ....

    ....

    ....

    ....

    ....

    ....

    ....

    ....

Learning objectives:

- To recognise that international organisations have a profound influence on many areas of our lives
- To learn about the aims, objectives and membership of four international organisations

Resources:

- PowerPoint 18.1 (print out 4 or 8 copies of the slides)
- Worksheets 18.1a and 18.2b
- Link to KS3: Book 2, Unit 15.2

Key vocabulary:

UN, EU, Council of Europe, NATO, human rights, member state, sovereignty

Get them thinking! (5 mins)

- Ask students if they have heard of any of the following organisations and whether they know what they do: the UN, the EU, the Council of Europe, NATO. Write their answers on the board.

Core learning (25 mins)

- Ask students what they think the word 'sovereignty' means. Link it to power (definition: 'Power is the ability of A to make B do what A wants against B's will', Max Weber). Explain the idea of shared sovereignty – where countries give up some of their own sovereignty in order to achieve shared sovereignty over a larger area.

- Divide the class into four or eight groups. Read through **Slide 1** as a class. Then, using **Slides 2–5**, give each group (or two groups) a copy of one of the slides you have printed out in advance. Ask them to look at the institution on their sheet, consider and discuss whether they have heard of it, how old it is, and what it does, for 5 minutes. Then rearrange the groups into new groups that have a least one person representing each institution and ask them to explain their institution to the rest of the group.

- Get the students to feed back as a class, summing up what they have learned.

Additional learning (15 mins)

- Ask students to complete Worksheet 18.2a in pairs or groups, and then compare as a class. As an extension activity for fast finishers, students can use the blank rows to fill in how else these institutions affect their lives. Then get students to discuss the answers in groups or as a class, giving reasons for their views. (*Suggested answers: 1. All; 2. EU; 3. All; 4. All; 5. UN and EU; 6. UN and EU; 7. UN, EU and Council of Europe; 8. EU; 9. EU and Council of Europe; 10. UN).*

- Students could discuss which of the organisations involve giving up some sovereignty. (*Answers might be the Council of European and the European Union, both of which have courts that member states are legally bound by. A definite no is NATO, which is a member organisation. The UN is less clear – there is international law, but member states often break it.*)

- Point out to students that the EU and the Council of Europe are two separate organisations. The latter only deals with human rights, whereas the EU deals with a wide range of areas (fishing, the single market, etc.). Point out that to be a member of the EU, you have to be a member of the Council of Europe.

Plenary (5 mins)

- Hold a brief class discussion about which institution most affects students' lives (*the UN or the Council of Europe).*

Assessment

- Get students to complete the quiz on **Worksheet 18.2b** and use this to assess their understanding. (*Answers: 1. UN; 2. EU; 3. Yes; 4. No; 5. UN; 6. EU; 7. Belarus; 8. France; 9. Brussels; 10. New York, 11. Strasbourg; 12. Brussels.)*

Extension or home learning

- Extension: Ask students to prepare a PowerPoint, with at least three or four slides which they can speak about for 2 minutes, on one of the four institutions in this lesson, using the following websites as a starting point: https://www.un.org/en/https://www.coe.int/en/web/portal, https://europa.eu/european-union/index_en, https://www.nato.int/.

- Home learning: Ask students to use the internet to research and then write two or three paragraphs about what has been reported in the news about the work of one of the four organisations, either over the last week, the last month, or the last year, depending on how much information they can find.

Worksheet 18.2a You and the world

Look at the following list and the table below. Which organisation does what? Note that more than one organisation can be listed for each answer. Use the internet to help you. Do this in pairs and when you have finished, compare your answers in groups or as a class.

- UN: https://www.un.org/en/
- Council of Europe: https://www.coe.int/en/web/about-us/who-we-are
- European Union: https://europa.eu/european-union/index_en
- NATO: https://www.nato.int/

Statement	UN	EU	Council of Europe	NATO
Helps prevents wars.				
Can help lower my mobile phone bill.				
Helps protect human rights.				
Allows me to live in safety and security.				
Creates trade and job opportunities.				
Helps prevents climate change.				
Helps provide education.				
Has its own parliament.				
Has only European members.				
Is the largest organisation listed.				

Worksheet 18.2b You and the world quiz

Complete the quiz below. Research any answers you don't know.

1. Which is the oldest organisation – the EU, the Council of Europe, the UN or NATO?

   ....

2. Which is the smallest organisation – the EU, the Council of Europe, the UN or NATO?

   ....

3. If you are a member of the EU, do you have to be a member of the Council of Europe?

   ....

4. If you are member of the Council of Europe, do you have to be a member of the EU?

   ....

5. Which is the largest organisation – the EU, the Council of Europe, the UN or NATO?

   ....

6. Which organisation is the UK not a member of – the EU, the Council of Europe, the UN or NATO?

   ....

7. One European country is not a member of the Council of Europe – which is it?

   ....

8. Which country is a member of NATO but has its troops under its own independent command structure?

   ....

9. Where is NATO HQ based?

   ....

10. Where is the United Nations based?

    ....

11. Where is the Council of Europe based?

    ....

12. Where is the European Commission – which runs the European Union – based?

    ....

Learning objectives:

- To distinguish between a free market, a mixed economy and a command economy
- To understand what economic growth is
- To examine other ways of measuring economic progress

Resources:

- PowerPoint 19.1
- Worksheets 19.1a and 19.1b
- Link to KS3: Book 1, Unit 16.2; Book 2, Unit 13.2; Book 3, Unit 15.2

Key vocabulary:

free market, mixed economy, command economy, globalisation, economic growth, GDP

Get them thinking! (5 mins)

- Ask students what they think is meant by a 'free market'. Then ask: 'What is the role of the government in a free market?' Note ideas on the board. *(A free market is one where economic decisions are made by private individuals and companies. The role of the government is limited to providing an environment where the free market can operate – e.g. a police force, the rule of law and an army for foreign defence.)*

Core learning (25 mins)

- Go through **Slide 1** with the students. When you are sure they understand the concept, move on to **Slides 2** and **3**. Then hand out copies of **Worksheet 19.1a** and ask students to read through the case studies and decide which system they prefer and why.

- Hand out copies of **Worksheet 19.1b** and get students to complete this as a sorting exercise, first in groups or pairs and then as a class. *(Possible answers: free market: 2, 5, 6, 9; mixed economy: 3, 8; command economy: 1, 4; free market + mixed: 7; mixed and command: 10.)*

Additional learning (15 mins)

- Ask students what they think is meant by 'economic growth'. Go through **Slide 4** to clarify. You can use statistics from the internet to show the latest growth figures for the UK from GOV.UK, the Office of Budget Responsibility or the *Financial Times*. International comparisons for growth figures can be found from the Organisation for Economic Co-operation and Development (OECD).

- Ask students whether they think other measures for progress should be used rather than just a narrow definition of economic growth, such as life expectancy (how long a person lives) and income inequality (how evenly wealth is spread across a population). Note these ideas on the board, then show and discuss **Slide 5**.

Plenary (5 mins)

- Get students to discuss what they think life might be like in a command economy such as Cuba or North Korea. *(Suggestions: a lot stricter; government, not private companies, making all major decisions; lack of free travel as the government decides who travels abroad and limits passports for the general population.)*

Assessment

- Check that all students have completed **Worksheets 19.1a** and **19.1b**.

Extension or home learning

- Extension: Ask students to choose a country and write a short report on why they think it is a free market economy, mixed economy or command economy. Examples might include the USA and Singapore (free market), Denmark and Finland (mixed economy) or Cuba and North Korea (Command economies). As an extra challenge, students should consider how the UK and China fit into these categories.

- Home learning: ask students to research New Zealand, which is one of the happiest countries in the world. Tell them to look at the idea of whether reducing wealth inequality (the gap between the richest and poorest in society) can make a country happier. Further information on New Zealand's Happiness Index can be found at https://www.forbes.com/sites/jamesellsmoor/2019/07/11/new-zealand-ditches-gdp-for-happiness-and-wellbeing/#390ccaf11942.

- Extension: Hold a discussion (or debate if you want to extend the class) on the following motion: 'Forty per cent of the UK economy is government spending. Therefore, there is no such thing as a free market because the government is in monopoly position – it can dictate to everyone what to do.'

Worksheet 19.1a Key economic concepts and systems

Case study 1: Cuba – a command economy

Juan lives in Cuba, which has been a communist country with a command economy since the 1950s. Because it is a command economy, the government takes all major economic decisions. It's the government, not the free market, that decides the exchange rate in Cuba. Ordinary Cubans are not allowed to own large amounts of foreign currency like US dollars – the government, not private businesses, decides most of the foreign trade that occurs with other countries.

In Cuba, the government has also decided that there will be economic equality. It does this by ensuring that everyone is paid the same hourly rate, no matter what job they do. So an eye doctor will earn the same amount as someone serving in a bar. Ironically, the barperson is better paid in tourist resorts than the doctor, because the barperson can earn tips.

All of the major businesses – water, gas, electricity – are owned by the government in Cuba, along with many other businesses, such as many hotels and a number of major sugar companies. Everyone has a job, because the government manages the economy in a way that ensures this, along with free healthcare and guaranteed housing. Literacy rates in Cuba are higher than in the USA, along with life expectancy. But people cannot criticise the government. It is difficult to leave Cuba, because the government restricts who has a passport.

Case study 2: The United States – a free market economy

Louisa lives in the United States, which has a free market economy. Here, as many economic decisions as possible are taken by private individuals and businesses. Where demand for a good is high and supply is low, there will be a shortage of the good or service. Therefore, to reduce demand, prices for the good or service rise until the demand equals supply. This is known as the price mechanism – prices are decided by supply and demand.

When demand for a good or service is low and supply is high, there will be excess supply of the good or service. Producers won't be able to sell their good or service so easily, so they will drop their prices until demand equals supply again.

The vast majority of major businesses, including water, gas and electricity, are owned by private companies. The market system is more efficient at providing a range of goods and services in general than a command economy, so there is greater choice. Taxes are lower than they are in a command economy, and there is more freedom – including free trade – and anyone who was born in the USA can apply for a passport. However, there is unemployment and people have to buy their own private health insurance. There is also less paid holiday in the USA than the UK, and less maternity leave. In addition, there are high levels of inequality, meaning that some people are very rich while others are very poor, living in poverty.

Case study 3: Denmark – a mixed economy

Peter lives in Denmark, which has a mixed economy. Like a free market economy, many parts of the economy are determined by the prices set by supply and demand. There are many private businesses and a wide choice of goods and services.

However, unlike a free market economy, Denmark has recognised that the market doesn't always work. For example, people have no choice when it comes to using water and electricity – if left to the free market these would be monopolies that would be free to charge what they like. So, water and electricity are nationalised in the Denmark – the government owns them. Taxes are also higher than in a free market economy.

In return, there are more generous state benefits for the sick, the elderly and the unemployed than in a free market economy. Denmark's economic growth may be lower as a result, but its wealth inequality – the gap between the richest and poorest – is also lower. This has led to Denmark being surveyed as a happier country than many free market economies.

Worksheet 19.1b Which type of economy?

Look at the Venn diagram.

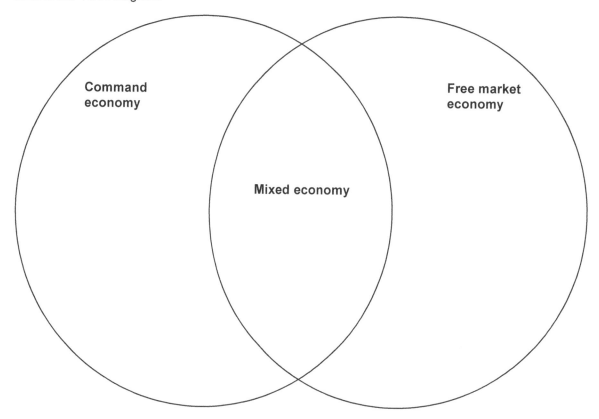

Write the number of each of the statements below into the correct part of the diagram.

1. All economic decisions are made by the government.

2. As many decisions as possible are made by the free market.

3. Some decisions are made by the government, others by the free market.

4. All major industries are nationalised – owned by the government.

5. The majority of major industries are privatised – owned by the private individuals or businesses.

6. Full employment is a priority – making sure everyone has a job – even if this means the economy isn't as efficient.

7. Economic growth is a priority.

8. This is a mixture or public and private services.

9. Usually involves higher levels of taxation.

10. Usually involves lower levels of taxation

Now compare your answers with another student, pair or group. Give reasons for your views.

The World Trade Organization

Learning objectives:

- To understand what trade is
- To learn about the WTO, its role and objectives
- To evaluate whether free trade is good or bad in the UK

Resources:

- PowerPoint 19.2
- Worksheets 19.2a and 19.2b
- Access to the internet
- Link to KS3: Book 1, Unit 16.2; Book 2, Unit 13.2; Book 3, Unit 15.2

Key vocabulary:

WTO, export, import, tariff, quota, voluntary export agreement, embargo, protectionism, free trade

Get them thinking! (5 mins)

- Ask students: 'What is trade?' (*the exchange of goods and services between two or more people, companies or countries*). They may have prior knowledge from discussions of fair trade.

Core learning (25 mins)

- Ask students if they have heard of the WTO. What does it stand for? *(World Trade Organization)* What does it do? How might it affect our lives and country? Collate ideas on the board.

- Play the video 'Is the WTO still needed?' (5 mins), which can be found on YouTube or via this link: https://www.dw.com/en/is-the-wto-still-needed/av-39908022.

- Show **Slide 1** and say to students: 'Imagine you want to buy a new phone from China. Yet for some reason the Chinese phone suddenly costs £100 more than it did last month. This could be because of a trade dispute (where two parties can't agree the terms of trade – how much a good or service should cost between the two parties) between the USA and China.' Point out how taxes on foreign goods in one country (called a tariff) can make goods from another country more expensive. Explain the four bullet points about the WTO and point out that its job and purpose is to prevent and solve trade disputes.

- Go through **Slide 2** with the class and, if possible, show the video 'What is the WTO and how does it work? (2 mins), which can be found on YouTube from CGTN America.

- Ask students, in pairs, to rank how they think the effects of a trade war listed on **Slide 2** would most affect them personally. Then compare their answers as a class, encouraging discussion. *(Answers may include: more expensive goods or services; less choice (particularly if there is quota or a boycott); greater unemployment and lower economic growth, as firms make less profits from foreign markets.)* Then ask students to complete **Worksheet 19.2a**.

Additional learning (15 mins)

- Show **Slide 3**. Explain that the WTO has to deal with many barriers to trade. Ask students to spend 5 minutes in pairs matching up the definitions. As a stretch activity, students could think of real-life examples of each. Check the answers as a class (*1D, 2E, 3B, 4F, 5C, 6A*).

- Show **Slide 4**. Ask students which points could be used in arguments in favour of protectionism or free trade. (*Suggested answers: protectionism – 2, 3, 6, 9, 10; free trade – 1, 4, 5, 7, 8.*)

Plenary (5 mins)

- Hold a discussion on whether the UK should encourage more free trade. What are the advantages?

Assessment

- Ask students to complete the crossword on **Worksheet 19.2b** (*Answers: Across: 2. exports, 6. tariff, 7. USA, 9. China, 10. imports; Down: 1. free trade, 3. protectionism, 4. trade, 5. quota, 8. boycott*). Use this and their responses to **Worksheet 19.2a** to assess their understanding.

Extension or home learning

- Extension: Ask students to look at the objectives of the WTO at https://www.wto.org/english/thewto_e/whatis_e/what_stand_for_e.htm The objectives include overseeing trade negotiations between countries, implementation and monitoring of trade negotiations, dispute settlement between countries, building trade capacity across the world and outreach work to help this. Check that students understand each objective and then ask them, in pairs, to rank the objectives in order of importance. Then ask them discuss, in groups, the reasons for their choices.

- Home learning: Ask students to research and write few paragraphs about the WTO Youth Ambassador programme https://www.wto.org/english/forums_e/students_e/youth_amb11_e.htm

Worksheet 19.2a The World Trade Organization

Look at the following table. Decided which of the effects listed is an advantage of free trade and which is a disadvantage. Then decide how important each advantage and disadvantage is by ranking them 1–8, where 1 is the most important. Finally, decide whether or not you think free trade is a good or bad idea overall. Then compare your answers in a group or as a class, giving reasons for your views.

Effect	Advantage or disadvantage?	Ranking
Higher unemployment in some sectors of your country.		
Lower unemployment across the world as a whole.		
Specialisation (where certain countries produce certain goods or services).		
Higher interdependency, where countries are more dependent on one another.		
Less revenue for government as tariffs are eliminated for free trade.		
More revenue for governments as the world economy grows more quickly.		
Higher environmental costs contributing to climate change, as goods are moved around the world.		
Greater choice and quality for consumers in a whole range of goods and services.		

Worksheet 19.2b The World Trade Organization crossword

Complete the crossword.

Clues:

Across

2. Goods that a country sells abroad (7)
6. Tax you pay on a good from abroad (6)
7. Largest economy in the world (3)
9. Second largest economy in the world (5)
10. Goods that a country buys from abroad (7)

Down

1. Trade where there are no barriers (4, 4)
3. Creating barriers to stimulate your own domestic businesses and limit competition (13)
4. The exchange of goods that drives economic growth across the world (5)
5. Limit on the number of goods that can come into a country (5)
8. Refusing to buy a certain good from a certain country (7)

20.1 Reflection and feedback

Learning objectives:
- To understand how reflection helps us to improve
- To recall three positive experiences and what these memories have in common
- To understand how to give feedback effectively

Resources:
- PowerPoint 20.1
- Worksheet 20.1
- Link to KS3: Book 1, 15.1, Book 3, 1.4

Key vocabulary:
reflection, feedback

Get them thinking! (5 mins)

- Define the word 'reflection' in the context of learning *(looking back at what we have seen, heard and done in order to improve it)* and write it on the board. Ask students to reflect on what they have learned from their PSHE course by completing the first part of **Worksheet 20.1**. Go through **Slide 1** to introduce the importance of reflection and feedback.

Core learning (25 mins)

- Point out to students that reflection and giving yourself feedback is a key part of improving – and there is always room for improvement! Go through **Slide 2** and give a positive example of feedback and reflection that made a difference to you.

- Go through **Slide 3**. This slide asks students to think about any useful feedback they have received in the past. Ask them to think about what image comes to mind when they think about this feedback. What did it sound like? How did it make them feel, and where could they feel this in their body? How did the feedback help them?

- Ask students, working in groups of three, to talk through their memories of helpful feedback, so each group of three hears three positive memories. For each turn, one person explains, one listens, and one writes down what they are hearing. Then ask students to summarise as a group the positive experiences they have recalled in a discussion. Were there any common features to the memories? Invite groups to share their summaries and findings with the class

- Now introduce **Slide 4** and the tips about giving others effective feedback.

- Ask students to complete the second part of **Worksheet 20.1** individually to prepare to give feedback on the course. Further details of effective feedback techniques have been included on the worksheet.

Additional learning (15 mins)

- Hold a discussion to agree as a group what the best things about the course have been, and one or two things that they would improve or change. What did they find most helpful? What did they most enjoy? Was any other topics they would like to have covered? Was there anything they felt should have been covered in more depth?

Plenary (5 mins)

- Ask the class to vote on the top three things about the course, and the one thing that they would change or improve. You could use this information when you are planning the course for the following year.

Assessment

- Check that students have completed **Worksheet 20.1** and listen to students' responses in the discussion and plenary to assess their understanding and how effective they are at giving feedback.

Extension or home learning

- Extension: Ask students to write a short review of the course to give Year 9 students who are about to start the course next year. Students should outline what the Year 9s will learn from the course and what the best parts of it were for them.

- Home learning: Ask students to imagine their perfect future in three years' time, and to write two or three paragraphs about what they see themselves doing in their perfect future. They should include what their perfect future looks like, sounds like and feels like, going into as much detail as possible. Ask them to consider the following questions: 'What have you managed to do successfully? How does it make you feel in your heart? How did you get there? What does your head think you need to do achieve your perfect future? What skills do you need to acquire? How does this relate to your gut values? How are you prepared to act now, to achieve that perfect future in three years' time?'

Worksheet 20.1a Reflection and feedback

Reflection

Look at the list of units from the course below. What have you learned from each unit? What will you do differently in the future as a result? Fill in the table below.

Unit and title	What have I learned from this unit?	What I will do differently in the future in my own life as a result?
1. You and your life		
2. You and your relationships		
3. You and society		
4. You and your values		
5. You and your future		
6. Your healthy body		
7. Your healthy mind		
8. You and your money		
9. Sexual relationships		
10. Sexually explicit content online		
11. Sexuality and gender identity		
12. You and your choices		
13. You online		
14. You as a consumer		
15. You and the future of our planet		
16. Fake news and disinformation		
17. You and the law		
18. You and the world		
19. You and the global economy		
20. Reflecting on your choices		

Feedback

Looking at the table, what have been the best three things about the PSHE course, and why?

1. ....

....

....

2. ....

....

....

3. ....

....

....

What do you think could be improved or changed about the course

....

....

....

Giving feedback – top tips

1. Use the sandwich approach – say something positive, then something negative, then something positive.

2. Remember that negative comments are three to five times stronger than positive comments. So, for every negative criticism, make sure there are at least three positive pieces of praise.

3. Make any criticism specific to a situation and time limited, rather than specific to a person. Saying, 'That conversation was quite loud,' is much better than saying, 'You always speak too loudly.'

4. When disagreeing with somebody, acknowledge what they have said first. 'Some people might agree with you that…, but…' is a good phrase to use here.

5. Achieve what you can. It's better to get somebody to agree with 75% of your feedback than to try and force them to agree with everything you are saying.

20.2 Your choices

Learning objectives:

- To learn how to balance breathing
- To learn how to set SMART targets
- To learn how to set PURE targets

Resources:

- PowerPoint 20.2
- Worksheet 20.2 (two copies for each student)
- Link to KS3: Book 1, Unit 10.1

Key vocabulary:

balanced breathing, internal and external motivation, SMART, PURE, ecological

Get them thinking! (5 mins)

- Get students to notice how they are feeling in their heart, their head and their gut. Then take them through the balanced breathing exercise on **Slide 1**. Afterwards, ask them how they are feeling. Get them all to notice the change and the more relaxed atmosphere in the room.

Core learning (25 mins)

- Explain that there are two types of motivation – internal and external. Give students an example of both types of motivation, e.g. 'You have to do your homework or you will get into trouble' (external), versus 'I want to do my homework so I will get the grades to go to college and get a good job' (internal).

- Ask students for an example of a target and write this on the board – e.g. 'I will be learning to play the piano over the next six months. I have confirmed that I can use the school piano and my parents have agreed to pay 50 per cent of the cost of the lessons.' You are now going to work together to improve this target, using two different methods for setting targets.

- Go through **Slide 2**, which contains a worked example of a SMART target. Then use questioning from the SMART model to improve your shared target on the board (e.g. Is it achievable? Who is paying for the other 50 per cent of the piano lessons? How often are you doing the lessons?)

- Go through **Slide 3** and make sure students understand what PURE targets are. Pay particular attention to what is meant by 'ecological' – a target that fits with all your personal beliefs (it will feel good in your gut) and which fits in with the environment around you (by helping both you and others). Use questioning based on the PURE model to improve the shared target on the board (e.g. Is it positive? Are you denying access to anyone else when using the school piano? What about the noise? When will you use it?).

- Now ask students to use **Worksheet 20.2** to write their own target for the next term, using what they have learned from the activities above. They should fill in the first column of each table to make their target SMART and PURE.

- Go through **Slide 4**, asking students to check their targets with the heart, their head and their gut. The order is important! They should go round these three perspectives until they are happy with their target.

Additional learning (15 mins)

- Ask students to work in pairs using **Worksheet 20.2** to review their targets and give each other feedback. They should fill in the second, third and fourth columns during or after their discussion, and decide whether they want to amend details of their target in light of their partner's feedback.

Plenary (5 mins)

- Ask students which part of target-setting they find the most useful or difficult – SMART targets, PURE targets or checking in if they are happy with their target in their head, heart or gut – and why. Discuss as a class.

Assessment

- Ask students to complete a second copy of **Worksheet 20.2**, filling in the first column of each table with a different target for themselves to be achieved over the next academic year.

Extension or home learning

- Extension: Students can go through their additional targets on the second copy of **Worksheet 20.2** with a partner, if they wish, completing the other columns in the worksheet.

- Home learning: Ask students to write a detailed plan for the next three years with targets they wish to set themselves. They may choose anything, from an individual target they have discussed in class to something that applies to their whole lives. Tell them you would like them to share these in a future class.

Worksheet 20.2 Setting your own targets

1. Write your own SMART and PURE targets for the next term in the first column of the two tables below.

2. Work with a partner, taking it in turns to give each other feedback on your SMART and PURE targets. Then fill in columns 2, 3 and 4, deciding whether you need to rewrite your targets in light of the feedback, and if so, how you would change them.

SMART target (specific, measurable, achievable, resource based and timetabled)

What is the target?	What sort of feedback did your partner give?	What do you think of this feedback – was it positive, negative or constructive?	How would you change your target following your partner's feedback?
S			
M			
A			
R			
T			

Worksheet 20.2 Setting your own targets *continued*

PURE target (positive, understandable, resource-based and ecological)

What is the target?	What feedback did student B give?	What do you think of this feedback – was it positive, negative or constructive?	How would you change your target following your partner's feedback?
P			
U			
R			
E			

Acknowledgements

The publishers gratefully acknowledge the permission granted to reproduce the copyright material in this book. Every effort has been made to trace copyright holders and to obtain their permission for the use of copyright material. The publishers will gladly receive any information enabling them to rectify any error or omission at the first opportunity.

We are grateful to the following for permission to reproduce copyright material:

Texts

Details in 1.1, 1.2, 2.3, 7.1 from Childline, www.childline.org.uk. Reproduced with permission of NSPCC; Definition in 2.3 from "Domestic Abuse", https://www.cps.gov.uk/domestic-abuse, © copyright 2017 CPS. All rights reserved Open Government Licence v2.0; Definitions in 3.1, 13.2, 'hate crime,' 'stereotyping,' and 'Harassment' from the Collins Dictionary. Reproduced by permission of HarperCollins Publishers; Figure in 6.1 'The Eatwell Guide', Public Health England, https://www.nhs.uk. © Crown copyright 2016; Extracts in 7.1 adapted from 'What is mental health?' and 'What are mental health problems?' Mental Health Foundation, https://www.mentalhealth.org.uk. Reproduced with permission of Mental Health Foundation; Section titles in 7.2 from You Can't Revise for GCSE English! Yes you can, and Mark Roberts shows you how, HarperCollins 2020. Reproduced with permission of HarperCollins Publishers; The chart in 9.2 'Contraception at a glance', from https://www.sexwise.org.uk, Sexwise. Reproduced by permission of Public Health England, FPA and Sexwise; Image in 10.1, slide 3 from Social Toaster, https://www.socialtoaster.com/. Reproduced with permission of Social Toaster; Extracts in 10.1 from "Sexting in schools and colleges: responding to incidents and safeguarding young people", https://assets.publishing.service.gov.uk/government/uploads/system/uploads/attachment_data/file/759007/6_2939_SP_NCA_Sexting_In_Schools_FINAL_Update_Jan17.pdf, December 2020, UK Council for Child Internet Safety, © Crown copyright 2020; Extracts in 11.2c and 16.1a adapted from "National Coming Out Day: Connor Franta explains what revealing your sexuality to millions of people on YouTube is like" by Olivia Blair, The Independent, 12/10/2016; "Being a gay rugby referee has been tough, but coming out was like being born again" by Nigel Owens, The Independent, 31/03/2015; and "Coronavirus: 5G conspiracy theory now most common fake news story surrounding pandemic, Ofcom finds" by Adam Forrest, The Independent, 21 April 2020, copyright © Olivia Blair, Nigel Owens, Adam Forrest/The Independent, 2020, www.independent.co.uk; Extract in 12.1, from "Addiction: what is it?" https://www.nhs.uk/live-well/healthy-body/addiction-what-is-it/, NHS, © Crown copyright; Extract in 12.2 from "Drug penalties" https://www.gov.uk/penalties-drug-possession-dealing, © Crown copyright; Extracts in 12.3 from "Guidance. Criminal exploitation of children and vulnerable adults: county lines, https://www.gov.uk/government/publications/criminal-exploitation-of-children-and-vulnerable-adults-county-lines/criminal-exploitation-of-children-and-vulnerable-adults-county-lines, Home Office, updated 7 February 2020, © Crown copyright 2020; Extract in 16.1c from "MPs slam tech giants for failing to 'answer basic questions' on disinformation" by PA Mediapoint, https://www.pressgazette.co.uk/mps-slam-tech-giants-for-failing-to-answer-basic-questions-on-disinformation/. Reproduced by permission of PA Media Group Ltd; and an extract in 16.2a adapted from "What is cancel culture?" by Caroline Westbrook, Metro, 8 August 2020, copyright © Solo Syndication 2020.

Images

1.1, Worksheet 1.1c: Sue Woollatt, Graham-Cameron Illustration; 1.1, Slide 1: inimalGraphic/Shutterstock; 1.2, Slide 1: DGLimages/Shutterstock; 1.2, Slide 1: Dragon Images/Shutterstock; 1.2, Slide 1: StockImageFactory.com/Shutterstock; 1.2, Slide 1: Romrodphoto/Shutterstock; 1.2, Slide 1: Monkey Business Images/Shutterstock; 1.2, Slide 1: legenda/Shutterstock; 1.2, Slide 2: tynyuk/Shutterstock; 1.2, Slide 6: fizkes/Shutterstock; 2.1, Slide 4: DGLimages/Shutterstock; 2.2, Slide 3: Alexey Boldin/Shutterstock; 2.3, Slide 1: Dean Drobot/Shutterstock; 3.1, Worksheet 3.1b: Halfpoint/Shutterstock; 3.1, Slide 3: Zurijeta/Shutterstock; 3.1, Slide 3: WAYHOME studio/Shutterstock; 3.1, Slide 4: Christopher Penler/Shutterstock; 3.1, Slide 5: Dmitriy Domino/Shutterstock; 3.2, Slide 1: Lukas Maverick Greyson/Shutterstock; 3.2, Slide 3: CLS Digital Arts/Shutterstock; 3.2, Slide 3: vic josh/Shutterstock; 3.2, Slide 4: Naypong Studio/Shutterstock; 3.2, Slide 5: Aspects and Angles/Shutterstock; 3.2, Slide 5: John Gomez/Shutterstock; 3.2, Slide 5: Fiora Watts / Stockimo / Alamy Stock Photo; 3.2, Slide 5: David Grossman / Alamy Stock Photo; 4.1, Slide 1: Alexey Fedorenko/Shutterstock; 4.1, Slide 3: Gary Perkin/Shutterstock; 4.2, Slide 1: JessicaGirvan/Shutterstock; 4.2, Slide 2: Chris Dorney / Alamy Stock Photo; 4.2, Slide 3: Colin Underhill / Alamy Stock Photo; 4.2, Slide 4: rahalarts/Shutterstock; 4.2, Slide 5: Fiora Watts/Shutterstock; 5.1, Slide 1: ESB Professional/Shutterstock; 5.1, Slide 5: fizkes/Shutterstock; 5.2, Slide 1: VectorKnight/Shutterstock; 5.2, Slide 2: MOLPIX/Shutterstock; 5.2, Slide 3: Monkey Business Images/Shutterstock; 5.2, Slide 4: Jaromir Chalabala/Shutterstock; 5.2, Slide 5: BBSTUDIOPHOTO/Shutterstock; 5.3, Slide 1: Everett Collection/Shutterstock; 5.3, Slide 3: Planar/Shutterstock; 5.3, Slide 4: Peshkova/Shutterstock; 5.3, Slide 5: Jenson/Shutterstock; 5.4, Slide 1: aerogondo2/Shutterstock; 5.4, Slide 1: Max Topchii/Shutterstock; 5.4, Slide 3: goodluz/Shutterstock; 5.4, Slide 2: ESB Professional/Shutterstock; 5.4, Slide 5: Odua Images/Shutterstock; 5.4, Slide 5: Vgstockstudio/Shutterstock; 5.4, Slide 6: NDAB Creativity/Shutterstock; 6.1, Slide 1: Monkey Business Images/Shutterstock; 6.1, Worksheet 6.1b: Monkey Business Images/Shutterstock; 6.1, Worksheet 6.1b: ILYA AKINSHIN/Shutterstock; 6.1, Slide 4: ILYA AKINSHIN/Shutterstock; 6.1, Slide 5: Monkey Business Images/Shutterstock; 6.2, Slide 2: Photographee.eu/Shutterstock; 6.2, Slide 4: oneinchpunch/Shutterstock; 6.2, Slide 4: photofort 77/Shutterstock; 6.3, Slide 2: SpeedKingz/Shutterstock; 7.1, Slide 1: vasabii/Shutterstock; 7.1, Slide 4: Antonio Guillem/Shutterstock; 7.2, Slide 1: Ollyy/Shutterstock; 7.2, Slide 3: zendograph/Shutterstock; 8.1, Slide 5: ShaunWilkinson/Shutterstock; 8.2, Slide 2: tommaso79/Shutterstock; 8.2, Slide 4: wk1003mike/Shutterstock; 9.1, Slide 4: Rido/Shutterstock; 9.2, Slide 3: ldutko/Shutterstock; 9.2, Slide 5: pim pic/Shutterstock; 9.2, Slide 5: JPC-PROD/Shutterstock;

9.3, Slide 1: Andrei Yarashevich/Shutterstock; 9.3, Slide 2: Lukiyanova Natalia frenta/Shutterstock; 9.3, Slide 3: Rawpixel.com/Shutterstock; 9.3, Slide 4: Monkey Business Images/Shutterstock; 10.1, Slide 1: ducu59us/Shutterstock; 10.2, Slide 1: Suradech Prapairat/Shutterstock; 10.2, Slide 2: astara19/Shutterstock; 10.2, Slide 4: solarseven/Shutterstock; 11.2, Slide 2: hydra viridis/Shutterstock; 11.2, Slide 6: New Africa/Shutterstock; 11.1, Slide 4: taa22/Shutterstock; 11.1, Slide 5: Ronnie Chua/Shutterstock; 12.1, Slide 1: Shaiith/Shutterstock; 12.1, Slide 1: one photo/Shutterstock; 12.1, Slide 1: Wpadington/Shutterstock; 12.1, Slide 3: Trifonenkolvan; 12.1, Slide 4: Dmytro Zinkevych/Shutterstock; 12.1, Worksheets 12.1a and 12.1b: Lidiia Koval/Shutterstock; 12.2, Slide 1: Butterfly Hunter/Shutterstock; 12.2, Slide 2: wanshutter/Shutterstock; 12.2, Slide 3: Marcus Morgan/Shutterstock; 12.3, Slide 1: OneSideProFoto/Shutterstock; 13.1, Slide 1: Artseen/Shutterstock; 13.1, Slide 3: chrisdorney/Shutterstock; 13.1, Slide 4: nito/Shutterstock; 13.2, Slide 2: Marcos Mesa Sam Wordley/Shutterstock; 13.2, Slide 3: simez78/Shutterstock; 13.2, Slide 4: Monkey Business Images/Shutterstock; 14.1, Slide 1: Rawpixel.com/Shutterstock; 14.1, Slide 2: David Tonelson/Shutterstock; 14.1, Slide 5: Rawpixel.com/Shutterstock; 14.2, Slide 2: Maddie Red/Shutterstock; 14.2, Slide 3: SB_photos/Shutterstock; 14.2, Slide 5: Sk Hasan Ali/Shutterstock; 15.1, Slide 1: Monphoto/Shutterstock; 15.1, Slide 2: Vlad61/Shutterstock; 15.1, Slide 3: elenabsl/Shutterstock; 15.1, Slide 5: Din Mohd Yaman/Shutterstock; 15.2, Slide 2: IndustryAndTravel/Shutterstock; 15.2, Slide 3: Zoltan Acs/Shutterstock; 15.2, Slide 4: geniusksy/Shutterstock; 15.2, Worksheet 15.2b: Karl Nesh/Shutterstock; 16.1, Worksheet 16.1a: Kphrom/Shutterstock; 16.1, Slide 1: M-SUR/Shutterstock; 16.1, Slide 3: Kphrom/Shutterstock; 16.1, Slide 5: buffaloboy/Shutterstock; 16.2, Slide 3: jirawatfoto/Shutterstock; 16.2, Slide 4: Lightspring/Shutterstock; 17.1, Slide 1: Spiroview Inc/Shutterstock; 17.1, Slide 4: Diana Parkhouse/Shutterstock; 17.2, Slide 1: ozgur_oral/Shutterstock; 17.2, Slide 2: New Africa/Shutterstock; 17.2, Slide 4: Sam72/Shutterstock; 18.1, Slide 3: PeskyMonkey/Shutterstock; 18.1, Slide 4: Pyty/Shutterstock; 18.2, Slide 2: Roman Tiraspolsky/Shutterstock; 18.2, Slide 3: Leonid Andronov/Shutterstock; 18.2, Slide 4: VanReeel/Shutterstock; 18.2, Slide 5: Alexander Zavadsky/Shutterstock; 19.1, Slide 4: Number1411/Shutterstock; 19.1, Slide 5: Voin_Sveta/Shutterstock; 19.2, Slide 1: Bernsten/Shutterstock; 20.1, Slide 1: fizkes/Shutterstock; 20.1, Slide 3: Sudowoodo/Shutterstock; 20.2, Slide 1: buzzbee/Shutterstock; 20.2, Slide 2: waewkid/Shutterstock; 20.2, Slide 4: Kittichai/Shutterstock.

DALCROZE EURHYTHMICS IN TODAY'S MUSIC CLASSROOM

Virginia Hoge Mead

Kent State University

Teaching

Teaching offers something – it offers love.
Not only the love of learning and love of books and ideas,
But also the love that a teacher feels for that rare student
Who walks into a teacher's life and begins to breathe.
I teach because, being around people who are beginning to breathe,
I occasionally find myself catching my breath with them.

Peter G. Beidler
Lehigh University

Acknowledgements

To my music editor, Jane Frazee, whose teaching and musicianship I have admired for
years; who gave me courage to start the book and, with her husband, the help and
encouragement that supported me every step of the way –

To those who inspired my musicianship and teaching and introduced me to the joys and
gratification of teaching music through eurhythmics: Dr. Hilda M. Schuster and
Dr. Frances W. Aronoff –

To Dr. Arthur F. Becknell, a classmate from Oberlin and a close, supportive friend and
colleague who unfortunately passed away just months before the completion of the
book –

To those students and teachers eager to gain understanding and insight into the Dalcroze
approach; especially Maria Foustalieraki who read most of the early manuscript and
tried out many of the experiences with her classes –

To all my students, young and old, who loved music, who wanted to make music and who
wanted to move –

I extend my sincerest thanks and appreciation.

All known sources have been acknowledged. Omission of
any acknowledgement is regretted and will be corrected if
brought to our attention.

ISBN 0 930448 51 0

Designed by Geoffrey Wadsley
Typeset by August Filmsetting, St Helens
Music set by Barnes Music Engraving
Printed in U.S.A.

Contents

Introduction

Dalcroze Eurhythmics in Today's Music Classroom is written for, and dedicated to, all those teachers who continue to ask for help in understanding and adapting Dalcroze techniques to the teaching of music in the elementary school. Many teachers who have had an introduction to Dalcroze eurhythmics are often surprised to learn that the whole approach includes solfège and improvisation. Some workshops or conference sessions have touched upon the ideas and philosophy behind the approach, but participants have had little time to absorb the experiences and realize the benefits to themselves as musicians and teachers.

In this book, I have tried to provide a guide for teachers who wish to learn more about the Dalcroze approach and how it can become an integral part of the music education of elementary school children. It is not a methods book for teaching music. Every music teacher is unique in philosophy, music skills, and teaching abilities. In addition, there are marked differences among students and even grade levels in various schools. As a result, it is not possible to dictate a specific or precise sequence of resources and activities for teaching music. Yet, the goals for developing musical awareness, skills and understandings are usually quite similar in all situations. This book attempts to help teachers understand the essence of the Dalcroze approach and to guide them, through suggestions and sample experiences, to incorporate some of these ideas and techniques into their lessons.

Although my attention is directed to those of you who teach elementary school music, these pages should also be of interest to applied music teachers and college music education faculty and students. Because the nature of the eurhythmics experience involves the whole body, mind and emotions, many leaders in areas of special education and therapy have applied the approach to their work and they, too, may find the book helpful.

The Dalcroze approach is used in many private schools and in private studio teaching, and yet there is no doubt that achieving successful eurhythmics experiences in many public schools is difficult. When the classes are large and diversified in musical ability, and when space is limited, it takes a special kind of thinking to include eurhythmics experiences in a music program. This was my challenge in writing this book.

Part One introduces Emile Jaques-Dalcroze, the musician and teacher. It traces the evolution of his approach and his ideas and techniques for teaching music. Chapter Two explains the three main areas of the approach – eurhythmics, solfège (ear training) and improvisation – and describes how and where these are used at all levels of musical development. Some discussion is given to the way Dalcroze intended the three areas to be integrated in the learning process. The third chapter proposes ways in which these experiences can be adapted to an elementary school setting and become an integral part of an elementary music program.

Part Two addresses three levels in the elementary school: primary, intermediate and upper grades. At each level, sample Dalcroze 'games' or exercises are described along with their intended purposes. Many of these eurhythmics, solfège and improvisation experiences use musical material which is common to students of elementary school age. Since eurhythmics is the unique part of the Dalcroze approach, emphasis has been given to such activities. However, you will soon realize how easily the movement, solfège and improvisation experiences can be integrated in a lesson – just as Dalcroze envisioned.

In many cases, the strategies will appear to be in sequential order, that is, they will fit both the sequence of learning and the sequence of seasons of the year, but teachers need not follow this plan rigidly. In fact, it is very possible that some ideas suggested for one age level can be used at a later time. The experiences and suggestions along the way should be clearly understood before they are tried in class. I hope they will become examples of activities for student exploration of new and different ideas.

Since there is so much emphasis on keyboard improvisation in the Dalcroze approach, a rather lengthy self-help essay appears as Appendix A, in addition to the many notated examples sprinkled throughout the book. While it seems contradictory to suggest that the teacher improvise for an exercise and then for me to offer a notated example, these are merely illustrations to help teachers who are unsure of their own abilities to have an idea with which to begin.

I believe that someone who incorporates Dalcroze techniques in teaching is one who has experienced that joyful awareness and understanding of the power of an integrated physical, emotional and intellectual experience with music. Many music teachers admit that their background in music has not included much freedom to move, improvise or create. Those persons should not allow their own inhibitions to determine the learning activities they plan for their students. It is a natural thing for a young person to swing to the music, to tap the beat on a hard surface, or to improvise a clapping rhythm. They are born movers! The students will have many suggestions for how to show a beat, or how to 'dance' that rhythm pattern with a partner, or how to feel the long notes at the end of the phrase. The teacher should capitalize on the natural movement instincts and creative impulses of the students. If the teacher recognizes the responses of the students and can incorporate them into the lesson with the whole class involved, everyone will enjoy the lesson. Students learn by this kind of participation more quickly than when explanations, or even demonstrations, are given. This does not mean that the teacher never explains or demonstrates, but all too often students are not given the opportunity to try something for themselves. They will tell you it's more fun to do it themselves!

There are several ways that teachers may find this book helpful. I have made a sincere effort to organize the book so that it is practical for the teacher. And because busy teachers do not have time to read long dissertations about special approaches to music education, I have kept the explanations to a minimum.

In order to incorporate any idea effectively or successfully into a teaching mode, a teacher must understand the philosophy and basic premises which underlie the approach. There are four premises which are the structural foundation of the Dalcroze philosophy; these are threaded throughout this book.

1 Eurhythmics awakens in one's mind physical, aural and visual images of various aspects of music.
2 With the integration of eurhythmics, solfège (ear training) and improvisation, a student's listening, performance and creative skills are solidly based on expression or communication rather than intellectual understanding alone.
3 All basic aspects of music can be experienced in speech, gesture and movement. Likewise, speech, gesture and movement are experienced in time (when something happens), space (where and how far something happens) and energy (how forceful something is).

4   All initial learning is through the senses. Thus, an approach which integrates the kinesthetic, tactile, aural and visual senses, as does the Dalcroze approach, becomes a strong and viable catalyst for learning.

I strongly suggest that you study Part One before trying the experiences with students in the classroom. Understanding the approach will help give you confidence in using the techniques and should result in successful and effective teaching. The variety of ways you find to 'spin off' from these ideas when combined with your own will determine the success of the book.

Part One
The Essence of the Dalcroze Approach

1. Dalcroze – The Man and His Ideas

Movement is an important part of much music education today. That integration has been slow to develop. The synthesis of mind, emotions and body is now understood as fundamental to all learning, but was not sufficiently acknowledged at the turn of the century. In 1905, Emile Jaques-Dalcroze, a professor of music with rather provocative ideas, spoke at a music conference on the subject 'Proposals for a Reform of Music Instruction in the Schools.' With this presentation the seeds of his approach to music education were sown, and he would continue to experiment and refine his teaching ideas throughout his lifetime.

Emile Jaques-Dalcroze was born in 1865 of Swiss parents. Soon after completing his studies at the Paris Conservatory and in Vienna, he was appointed Professor of Harmony, Solfège and Composition at the Geneva Conservatory. In his earliest years of teaching he questioned the musical training in schools and colleges. He was particularly concerned about his solfège students. He was appalled at the theoretical emphasis and fragmentation of all music study. Students studied theory by rules and writing, but not by sound. As instrumentalists and vocalists, they were taught the notes and mechanics of performing, but were not taught how to listen or hear. Often, the expressive qualities of music eluded the student. Dalcroze began to devise ear training exercises for students in his solfège classes and, because he realized the importance and potential of beginning this training early, he also tried his ideas out with children's classes. In 1898 in an essay entitled, 'The Place of Ear Training in Musical Education,' Dalcroze asked,

> Should it not be possible . . . to establish more direct communications between the feeling and understanding, between sensations which inform the mind and those which recreate sensorial means of expression?

He hoped that the singing exercises he was devising would develop his students' ability to hear music mentally as well as aurally. He characterized this as 'inner hearing' – being able to hear a musical example in the inner ear, or in the mind. This is easily understood when we realize our ability to recall a lovely lake in our mind's eye or hear the beginning of the 'Hallelujah Chorus' in our inner ear. Dalcroze believed that developing inner hearing would result in a more conscious awareness of the muscular sensations involved in singing pitch. The conscious sensation would alert the thought processes, and an understanding and mental awareness of musical sound would evolve.

While Dalcroze experimented with solfège aural training exercises, he noticed that his students instinctively accompanied their responses with movement. Their singing seemed to set in motion a muscular response – tapping a foot, nodding the head, swaying from side to side or gesturing the beat or phrase with a hand.

One day, while staring out the window and pondering his ideas, he was struck by the natural flow and animated movement of a student walking across campus. He began to think about the possibility that the natural rhythmic gait of the body and the regularity of a person's breathing could be at the core of a musical response. At the next class he asked his students to step the beat around the room as they sang their solfège exercises. He saw in this movement the importance of a well-functioning and integrated sensory, muscular and nervous system which could then free the imagination and spirit for an expressive musical performance.

To capitalize on these natural movements of the body Dalcroze asked his students to walk, conduct, swing their arms or gesture the beat of the music as they sang. These 'game-like' exercises took on a deeper purpose: that of improving the response time and accuracy in communication and co-ordination between the ear, the nervous and muscular systems, and the mind. It was at this point that eurhythmics was born. The result of expressing music in movement was that the mind held in memory muscular sensations of time, duration, energy, articulation, accentuation, and many other aspects of music.

Some of his teaching methods were considered questionable at the time. Students were on their feet, with their shoes off, moving around the room; the 'ladies' had their long dresses hiked up to give them more freedom of movement. He challenged his students with a myriad of movement experiences designed to alert the whole being to the many aspects of time and energy in music. He called this study of music through movement 'eurhythmics,' from the Greek roots *eu* and *rhythmos*, meaning good flow or good movement. Dalcroze continued to improvise musical examples to help his students to realize fully the connection between timing and energy or dynamics in music, between pitch and movement in space, and between the music and its temperament or character. Gradually the movements became freer and more individually expressive.

As Dalcroze began to apply these same ideas to the teaching of harmony, form and keyboard study, he realized that students also needed further opportunities to use the musical materials and their new understanding. This could be accomplished by improvising with movement or by using their own instruments or voices. He favored the piano for improvising because even the simplest musical idea of two pitches can simultaneously imply melody, rhythm and harmony. Dalcroze believed that improvising was an opportunity for the students to synthesize the ear training and eurhythmics experiences with their imaginative and creative ideas. And so improvisation was added to movement and solfège to become the third part of Dalcroze's approach to music education.

Those who studied with Dalcroze say that he was an unusual person who combined all the attributes of a caring human being with deeply held convictions. He was warmhearted, lively, intensely observant and caring and had a keen sense of humor. He was an accomplished musician who expected nothing but the best responses from his students. He could be stern and very demanding, but some students have spoken of his shy and gentle apologies whenever he was too harsh with someone. All of his students remember, with admiration and awe, his piano improvisations. He believed that the musical examples used in class should, for the most part, be improvised; thus the music was always fresh and new and never could dull the senses with its predictability. (For those teachers who are not comfortable improvising at the piano, suggestions and options are given throughout the book and in Appendix A).

Dalcroze added a strong interest in theater, opera and dance to a fascination with psychology and people; given his gift for teaching it was only natural that he chose a career in music pedagogy. In the first half of this century his influence was strongly felt in all of the above professions. He was invited to work with the Paris Ballet to help its dancers understand and execute the difficult rhythms of Stravinsky's *Rite of Spring*. He collaborated with Adolphe Appia, the scene designer for Wagnerian operas, and together they made significant contributions to the theater in stage lighting, set decor, and the choreography of crowd scenes. His belief in teaching for the integration of the whole being – the senses, the nervous and muscular systems, and the mind – has been an influence on individuals in the fields of general education, therapy, special education and psychology.

Dalcroze had many followers. In the early days of his teaching they were mainly his students and the parents of the children he taught. These were the people who were inspired by his teaching and who recognized the benefits of his approach. Those teachers of music who had not yet experienced his classes were not convinced, yet he was soon in demand for demonstrations and courses all over Europe. As his influence spread he began to train teachers to carry on his work. He established stringent standards for teachers, but despite his exacting requirements Dalcroze schools were soon established in many countries, including the United States (in 1915). Dalcroze continued to question and refine his approach to teaching music until his death in 1950. To students of Dalcroze himself or to those of us who have studied his approach, these ideas seem basic to developing all levels of musicianship: **ear training and solfège**, to develop the inner ear to hear and listen acutely; **eurhythmics**, to train the body to feel the muscular sensations of time and energy as they are manifest in space; and **improvisation**, to give students opportunity to express consciously, and with their own freedom of imagination, what they hear, feel and understand.

2. The Dalcroze Approach to Music Learning

Before considering how to adapt Dalcroze techniques to the elementary music classroom, it would be helpful to examine further the whole approach and give thought to the ideas and premises from which the methodology evolved. This chapter will attempt to explain in more detail the various types of experience and the purposes behind them.

In Chapter One you were introduced to the Dalcroze approach to teaching music. Three areas of study were identified: eurhythmics, the experience of physically feeling the various aspects and expressive qualities of music through movement; solfège, that is, the experience of singing with pitch syllables to develop a keener sense of hearing; and improvisation, the opportunity to express immediate musical ideas through movement, the piano, the voice or other instruments. Closer study reveals the integration of these three areas of study results in more perceptive listening, more sensitive performing skills, as well as the ability to read and write music. Many of the activities described in Part Two will incorporate ear training, solfege and improvisation in the eurhythmics experiences.

What is Eurhythmics?

The essence of eurhythmics is the spontaneous and individual realization in movement of what you hear in music. Unfortunately, reading about it doesn't allow you actually to realize or enjoy the fusing of the senses, body, mind, and emotions into one experience, which is what happens in eurhythmics.

Eurhythmics can be the joy of actually 'living' the music as it is being heard. It can be an opportunity to realize in movement the relationships of timing and energy in the music as they manifest themselves in space. Consider how you would move freely to the tempo or timing of each of the following examples:

'Farandole' from *L'Arlésienne* Suite No. 2 by Georges Bizet.

The Shaker song 'Simple Gifts,' as it appears in *Appalachian Spring* by Aaron Copland.

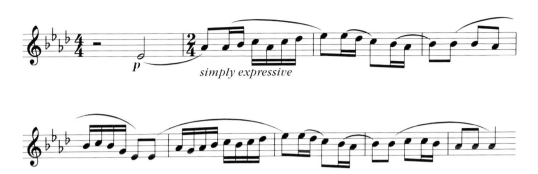

In eurhythmics, the whole body becomes an instrument and 'performs' or translates into movement some aspect of the music, for example, timing, measure, irregular accents, pitch contour, or crescendo. The timing (duration, tempo), the energy (weight, dynamics, accentuation), and the space used to express it in movement are recorded in the muscles as a kinesthetic image. A gymnast develops a kinesthetic memory, or image, of the timing and force of the thrust in a backward somersault; a painter develops a kinesthetic image of the weight and rhythm of brush strokes needed to paint the shape of a hemlock tree; a musician develops a kinesthetic memory or image of the relationship of ♩ to ♩ or, something more difficult, ♩♪ versus ♩♪ .

Dalcroze believed that in the study of music students should continually be cultivating a memory bank of aural, visual and kinesthetic images which could be recalled at any time for reading, writing, performing or creating music. The stronger and more carefully defined the images, the longer and more precisely they remain in the memory. The wide variety of experiences in the Dalcroze approach can often complement and strengthen the image.

What Are the Unique Aspects of a Eurhythmics Experience?

How does a eurhythmics experience differ from other approaches to teaching music? I believe it is the total absorption of mind, body and emotions in the experience of actualizing the musical sound. You imagine your body as the instrument and you sense the excitement of being the interpreter, the performer and the listener all at the same time. You imagine that you and the music are one.

When speaking of movement with music, we often say we are 'feeling the music.' The word 'feel,' or 'feeling,' implies several things. It is often said, 'He plays with feeling,' or, 'She feels the rhythm of the music,' or simply, 'He feels the music.' In a eurhythmics experience, one feels the physical sensation of moving through space in the timing and with the energy prescribed by the music. One also feels the expressive qualities of the music, such as a well-timed ritardando or the gradual excitement of a rising sequence in a melody line. The word 'feel' implies that a message was received through the senses, transmitted through the nervous system to the mind, which tells the muscles how to respond.

There is a sense of being awakened to the life of the music when experiencing eurhythmics. We speak of it as activating and integrating the

- senses,
- nervous system,
- intellect,
- physical body,
- emotions, and
- creative and expressive self.

When we can understand the uniqueness of this kind of experience we can understand why Dalcroze eurhythmics has influenced and complemented so many other branches of education and medicine. One may read of the teaching of eurhythmics in all areas of special education including the physically, mentally or emotionally handicapped. Physical and musical therapists have found eurhythmics techniques to be beneficial in helping their patients. As early as 1917, eurhythmics classes were given in Geneva, Switzerland for children with special needs.

In his writings, Dalcroze spoke often of the need to develop 'a consciousness of bodily rhythm' and the need to strengthen communication between the senses, the muscles (body) and the mind. He believed that if students could become conscious of their own natural rhythms and inner sense of hearing and feeling music, they would make great progress toward developing their own musical sensitivity and understanding. As Dalcroze observed,

> I look forward to a system of musical education in which the body itself shall play the role of intermediary between sounds and thought, becoming in time the direct medium of our feelings ...[1]

What Activities Comprise a Eurhythmics Experience?

Dalcroze teachers can employ a wealth of activities to enable their students to develop an understanding of musical sound. Let me suggest a few of these:

1 Students should have opportunities to respond freely to music – stepping, clapping, swinging, gesturing, or using the whole body. Students should be encouraged to move instinctively as they follow or express the music without inhibition or intimidation. When this happens, the ear, body and mind are alerted to the music and the movement can show increased awareness and sensitivity to the elements and nuances in the music. This experience can demonstrate awareness and understanding of various aspects of a composition.

2 Students may be asked to move in a specific way as they respond to the music. With young children, the movement may sometimes be motivated by suggesting a work or play rhythm as in activity (a) below, using the spinning song 'Sarasponda.'

Sarasponda

Sa - ra - spon-da, Sa - ra-spon-da, Sa - ra - spon-da, Ret-set-set! Sa - ra -

- spon-da, Sa - ra-spon-da, Sa - ra - spon-da, Ret-set-set! Ah - do - ray-oh! Ah -

- do - ray-boom-day-oh! Ah - do - ray-boom-day, Ret-set-set! Ah-say - pa - say-oh!

(a) The children can explore ways to show the movement of the spinning wheel. (Move one arm like a wheel, or roll one hand around the other.) They can also show the movement of carding the wool. (In the rhythm of half notes, pretend to comb through the wool in preparation for spinning.)

■ **On the first half of the song, show the spinning wheel. When you sing the second part, 'Ah-do-ray-oh!', show how you card the wool.**

(b) ■ **Take a partner and together decide on two ways to show the beat of 'Sarasponda' – one for the beginning part of the song and the other way for the second part.**

Older students might be directed to listen:

(c) ■ **I'm going to play two different rhythms. I want you to listen and then step** (*and/or clap*) **the opposite of what I play. Here are the two rhythms:** (Repeat each one several times until the students are responding correctly and with precision.)

3 Students may be asked to respond in a specific way when a signal or command is given. This quick-reaction exercise is a basic eurhythmics experience which can be designed for students of all ages. Signals are either verbal ('Hopp, hip, heep,' as used by Dalcroze, or 'Change'), or they are musical, for instance, an accented chord or a rhythmic motive such as ♪ ♩ . These exercises are designed to quicken the reaction time of the ear, mind and body, and improve the precision and clarity of the response. Specific examples of quick-reaction exercises are given with the experiences in Part Two.

4 Students may be asked to respond in an interrupted canon. It is similar to an echo response in that they imitate what they have just heard when the music is interrupted by rests. At first, the canon is interrupted after each measure, but as the children progress, a longer portion of music is heard before it is interrupted for the response. In this way, concentration and memory skills are strengthened. It is important, however, that the continuum of musical line or phrasing in the canon is adhered to; isolated measures do not create a musical line. Here are two short examples to be stepped or clapped. Students begin at the 'X.' (Notice that even though there are rests in the first example it implies a continual melody, as is demonstrated in the second example.)

5 Students may be asked to perform a canon in movement. In this experience, there are no interruptions or measures of rest. The second example above is actually a canon. Students must express movement through the whole notes. The students imitate or respond, a measure late, to what they have just heard, while hearing and remembering something new. In the earliest lessons, a teacher can simplify the task by inserting a measure of simple rhythm – for example, all quarter notes or a whole note – between each of the other measures. Later this task can become quite challenging, but the musical example can be designed so that the students finish the exercise feeling some success and accomplishment.

6 Students learn to conduct while stepping beats or rhythms in a eurhythmics lesson. At first they may be asked to show only the accented beats with a strong gesture using both arms. In the upper elementary grades, traditional conducting patterns can be taught;

8

students can learn to conduct while stepping a meter, or divisions of the beat. Older students can be challenged to conduct while stepping rhythm patterns, melodies or themes. This is an integral part of eurhythmics. Using both arms for conducting results in a more balanced physical feeling when moving the whole body. It is easier for students to learn to conduct when the arms are mirroring each other. They also respond more carefully to the dynamics and phrasing when both arms are involved in expressing the music.

7   Students, especially young people, enjoy using props such as balls, scarves, balloons, bamboo rods or sticks. They can be used to give the students a more concrete physical and tactile sensation of the weight (force), the articulation and timing of the movement, and a sense of the follow-through. Although their main purpose is to help students become aware of the kinesthetic sensation felt in the movement, props can free a student from feelings of inhibition and motivate or bring focus to the activity. They also help the student respond with more confidence and independence. Props also give a visual picture of the timing, energy and space relationships used in movement. For example, when students bounce–catch a ball on quarter notes, toss–catch a ball on half notes, or roll a ball from hand to hand on eighth notes, they can feel and see the energy and space needed for each activity as the timing changes. You'll understand if you try these yourself.

B   bounce
C   catch
R   roll
T   toss

Students may play a drum or other small percussion instrument while moving. This could be considered a prop, but it becomes much more than that when the children can play the instrument sensitively while moving.

8   Students may be asked to try an activity with a partner or in a small group. In addition to the help others provide in stimulating and reinforcing expressive responses, group activity promotes appreciation for the efforts of all its members.

What Music Is Used for a Eurhythmics Experience?

Both improvised and composed music are used. Teachers improvise at the piano, with the voice or with other instruments. Dalcroze believed that improvised music was best for ear training exercises. As a master improviser and composer, he improvised for most of his classes. Today's Dalcroze teachers often supplement piano improvisations with composed and recorded selections to highlight a particular learning concept; for instance, a form, a change in meter, or a rhythmic device such as hemiola. Once students have explored an element or concept by responding to clear-cut examples improvised by the teacher, they are ready to discover the same thing in a familiar or unfamiliar selection. Their learning experience is rewarding and meaningful because it relates to 'real' music.

The students should experience composed music in the medium for which it was written; for this reason, transcription to the piano is limiting. A live performance is the most rewarding way to listen and respond in movement, then listen again.

Composed music often seems to have such an inevitability about it that students are not always ready for quick or subtle changes in the music. They tend to let themselves be bathed in the overall sound.

Improvised music can minimize these limitations. The improvising teacher can make sudden or gradual changes in the music to keep the student alert and hasten the response time between the ear, mind and body. There are innumerable possibilities for changes in the music: meter, rhythm pattern, articulations, texture, or key, as well as the obvious ones such as tempo and dynamics. Sometimes the teacher will modify the music slightly (tempo or accent, for instance) to help the students feel the response more precisely. Some teachers improvise examples of music in many different styles and in many extremes of character and mood to elicit a variety of appropriate responses.

A composed and/or recorded selection can be particularly important as a culminating experience in a lesson. The students need to listen closely to the music and recall what they have just learned. All of their discovery and learning is then synthesized into their own individual movement response to the music.

What Can Be Learned Through Eurhythmics?

Virtually all aspects of music can be explored through eurhythmics. However, much time and extensive participation are required to appreciate these possibilities fully. Here are a few examples of the various awarenesses, skills and understandings that can be realized through movement activities.

1   The overall timing and energy of the music are often the aspects which motivate the initial response. This step is valuable in assessing the students' first perception of the music. Their instinctive reaction expresses the character or mood of the music.

2   A basic study of such elements as tempo, timing, accents, measure (or meter), note values, dynamics and phrasing can be made enjoyable and challenging through eurhythmics experiences.

3   Various concepts or topics in rhythm are explored in exercises or 'games.' Some of the following examples are relatively simple, others which are more difficult could be explored with students more advanced in their musical development:

- The relationship of quarter and eighth notes.
- The beat and divisions of the beat.
- Timing: twice as fast and twice as slow.

10

- The quarter versus the dotted-quarter beat feeling (♩ versus ♩.)
- Accents and groupings of eighth notes.
- Rests in music.
- Syncopation.
- Hemiola.

4   Concepts dealing with other aspects of composition, such as melody, harmony, form and expression are also explored in eurhythmics. For instance, students may be asked to show the phrasing or shape of a melody in movement. They could be asked to respond to changes in harmony or to contrasting sections in the music.

5   The relationship of layers of timing or rhythm in a song can be explored in movement. The individual layers should be identified, such as beat rhythm, measure rhythm, melodic rhythm, phrase rhythm and harmonic rhythm. Students can express each layer of rhythm in movement and then groups of students can design a movement sequence which expresses the composite of these layers. Here is an example of such an activity for upper elementary students, using the Russian folk song 'The Little Birch Tree.'

(From *A Russian Songbook* by Rose N. Rubin and Michael Stillman)

1. ‖: Growing all alone is the birch tree :‖
   No one comes to the meadow.
   All is still in the meadow.

(Wintertime)   2. ‖: Snow is falling all 'round the birch tree :‖
   Ice is glistening on the branches;
   Branches bending in the cold wind.

(Springtime)   3. ‖: Sun is shining bright on the birch tree :‖
   Leaves are dancing in the sunlight;
   Flowers blooming in the meadow.

The students will need to listen to determine the timing or length of each layer of rhythm, for instance, the length of the phrase or the length of each harmonic change. Each of these layers can be notated. Here are the simultaneous rhythmic layers for the first phrase of 'The Little Birch Tree.'

The beat rhythm is:

The measure rhythm is:

11

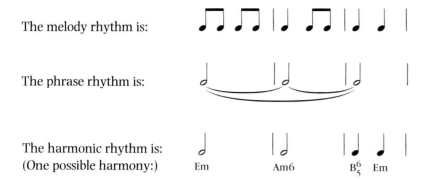

The melody rhythm is:

The phrase rhythm is:

The harmonic rhythm is:
(One possible harmony:)   Em   Am6 B_5^6 Em

What is Dalcroze Solfège or Ear Training?

One of the greatest strengths of the Dalcroze approach is the potential for significant development in ear-training skills. These skills are reinforced through the interaction between physical and aural experiences. Whatever can be heard or sung can be felt through movement or gesture and vice versa. One strengthens the image of the other. Many of the eurhythmics experiences described in Part Two of this book will include solfège or ear-training exercises which relate to the movement.

Students in a Dalcroze class sing with *so–fa* syllables, as the word 'solfège' implies. In addition, they sing with nonsense syllables, such as 'loo,' or with letter names. There are two systems of syllabication: the moveable-*do* system and the fixed-*do* system. Dalcroze training centers throughout the world typically use the fixed-*do* system which 'fixes' the syllable *do* always on C. That means that no matter in what key you are singing, C is always *do*, D is *re*, and so on. It is believed that this develops a keen sense of relative or even near-perfect pitch. Because the moveable-*do* system is more widely practiced in music education in this country, teachers who have studied the Dalcroze approach use this system successfully in ear training and solfège experiences. Whenever singing with syllables is suggested in the experiences in Part Two of this book, the moveable-*do* system will be used. Syllables are not difficult for children in the elementary school to learn, especially if started early. They easily recognize patterns such as *do–mi–so* or *mi–re–do* and attach syllables to the sound of these patterns as easily as they sing nonsense words to songs. The sound of the syllable invites a good tone quality and gives a more concrete identification with the actual pitch being sung than the more neutral 'loo.' Syllables also help to affirm the sound of a particular pattern in any key. For example, the *do–mi–so* pattern sung in the keys of C, F, or G, always will sound like 'do mi so.'

Ear-training exercises are always accompanied by movement, gesture or conducting. Movement helps the ears, eyes and mind 'attend' more closely to the task – actually, the movement can mirror the sound being sung. It can reinforce the timing, the flow or line of phrasing and the dynamics. Students are also alert to details of expression when they are so involved. Sometimes the term 'solfège-rythmique' is used for this experience of integrating singing and moving. Choral directors have found that incorporating solfège-rythmique techniques into their rehearsals will result in renewed vitality in the singing, more alert minds, ears and bodies, and thus a more musically sensitive performance.

What Are Dalcroze Solfège Games and Exercises?

The same lively and challenging exercises that one sees in eurhythmics can be seen in a solfège experience. Quick-reaction exercises of addition, omission, subtraction, variation, and 'change' games, canons, and improvisation all develop a keen sense of pitch and timing relationships. The most important result of these exercises is the development of an inner sense of hearing, and eventually the ability to hear what you see in notation and see what you hear. Anyone who has experienced these exercises can recall feelings of intense concentration, of frustration, triumph, and even laughter, in response to the challenges. Here are examples of three solfège exercises in which the students must sing from notation.

1. ■ Sing the following example with syllables.
   ■ When you hear the signal 'Hopp,' continue singing but twice as fast. When you hear 'back,' return to the original tempo.

2. ■ Sing the same example but with a different meter signature for each measure – in this order:

3. ■ Sing the example but change the first note in each measure to a half note. For example:

What Did Dalcroze Mean by 'Inner Hearing'?

The idea of 'inner hearing' began in harmony classes when Dalcroze experimented with specially designed singing exercises which linked the ear, mind and voice in one avenue of communication. He recognized a connection between the ear and voice by observing that there was a muscular sensation in the back of the throat when one thinks a melody. This

13

led him to emphasize the use of the singing voice to help the students internalize the aural image of a musical sound. He spoke of this as 'inner hearing.' A student of mine once described this as hearing music in our 'thinking voice.' This is probably what you experienced when you looked at the two musical themes near the beginning of this chapter. 'Farandole' by Bizet and 'Simple Gifts' by Copland. Look at them again and hear them in your 'thinking voice.' Did you notice any physical sensation at all, as though you were singing them?

What Part Does Improvisation Play in the Approach?

Improvisation is an important part of the Dalcroze approach. It is a natural continuation of the ear-training and movement experiences. When Dalcroze noticed that his students were responding musically and at the same time discovering new sensations of sound and movement, he invited them to express musical ideas with their voices or at the piano. He recognized the piano as an important medium for improvisation because he viewed the movement of the fingers and hand as an extension of the movement of the body with music. He stressed the idea of simplicity and helped his students realize that even if only two pitches were used, a melody, rhythm and harmony would be implied. His students also improvised with other instruments as well as with movement.

Dalcroze thought that improvisation should be encouraged as a natural form of expression, very much like speaking. Unfortunately, many people have learned to think of it as a threatening experience, or something they 'couldn't possibly do!' Yet, they improvise all the time when they carry on a conversation, decide what to wear, plan their days, and so on. Except for the worlds of jazz musicians and fine church organists, improvisation is sadly neglected in today's world of music and music education. It is ironic to realize that improvising is such an inherent behavior in children. They learn so much on their own,

- by being curious,
- by exploring possibilities,
- by trying something out, and
- by expressing what they feel or what they know.

A person who is curious is interested in exploring, is imaginative, is fascinated by creating in a medium such as drawing, painting, music, design, or writing. Why is so much emphasis placed on creativity, exploration and self-expression in many fields, when in music, except with very young children, there seems to be time only to imitate (and imitate exactly) that which has been created before – the written notation including the given expression marks?

Teachers with some courage and determination are trying simple keyboard improvisation in their own music teaching. They are generally more comfortable using percussion and Orff barred instruments than the piano, but even those instruments could be better used in the service of improvisation. As part of the learning process, all students should be encouraged to improvise on various instruments, the piano and the voice, as well as with movement.

Here are three sample improvisation ideas which might be used in a classroom situation:

14

1 At the piano, choose an interval of a second and improvise a tune called 'Popcorn.'
2 With a partner, improvise a movement sequence (without music) which demonstrates
   staccato and legato.
3 Sing this phrase and then improvise an answer:

Students should be given examples or suggestions in preparation for the task of improvising. They need opportunities to explore possibilities before trying to improvise their musical ideas. It is actually the doing or the experience of spontaneously creating rather than the product that matters here. The fact that the students are using their imaginations, their musical knowledge and skills, and that they are expressing their own thoughts and feelings is what is most important.

Those persons who are teaching Dalcroze classes are improvising all the time. Somewhere along the way they had to develop their own improvisation skills. Can someone who is bound to written notation learn to improvise? It is definitely possible for teachers wishing to use Dalcroze techniques in the classroom to develop some interesting original musical ideas to use in their teaching. The guidance on keyboard improvisation in Appendix A should be of help to beginners.

Teachers who are studying the Dalcroze approach practice improvisation with a purpose in mind. Not only must they develop their own creative ideas but they must explore a wide variety of musical materials such as modes, clusters, harmonic progressions, styles of music, unusual scales, and so on. All practice improvising and some keep a notebook of musical ideas, such as melodic and rhythmic motives and harmonic progressions.

Why is improvisation such an important part of Dalcroze training? Because student improvisation can:

● help the student synthesize what has been learned from an experience;
● demonstrate what the student has learned or understands;
● motivate students to want to express musical ideas of their own;
● stimulate the students' powers of concentration and listening;
● stretch students' imagination and exercise their musical thinking;
● bring about a sense of accomplishment and satisfaction to the one who is improvising.

It seems clear that the improviser becomes a better listener, interpreter, performer and certainly understands more about music. Dalcroze added a further dimension when he noted that 'He who is able to express himself succeeds all the sooner in expressing the feelings of others.'[2]

In summary, this chapter has attempted to introduce more specifically the exercises, aims and techniques used in the Dalcroze approach which includes eurhythmics, solfège or ear training and improvisation. Because of the nature of this book, most of the emphasis has been given to eurhythmics. Careful consideration of all three parts of the approach will reveal that they are not three separate subjects for study but three avenues of expression with many interrelating possibilities. In fact, in many instances, the term 'eurhythmics' implies a study of music which involves the student in movement, solfège or ear training and improvisation. Eurhythmics in the elementary music class is the focus of the remaining chapters of this book; however, solfège and improvisation suggestions will also be included.

3. Eurhythmics in the Elementary Music Program

How are the ideas and teaching techniques of Dalcroze the musician and teacher related to music training in the elementary school? Is it possible to incorporate eurhythmics, which is the core of his approach, into an elementary music program? How can you adapt Dalcroze techniques into your own music teaching?

This chapter is designed to answer those questions by helping you consider ways of using some of the traditional Dalcroze games, exercises and other teaching techniques, as described in Chapter Two, in your music lessons. I would like to share with you some of the ways that I have found to incorporate eurhythmics in a limited space and/or with a large and exceedingly active group. This chapter also includes suggestions and guidelines for planning and initiating these experiences. You may wonder why these suggestions and techniques appear in this chapter rather than with the experiences outlined in Part Two. I hope that this chapter will serve as an introduction to many useful ideas that can be used at any level of music teaching. Rather than explain a technique each time it appears in Part Two, it will be assumed that you already understand it and can adapt it to particular situations.

A Circle of Involvement Leads to Music Literacy

Many of you would probably agree that our goals for teaching music in the elementary school have been formulated on the premise that the students' involvement in music throughout their lives will probably be either as listeners or performers of music. A few especially talented ones may become professional musicians; some will enjoy music as amateur performers. We hope that some will be interested in joining community performing groups. We also hope that some will become enthusiastic supporters of cultural and ethnic music organizations. We need to consider the possibility of future involvement in music for all students in our planning. Therefore, our lessons must include opportunities for each student to

● enjoy music through listening, enhanced with perception and understanding;
● express ideas and feelings in singing, in moving and in playing instruments; and
● become familiar with examples of music from various times, places and people.

A well-planned, goal-oriented music program in the elementary school should lead to some degree of music literacy. What does literacy actually mean? Webster's dictionary states that a literate person is one who is educated, is able to read and write, and is versed in literature and creative writing. Doesn't music literacy imply the same thing, with music as the subject matter?

The following figure, especially adaptable to elementary school students, illustrates the continuing circle of activities and involvement which lead to music literacy.

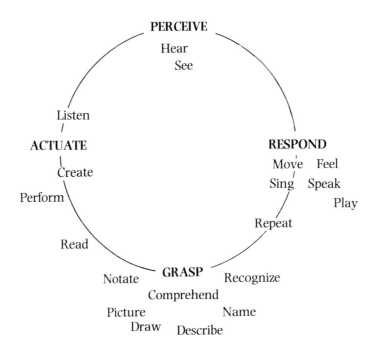

All music learning begins with the *perceiving* or *hearing* of sound, then as the student *responds* in some way, the mind begins to *grasp* bits of understanding and the student is ready to *actuate*, or *create* his own music either by *performing*, *improvising* or *composing*. The satisfaction enjoyed through performing or creating music can cause the student to listen with a keener ear. At that point the learning continues around the circle again. The activities listed on this circle represent a sample of the variety and sequence of involvement needed to develop music literacy.

Why Include Eurhythmics in the Music Lesson?

Eurhythmics experiences in the elementary classroom relate to all of the activities around the circle. Students will hear sounds and music and see them translated into movement in space; they can draw the movement in the air or on paper. As students step and clap quarter, eighth or half notes on command, they experience the relationship of timing between the three note values and should observe a change in the size of their movements. As they continue to develop this sense of relationship they can improvise music for their classmates to move. Or they can listen to a composition which reflects one or all of the note values, and then create a movement sequence using the three durations of notes. The 'Troika Song,' to a tune from *Lieutenant Kije* suite by Prokofiev, is a good opportunity for this activity. Students can discover the quarter-, eighth- and half-note rhythms and create a movement sequence to be performed with the music.

Troika

Music: Sergei Prokofiev
Words added by: Phyllis Stycos

Music, like any other art form, stimulates a response that is instinctive and personal. Consider your own response to a watercolor painting of an English garden, to a strikingly tall building mostly of glass, or to a lively Russian dance tune. Your response could be intellectual, emotional or even physical. With children and music, the initial response is usually physical. Children move naturally. We want them to be eager and curious learners, and at the same time we must recognize their innate need to be active. The challenge for the teacher is to channel their energy in the right place at the right time. We must not underestimate the children's natural tendency and need to move.

Let's take a moment more to think about children. They instinctively respond to something that they hear, see, touch, taste, smell or feel. Their response connects thoughts, imagination and feelings – the real beginnings of learning. That wonderful curiosity of children is activated and they are motivated, eager and ready to learn. In a classroom situation, the physical response is often stifled for lack of space or time and because of the need to 'keep the students under control.' This is often realistically true but it is a shame – especially in the music classroom where emotions and feelings run high. The natural, spontaneous response, if encouraged, can be a catalyst for learning.

It is the students who demonstrate the need for and the importance of Dalcroze eurhythmics as a vital way of learning music. Two main premises emerge:

1   Eurhythmics affords students opportunities to experience the discipline as well as the expressive qualities of music in a way that is indigenous to their style of learning – one of activity, curiosity, energy, and play.
2   Eurhythmics, embodying ear training and improvisation, can be planned to lead students through sequential and logical steps towards music literacy.

What Is Important in the Eurhythmics Experience?

Movement experiences in the classroom are often planned as enjoyable accompaniments to the music without a focus on specific objectives. In a eurhythmic experience, the simplest movements or gestures are meant to develop an awareness of any number of aspects of music such as tempo, dynamics, phrasing, repetition and contrast. Depending on the activity, these experiences will also develop other skills, such as physical, social and thinking skills. In eurhythmics, emphasis is placed on a keen sense of listening and a natural physical response which helps connect the ear that hears, the mind that recognizes and the body that expresses in movement. Any musical response comes from an inner sense – that sense of hearing in the mind, or the 'thinking voice,' and feeling in the body, the timing, flow and energy of the music. When this happens, the response reflects the essence of eurhythmics.

Another important aspect of the eurhythmics experience is the perception of a musical line. A study of eurhythmics reveals an awareness and understanding of a threefold action in movement which is mirrored in music. In the performance of music, each sound, like each physical gesture in movement, comprises a *preparation*, a *point of arrival* and a *resolution* or *follow-through*, which can become the *preparation* for the next sound. Awareness and attention to this in performance results in an acute sense of *line* in music. It is too sophisticated a concept for elementary school students, but the idea should be reflected in everything the teacher does in the classroom, for example, clapping a pattern, singing a song or playing an accompaniment on the piano. Since young children instinctively mirror what a teacher does, they will be performing with some sense of a musical line from their earliest times with you.

If you were to step or clap a phrase of rhythm, you would experience more than just sounding the notes in the right time. Each note is a part of the whole phrase; it is connected to the preceding note and the one that follows. When the mind and the ear are aware of this connection, the phrase is instinctively expressed with the whole body. The following three exercises should help you experience 'line' in music.

1   Perform the following two-measure example in each of the three ways described below.

    (*a*)   Sing the example at a moderate tempo and let the breath flow through the long notes.

    (*b*)   Move one arm as if painting the rhythm with a brush. Be sure to paint through the long notes.

    (*c*)   Clap the rhythm of the example and let your arms carry the sound through the long notes.

2   Clap the theme from *Finlandia* by Sibelius. Imagine that each sound is spurting from your hands like water being ejected from a fountain. On the long notes, let your hands show the water moving higher and higher.

(Winds)

mf *espress.*

3   Paint the *Finlandia* theme in the air (with an imaginary brush), being careful to paint through the duration of the long notes.

Notice that with each exercise, the amount of space involved in movement or gesture is determined by the timing and energy needed to perform the rhythm. The word energy refers to force or dynamics. If one of those examples were to be performed *allegro* (timing) or *fortissimo* (energy, dynamics), can you imagine the relationship of space needed for movement? The performance of a fine musician will reflect an inner physical sense of this relationship of timing, space and energy in the music. The realization of this relationship can be developed in the varied activities of a music program. These include:

- singing games, folk dances, and songs with movement;
- eurhythmics exercises and games;
- echoing or copycat experiences;
- singing or playing instruments;
- using balls or other props;
- gesturing the movement of music (the rhythm, beat, melody, line, etc);
- conducting; or
- creating movement to express a musical idea.

Planning and Managing the Eurhythmics Experience

When planning any type of music lesson, careful thought must be given to:

1   determining the specific objective for the lesson;
2   choosing the most appropriate experiences;
3   sequencing them wisely;
4   choosing the best musical examples;
5   planning for varied repetition (and contrast) in activities and music; and
6   involving students in a pleasurable experience.

When including eurhythmics in the music lesson, teachers find much thought and planning must be given to managing the group. I have given a great deal of attention to this section because I feel that initiating the eurhythmics experience must be a priority matter in planning.

1   There must be a good rapport between you and the students. For me, that means a mutual respect and expectation. The students respect you and expect to be engaged in an interesting musical experience in which they will learn. You respect them as creative and

thinking learners and expect them to be co-operative participants in the activities you have planned. This is my 'respect and expect' philosophy.

2   Plan experiences so as to balance students' feelings of success and challenge. In the early stages of eurhythmics, students of any age are often self-conscious and show it in their behavior, either by being silly, boisterous, or uncooperative. You will initially need to consider a balance between something easy and something challenging which will capture their attention; they need to feel successful as well as challenged.

3   Keep in mind the students' natural inclination to move. Try to incorporate their natural movements into the lesson. Besides students' spontaneous expressions of movement in music, work and play rhythms, the movements and sounds of machines, and other types of imagery are excellent sources for suggesting and encouraging movement. Keep in mind the use of speech, gesture and body language to express a thought or feeling. Often some aspect of music can be realized through speech or expressed in a gesture so that students connect the hearing–feeling–understanding threads.

'Hel-lo there!': ♪♩ ♩♩ versus 'Hi there!': ♩♩

4   Good preparation for each step in the experience will give students confidence to continue trying. Begin preparing the experience while they are responding co-operatively and purposefully – probably while they are still seated. They can simulate the timing, direction, and left-/right-side activity with their hands on their laps or desk tops, if necessary. This is similar to preparing an Orff accompaniment by patting the rhythm on thighs before playing it on an instrument.

5   When you are ready to have the class move in open space, be certain that

(a)   the space has been identified and they know how much or how little is available. For young children, if the room is quite large, it may be wise to block off part of it with chairs. Too much space can be as much of a problem as too little for some children.
(b)   they understand the task;
(c)   they understand the directions;
(d)   they understand all the parameters of the activity: when to begin, when to end, which direction to go, and the part of the music to which they will respond.

Let me caution you to keep your verbal directions to a minimum. They should automatically know to begin and end with the music, or the signal.

6   Each step of your plan should be thought of as a building block, starting with something easy or well known. Design the movement sequence so that each step is a variation or an extension of the previous one. Ask yourself, 'What do the students need to be able to do before they can do this?' Not only do the steps need to be sequenced carefully, but the musical examples must also be chosen carefully. This is why improvisation by the teacher is so important. It can focus students' ears on specifics in the music.

7 Consistency in many aspects of the eurhythmics lesson will result in students feeling confident and comfortable in it, especially when working in a large space. A quick-reaction game is a good beginning experience and will alert minds, ears and bodies and prepare the class for what will be developed in the lesson. A musical game, folk dance, or even structured or free movement with a well-known piece of music can be an enjoyable culminating activity for the end of the lesson. It can help summarize the learning experience.

8 Use consistent signals, appropriate to the age level, which will help when students become overly excited or lose self-control. For example, with young children, a prop such as a clown's face painted on both sides of a card and held up high can signal the children to freeze. It keeps their eyes on you, the teacher, rather than other children in the room. Use musical signals whenever possible: a rhythmic, melodic or harmonic signal. Use some consistency in voiced signals, such as 'Change,' 'Walk,' 'Begin,' or signals that Dalcroze used, 'Hopp,' or 'Heep.' There is a skill to giving signals with your voice. It helps to practice this skill. Suppose you asked the class to change their walking to running at your signal 'Change.' The timing of the signal on the beat prior to the change and even the tone of your voice must be sufficiently rhythmical to ensure the new response. The invitation is an anacrusis, the pick-up or breath before the downbeat of the change. Try this example and imagine yourself as the leader giving the signal and the student moving or clapping.

9 Alternating periods of structured and creative movement will help to keep students on task. Specific directives for the movement will keep them alert and inspire confidence in knowing what you are expecting them to do. Sometimes you can wake up a lethargic or inattentive class with a surprise or deceptive signal. Even with adults, this can result in laughter which relaxes or alerts the students and brings them back to task. Here is an example to illustrate the point. If fifth graders are asked to walk forward on the tonic chord and backward on the dominant chord, set up a pattern of change at the beginning of each measure and then, suddenly, break your pattern and change the chord at an unpredictable place. Watch their expressions as they try to figure out what happened and try to anticipate when you will change next.

10 Clear and concise instructions, each one resulting in an immediate response, seem more successful than a long string of instructions which no-one can remember. This is especially true if students are asked to stand before they know the instructions. When they are on their feet, they want to do something, not stand quietly and listen to the teacher talk.

11 Before introducing new music to the class, you should think about the timing (such as tempo and note values) and the energy (dynamics) of the music. Consider any characteristic tonal patterns. Ask yourself what might be most obvious to the students and what could be explored or experienced through movement. Identify the element, concept or aspect of

23

the music you want to highlight and then make a list of a variety of possible activities before you design your plan. Can they dance it with their fingers on a desk or floor? Can they draw it in the air? Can they conduct it? Can they mirror it in movement with a partner? Would a prop help to encourage a good feel for the movement – something like a ball, a light rhythm stick, even an instrument held in the hand?

12 Repetition without purpose doesn't necessarily accomplish much and can lead to boredom. However, repetition of any eurhythmics experience is needed in order for students to become comfortable with the movement. Out of 'the comfort zone' comes a mental awareness and recognition of what is happening. It is important that variations are present in repeated experiences. For instance, if the students are learning to recognize the difference between a $\frac{2}{4}$ meter and a $\frac{2}{4}$· meter, they should experience examples in different tempos, with different dynamics and articulation in completely different settings, for example, a song, a folk dance or a piano composition. Students should understand that some experiences, especially those that develop skills, need to be repeated, improved, refined, and mastered.

13 Music can be the best classroom manager! If the experience is based on listening and responding, then whether the activity is highly structured or creative, it happens within the time and space of the music. The music is also a manager because whatever the students are doing should reflect some part of that music and therefore the activity has purpose and meaning.

14 Last of all – but most important – let the music do the teaching! Too often we teachers get in the way of the students' personal experiences with the music. We must be careful to monitor our talking, pointing, gesturing, motioning and other teacher behavior which distracts students. I have found that an attitude of sharing my knowledge, enthusiasm and enjoyment of the music and then 'stepping back,' so to speak, and letting the students experience the music, is the most effective motivation for their involvement.

What about Space for Eurhythmics?

The amount of space usually determines the type and extent of the movement. Dalcroze eurhythmics is meant to be experienced with the whole body moving freely in open space. The opportunity to express the elements, character and nuances of music in a free and unrestricted expanse of space is what makes eurhythmics so vital to developing musicianship. When that happens, a student is likely to discover an ability to hear, feel and recognize much that is happening in the music. Exemplary eurhythmics programs are rarely possible in elementary schools because of space limitations, but there are several ways of solving space problems and planning activities which allow students to gain as much as possible from the movement experience. Let's begin with the space we know we have. In the primary grades, if the music is taught in the classroom rather than in a music room, there may be more space for movement than in an upper grade classroom where there are moveable desks and maybe tables and chairs, globes, charts and a reading center. In those classrooms, unless some rearranging is done, the children can move while sitting, standing or find a spot where they can move with a partner or in a small group. I have actually seen some excellent ball games with whole classes standing in a circle around the desks in a crowded classroom. Try challenging your students to explore space around and above them, or ask them to 'glue' their feet to the floor and use only the immediate space available.

When the music lesson is taught in the classroom, in spite of much rearranging of desks and tables, the space will seem confining to students who hear music that is running, skipping, circling, falling, syncopated, strongly accented, legato or staccato. The movements of walking and swinging arms are the beginnings of eurhythmics; when the space does not permit these natural movement responses it is difficult to motivate any kind of movement. All is not lost, however. Sometimes students find creative ways to use the available space. Here are a few suggestions to keep in mind:

- Ask a few students move at a time in the space allowed.
- Challenge the students who are sitting and waiting a turn to find their own ways to solve the same problem – perhaps with a partner.
- Invite students to move forward and backward in the space between the desks or tables.
- Ask the students to arrange desks or tables closer to the center of the room so they can move around them. Most students enjoy the responsibility and challenge of accomplishing this in record time, with the least amount of confusion. This could be a procedure for each class to learn through practice.
- If you have a large music room, ask students for before-school help to move chairs so that your lessons on those days can be based on eurhythmics in an open and comfortable space.
- Some music teachers have worked out schedules with other teachers who use the gym or multi-purpose room so that a music class can use that space occasionally. This would probably allow only minimal time for the kind of eurhythmics experiences you would like to include in the music lessons; however, it is better than nothing. To really see results, the experiences should be an on-going and integral part of the total program in music. In Part Two of this book, there are experiences for a variety of spatial areas; you are encouraged to be imaginative in adapting these experiences to the space you have available.
- Students enjoy solving problems, so from the beginning, challenge them to find their own ways to move with the music in the space available. I believe that you will enjoy their amazing creativity. Suggest things that cause their movement to look and feel as though they are in a large, open space.
- **Imagine that you are running with lots of energy.**
- **Lift your knees high!**
- **Let me hear a loud, silent clap!**

I am well aware of the space problems for the experiences suggested in this book and so I conclude this section by reminding you that it is the inner sense of movement and hearing which you want students to experience and the quality of the movement is more important than the expanse or quantity of movement.

Moving in a Circle

Let's think for a moment about students moving in a circle. This is often a teacher's first thought when asking young children to step the beat of the music. Moving in a circle for initial beat experiences is a wise choice. The circle gives a sense of security and sets boundaries or limitations. I usually start elementary school students in circles, even sit-down circles, but as soon as possible I plan ways to free them from the circle, even if it is only for part of the exercise or musical example. The circle does help to control a group but trying to have a large group of students moving in a constricted space does not result in the most successful eurhythmics experiences. If they are asked to walk a steady beat with the music, you might think that a circle would be appropriate; however, the stride of one child as compared to another is probably different. Also, just seeing another person directly in front of you in the circle impedes your own individual movement sense and can distract you from the music. I often see a student trying to keep from stepping on Johnny's shoes in front of him (or else, making every effort to do just that!).

When you think your students are ready to move independently and away from a circle, plan an experience which will cause them to break the circle at a specified point in the music or at a signal, and return at the end or at another signal. The two typical eurhythmics exercises which follow illustrate this activity. The first is for young children and the second version is for older students.

1   Moving out of the circle for eight counts. With a click of the fingers, start the class walking in a circle around the room.
    ■   **When I say 'Go,' walk eight steps away from the circle as though you are going on an errand. Be back in your spot on the eighth step to continue walking in the circle.**

2   For an older class that still needs to work in a circle, change the commands slightly:
    ■   **Step quarter notes. When I say 'Eighth,' step eight eighth notes away from the circle but be back in the circle ready to continue stepping quarters. If I say 'Half,' step eight half notes out of the circle and then be back, ready to step quarters again.**

The sequence of movement might be something like the following:

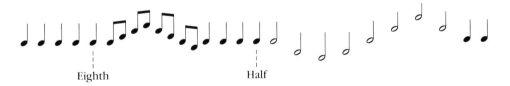

Eighth   Half

Ever since satellites and space modules began circling the earth, students have enjoyed and understood what was meant by
■   **Move in your own orbit around the room.**

If you can encourage them to move 'with the traffic' but without following anyone, you will notice that they concentrate more on the lesson and on the music. Also, the movement is much more individualized and natural. Students will find a great deal of satisfaction in moving freely around the room, responding to the music and the signals in your exercises. It may be a wonderful opportunity for them to develop self discipline as well as their individual listening skills. The vivid physical image that remains from the experience can, then, be used to great advantage in further developing their understanding and performance skills.

Variations on Clapping

Clapping seems to be the most common movement response in a music class; nevertheless, I have found that too often the clapping is more like applause than an expression of the music being heard or performed. Using a variety of ways to clap adds a creative dimension to your lessons. In addition, the variations can reflect the nuances in the music. Students will be responding with more musical sensitivity than if the clapping were all the same.

First of all, your clapping should reflect the timing, precision and nuances of the written or heard sounds. Young children tend to imitate the teacher and therefore, if you begin in the kindergarten to show the duration of sounds in your clapping, the children will mirror you until it gradually becomes automatic.

There is a variety of ways to use the hands, fists and fingers to achieve different sounds and to feel physical gestures of accented versus unaccented sounds, divisions of the beat, or changes in rhythmic units, such as ♫ and ♩♪ . For instance:

(a)   With only one or two fingers of one hand, tap into the other palm.
(b)   Strike a fist into the open palm on accents or to achieve a dramatic effect:

(c)   Sweep one palm against the other on long notes.
(d)   Lightly, brush the back of the fingertips of one hand against the fingers of the other hand to feel an anacrusis (or pick-up), then clap the rest of the pattern as usual. For example:

(e)   Alternate hands on each measure: the left hand claps into the right hand on measure one; the right hand claps into the left hand on measure two. Continue alternating hands from one measure to the next.
(f)   To feel an accent, slap the fingers of one hand against the thumb joint of the other hand, in the direction of the opposite shoulder. For instance, if the left hand slaps the right thumb joint, it will pull back towards the right shoulder. This feels a little like the cowboy slapping his thighs as he yells, 'Giddy-up!' This slap can be used effectively on 'pop' in the song 'Pop Goes the Weasel.'

Pop Goes the Weasel

2

C   G7   C   G7   C

1. All   a-round the   cob - blers bench,   Mon - key chased the   wea - sel,
(2.) paint - er needs a   lad-der and brush, The   art - ist needs an   ea - sel,

C   G7   C   F   G7   C

Mon - key thought 'twas   all___ in   fun,   Pop   goes   the   wea - sel.
Danc - ers   need   a   fid - dler's tune,   Pop   goes   the   wea - sel.

D7   G   D7   G

Pen - ny   for   a   spool_ of thread,   Pen - ny   for   a   nee - dle,
I've   no time   to   wait or   to sigh. No   pa-tience to wait   till by and   by,

Dm   G7   C

That's the way   the   mon - ey goes,   Pop   goes   the   wea - sel. 2. The
Kiss   me quick   I'm   off, good-bye,   Pop   goes   the   wea - sel.

The simplest clapping can become more alive and expressive when students are standing instead of sitting. It is much easier to show measures or phrases while standing and clapping. It helps to ask the students to 'send it' or 'sell it' to a partner. I remember the first time I gave this direction to a group. The students were improvising on percussion instruments as I was improvising on the piano. They were so timid and circumspect in their responses that I asked them to pretend they were in a store window and I was outside considering buying one of the instruments. Each time I looked at them (or cued them) they were to try to 'sell' their instrument to me by showing off its unique musical possibilities. What a difference it made in their playing and in the sound of the instruments! The students heard the difference, immediately. Their bodies, facial expressions and their music became much more interesting and alive as they tried to sell the instrument to me. A clapping pattern which you have notated on the chalkboard is hardly as interesting an activity when compared with pretending that you are giving it or selling it to another person. This idea truly results in a more sensitive and artistic performance of music, whether one is clapping, playing an ostinato, singing a folk song, or performing music in any way.

If students are asked to clap something they hear in the music, their attention should be focused on that particular detail. Many different aspects of music can be expressed by adding variety to the clapping. When performed in a limited space, the clapping can even show the contour of a melody, or the beginning and ending of phrases. Besides the beat or a rhythm pattern, you might ask your students to clap any of the following, which represent only a sampling of the possibilities:

- tempo and dynamics;
- note values, demonstrating the duration of the notes;
- accents or groupings of pulses;
- beats organized into measures – clapping from left to right as if reading music;
- patterns and phrases which may or may not include an anacrusis but will include cruses (accents).

Here is a variation on clapping which can be used with older students to help them feel the division of a beat – duple or triple. It is difficult to describe and should be taught through demonstration. For lack of a better term, call it a 'wrist-tip.' To feel the beat of music, 'bump' the wrists of both hands together with an outward motion as if tossing a balloon up and away. It should feel like a gentle 'bump.' Then, to feel the division of the beat, rebound the fingertips together on each beat division. For example: ♩♪♪ = Wrist–tip–tip (W T T)

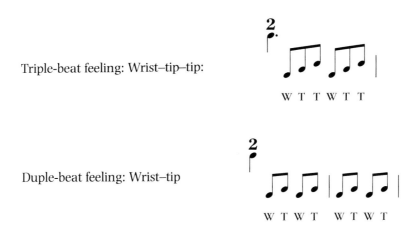

Triple-beat feeling: Wrist–tip–tip:

W T T W T T

Duple-beat feeling: Wrist–tip

W T W T   W T W T

A popular partner activity is the 'paddy-cake.' We all think of 'paddy-cake' as something to do with a young child but this activity can be used for a simple ear-training exercise as well as for an advanced experience. Partners face each other with both hands held up, ready to 'feed' a musical idea with one hand (tap it out) and 'receive' another musical idea in the other hand. An example: Partner A listens for music played in the treble range and taps it into Partner B's right hand. Partner B listens for the bass range and taps it into Partner A's right hand. This means that each partner is only listening for one thing but is receiving (feeling) something else. Here is an example of a piano improvisation using treble and bass registers so that the students can easily distinguish their parts:

Combining claps with other sounds and motions allows many more possibilities for varying the simplest response. Patterns of stamps, patschen, claps and snaps which are used so effectively by Orff teachers can certainly be used to an advantage in Dalcroze experiences. These may be anything from a simple stamp–clap to a rather complicated pattern which takes concentration, co-ordination and memory to master. Students will enjoy exploring and creating new ways to use these movements in order to express the music they are studying. A reminder however: a stamp of the foot, a pat of hands on the knees, a snap of the fingers or a clap of the hands does not express the duration of a note value. It only expresses the attack of the note, placing it in time. With some attention paid to the music, a stamp can become a slide on a half note; likewise, the hands can slide across the thighs through long notes. If a snap or clap is suggested for a long note, the duration of the note should be shown and felt through a wide circular motion of the hands and arms.

I hope that this brief overview of Dalcroze eurhythmics experiences and techniques suggests new ways to teach musical objectives with all of your students. Perhaps you already have imagined ways to adapt some of these ideas to your own teaching.

Part Two:
Experiences and Guidelines

4. Experiences in the Primary Grades

The easiest and most logical way to begin to use eurhythmics with young children is with the motions and actions suggested in songs. When children's imagination is engaged the words and/or the music will evoke an instinctive response in gesture or movement. As they learn to listen with a keener ear, they will be more perceptive to the timing and dynamics of the music. Soon other aspects of the song such as phrasing, rhythm and tonal patterns, repeating and contrasting ideas and melody direction will become apparent and can be expressed and further explored with movement and singing.

This chapter includes sample activities and music which will help children focus on what they hear in music. These eurhythmics experiences will awaken physical and mental images which can be the basis for all musical skill development and understanding. An important premise behind every activity in this book is that before students can develop any understanding or concept about music, they must first experience it aurally and physically, explore it in different guises and then recognize it as something familiar.

Exploring Movement

The movement in a eurhythmics experience is one that grows out of the imagination, feelings, awareness and basic physical skills of the student. At first the children will need to feel comfortable moving expressively. They will need opportunities to explore the space available for movement and the possibilities for using the whole body to creatively express the idea or the music. These first few experiences can be used to stimulate the imagination and motivate primary children to move freely.

1   *Experiencing different ways of walking.*

Don't use music for this experience. The children need to be completely absorbed in your story and they need to be free to determine their own tempo and energy for walking. Tell the story with expression, and pause after each statement to give them time to respond.

- ■ **Let's take a walk.**
- ■ **We could walk fast, or we could walk slow. There's no hurry.**
- ■ **Sometimes it's fun to walk zigzag.**
- ■ **Can you walk sideways?**
- ■ **Backwards?**
- ■ **How do you walk in deep snow?**
- ■ **On ice?**
- ■ **In mud?**
- ■ **Walk in your bare feet. Ooh, the sidewalk's hot.**

- There! It's better here in the cool green grass.
- Walk on cotton balls;
- On pebbles. Oh, you're limping! You must have stepped on a sharp stone!
- It must be better now.
- Can you walk like a robot?
- Walk on the moon! You look like a ghost walking on air.
- Thump!
- Why look here! You're back home again.

2   Imagining movement in pictures.

Suggest to the class that you have a picture in your living room of a farm.

- It's a wonderful picture with animals, trees and farm machinery – so many things that you might see on a farm. Wouldn't it be fun to have a knob to turn to make everything in the picture start moving? Show me what you might see moving in the picture.

The first time I tried this I couldn't believe the result. When I clapped my hands, the picture froze again. I was so fascinated by that first attempt that I tried a city picture, and later a seaside and a factory picture. Once, when I suggested that the farm picture also had sound, I got into trouble; the result was a clamor of barnyard sounds – unrelated to movement. I quickly clapped my hands to 'turn the sound off' and then changed the subject. Usually the children are delighted to add vocal and/or instrumental accompaniment to these stories, but this particular experience was to motivate the movement.

3   Telling a story in movement.

Children love to act out stories improvised by the teacher. The music that you improvise to accompany your story can motivate the children to move expressively. Children like to have these stories repeated and as you watch their movement and listen to their spontaneous suggestions, the story becomes more and more detailed. I have sometimes encouraged vocal and instrumental sound accompaniments with these stories and some children even want to improvise sounds on the piano. The main purpose of the story, however, is to encourage the children to reflect the imagination of the storyteller and the accompanying music in movement. The story should invite a variety of movement qualities such as: quick, heavy, plodding, sliding, falling, rising and fluttering. The accompanying music should encourage those responses. Watch the children carefully and try to duplicate the movement of individuals. Don't be surprised if, at first, the children respond to the story and ignore your music; later, let your music do most of the storytelling.

- Let's go for a walk.   (*Insert walking music*)
- My, isn't it a lovely day.
- Look up at those beautiful leaves!   (*High, fluttering*)
- But look at all these that have fallen.   (*Falling, fluttering*)
- Swish, swish   (*Brush hands across black keys, middle register*)
- Let's go through that pile of leaves?   (*More excited sound*)

34

■ I like to jump in piles of leaves	(*Accented chords for jumping*)
■ Toss them high in the air	(*Quick arpeggios, low to high*)
■ Wait!	(*Silence, then, one soft, staccato sound*)
■ Do I feel a raindrop?	(*Then another, and another*)
■ Yes, its raining.	(*Many soft, falling staccato sounds*)
■ And it's beginning to rain harder.	(*Continue, faster*)
■ We'd better go back.	
■ Oops! The walk is muddy.	(*Pedal: thicker and heavier chords*)
■ I'm sliding!	(*Short glissando*)
■ Uh oh! My feet are sticking in the mud!	(*Settle on one slow, thick and heavy repeated chord*)
■ There! That's better.	(*Snap free from that repeated chord and begin the walking*)
■ I'm out of it.	
■ But look at that big puddle.	(*Tremolo on a full, low chord*)
■ Guess I'll have to jump over it.	(*Continue*)
■ Here I go! One, two, three!	(*Three chords; third, accented*)
■ There!	(*Silence – a sigh*)
■ Is the rain stopping?	(*Less and less rain falling*)
■ And it's really getting hot and sticky!	(*Ritard; labored walk*)
■ I certainly am tired. Glad I'm almost home!	(*Continue*)
■ Better tiptoe in so nobody sees how wet I am!	(*Light, delicate*)

4   *Expressing music with fingers, hands and arms.*

Using 'The Aquarium' from *Carnival of the Animals* by Saint-Saëns, let the children first talk abut an aquarium; how the fish move and what else might be seen moving in the tank (bubbles, seaweed, snails). As the class listens to the music, let your hand follow the movement of the fish. Show the children how they can squeeze one hand in an elongated shape to look like a fish ⌁ with the fingers and thumb pinched tightly together. Let your fingers imitate the trickling and descending melody when the food floats down to the bottom of the tank or the rising bubbles (near the end of the composition). Children become very absorbed in this activity and will listen closely and respond creatively to the music. During a lesson in one of my classes, a small group of about six children grouped themselves together on the floor and, without talking or planning, created a giant aquarium. As they began to respond to each other's hand movements, some of them were weaving their 'fish' in, out and around each other's 'fish.'

Sound and Silence; Beginning and Ending

It seems to me that there are many experiences in classroom music when children participate just by following along. There is so much happening in the music at one time that they can't really focus on any specifics. My awareness of this fact and the solution I found to the problem has made the biggest difference in my teaching since my study of the Dalcroze approach. These first experiences in sound and silence seem very simple, but the aim is to draw children's ears to sound and their minds to another one of their 'loves' – movement.

1   *Drawing sound in the air.*

- **Pick up a magic pencil** (*imaginary*)**. Listen; whatever you hear, draw it with your magic pencil high in the air.**

Use a variety of vocal sounds: clicks, whistles, buzzing and humming, with many beginnings and endings and silences in between. When you see that the children are beginning to hear other aspects of the sound (direction, tempo changes, articulation, dynamics, and so on), focus on that one aspect for several examples to give them time and opportunity to develop further awareness.

2   *Moving like parts of a machine; starting and stopping.*

This can be done either sitting or standing.
- **Take a partner and link up in some way with arms, fingers or feet, so that you are two parts of a machine.**
- **How would your machine move with this music? Let the music turn the machine on. Listen carefully.**

Improvise machine-like rhythms or sounds on an instrument. I use the piano, but you can use percussion instruments. Continue each example for a few seconds; stop, pause, then begin another example. In another lesson, tempo changes can be added. Try these examples first, extend them and try some of your own.

Remember to use extremes in timing, accentuation, dynamics and texture. The objective is starting and stopping, but when your students begin to respond to other aspects of the music, encourage them and label what they are doing, for instance,

- **That music certainly made your machines go faster.**

Many years ago, I had a small but obstreperous group of six-year-olds in a eurhythmics class. For many of the experiences planned for that class, I purposely included signals which would give them an opportunity to release their energy and then other signals which would bring their attention around to the music again. For this machine game, I included in my improvisation a gradual rush of sound or slowing down of sound to signal a breakdown of the machine. They loved, it, especially when they decided to collapse on the floor in gales of laughter. However hysterical they thought that was, I never interrupted my improvisation but paused a second and then played something that suggested a repairman had come to fix the machine. I played a tap here, a twist there, and a slow winding up of the machine again. They recognized exactly what I was doing and responded as I had hoped. I must say that they had fun, but I was rewarded to see how the music could bring them back to a perceptive and appropriate response.

3 *Listening and anticipating sound and silence in music.*

- **Find a spot in the room to call 'home'.**
- **Take a walk with the music. Along the way you will have to cross some streets so listen for the lights. You will know when you are at a crossing when you hear this (*a quick, high-pitched interval of a second*). If the music stops, the light will be red. If the music holds on one pitch, the light will be yellow. You will know when the light is green. Are you ready?**

Let them decide what they should do when the light is yellow. The music for this experience can be a simple melody of all quarter notes, something like the example given below. If you are not sure of the children's walking tempo, ask one or two of them to show you how they would walk to a friend's house. Then, use that tempo for your musical examples. This is why improvising is so important. If you must use a recording, be sure that the music suggests walking and the tempo is appropriate for the children of their age. Also, be sure that the volume can be manipulated quickly and easily so that you can stop and start the music precisely. Here is the keyboard example. A quarter-note ostinato of F–C–D–C would be appropriate for the left hand.

4 *Listening and anticipating the length of a song.*

This idea is similar to the previous exercise. Ask the children to take a walk with a song you will sing, or they can sing.

- **See if you can be back home on the last note of the song!**

One suggestion for the song might be 'Go Round and Round the Village,' but with words changed slightly (in parentheses) to give them a better feel for the quarter-note walking tempo.

Go Round and Round the Village

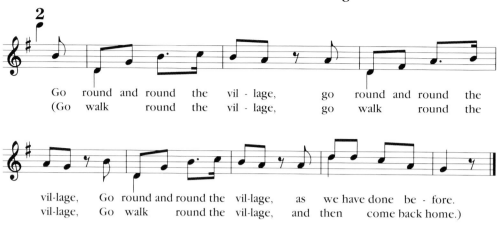

Go round and round the vil-lage, go round and round the
(Go walk round the vil-lage, go walk round the

vil-lage, Go round and round the vil-lage, as we have done be - fore.
vil-lage, Go walk round the vil-lage, and then come back home.)

5 *Singing, moving, and responding to signals – all at the same time.*

For this activity, use a song that the children know and can sing by memory. 'Mighty Pretty Motion' is rhythmical and encourages spirited movement. Suggest that the children rake leaves or sweep the walk on a fall day as they sing this song.

■ **Sometimes people sing to help them move in rhythm when they are working.**

Mighty Pretty Motion

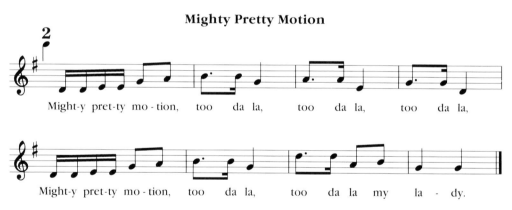

Might-y pret-ty mo - tion, too da la, too da la, too da la,

Might-y pret-ty mo - tion, too da la, too da la my la - dy.

■ **Sometimes people need to stop and rest when they are working. Sing the song again and when you hear the woodblock stop working but keep on singing. When you hear the woodblock again, go back to working.**

The children will have to listen carefully to respond to this quick-reaction exercise.

Timing, Beat and Tempo

These are the main elements of movement in music and the development of skill in recognizing and responding to these essential aspects of music must not be rushed or overlooked. The following exercises are mostly quick-reaction games to develop young children's skill in responding sensitively to the timing, beat and tempo aspects of music.

1 *Watching the movement of a pendulum.*

Tie something with a little weight to the end of a string – like a key or a ring. Start the pendulum swinging. You may have to manipulate it slightly so that it continues at the same tempo. Have the children stand and swing their arms freely to imitate the pendulum.

■ **Clap when it touches each side.**

Ask them to speak with it:

■ **Swing, swing.**

Try starting the pendulum at different tempos.

2 *Creating a swinging pendulum with a partner.*

■ **Take a partner and make a pendulum with your partner's hands. Let your pendulum swing from side to side.**

The children should stand with feet slightly apart and swing their arms on the ♩. beat. Play or sing this song.

Hickory Dickory Dock

3 *Responding to the timing in a singing game.*

For our purposes, timing refers to anything having to do with when, how long or how fast or slow. In the following two versions of 'Hickory Dickory Dock,' the children must attend to the following elements of timing:

● Begin and end exactly with the group.
● Sing and move in a steady tempo, with the rest of the group.
● Change the motions at the correct place in the song.
● Clap only once when the clock 'strikes one.'

These goals of responding to timing may seem too obvious, but they are important beginning steps in the study of rhythm and I believe that they should be identified. I designed the 'sit-down' version of this game as an initial experience for a lively class. After they had successfully accomplished that version, I introduced the second version which will be familiar to some of you. It was met with immediate success.

Version one: Hold up one arm, bent at the elbow so that the hand can swing from side to side at the wrist. Explain that this is like a grandfather clock.

Measures 1 and 2:   Swing the hand from side to side on the beat ♩.

Measures 3 and 4:   Let two fingers of the other hand (the mouse) run up the clock (arm), arriving at the top on the word 'clock.'

Measure 5:   Clap once on the word 'one.'

Measure 6:   Let the two fingers (mouse) run down the clock (the arm).

Measures 7 and 8:   Repeat the first two measures.

Version Two: Stand and face a partner.

Measures 1 and 2:   Partners hold hands to make a pendulum which swings from side to side on the ♩. beat.

Measures 3 and 4:   Partners exchange places using small running steps.

Measure 5:   All clap hands on 'one.'

Measure 6:   All run back to their original places.

Measures 7 and 8:   Repeat the first two measures.

4   *Watching and imitating the timing of a bouncing ball.*

As the children watch one child bounce and catch a ball, they can speak exactly what they are seeing, that is, 'bounce–catch.' Notice that it is not dribbling the ball. The movement should have a steady duple feeling of bounce–catch. Ask the children to let their voices follow the direction of the ball as it bounces down and then up again.

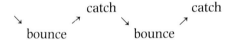

5   *Accompanying songs with work and play rhythms.*

Sing the song 'Sing, Sing Together,' with the words changed slightly ('Swing, Swing Together'). The tempo should be slow, with a strong accent so the children can imagine pushing a swing high up in the air. Push only on the first beat of the measure and then pull back on the secondary accent (on 'and'), ready to push on the crusis of the next measure. Notice the second verse suggested here.

Sing, Sing Together

Sing   sing   sing   sing.
Push   and   push   and   push   and   push   and

Here is a similar activity for the song 'Rig-a-Jig-Jig.' The children can pump up their bicycle tires for a ride in the park.

Rig-a-Jig-Jig

Rig - a - jig - jig and a - way we go,   a - way we go,   a - way we go.
Pump   and   pump   and   pump   and   pump   and

Rig - a - jig - jig and a - way we go,   Hi ho, hi ho,   Hi ho.____
Pump   and   pump   and   pump   and   pump and.

6   *Using small rhythm sticks to feel a steady beat.*

(Directions for making the sticks are included in Appendix B.) Students of all ages enjoy using these lightweight sticks to play the beat and/or rhythm, to learn to conduct, or to use them for special effects, such as a clock ticking. Here are two ways that I have used these sticks for experiencing a steady beat.

A   The children will walk the beat of a familiar song, for instance, 'Go Round and Round the Village,' while you play or sing it. As they walk, they will hold a stick in one hand and tap a beat into the palm of the other hand. For a quick-reaction change, when you stop playing or singing, they should interrupt their stepping and tap the stick on the floor. When the music begins again, they resume walking and tapping the stick into their hands. Later, for a quick-reaction change, signal a specific number of beats to be tapped on the floor and counted out loud. For instance, on the last beat of a measure, you might signal 'six' and the children count and tap six beats on the floor; then the song begins again with the initial activity.

B   This is a fun activity in which the children imagine the stick is a prop – a tool, or a toy. They must think of lots of things the stick could represent, for instance, a broom, hair brush, hammer, paint brush, spoon, golf club or umbrella. In small groups of six or eight children each, they listen to music that has a strong, obvious beat to it. One suggestion is 'March' from *Summer Day Suite* by Prokofiev. The first child holding the stick listens, and moves the prop in time with the beat of the music. On a signal from you, the stick is handed to the next child who begins moving it a different way – still on the beat. The children may want to call out guesses as to what the stick is supposed to be, but don't let them drown out the music.

The sound of these sticks is so insignificant that it doesn't detract from the music. Because of the size, the subtle nuances of accent, dynamics and articulation are easily controlled. The sticks are an extension of the students' arms and the movement seems more apt to come from an inner realization of what is happening in the music. Besides, students' attention is more on the stick, the activity and the music, than on themselves.

7   *Feeling a steady beat twice as fast and twice as low.*

It is important for children to feel a strong sense of steady beat while performing or hearing music, but in the beginning they tend to hear and move with the rhythm of the words – the part they are singing and enjoying. In many of the exercises in this book, children must concentrate on the steady beat. I have found that sometimes the beat of a song is perceived by the children to be faster or slower than my perception of it. They may hear it twice as fast or twice as slow. This can happen with students at any age. In my classes, we often explore the three possibilities: a comfortable walking tempo, a tempo that is twice as fast, and one that is twice as slow. After exploring the three possibilities, I can usually suggest that they find the most comfortable walk and as a group, they settle into a common tempo.

Here is one idea which I used to help a group feel the three tempos. Using the song 'Hot Cross Buns,' let the children imagine that they are preparing the dough for the buns.

Try each of the following steps continuously throughout the song. Much later, when they can read the three note values, ♩ , ♫ , 𝅗𝅥 , they can sing and do whichever motion you signal.

(*a*)   Pat the dough into a ball on the quarter-note beat
(*b*)   Pound the dough with the side of the hand on the eighth notes.
(*c*)   Knead the dough on half notes.

They could also beat the icing for the buns, by hand. Holding an imaginary bowl under one arm and a spoon in the other hand, beat the icing at a moderate quarter-note tempo ♩ . On a signal, they can beat the icing twice as fast ♫ ; then, as if resting, beat it twice as slow 𝅗𝅥 .

After starting the activity, I use the signals

■   **Fast,**
■   **Back,**
■   **Slow**

It is important that the children physically feel the difference in a movement that is twice as fast or twice as slow as the original. In all Dalcroze exercises signals must be given precisely and rhythmically, and for that reason Dalcroze teachers often use the signal

■ **Fast,**

meaning 'Change to twice as fast.'

■ **Back,**

meaning 'Go back to the original tempo,' and

■ **Slow**

meaning 'change to twice as slow.' In Chapter Six, some attention is given to the musical terms 'diminution' (twice as fast) and 'augmentation' (twice as slow). When using those terms with older students, I usually write the terms on the chalkboard and call out the corresponding letter.

A Augmentation
B Original
C Diminution

8 *Playing a game of timing and energy.*

In groups of five or six, children line up behind a leader. They listen to a musical example and the leader determines how to step the beat in character with the music. The music must suggest a way to move – feeling proud, happy, silly, sad, anxious, weak, or strong, for instance. The rest of the group follows. When the music stops, the followers freeze and (without missing a beat) begin to count from one to eight in the same tempo while the leader steps those eight beats to the back of the line. They can all give a hearty clap on the eighth count. When you play music for this game, try any of the following:

(*a*) short examples, improvised;
(*b*) simple piano music; or
(*c*) familiar songs played in various moods.

Whatever you play, be sure that you are expressing each example with a distinct beat and character. For example, 'Sandy Land' could be played in a fast, staccato tempo or in minor, at a slow, plodding tempo.

Sandy Land
A variation in diminution

Sandy Land
A variation in augmentation

9 *Passing a ball to develop a sense of timing and beat.*

There are many possibilities for using balls to develop musical skills and understandings. When a ball is bounced, caught, tossed or rolled, the person experiences the natural physical feeling of preparation, impulse and follow-through which is experienced in any natural gesture or movement. These three aspects of movement relate closely to the anacrusic, crusic and metacrusic gestures in a musical phrase.

Also, when we use a ball with music, we experience a relationship in the timing and energy of the motion, and the amount of space in which the ball travels. In musical terms, when one is playing, singing, or moving, the muscles of the body automatically determine the relationship of how much breath or energy (also space, when playing or moving) is needed for the timing of the music. The most important concept of the relationship of time, space and energy can be experienced with passing a ball on a steady beat. This first experience with balls in a music class is played in a circle with a yarn ball. The soft and springy feel of this ball makes it inviting to a young child and does not suggest throwing or bouncing as another type of ball might.

In preparation, I usually walk around the inside of the circle, letting the ball touch each pair of outstretched hands as I say

■ **Pass, pass, pass**.

That way, the class can see how the ball will travel from one person to the next in a steady tempo. When the children are ready, with hands outstretched, start them speaking

44

■ **Pass, pass, pass.**

Then start the ball around the circle.

As the children become more skilled at this passing game, you may change the directions of the game and create quick-reaction exercises to develop their listening skills and require them to respond with a keener sense of timing. A larger or smaller ball can be used to meet the needs of children of different ages and abilities. Here are five more ball games for primary children, sequenced in the order in which I would present them.

A   *Hearing a steady beat.* Ask the children to listen to a drum beat and pass the ball with the beat. When the drum stops, they must stop passing the ball; when the drum begins again, they resume passing the ball around the circle.

B   *Thinking the steady beat and listening for a signal to start and stop.* Ask the children to put the word 'pass' in their thinking voices and pass the ball. You will have to give them a good start:

Red,   red,   rea-dy be-gin   (pass)

C   *Listening for a signal to change the response.* Call out another quick-reaction signal which tells the children to pass the ball in the opposite direction. For something different, I have signalled a 'whoop' to change direction and then 'and' (spoken as an anacrusis) to change back again.

D   *Listening for tempo changes when passing the ball.* Use a drum or another instrument and change the tempo slightly. Combine this exercise with the starting and stopping exercise. The children will be challenged to listen for tempo changes and the drum stopping and starting again.

E   *Responding to the form of the song 'Clap, Clap, Clap Your Hands.'* Teach the song before you try this experience. The children will pass a ball around a small circle on the verse, but let them suggest how they want to move or use the ball on the chorus ('La, la'); that way they will be identifying the two distinct parts of the song. After they have decided what they will do on the chorus divide the class into small groups, each with one ball. One possibility for the chorus: whoever is holding a ball can step the rhythm of the eighth notes anywhere outside of the circle but return 'home' in time to begin the verse again.

Clap, Clap, Clap Your Hands

Clap, clap, clap your hands, clap your hands to - ge - ther
Pass, pass, pass the ball, pass the ball round the cir - cle

clap your hands to - ge - ther.
pass the ball round the cir - cle.
La la la la, etc.

Hearing and Singing Pitch

I believe that the most important aspect of all we do in music education is ear training. In the Dalcroze approach, solfege and eurhythmics go together closely to train the ear. You have already learned that the focus of the book is eurhythmics; yet, because we all know that rhythm and pitch go hand in hand, it is important to understand how easily the Dalcroze games or exercises can be adapted to learning pitch.

The first thing that needs to happen before we start concentrating on pitch is that children need to discover their own voices and recognize what they can do: whisper, call out, sing high, sing low, speak, plus make a variety of vocal sounds. There is a sizeable literature on the teaching techniques used to help children develop their best singing voices. However, I do want to stress the importance of the first step – that the children are truly conscious of their own voices and the sounds they can make. Whenever possible, create opportunities for children to sing alone. They need to hear themselves sing. One particularly helpful step is to ask them to cup their hands over their ears. It is amazing how their own voice sounds different to them and they can hear it in a more intimate way. We need to create more opportunities for children to sing alone or in small groups, for instance, parts of songs, or phrases which call for individual expressiveness or a sense of drama. I have always wondered what would happen if the reading groups in school only read aloud as a group – as most of the singing is done.

Many of the other activities appropriate to young children involve movement which can imply high and low pitch as well as pitch moving up and down or staying the same. It is possible to create many examples of pitch placement and movement within the stories and games we often include in a music lesson; for instance, birds fluttering about in the high register, the snake slithering along in the bass, or the hopping bunny in the middle register. I have chosen to include a few ideas of my own which have been particularly successful in order to illustrate this point.

The following experiences are included to show how eurhythmics can reinforce the placement and movement of pitch just as it reinforces rhythmic elements.

1   *Hearing and responding to high and low pitches.*

■   **Come, let's take a walk in Mr. Appleseed's orchard. If you hear a high sound on the piano, like this** (*play an interval of a second in the high register of the piano*), **reach up high and pick a bright red apple. If you hear a low sound, like this** (*a low sound*), **pick one off the ground**.

The children can carry an imaginary basket to hold the apples. Your improvisation for this exercise can be very simple. Play a sprightly (but not too fast) walking tune with quarter notes in one hand and reach with the other hand, to scatter high and low cues at irregular intervals of time.

2   *Singing the direction of a bouncing ball.*

■   **Watch how the ball travels when I bounce and then catch it.**
■   **Can you make your voice slide down and then up as the ball is doing?**

If they seem to hesitate because they don't know what to say, suggest the sound 'woo.' Let them try something before you demonstrate. Choose a slow tempo at first; then change it and see if they will follow you. This would be a good time for them to cup their hands over their ears and hear themselves. After they follow the direction of the ball on the bounce–catch, try toss–catch at different heights or roll the ball from one hand to the other. Toss it high to someone in the class or roll it across the floor to someone. Repeat each of these several times so that they really are making the sound follow the direction of the ball. Encourage the children to exaggerate the direction of their voices. It might be wise to have them use their hand to draw the movement of the ball in the air so they reinforce what their voices are doing. This helps them make the mental connection between sound and a visual picture.

3   *Gesturing the direction of pitch in a simple song.*

Climbing Up the Elevator

Mead

Climb-ing up the e - le - va - tor. Climb-ing down the e - le - va - tor.

Start at the bot-tom and end at the top.   Start at the top and end at the bot-tom.

Ask each child to hold up the left arm, bent at the elbow; imagine that this is an elevator. The index finger of the right hand slides up and down the elevator from the elbow to the fingertips as the song is sung. On the third and fourth phrases, slowly slide the voice up and down as the text suggests. This is simply to reinforce the sound of the pitch going up and down. Later, hold your finger at one 'floor' so that the voices hold that pitch until the elevator moves on up or down. Sometimes I have asked children to suggest what might be sold on each of the eight floors of the store, for instance,

Third floor, toys.

They love to suggest something and then sing their suggestions. It amazes me how easily they remember what is sold on each of the eight floors from one lesson to the next.

Solfège Games

Traditionally the Dalcroze solfège training begins with C major scale patterns. I personally believe that it is more appropriate and practical in our school situations to begin with the common *so–mi* pattern and then gradually extend that to the rest of the pentatonic scale before introducing the major scale. You will notice that the solfège training in this book emphasizes tonal patterns familiar to much of our Western folk music. Our school children must experience music of the world's people by listening, singing and playing instruments, but their hearing and singing skills can be developed to better advantage by using the natural pitch patterns of their childhood. Dalcroze solfège study is a well-thought-out and sequenced plan and it would be impossible to present a complete, or even partial description of it here. As has been stated before, it is difficult not to present some ideas which explain Dalcroze's integration of solfège with eurhythmics. The following exercises, or games, illustrate ways of beginning to use syllables with children.

1   *Hearing and singing the tonal pattern* so–mi.

Imagine yourself taking a walk on a beautiful fall day and singing quietly to yourself. Improvise a melody and sing it on the syllable 'loo.' Call out to friends (individual children), singing 'Hi there' on the *so–mi* pattern. The individuals can answer with the same pattern. The children can pat the walking tempo on their knees. Invite individual children to take a walk and sing to some friends along the way. Show the children a special wave – one that looks like the hand signs for *so–mi* – vertical open hand on *so* and a horizontal open hand on *mi*.

2   *Showing the placement of* mi–re–do *in space.*

Sing the song 'Hot Cross Buns' with the following motions which illustrate hand levels for the pitches *mi, re, do.* With both hands, pat *mi* on your head, *re* on your shoulders, and *do* at your waist. Ask the children to try the motions with you as you sing the syllables. By doing this, the children can see and place the three pitches with a distinct sensation of touching and moving in space. They should practice this until they can sing and motion the syllables with ease. At another time, ask them to watch where you place *mi–re–do.* Pitch it a little lower and pat *mi* on the shoulders, *re* at the waist, and *do* on the thighs. This establishes *do* with a strong sense of arriving 'home.' (Later, 'home' translates into the tonic, or keynote of a song.)

3   *Playing solfège games to practice one tonal pattern.*

Once a pattern has been introduced and the children recognize it and are able to sing it independently, games can be devised to further their listening and responding skills. A game will not accomplish much for a child who can't hear, recognize or sing the initial pattern and so this learning process cannot be rushed. Here are a few sample games.

A   Sing any three-note pitch patterns with 'loo.' If the children hear you sing m r d exactly as it appears in 'Hot Cross Buns,' the class should echo with syllables and hand levels. For any other pattern, they should remain silent.

B   Sing other combinations of *m–r–d*, with syllables. The class echoes whatever you sing and then adds the *m–r–d* pattern from 'Hot Cross Buns.' They are experiencing new patterns but reinforcing the familiar one. An example:

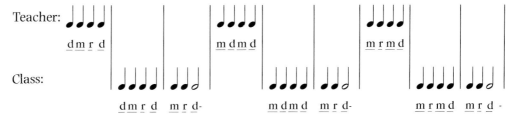

C   Sing an improvised four-beat, *m–r–d* pattern with 'loo.' The class should repeat it with syllables.

The children will benefit from practicing this exercise often but as their responses improve, the number of syllables and the complexity of the patterns can increase.

D Choose individual children to be leaders and sing or play patterns on resonator bells, Orff instruments or the piano for the class to echo. A new game may result from the creative ideas.

4   *Recognizing variations of a familiar pattern.*

The melody of the song 'Love Somebody' includes the *m–r–d* pattern in a variation. It is rhythmically disguised from the original 'Hot Cross Buns' pattern. Instead of *m–r–d*, in this song it is:

Love Somebody

This is a good way for children to realize that music is made up of familiar (and unfamiliar) patterns disguised in many ways. When the children know this song, see if they can discover the *m–r–d* pattern and substitute the syllables for the words on that phrase.

Children delight in singing syllables as a substitute for words in a song; they respond because it sounds humorous to them. Ask them to find a familiar pattern for instance *d–m–s*, then sing the song and substitute syllables for the words and sing the syllables, or if you want them to develop some facility with the syllables, tell them you have a new verse to a song and let them listen and learn the whole song with syllables.

■ **Listen and see if you can find the *d–m–s* pattern in the song 'Love Somebody.'**
■ **Sing the song and substitute the *d–m–s* syllables wherever they belong.** (Example below)

Use every possible technique to help the children become familiar with these simple patterns. To connect the sound of the patterns with a visual picture of pitch direction, use hand levels and whole arm movement, play step bells, draw with a magic marker, or other possible techniques.

When children are asked to play an ostinato or a particular pattern when it occurs in a song, give them the notation on a card or put a picture of the notation on the chalkboard even if it is as simple as:

$$d \quad d \quad d \qquad = do \quad do \quad do \qquad or \qquad \begin{array}{l} s \quad s \\ \quad\quad m \\ \quad\quad\quad d \end{array} \qquad = \begin{array}{l} so \quad so \\ \quad\quad mi \\ \quad\quad\quad\quad do \end{array}$$

We must give children the opportunities to read music whenever possible. Notating the syllables to show the direction of the melody demonstrates the idea of sound moving up or down or staying the same. In the early stages of children's learning, I illustrate the patterns this way:

$$\begin{array}{l} \quad\quad\quad\quad l \\ \quad s \quad s \quad\quad s \\ m \quad\quad\quad\quad m \\ d \end{array}$$

(After all, this is the way sound appears in scores!)

I have sometimes pictured a pattern as a 'package of sounds.' As I introduce new patterns, I show a new package. In the song, 'Love Somebody,' there are really only three packages to work with (1, 2, 3).

$$1 \quad \left(\begin{array}{c} s \\ m \\ d \end{array}\right) \quad 2 \quad \left(\begin{array}{c} f \\ m \\ r \end{array}\right) \quad 3 \quad \left(\begin{array}{c} m \\ r \\ d \end{array}\right)$$

Notice the simplicity of this. After they have used hand levels and sung the whole song with syllables, let one child lead the class by pointing to the syllables in the packages. From these packages on the chalkboard, notice how you might begin to show a picture of the notation. The lines that I have included in the example are a hint of the staff. The relationship to the staff will become obvious later.

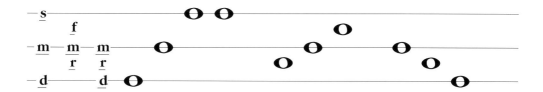

Encourage individual children to create a new song which uses the same three packages. Perhaps they can do this outside of school, notate it, and play it for the class another time.

5 *Listening for familiar tonal patterns in a new song.*

Teach 'The Shoemaker Song,' then continue some of the same solfège or ear-training experiences with this song. The first measure of the second part begins with *r–r–s,–s,* which you might want to omit from the games at first. It is a more difficult pattern to sing. When this happens in a new song, I often say that that particular pattern is mine; only I can sing it. That way, they will hear it sung correctly several times.

6 *Listening to 'The Aquarium' from* Carnival of the Animals *by Saint-Saëns for melody direction.*

This experience was described at the beginning of the chapter as a way for children to explore movement, especially smooth, extended movements of the arms and hands. Review it with more emphasis placed on listening for melody direction.

7 *Listening for the direction of melody in a more challenging example, the third movement of Symphony No. 8 by Dvořák.*

Concentrate on the movement of the melody line. It is quite difficult to expect young children to hear and follow the direction of the melody in a listening example which includes melody, accompaniment and instruments and so I would suggest that they follow your hand movement as they hold small kites attached to their hands. The kites are easy to make; the directions are in Appendix B.

52

In preparation for this lesson, listen to the music and follow the theme score. Imagine the kite being lifted into the air then dipping down or gently gliding down – sometimes being caught on a fickle wind. There are times when it seems as though the kite flutters down, gradually lower and lower, until it almost settles on the ground but just in time it is swept up high into the sky again. (Use only this first section of the music.)

Symphony No. 8

Third movement

Dvořák

Duration and Rhythm

After games and exercises with many components of timing in music (beat, tempo and duration), children should start experiencing the relationships between note values and then the combining of note values into rhythm. It is important that duration and rhythm are first experienced in movement as were the elements of timing, tempo and beat. I begin my focus on duration with quarter, eighth and half notes. Here is a sampling of the eurhythmics experiences I use to teach duration and rhythm.

1   *Responding to four basic note values in a story.*

This activity can be called 'Let's build a house.' Invite the class to help build an imaginary house in the center of the room.

- ■ **Let's build an imaginary house right in the middle of this room. We will need some construction workers to saw wood. This is how they will work.**

Play an example (♩) and choose that group of children.

- ■ **Next, we will need some carpenters with hammer and nails. Here is the way they will work.**

Play an example (♫) and choose the group of children.

- ■ **We will need painters to paint the house.**

Play their music (♩) and choose the children.

- ■ **We need workers to do some heavy work and guide the big cranes.**

Play strong, full chords (o).

I don't believe it is practical to teach the whole note to young children because they won't often encounter it and they find it difficult to hold a note for a long time. I have included it in the building of the house, however, and that group of children always enjoyed being responsible for the heavy loading, lifting, pulling or pushing.

Each group is assigned to a corner of the room. When they hear their music, they come to the building site and start to work as they follow the timing and energy of the music. They retreat quickly to their corner when their work rhythm is no longer heard.

Try to draw the children's attention to high and low pitches as well as pitch moving up, down or staying the same. You might have to casually insert suggestions such as

- ■ **Paint up high above those windows;**

or

- ■ **Hammer those floor boards.**

Be sure your music suggests this. Subtleties in dynamics, articulation, register and accentuation may be reflected in their movement. I am always thrilled when they tell me they are moving a certain way 'because the music sounds like that' or 'the music is doing that.'

Now, what about the music for this experience? It must be improvised because the whole experience is focused on children listening for the rhythm of their assigned work. The objective for this experience is for them to hear and respond to an exact relationship between the three (or four) note values. I use the piano almost as a percussion instrument for this activity. If I were to give you a notated example, it would probably never reflect the actual movement that you want the children to experience. You must feel it yourself, as if you were doing the action. Practice, by going through the actions that you would expect the various workers to do. Then literally drop your hands on the keyboard and express that physical feeling and movement in clusters. Here are a few ideas to illustrate my point. Begin with your hands in these positions.

Large, heavy, labored movement.   Feel long, steady painting strokes.

Accent each swing of the   The hammering sounds can
saw, back and forth.   move in close, half steps.

There is another possibility for music to accompany the building of the house. I have seen wonderful creative movement with sounds improvised on a collection of percussion instruments. Suspend a rod or broom handle between two chairs. Attach three or four instruments to the rod which you can strike, shake, or knock. Experiment with various instruments until you have a good variety of sounds possible for building this house. You will need sounds which express the four notes values used in building the house. (♩ , ♫ , 𝅗𝅥 , 𝅝)

Two important reminders:

● You must determine the tempo of each note value before you begin the game. The relationship between durations must be correct and the children must be able to move in that tempo.
● Begin with the quarter-note tempo (sawing wood) even though that would not be the first step in building the house. In early eurhythmics experiences, it is best to establish

the walking tempo first – the basic timing which is closest to the student's heartbeat and walking tempo.

2   A Halloween game with ♩ , ♫ and ♩ .

For some groups of children, this game should be clapped or patted on their thighs first, until they understand the directions. With one class, I simply told the story as they were standing in a space in the room.

- **Show me with four steps how you would creep slowly up to someone's front door on Halloween Night.**
- **Count: 1 2 3 4.**
- **Knock four times: 1 2 3 4.**
- **Take eight running steps away: 1 2 3 4 5 6 7 8.**
- **Call out 'Boo.'**

Repeat the same activity. An example of the music you could play for this:

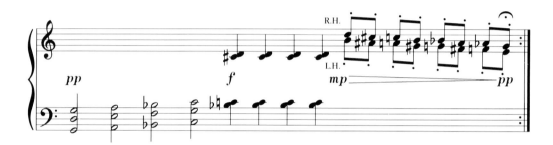

If you use a drum for this activity instead of the piano, the duration of the half notes will not sound. Try to create the long sound of the half note by sliding your hand or fingernail across the head of the drum. The purpose is to have children experience the duration of the note values. Add dynamics to your improvisation and they will begin to respond to this element. Here is a good opportunity to introduce crescendo and decrescendo marks. Further, if your children know what the three notes used in the game look like and can identify how they were stepped (either walking, running, or gliding) ask them to help you notate these movements.

Two variations:

A   Since I am a great believer in children voicing sounds to match what they are feeling physically, I asked my class to speak the movement with words.

    ♩ = Creeeeeeep
    ♩ = Knock
  and
    ♫ = Run-ning.

56

B   Ask the children to suggest instruments which could be used to perform this as a Halloween composition. If they are not familiar with the instruments, select a few possible ones, place them on the table, let them explore possibilities, then determine which they want to use. Use pitched and unpitched instruments and even encourage the use of the piano as they improvise the music. Let the children determine how many times they should repeat the idea and whether it is repeated exactly each time.

■   **What will be our plan?**
This is a good way of introducing the idea of form in music to children. It makes more sense to the children to talk about the 'plan' of the music rather than the 'form' of the music. You can easily exchange the two words later.

3   *Creating machine-like movements for certain note values.*

'The Machine Game' was introduced earlier in this chapter, but there are other more challenging versions of it. When the children are beginning to respond independently to the relationship of quarters, eighths and half notes, group them in threes and have them count off; they may either sit or stand. The 'ones' will design a way to move on quarter notes, 'twos' on eighths, and 'threes' on half notes. For a musical accompaniment here are three possibilities:

A   Suspend three percussion instruments as described before and play them for the machine to move.
B   Play a constant, soft quarter-note beat (to keep the timing steady), and signal the individual parts of the machine to move. You will have to reinforce the parts with another sound.
C   Improvise with the three note values at the piano, one or two at a time.

When this is being performed accurately, encourage the groups to let their movement work together just as parts of a machine would be synchronized both in time and in space.

Some variations on the Machine Game:

A   You can try to cause the machine to speed up (somewhat) or slow down by changing the tempo of your quarter notes on the drum. If this happens, the movement of the machine should reflect the timing (tempo): slower = larger movement; faster = smaller, more compact movement.
B   When the children have reached the place where they can hear a given quarter note and on their own, establish the eighth and/or half notes, they also can be asked to create sounds which fit their movement. Encourage vocal sounds to accompany the movement. This can be done without any music from you.
C   Invite children to come to the piano. Using the black keys, one child establishes quarters and two others add the eighths and half notes.
D   As other rhythms are studied, for instance, ♩♫ or ♩.♪ , these can be used in the Machine Game. Always establish the beat as the basic movement, then add others.

4 *Feeling the rhythm of a song in arm and hand gestures.*

Imagery often helps children express an idea more easily and more vividly. Try this activity with the song 'Hot Cross Buns.' Begin by asking the children what it would be like to work in a bakery.

- ■ **Imagine having to put icing on dozens of hot cross buns.**
- ■ **If you do it in rhythm it is easier. With a spreader, make a cross then slide the bun aside.** (*Demonstrate this as you speak*) **Sometimes, you have to brush away the crumbs.**
- ■ **Sing the song and follow me.** (*For another verse, sing the following words which describe the motions*

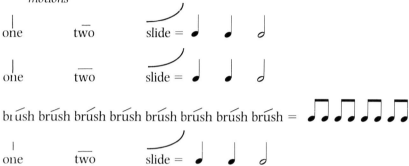

Here is another verse to sing with the same tune:

> Jumping beans, jumping beans
> In my hand I have a dozen jumping beans.

To feel the rhythm in the hands and fingers, pinch the thumb and two fingers of one hand together and make them 'jump' in the palm of the other hand, in the rhythm of the song. Be sure that the size of the jump is in relationship to the duration of the note values. The motion of your hand will look something like this:

5 *'Notating' rhythm with a finger or rhythm stick.*

Minka

Russian Folk Song

1. Min - ka, Min - ka, when I leave thee, How my sad heart al - ways grieves me.
2. When I hear sweet mu - sic play - ing, Ev - 'ry note to me is say - ing,

When I'm gone I long to be with Min - ka, Min - ka mine.
"Min - ka, Min - ka, fair - est maid - en, Min - ka, Min - ka mine."

When I see the full moon shin - ing. Then I will for thee be pin - ing,
When the win - ter snow is fall - ing, I must go, for love is call - ing,

Min - ka, Min - ka, fair - est maid - en, Min - ka, Min - ka mine.
Call - ing me to be with Min - ka, Fair - est Min - ka mine.

Many aspects of rhythm can and should be experienced with smaller motions of hands and fingers as a preparation for notating rhythm as well as in preparation for playing instruments. I use small rhythm sticks much like a pencil. After the class knows a tune, for instance, 'Minka' (sung with a neutral syllable), let them feel the movement of the eighths and half notes in their hands, fingers and arms by using the sticks to draw the sound of the rhythm across a desk or even across the floor. The tempo will have to be slower than usual for this song. Notice that the directions say 'draw' or 'write,' and not 'tap' the sound. The reason for this is that in eurhythmics, students are moving through space and time when they step and clap rhythm, so it seems logical for the sticks to move through space as they note the timing of the rhythm. You will recall that timing refers to the duration of the note values and when they are sounded. With luck they will have seen you notate rhythm on the chalkboard in this manner. I find that I do this instinctively; I hear it in my mind and write it simultaneously and when students are watching, they can hear the chalk sounding out the rhythm. If students express half notes with a sustaining movement such as gliding, they should show this at the end of the long phrases in the song, 'Minka.' This pre-reading and -writing activity can be done with many songs and especially with patterns that you are highlighting in a lesson.

6   *Physically feeling the relationship between quarters and eighths.*

Here are three sequential exercises to develop an awareness of the relationship of these two notes.

A   Ask the children to step whatever they hear you play (♩ or ♫). They should also speak what they are stepping: 'walk, walk' or 'run-ning, run-ning.'

B   Next, ask them to step the opposite of what you play, either quarters or eighths. They should begin to be aware of the relationship of two eighths to a quarter, but there is no reason to mention quarters and eighths yet. At this point I would ask them how they are moving (walking and running), and then begin to use those terms. I will begin to call them quarters and eighths when they are clearly aware that they are responding to specific note values.

C   Start the children stepping and speaking quarters. When you signal,

■   **Change,**

they should change to eighths and then change back on your next signal. When you accompany this exercise, play the eighths so that the music clearly articulates two sounds to one quarter.

Example:

Change

The children should be speaking:

■   **Walk, walk, . . .**

then

■   **Run-**   **ning,**   **run-**   **ning**

Encourage them to speak the eighths with the same inflection shown here and shown in the musical example above. This will help them realize the relationship. (Notice that eighth notes are written this way in many places in the book.)

Once the children can tell you that there are two sounds for 'run-ning' and one for 'walk,' you can call the quarter note a beat and then signal so many beats of eighths, for instance, if you signal 'three,' they should step ♫♫♫ .

Later on, try a variation of Exercise C with a song or a recorded selection. The theme from the movie *Peter Gunn* and the Russian folk song 'Minka' are two examples which have a strong feeling of relationship between the quarter-note beat and eighths. The words of 'Minka' are not particularly interesting to children in the primary grades but it is a good folk tune to help them feel eighth notes related to a beat. They can step or clap the eighth notes as they hear the song. When you call out a number (one to eight), they should step that number of quarter beats and then return to eighths again.

7   *Notating simple rhythmic examples.*

After the children have experienced gesturing the movement of rhythm in their arms, hands and fingers, they can translate that experience to notating simple patterns or songs. When we notate something, I insist on a stepwise procedure which the whole class follows. Each step will need to be practiced several times. At first, we notate something with the sticks on a hard surface. To notate a phrase from 'Minka,' ask the class to:

A   Sing the first (long) phrase with 'ta' and at the same time, with a small rhythm stick or the eraser end of a pencil, tap the 'feet' of the notes across the page, just as if their feet were moving across the floor. For the long note at the end, let the stick draw a curve as it extends through the length of the note.

B Immediately, the arm should swing back, ready to draw 'legs' on the same notes. The phrase should be sung again so that the notating is an extension of the singing.

| | | | | | | | | | | | | | | | | | | | | | | | | | | | | | ⌡

Don't worry if each 'leg' (stem) isn't attached precisely to a 'foot' (notehead); the steady stream of eighth notes allows the children ample opportunity to practice the notation procedure before they attempt to notate simple songs.

C Everything else – beams and bar-lines – is put in last, not in rhythm.

♫♫|♫♫|♫♫|♫♫|♫♫|♫♫|♫♫|♫♫|♫♩ |

This whole procedure should recall the first introduction of what notes look like:

- ■ **To walk, we use our feet and our legs.**
- ■ **Here is a foot ▬ , and here is the leg | .**
- ■ **We call this a quarter note ♩ .**
- ■ **A running note has a wing, or a flag ♪ .**
- ■ **These are called eighth notes.**
- ■ **Often, two eighths are joined together ♫ .**

When a half note is drawn, the line for the 'foot' of the note can be curved around so that it resembles a half note ➷ , then ♩ .

A song as simple as 'Hot Cross Buns' is an excellent one to try this procedure. I urge you to follow the procedure above by having the class do each step together, always singing, and always moving the hand in rhythm. The song can be sung with movement words: (The first step for notating is shown here.)

Walk,	walk,	glide	▬	▬	➴
Walk,	walk,	glide	▬	▬	➴
Run-ning,	run-ning,	run-ning, run-ning,	■ ■	■ ■	■ ■ ■ ■
Walk,	walk,	glide.	▬	▬	➴

Whenever possible, prepare this activity by having the children step the rhythm in space. The notation can be done on the chalkboard with chalk, on newsprint with markers, and later, with pencil and paper. The results may not look very neat when their whole arm is involved in the movement, but it is the process that is important, and the notation can always be cleaned up later.

8 *Listening for specific rhythmic patterns.*

This game challenges children to listen and echo rhythm patterns from well-known songs. Select four children to 'travel' around the room. Two of them will travel by echo-steppping only the patterns they hear from the song 'Hot Cross Buns' and the other two will echo-step only the patterns they hear from 'Are You Sleeping?'. The children at their seats will echo-clap all other patterns. If you use a pitched instrument such as the piano or a recorder, the melody will give the answer away. The focus in this exercise is on the rhythm; an unpitched instrument will better suit your purpose for the game. Here are examples of patterns you can use. Notice that one pattern exists in the two songs. See if the children discover that.

Go back and forth between patterns. The same game can be played with rhythm patterns from other songs that the children know.

Accents

Accentuation is an important and natural part of speech and music. In eurhythmics, we speak of several types of accents or crusic points in the music:

- a dynamic accent (*sf* or >),
- a melodic accent (a high pitch),
- a metric accent (an accented beat in the measure), and
- an agogic accent (a long note on a weak pulse).

These accents are all crusic but some are more obvious or more subtle than others. Children enjoy discovering strong accents in music and expressing them in movement. We need to help them discover and express subtle accents in meter and phrasing. The most logical place to begin to develop awareness is with their own names or familiar places and people. Let them determine accented and unaccented sounds in their names. Ask them to explore ways that they can show the difference between the accented and unaccented syllables when they clap their names. Here are several ideas to try with lists of names, foods, places and months of the year.

1 *Using hand motions on accented and unaccented syllables.*

With one hand, clap the accented syllable into the open palm but tap the unaccented syllables with the fingertips. Or pat thighs on the accented syllable and clap the unaccented syllables lightly. Make sure that the children's wrists and hands are relaxed during this activity. Their hands should almost drop onto their thighs for the accent.

2 *Bouncing a ball on accented syllables of words.*

Children can kneel on the floor, each holding a tennis ball, and recite the months of the year in a duple rhythm – drop the ball to the floor on the accent(s), then catch it on the rebound.

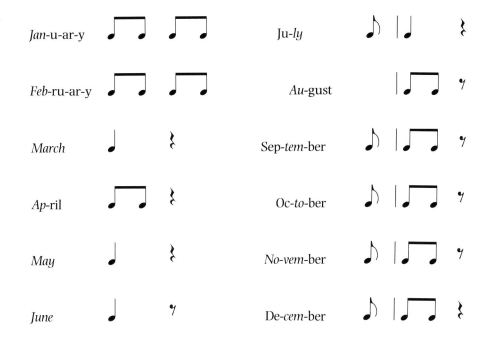

Another time, do the same exercise with other balls or things that can be tossed: a soccer ball, a pingpong ball, beanbag or balloon. You'll be surprised at the subtle differences in the timing and energy needed to perform the accents.

3 *Listening and bouncing a ball on metric accents in music.*

Before the balls are distributed, have the children listen to music in which the meter is clearly defined with accents. Try improvising on the example given below. First, ask the children to find the beat and clap it lightly. Then,

- **Find the beat that seems to say 'bounce.'**
- **Pat your knees on the 'bounce' beat. That beat is accented.**

When they have a good feel for this, they can stand and bounce a ball to a partner on the accent. The partner should catch the ball on the next beat. At first, the accents in the music should be quite obvious; then, try other selections in different meters, tempos and with different subtleties of accents.

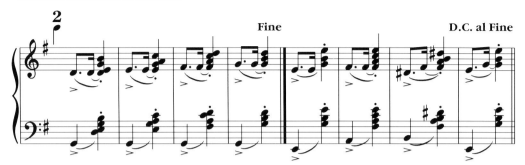

Familiar songs or recorded compositions can be used for this experience. Here are some suggestions:

- 'Minuet' from the *Music for the Royal Fireworks* suite by Handel
- 'Chim Chim Cheree,' from the movie *Mary Poppins*, by Richard and Robert Sherman
- 'The Changing of the Guard,' from *Carmen*, Suite No. 2 by Bizet
- 'March' from *The Love of Three Oranges*, by Prokofiev

4   *Finding accents other than the first beat of the measure.*

In Gossec's 'Gavotte' there are several examples of melodic accents in unusual places in the music. They take on the element of surprise. For this experience, I use only the first 16 measures or two periods, although the second half of the composition is equally interesting for finding melodic accents.

Gavotte

F. J. Gossec

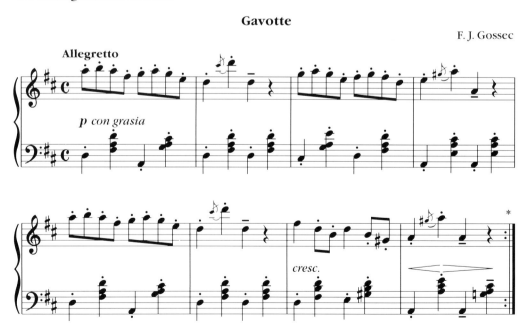

65

*No repeat on recapitulation

The accents in the 'Gavotte' are the result of grace notes and octave leaps. In measures 9–16 these accents are omitted except for the last measure. Suggest that the children listen to this music and then describe it in terms of what they heard. I think it is important for them to have an opportunity to talk about the music and hear what their classmates heard. Ask questions:

- **Can you describe the music?**
- **What did you hear?**
- **If you were to see someone dancing to it, what would you see?**

They will probably hear the accents as a 'jump' or a 'pop.'

- **What happens in the music when you hear an accent?**

Call it an accent and when you play it again, ask them to clap all those accents.

Invite children to step the rhythm of the melody. The challenge will be to step exactly what they hear. Some of them will be very successful and step the rhythm pattern as if running towards a spot, preparing, jumping, and then landing. This is a good example of an anacrusis leading to a crusis.

In the second eight measures, the accentuation is slightly different except in the last measure. There are melodic accents but they are not as prominent. Don't try to explain too much about the difference, but after the children listen, encourage them to share their thoughts about this part. If they do notice the difference in the accentuation of the two parts, encourage them to express the music in movement and/or gestures and show the difference.

5   *Expressing accents, meter and rhythm in creative movement.*

Children will enjoy getting to know the lively Bartók 'Jeering Song' from *For Children*.[1] After several hearings, they can find the beat, the accents, the rhythm, and the general spirit of the music. They will enjoy expressing the music as if they were clowns.

Jeering Song

Béla Bartók

Rests

Movement plays a big part in developing children's awareness of rests in music. I have found that something needs to happen on the rests in order for children's attention to be drawn to the silence. Rests can be experienced as a physical gesture or motion. In the beginning, besides gesturing on a rest, I have asked children to touch their temples in order to actually 'hear' the rest in their heads. If they are playing mallet instruments, they can touch their shoulders with the mallets. The following are some eurhythmics exercises that could be used to draw children's attention to rests.

1   Hearing and responding to silence in music.

One of the first eurhythmics exercises is starting and stopping with the music. This basic exercise could be reviewed at this time. It can be more challenging now if you give each child a packet or envelope with three 3 × 5″ cards in it:

The blank one is for the silence. Draw the notes on both sides of the cards so that they can be seen from anywhere in the room. This exercise can be played with part of the class moving on the floor and the others remaining in their seats. Whether you play quarters, eighths or rests the children will respond, either by stepping or patting their knees. Those who are stepping will hold up the appropriate card to identify what they are hearing. Those sitting in their seats will not have cards but will pat their knees on the quarters and eighths and, on the rests, they will hold both hands up, palms facing forward. The musical example that you play may be similar to the following:

2 *Feeling rests on different beats of the measure.*

This activity is like a dance routine. Not only will it help children feel and count steady beats, but it will give them a vivid sensation of rests in music. Teach the routine before you try substituting rests on certain beats. The directions for the routine are as follows:

> Four steps forward, four steps back. (turn to the right)
> Four steps to the right, four steps back. (turn back, forward)
> Four steps forward, four steps back.
> Four steps around in a circle, four steps in place.

When the children are successful stepping this routine and counting out loud, call out one of the four beats so they can substitute a rest on that beat. That substitution continues through each measure of the routine. They won't take a step on that beat but they can gesture a silent beat to show the rest. For instance, when you signal 'Three,' each line in the routine will be stepped, ♩ ♩ 𝄽 ♩ . If you say 'One,' each line will be stepped, 𝄽 ♩ ♩ ♩ .

3 *Reading rhythms which include quarter-note rests.*

When the children are ready to see what a quarter-note rest looks like, introduce it and draw it on the blank card in the packet they used in Exercise 1. A follow-up to the previous exercise would be to notate some rhythm patterns on the chalkboard and ask the class to read and speak the patterns as you point to them.

69

Skinnamarink

Traditional

When you introduce this song to the children be careful to add rests only where you eventually want them to be discovered. The eighth-note rest following 'afternoon' will be too short for young children so you will probably want to hold the note for one and a half beats. As you teach the song, create movement for the rests which reinforces the meaning of the text. For instance,

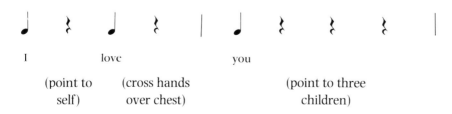

Write this pattern on the chalkboard:

It can be played on the woodblock as an ostinato. For a challenge, ask someone to rewrite this phrase so that all the rests are quarter notes and all the quarter notes are rests. The result would be:

Can the children suggest words for this 'complementary rhythm'? One possibility:

These two ostinatos can be combined and either spoken by two small groups or played on two instruments

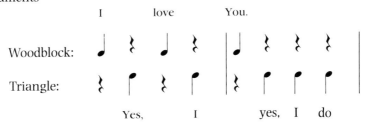

Listening Perceptively; Moving Expressively

'There and Back' by Ross Lee Finney[2] is a lively little piece which features dotted rhythms, accents and rests. By now, you can probably think of several ways to use this music in your classroom, but here is one suggestion. Begin by capturing the children's attention with a question:

- **Suppose you decide to visit a friend this afternoon. How will you go? Listen to the music and see how you will move.**
- **Will you just walk? Will you run? Will you go another way?**
- **See if you can find places in the music where you might stop to look at something** (*Notice the fermata in measure six and rests in all of measure eleven*).

Invite a few children to show you how they'd go (skipping, probably). If they don't show the accents, ask them to listen and find places in the music where they could jump and land with both feet at once. If you have already worked with accents, ask the children to find them and show them in movement.

If your children are ready for some problem-solving questions, try these.

- **What title would you give this composition? Why?**
- **Describe the accents in this music. What makes the accents?**
- **Why do you suppose a composer puts accents in the music?**
- **Ross Lee Finney titled this composition 'There and Back.' Did he choose a good title?**

There and Back

Ross Lee Finney

(from Contemporary Piano Literature, Books 3–4)

5. Experiences in the Intermediate Grades

Eurhythmics experiences in the intermediate grades should further the learning and skill development started in the primary grades. The emphasis here will be on developing understanding through discovery, recognition (aural and visual), performance, and creativity. The children should be encouraged to become independent in their responses but they will also have many opportunities to work in pairs and small groups. This should help them become more sensitive to ensemble performance. Do not be surprised to find certain experiences discussed which have been suggested in an earlier chapter. Eurhythmics experiences are often repeated from age group to age group but with a new challenge, new music, more difficult examples, or with a different emphasis.

Exploring Movement

I have often been asked at eurhythmics workshops, 'How should one begin with children beyond the primary grades?' I believe that the first step is to capture the children's desire to move and their willingness to explore music through a variety of activities. If you can imagine music in the movement that you see in children, it will help you plan for these activities. Unfortunately children in school are often reminded to curtail noise and movement in the classroom, and therefore they do not always feel comfortable or free to move in a music class. Yet it is important that they have an opportunity to explore possibilities in the space allowed so they can use the ideas later when following movement sequences or improvising movement.

Here is a simple activity which will allow your students to explore one way to move in different situations. If you are in a crowded classroom, ask two or three children to move at a time. They should choose their own space, direction and tempo to fit the situation that you are going to suggest. Although the whole activity could be done with walking, running, skipping or skating, these directions are for walking.

■ **Let's think about different ways of walking. I will give you a suggestion and you show us how you would walk. When you hear the toneblock (♩) stop right where you are and wait for the next suggestion. Find a space out on the floor and show me that you are ready to walk.**

Use many of the following suggestions and give the children time to explore each way of walking:

to catch a bus	with a sore foot
with the wind	in deep snow
against the wind	if you felt angry

on slippery ice	in puddles
in Fall leaves	while carrying something heavy
in hot weather	while carrying something hot
in cold weather	while carrying something very special

The children can be reminded of these experiences later, when they are listening to music or performing it. The various gradations of timing, energy, weight, and mood which they experience in these movement explorations are realized in what they hear or how they perform music. In other words, whatever they feel in movement is internalized and then can influence their performance or enjoyment of music.

Here are some other activities which give children an opportunity to explore movement – often in limited space but usually stressing aspects of timing: steady beats, accented beats, duration and measure. When these activities are accompanied by music they stimulate listening and responding and are considered eurhythmics experiences.

1   Feeling the duration of four beats.

Be sure the children understand and can do the following: push, pull, lift, press, stretch, curl, twist and dig. Ask them to show you how they would pull something while you count four beats. As you say the word and count, connect the elongated sound of 'pull 2 3 4.'

■   **Now, step four beats and listen for my direction. Do that motion for four beats then step four more. Let's try one.**

Establish the tempo with finger clicks and signal them to begin stepping.

A variation on the same exercise: The children can choose their own action for the alternate measures.

2   Changing back and forth from quarters to eighths.

The children choose partners. One person is the leader until you signal a change. Together they clap quarter notes until you signal either two, four, six or eight eighth notes. On the next (quarter note) beat, the leader of each pair either gestures or moves that number of eighths while partner B mirrors or copies the movement. For instance, the leader might clap the eighths in an arc overhead or a step in a circle. The person mirroring the movement must watch and respond simultaneously. The leader is responding creatively, the follower is copying as precisely as possible, and they are both keeping the timing and counting exact. Encourage them to move a different way each time eighth notes are signalled. As a basic exercise always signal an even number of eighth notes so that the children can resume clapping quarters without any difficulty.

74

This exercise can be done with or without music but be sure the tempo remains steady. If you use music, you might play chords for the measure of quarters and then a scale passage for the eighths. On the fourth quarter, always signal the number of eighths on the next measure. This example illustrates the sequence.

3 Timing movement precisely.

You can call this, 'Creating a Mobile'.

A group of five children forms a rather large circle and each takes a consecutive number from one to five. One by one, each child steps four eighth notes into the center of the circle and on the next count takes a pose as part of a statue. The tempo of the eighths must be established carefully before they begin. A good way to do this is to count eight eighths and begin on the next one. In this illustration, the X marks the point at which the pose is formed.

Teacher: '1 2 3 4 5 6 7 8'

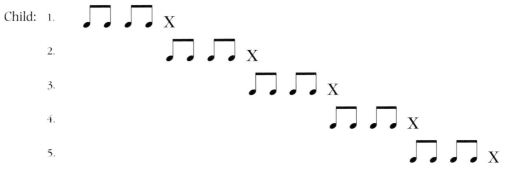

The timing of the eighths continues without hesitation until all five children have linked up to create the statue. They each hold their pose until all five parts of the statue are in place.

The statue can be dismantled by reversing the process; one child steps out of the center back into the circle with four eighth notes followed by another child and so on. To further the idea, the statue can become a mobile and move gently through the count of four half notes (♩ ♩ ♩ ♩) before it is dismantled (a reverse of the movement back into the circle). I sometimes put all these ideas together and create an ABA form. The A section is the creating of the statue, the B section is the mobile and the repeat of the A section is the dismantling of the statue.

After a few attempts, they should begin to realize how the parts of the statue can compliment each other. For instance, if the first two children have landed a pose which is directed downward, the next child can try to pose in an upward direction.

This idea of making a statue is more than fun for the children; it develops concentration and precision in timing as well as a sense of visual and aural form and design.

Further Response to Timing in Music

There are many ways to develop sensitivity to timing in music. The first four exercises described below are circle games with balls. Children enjoy these games; with careful planning and a wise and wide choice of music and directions, you can achieve many of your learning goals. The games are much more than simple bouncing and catching on the beat of the music; they challenge the children to listen and follow the beat or change the activity on a signal or a new section in the music. Encourage the children to show their awareness of the dynamics, tempo, articulation and accents of the music in their response with the ball. Moving, singing or playing experiences with music should always grow out of their inner sensation of these elements of expression. Their responses should and will reflect sensitivity to these elements. In Chapter Four, I suggested that yarn balls be used first, but at this level children can use a ball from the physical education class. The exercises in a circle formation may be accomplished in a crowded classroom, but when the children try to walk around the room while handling the ball, more space will be needed.

1 *Tossing and catching an imaginary ball.*

The children should stand in a circle around the room. Each should identify a partner across the circle to whom they will toss and catch an imaginary ball. The object is to follow the tempo and dynamics of the music as they imagine playing toss and catch with a friend. The music should be improvised on the piano so that you can change the tempo and the energy of the throw. Don't worry about harmonic voice-leading; tone clusters work well in this situation. Think of the piano as a percussion instrument; the music must help the children feel the thrust and energy of the throw as they send the ball, followed by the lesser amount of energy and impact on the catch. Here is a short musical example which you can develop further.

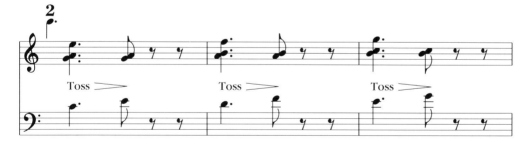

The first time you play for this exercise, it may help to feel the timing and dynamics if you ask two children to demonstrate tossing and catching an imaginary ball. Watch carefully and try to feel the timing and dynamics of their movement as well as the duration of the ball 'flying' across the room. Immediately, transfer the feeling of what you are seeing into your fingers and on to the piano. Ask the children on one half of the circle to begin on a signal from you. After they are comfortably into the tempo of the music, begin to change it slightly. It is helpful to watch individual pairs of children so as to give them a strong sense of tempo and accentuation. You should actually feel that your music is reinforcing their movement.

76

2   Passing the ball.

Now that your children's ball skills are more developed, review the quick-reaction games they learned in the primary years by changing to a larger ball. Be sure to establish an appropriate tempo before they begin.

3   Keeping a steady beat.

Ask the children to listen to a musical example and show you the tempo of the beat. Let them show it any way they wish; for instance, a hand gesture, a toe tap, or shoulder movement. This exercise is done in a circle.

■   **Pass the ball on the beat. When I call out a number, whoever has the ball should hold it for that many beats.**

At first, encourage the children to count the rests out loud, but eventually they should count silently. The simplest music for this experience would contain only quarter notes. It is best for you to improvise the music on the piano, for if you use a recording, stopping the music and tracking the rests can be difficult. Play one pitch softly on the rests to reinforce their steady counting; later, refrain from playing when they are counting silently.

4   Passing the ball and counting in a steady tempo.

This game is fun but challenging. It is played without music; the only sound is your voice calling out a number. Consequently, the children must concentrate on keeping the beat steady and counting carefully. This activity develops the inner sense of timing. The ball is passed one way and then on a number signal, it is passed the opposite way. You must always call out another number on the last count of each set. Establish the tempo by speaking the first few beats before you give the first signal.
For example:

■   **Pass, pass, pass, four**

When you say 'Four,' the child holding the ball passes it to the right. On the fourth count, if you say 'Six,' the ball is passed six counts to the left, etc. A sequence of passes might be:

■   **Four** (*to the right*)
■   **Six** (*to the left*)
■   **Two** (*to the right*)
■   **Nine** (*to the left*), etc.

Meter and Measure in Music

In the primary grades, the preparation for skill and understanding of meter and measure in music began with timing in songs and movement games. The sequence of activities presented in Chapter Four led the children to respond and recognize such concepts as:

●   We can move in time with the music.

- The timing is steady and continual and it is called the beat of the music. We can step, clap, swing, or even draw the beat of the music (e.g. ♩ ♩ ♩ ♩ ♩).
- Usually we can detect some beats that are stronger than others, called accented beats. These can be defined or highlighted by a specific movement.
- Accented beats can also be articulated verbally, with a word appropriate to the song or music ('yes' or 'here') or with a nonsense word ('du' or 'zip'). If the students call the accented beat 'one,' they can count the other beats in the grouping and identify the music as being measured in twos, threes, fours or fives, for example.
- The children recognize that the music has been measured.
- Beats and accents can be pictured or drawn. (e.g. **Xxx   Xxx   Xxx**). Help children realize that they can 'see' rhythm in movement; for beats measured in threes, use a strong slash movement followed by two gentler waves of the hand. (e.g. ‿ ⌣ ⌣   ‿ ⌣ ⌣)

The following experiences will continue to develop understanding and skill in feeling meter and measure in music. Some experiences will also help to develop music reading and writing skills.

1   *Organizing beats into measures by means of accents.*

Have the children stand in a circle.

- **With a soft-sounding clap, pass this beat around the circle, each one clapping one beat. (**Demonstrate the tempo as you give directions.***)*
- **When I call out a number, for instance, 'three', the next beat should be the accented beat in a measure. Continue to clap measures of three beats until I call out another number.**

I often demonstrate this experience by pointing to individuals around the circle and talking through an example. As soon as they understand the task, call out other numbers from two to seven. Let them continue in each meter for several measures before going to another one.

- **When you have an accent to clap, send it into the center of the circle like a pop or a small firecracker.**

Continue this activity long enough for them to actually 'see' the claps grouped into measures (accent–weak–weak   accent–weak–weak). Emphasize measures in two, three and four. Here is an example of the exercise:

x x x x x **X** x x **X** x x x **X** x x **X** x **X** x **X** x **X** x x x   etc.

Three   Two   Four

The above exercise not only develops a sense of meter, but it means that the children must keep a steady beat. At first, you may want to help by playing a drum or sticks softly. Be sure that you do not hint at a meter; keep the beats even in timing and dynamics. It isn't appropriate to use a song or a recording with this exercise because both will typically illustrate one meter only.

2 Bouncing a ball on the accent to feel meter.

Children enjoy bouncing a ball on an accent and catching it on the next beat.

Begin with a meter of two: bounce, catch: ↓ C / B

Then, try a meter of three: bounce, catch, hold: ↓ C H / B

or, a meter of four: bounce, catch, hold, hold: ↓ C H H / B

You won't have to explain all of this if they simply follow directions – to bounce the ball on the accent and catch it on the next beat. Encourage whatever motion they do naturally while holding the ball and waiting for the next accent. They will be responding to the other beats. Sometimes children roll the ball from hand to hand or gently toss it in the air to fill in the number of weak beats. It takes a few measures for them to decide on the sequence of movement for a particular meter.

3 Measuring the meter in familiar music.

You may want to follow these activities by playing excerpts of various musical examples which are in different meters. These can be taped ahead of time. Have the children identify the meter after they discover it with some kind of movement that acts as a 'measuring stick.' They should continue the movement until the music stops and then be ready to identify the meter. A few examples of music might be:

In three: 'Happy Birthday'
In two: 'Yankee Doodle'
In four: 'I've Been Workin' on the Railroad'
In three: 'Star-Spangled Banner'
In two: Haydn's 'Surprise' Symphony, 2nd Movement
In two: Rossini's Overture to *William Tell*

4 Understanding the terms and symbols for meter.

If the words 'measure' and 'meter' have not been discussed, this would be a good time to do so.

■ **We have been listening for the meter in music by measuring the way the beats are grouped around an accent. We have several ways of measuring things. How would you measure a door?** (*In yards, feet, inches*)
■ **What is the gas meter on a house?**
■ **Why do we have parking meters downtown?**
■ **Can you measure the meter of this musical example?**

Play an example in four, such as 'America the Beautiful.'

■ **What did you do to decide on the meter?** (*Listen for the beat and accents*)
■ **What is the meter?** (*Four*)

Put a four on the chalkboard (4); ask the children what kind of notes they were clapping (quarters). Put a quarter note under the four, with the stem turned down (4) and intro-

79

duce this as a meter signature. When the time comes, or you feel that they are ready, you can experiment with other signatures. If the children are clapping a tempo that is rather fast, they may say that the meter signature is ♪ or if they are clapping slowly, they may say that it is ♩ . Several years ago, when a group of second graders were particularly interested and responsive to this lesson, I improvised a simple example in seven. I carefully tried to play something rather fast with seven beats in a measure (♩♩♩♩♩♩♩) without the 3 + 2 + 2 grouping (♫♩♩♫). The children stepped the lively beat and clapped a strong accent on one. When I asked for a volunteer to write the meter signature on the chalkboard the children were eager to respond; the first child wrote $\frac{7}{♪}$!

5   *Picturing the grouping of beats in a measure.*

Many of these experiences should be considered as preparaton for reading and writing notation. Children 'see' beats measured into meter when they clap the beats and accents around a circle. Here is another way to show this: line twelve children up in front of the room to represent twelve beats. Ask those in their seats to call each child a beat and read when they see: 'beat,' 'beat,' 'beat,' 'beat' . . . Now, imagine the beats grouped in measures of three each. Read the line of beats again, but say 'there' on each accented beat. (They can also say 'strong, beat, beat' or 'one, beat, beat'). The child who is the accent can strike a pose on the accent.

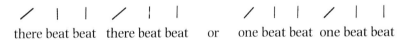

there beat beat   there beat beat   or   one beat beat   one beat beat

The word 'one' prepares them for counting beats later on. The twelve beats represented by the standing children can be grouped into meters of two, three, four, and six. Repeat each meter at least twice. If the children are particularly perceptive, you might try a quick tempo which they would identify as eighth notes, and then the meters could be $\frac{2}{♪}$, $\frac{3}{♪}$, $\frac{4}{♪}$, or $\frac{6}{♪}$.

6   *Reading beats and bar-lines.*

In further preparation for reading and writing notation, put a long line of note stems on the chalkboard. Ask the class to clap and speak this line, first without any meter and then in a meter of four. Speak the word 'du' on each note. The children have to watch the notes carefully to keep track of where they are on the line.

After they have tried this, ask them to speak the line again (in a meter of four), but watch what you are going to do. As they read, put bar-lines before each accent and then after they read the line once more, talk about how the bar-line helps them keep their place in the line.

80

7 *Singing in meters.*

Show the children the following example and have them sing it with syllables.

Now, sing it in a meter of three – each pitch as though it were in a measure of three beats : *d d d | m m m | s s s |*. They can sing it in other meters also. You may want to notate some of it for them so they can see the measures.

etc.

8 *Improvising music in a meter.*

Individual children may improvise a musical example in any meter of their choice for the class to identify. Ask them to use an Orff mallet instrument or the black keys of the piano. Although the example will be simple and obvious, it is still an excellent experience for a child to become the performer and to make his or her own musical decisions. The challenges for the performer are to determine the tempo and meter and to keep a steady beat. With this experience, I ask another child to find a way to move with the music being created.

Hearing, recognizing and reading divisions of the beat[1]

From the time children are born, they are imitating and exploring sounds with their voices and repetitive movements with their bodies. Soon, they are fascinated to find that they can also make sounds by tapping, striking or rubbing something. As language develops and they begin to sing songs, children quickly learn to imitate the rhythm of words and the rhythm of motions and movement that fit the song. When they sing songs, they often move instinctively with the beat of the music but at the same time they are experiencing the rhythm of the words as natural divisions of the beat.

Eurhythmics experiences in the primary grades build on this innate sensitivity to the timing and rhythm of music. In these early grades, the children have many opportunities to hear and respond to music that feels like walking (♩), running (♫), skating (♩), galloping (♪♪) and skipping (♫). By the intermediate grades, they should be able to hear, recognize, and respond well to these fundamental movements, in addition to the beat and divisions of the beat. More attention can be given to specific skills and understandings which lead to sensitive performing, reading and writing notation. Read the following phrases rhythmically, as though they were the words of a song. Try not to look at the suggested rhythm as you read.

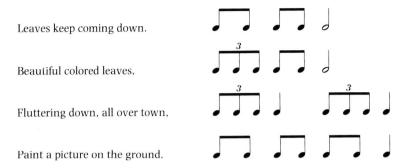

Leaves keep coming down.

Beautiful colored leaves,

Fluttering down, all over town,

Paint a picture on the ground.

There are several ways to read these in rhythm, but the important lesson here is that children are hearing and performing quarters, eighths, triplets and half notes in a meter, in phrases and with accentuation. When you ask children to clap beats or a rhythm, encourage them by your own example, to clap each beat as a unit or 'package.' When beats are clapped in circles with the motion of the hands looking like this, 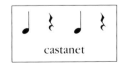 the children sense that they are expressing the sound rather than just applauding. I often notate rhythms on the chalkboard and charts to show the divided beat as a unit:

I challenge students of all ages to perform the example with expression.

In the intermediate grades children still need more experiences hearing and responding to music which focuses on the same aspects of rhythm and pitch as they experienced earlier. But now they are ready to recognize and understand these elements in music that they can read and perform. Because this will require notation skills, it is important that they see many examples of music notation. In some school music programs, it may be unrealistic to try to teach music reading in the time allowed for music instruction. However, it is my earnest belief that we should take every opportunity possible to engage children in reading notation. By the time they can hear and recognize quarters and eighths, they can begin to recognize notation which symbolizes what they can perform. I advocate showing ostinato patterns to children, no matter how simple or repetitive. They feel a sense of accomplishment and pride when they can read their part and play it on an instrument. It is important that they have already experienced those patterns by moving, singing and in ear-training exercises. Here are some sample visuals (they will have had to experience the rest):

drum

castanet

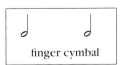
finger cymbal

You will need to focus the attention of your students on the picture of the music they are hearing, creating or performing. Reading and writing notation, whether it is abstract pictures, line drawings, or actual notation, should be a logical outgrowth of their listening, moving, singing and ear-training games.

Children should develop a strong inner sense of relationship between beat and division of the beat – a sense so strong that, given a tempo, they can perform divisions of the beat in two, three or four. Often, key words from songs can be recalled as examples of beat divisions.

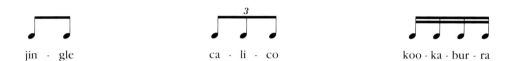

jin - gle   ca - li - co   koo - ka - bur - ra

They don't need to know the word 'triplet' or its meaning before they can tell you that 'ca-li-co' has three sounds and they can clap or step ca - li - co, ca - li - co, while you are playing a beat (♩) on the drum. However, when they hear and can recognize this division of the beat, they are ready to call it a triplet or 'trip-o-let.' Later, when you are teaching the dotted quarter as a beat (♩.), a word other than 'calico' should be chosen for the three eighth-note division (♪♪♪) to avoid confusion between the ♩ and ♩. beats.

The following eurhythmics experiences are intended to develop the skills of hearing and responding to divisions of the beat, as well as reading and writing simple rhythms using divisions of the ♩ beat. It will not be practical at this time for the children to attempt to step or clap a division of four unless the beat is slow. I like to have the children explore a beat divided into four sounds ♬ , but I don't spend much time on it. The important thing, at this stage, is dividing the beat into ♫ or ♪♪♪ .

1   *Feeling the beat and its simple divisions.*

As you play something with all quarter notes, have the children step or clap with you. The quarter-note tempo must be slower than their walking tempo so that they can feel and perform the divisions of the beat. When you signal

- ■   **Two** ♫
- ■   **Three** ♪♪♪
- or
- ■   **Four** ♬

they should think the division as they continue to step the beat. This is the point at which a familiar word from a song or a previously played ear-training game can help them hear the even division. After a few beats, when you say 'now,' they should begin to step the division, continuing until you signal them to resume stepping the beat.

2   *Stepping a division on one beat.*

Ask the children to step the beat you are playing. When you signal a division of two, three or four, on the next beat, they should step that division once and then resume stepping the beat. For example:

Four   Two   Two   Three

Try to speak the number as an anacrusis to their next beat so that they respond with good timing. Think of your signal as preparation for a downbeat feeling in their response. When you signal the number, lift your voice as though inviting them to respond on the next beat.

If you are not sure about how to do this, here is a trick. Imagine yourself as the director of a choral speaking group about to say the Gettysburg address. They are counting on you to give them a cue to breathe and then begin together:

- ■ **'Four score and seven years ago.'**

Try it. Now, think through the example given above and imagine that a class is stepping and clapping and responding to your signals.

3   *Hearing, then echoing divisions of the beat.*

Can the children hear and distinguish the division when they hear it in unfamiliar music? Play the following simple example. Ask them to gesture the beat with their hands and if they hear a division echo-clap it on the very next beat. The children's response is notated below the staff in this example.

4   *Differentiating between divisions of the beat in a song.*

Wally-ach-a

Wal - ly - ach - a,   Wal - ly - ach - a,   Dig - gi - ty doo   dig - gi - ty doo.

Wal - ly - ach - a,   Wal - ly - ach - a,   Dig - gi - ty doo   dig - gi - ty doo. It's the

simp-lest thing there   is-n't much to   it.   All you got-ta do   is   dig-gi - ty   doo.

I   like the rest, but the   part   I like best   is   Dig - gi - ty, dig - gi - ty   doo.

Teach 'Wally-ach-a' by rote. As the children are learning the song, invite them to incorporate movement into their exploration of the rhythm. They can discover the beat, divisions of the beat, accent, meter and phrasing. This would be a good opportunity to call attention to the two variations of four sixteenths which appear in the song ♫♫ and ♫♫.

Divide the class into four groups and assign each group one of the following rhythms in the song. As the children sing the song, each group will listen for their rhythm and respond with the wrist–tip (W T) motions.

Group One: The beat   ♩
             Bump wrists together.

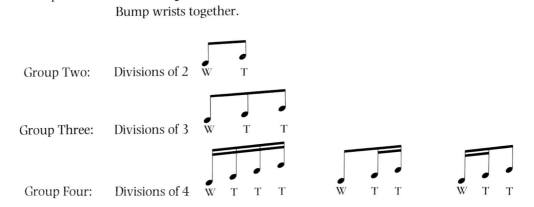

Group Two: Divisions of 2   W   T

Group Three: Divisions of 3   W   T   T

Group Four: Divisions of 4   W T T T   W T T   W T T

5   *Practicing reading rhythm with beat divisions.*

In the beginning stages of music reading, children need to practice moving their eyes steadily from left to right across a line of notes. Write a long line of note stems on the chalkboard, like this:

One child can point to the note stems as the class responds by speaking 'ta' and by clapping or tapping the small sticks on the desk. Try it without the leader pointing. Ask two or three children to come to the chalkboard and put a '2', '3' or '4' under one of the stems. This will tell the class to change that note to a divided beat. The whole class can then read the line but substitute the divisions as marked. For example:

At first, just the numbers will appear; then let other children come to the board and write in the notation for the division. Make certain that there is enough space for the division to be inserted.

6   *Practicing reading pitch and rhythm with beat divisions.*

Notate a four-measure melodic phrase in quarter notes, using tonal patterns which the children can read and sing. When they can sing the example with syllables, change the notation of one or two notes so that they will be reading divisions of the quarter note. Here is a four-measure phrase and an example showing a few substitutions.

7   *Creating music that uses beat and simple beat divisions.*

Notate several tonal patterns on the chalkboard which the children can use to create ostinato patterns. For example:

Invite individuals to improvise a two-measure ostinato in $\frac{4}{4}$ meter on an instrument of their choice. They should use one or two of the beat divisions in their ostinato. The tempo should be slow so they can play the divisions easily. Here are two examples:

Choose four of the ostinatos to be performed together. Start them one at a time and then end together or drop out, one at a time. Invite a child to improvise a melody using the pitches G–A–B–D–E, while the four ostinatos are played as an accompaniment. Be careful of balance. The ostinatos will have to play softly if the melody is to be heard. Here is an example of a melody that might be played on the recorder or another melody instrument.

Longer than a Beat

By now your children are well aware of long sounds in music, sounds that extend beyond the next beat. One exercise that was presented earlier in this chapter asked children to feel the duration of several beats through a movement such as pulling or twisting. In many previous eurhythmics experiences, the children were encouraged to show movement through the long notes, or to feel the sound travelling through the steady beats.

Here is a sequenced sampling of exercises which can help children develop their skill in hearing and responding to half notes. The same exercises could be designed to focus on any two or three note values.

(*a*) Move on ♩ and ♫ , but freeze on ♩

(*b*) Move on ♩ and ♫ , but stop and show the 𝅗𝅥 with a silent clap.

(*c*) Freeze on ♩ and ♫, but move on 𝅗𝅥

(*d*) Move on each note value but change directions on 𝅗𝅥

(*e*) As you hear ♩ and 𝅗𝅥, show the opposite one in movement.

For each of the above exercises, play a musical example which uses only those three note values. Continue each one for several beats. An example is given here, but you will have to lengthen it and develop your own interesting ideas. You could use just one hand.

When you ask children to freeze, they must be immobile for those few seconds when you can introduce a new element in the music or feature something to which they need to pay particular attention. I have found that they truly focus on that 'something' during the silence of freezing. They usually listen with anticipation to begin again at your signal, either musical or spoken. It is amusing to observe the way some children think they know exactly when you will give the next signal.

Children do not see many whole notes in their songbooks and when they are performing, whether they are singing or playing, it is very difficult for them to hold a note that long. Their bodies just won't stay still and they are not comfortable 'attending to' long notes. They can make long, extended movements when challenged, but a great deal of concentration and skill is required to keep a beat steady while counting a specific number of beats. When children perform or improvise independently, they usually rush through long notes. One way to help them realize the ongoing steady beat in a long note is to introduce the tie in music. In that way, they can actually see the beat even though they are holding the sound through the beat. Also, by introducing the dotted quarter and dotted half note through ties, the children have a concrete illustration of what the dot is representing.

My explanation of a tie may seem too simplistic, but it has worked with children.

■ **When two notes are tied together, the second one does not sound separately; it is held over.**

This seems to suffice for an explanation until the children can understand the meaning of 'articulating a sound.' Here are four experiences which can be used in introducing the tie and dot.

1 *Creating a long note with a tie.*

Draw a long line of quarter notes on the chalkboard:

Ask the children to read the line by speaking 'du' on each note. Draw a bow, tied between two of the quarter notes

- ■ **If I 'tie' this quarter to the next one, the second one holds on to the first one and doesn't sound separately.**
- ■ **Listen to my example: 'du–u'** *(Hardly articulate the 'u' at all.)*

Speak the line with the tie drawn in. As the children imitate you, insist that they gesture, with their hand, the sound of their voice.

Notation:

Hand gesture:

The hand gesture can be in the air or on a surface so that they have a tactile sensation of the movement of the sound. Let one or two children draw other ties (with bows) in the line of quarters and then repeat the line, speaking, and singing it on a single pitch.

Erase the bows and explain that the mark which ties two notes together looks like this: ⌣ . Tie other quarters together in the example, or change some of the quarters to half notes and add ties which will eventually create dotted half notes.

2   *Practicing reading and performing ties.*

This is a simple exercise designed to help children realize ties as substitutions for beats or parts of beats. It may be best at the outset to have the class observe a line of eight children performing the exercise. Notate the following patterns on the chalkboard or on a transparency. Position the line of children so that they and the rest of the class can see the notation. The children in the line will number off and then begin to count as they each clap one quarter note.

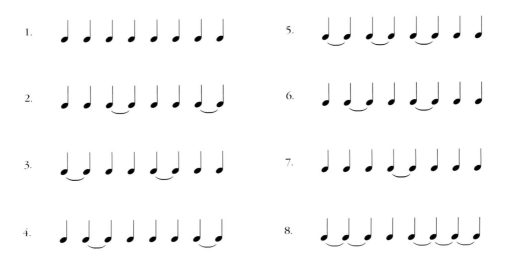

89

Wherever there is a note tied to the next one, the child should reach over as though to connect that note with the next person who doesn't clap but makes a slight motion. For instance, for the fourth example

children count:

one, two,_____ four, five, six, sev'n_____

All of this must be done with a steady beat. After the exercise, some of the children sitting in their seats can rewrite the rhythm substituting the correct note values for the ties. When they get to the last example and try to rewrite the three quarters tied together, you can explain to them that a dotted half note is the same as three quarters tied together.

Children sometimes ask about the 'period' or 'dot' after a quarter (♩.) or half note (𝅗𝅥.). If they are not quite ready to be introduced to those note values, you can name the note and demonstrate how it is to be performed. When the beat is a quarter note, the dotted quarter must be performed as part of a pattern. You must be careful to demonstrate a dotted quarter with the eighth that follows it, as well as the quarter-note resolution; not just ♩. , or even ♩. ♪, but ♩. ♪♩ or ♩. ♪𝅗𝅥

I believe that few students really understand the meaning of the statement, 'The dot equals half of a note it follows.' It can be understood mathematically – half of a quarter note is an eighth – but how do you perform half of a quarter? The concept has to do with how long something happens; it must be realized in some physical movement of all or part of the body. By introducing the dotted quarter and the dotted half through tied notes, the children have a concrete illustration of what the dot is representing.

3   Substituting a dot for a tied note.

As the following sequence of rhythm patterns is repeated several times, your children should begin to recognize how a dot is often substituted for tied notes. Establish a comfortable tempo for them to tap on their desks and speak with 'ta' each rhythm pattern twice.

Ask your children to read the first rhythm pattern below. Always have them to repeat it twice. Then challenge them to change the words to fit the rhythm of examples (*a*) and (*b*). (I have suggested words in parentheses.)

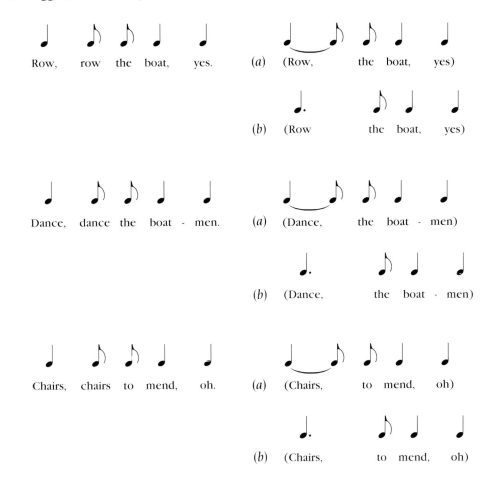

The above word examples came from the following three songs: 'Michael, Row the Boat Ashore,' 'The Boatmen's Dance' and 'Chairs to Mend.'

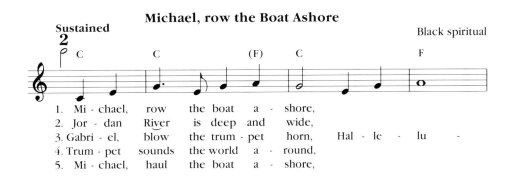

Michael, row the Boat Ashore

Black spiritual

1. Mi - chael, row the boat a - shore,
2. Jor - dan River is deep and wide,
3. Gabri - el, blow the trum - pet horn, Hal - le - lu -
4. Trum - pet sounds the world a - round,
5. Mi - chael, haul the boat a - shore,

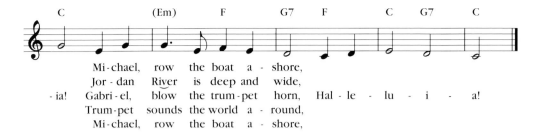

Mi‑chael,   row   the boat a‑shore,
Jor‑dan   River   is deep and   wide,
- ia! Gabri‑el, blow the trum‑pet horn, Hal‑le - lu - i - a!
Trum‑pet sounds the world a - round,
Mi‑chael,   row   the boat a‑shore,

The Boatmen's Dance

American minstrel song

1. The boat‑men dance, The boat‑men sing, The boat‑men up to ev‑'ry‑thing. And

when the boat‑man gets on shore, He spends his cash and works for more.

Refrain

Then dance, the boat‑men, dance! Oh, dance, the boat‑men, dance! Oh,

dance all night till the broad day‑light, And go home with your pals in the morn‑ing.

2. The oyster boat should keep to the shore,
   The fishing smacks should venture more,
   The schooner sails before the wind,
   The steamboat leaves a streak behind.
   Refrain

3. When you go to the boatmen's ball,
   Dance with your wife or not at all,
   Skyblue jacket and tarpaulin hat,
   Look out, my boys, for the nine-tail cat.
   Refrain

Chairs to Mend

Traditional

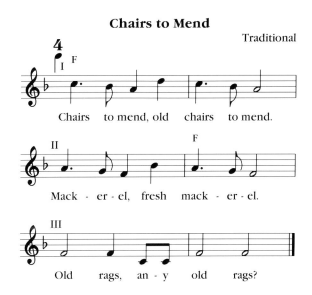

Chairs to mend, old chairs to mend.

Mack - er - el, fresh mack - er - el.

Old rags, an - y old rags?

4 'Solving' the rhythm of an unfamiliar song.

Show your children the notation for the song 'Early to Bed.' Divide the class into small groups and see if they can figure out how to speak the rhythm of the song. It would be interesting to invite the groups to share the ways they arrived at their solutions.

Early to Bed

Anonymous

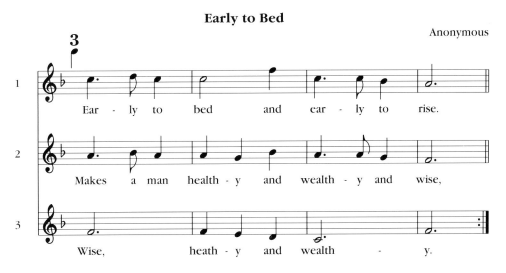

Ear - ly to bed and ear - ly to rise.

Makes a man health - y and wealth - y and wise,

Wise, heath - y and wealth - y.

(from *Round and Round They Go*)

Continue going over these same experiences with other songs and help your children find ties and dots in the notation of their favorite music. There are more experiences with dotted rhythms in the next chapter. Other good examples of songs which use the dotted quarter and dotted half notes are:

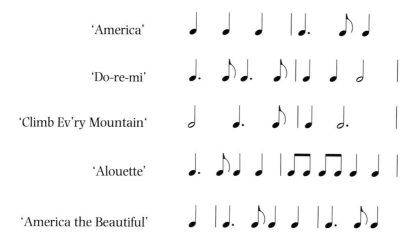

Using Note Cards to Develop Music Reading and Writing

Eurhythmics affords many varied opportunities to respond to specific aspects of music, and eventually it is important and logical that students see and read notation. The difficulty with looking at the notation of a song is that so much more is included in the notation than what you want the children to see in the early stages of note reading. For example:

- Pictures on the page attract their attention.
- Hyphenated words are distracting. Children like to read the words of the song; they are confused by hyphens.
- Notes written on a staff; the pitch is not necessary for reading rhythm.
- The notes are often spaced without attention to the underlying beat. This is illustrated in the following examples:

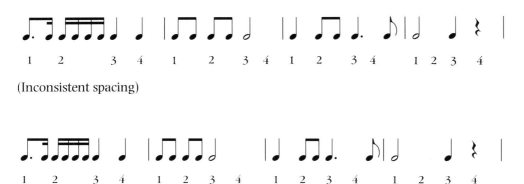

94

We must prepare visual examples so that the consistency of spacing and notation reflects the timing of beats (when the beat should occur), and the relationship of divisions of the beat. A visual aid is used to help develop a musical skill. At the same time it should aid the students' sense of accomplishment, not frustration.

I have found that children enjoy manipulating their own visual devices such as sticks, straws or note cards which they can line up in front of them on the floor or on a desk so as to see, touch, and read music notation. I made laminated 3″ × 5″ note cards, each with a beat on it. The following is an illustration of various note cards used in meter and rhythm games. Note that the half note is taped to a card the same size, and when it is needed in a game, it is opened and placed across two beats. (It becomes too complicated to work with three or four cards taped together so I present only the half note this way.)

1 *Measuring beats in a meter.*

Since space is needed for this game, it can be played with the children grouped in fours or fives. Each group is given a packet of twelve quarter-note cards which they line up in a row on the floor or on a table. You will have to encourage speed or else they will take forever to line them up in perfect order.

Individuals in each group take turns pointing to the note cards as the groups speak the steady quarter notes with 'du.' This keeps everyone involved, even though each child may not have a personal packet of cards. As you play twelve quarter notes in a meter – for instance, three – each group (with someone pointing) speaks the rhythm but substitutes 'now' or 'one' on each accent. (This is similar to a previous exercise where the children listened for the accent and spoke: 'NOW – beat – beat', or 'ONE–beat–beat.') Here is a simple musical example to illustrate how the class will speak: 'ONE–du–du ONE–du–du.'

When the children have found the accent and identified the meter, they can put a small rhythm stick (or colored straw) before each accent – like a bar-line. Sometimes I ask the child who is pointing to pat the accent with a flat palm and touch the other beats with the tip of the finger. That way, as the group watches the child's hand, they can see the different motion on the accented beat.

Here are three more examples of music to play for this activity. Notice that twelve beats can be organized in meters of two, three, four and six. Play each example as musically as possible in spite of the fact that you are only playing quarter notes. Try this first with the rhythm sounding on a rhythm instrument, and then try an example on the piano. A melody will often suggest a meter even in the absence of a rhythmical accent.

There may be other ways to speak the phrase besides 'du,' but for this beginning exercise, I feel that counting is too difficult. This is especially true when you start inserting eighths and half notes. The sound of the number gets in the way of speaking a phrase of music with a fluid line. Also, the children get so involved with remembering whether they are to say 'one,' 'two,' or 'three' and then if you add 'one and, two and' there is too much to remember. Whatever you choose to have them say to verbalize the beats, be sure they speak distinctly and rhythmically. In fact, ask them to exaggerate the enunciation. Here are some possibilities:

Since a long line of quarter notes reminds my classes of 'walking music,' I may begin by having them speak 'walk, walk.' I don't continue that too long because the word is difficult to say repeatedly and it may become a two-syllable word with a guttural 'k' on the end.

96

Worse yet, the children may become silly (as in one of my classes) and start quacking like ducks. It does, however, reinforce the basic movement of the quarter note when reading music. Also, notice that the word 'beat' almost sounds like a two-syllable word when repeated over and over: 'bea-te.' I use 'du' often because the 'd' sound is clearly articulated and the 'oo' sounds through the length of the note.

2   Substituting two eighth notes for a quarter-note beat.

Each packet should now contain the twelve quarter notes but also four cards showing ♫. Now you can begin to add rhythm to a phrase of beats in a meter. After your students line up the twelve quarter-note cards, tell them you are going to change one quarter-note beat to two eighth notes. As they watch one child point to the cards, play an example which includes one beat of eighths. For instance:

The children decide where they need to place the card of two eighths on top of a quarter note. They will be notating the new rhythm. This is just like rhythmic dictation but the children enjoy manipulating the cards. Notice that the word 'notate' can be used in this practical situation where the children are actually using the cards to manipulate notation symbols.

Any note value or rhythmic unit may be put on cards and incorporated into these games. The two cards taped together for the half note are folded when they are in the packet but when they are needed for notation, they are opened up and placed across the correct number of beats.

The usual sequence for introducing and teaching note values and units of rhythm begins with the first four movements to which the children respond in beginning eurhythmics experiences:

♩ = walk: ♫ = run-ning;   ♪♫ = skip-ty and   ♩ = slide

These words are used to verbalize the movement in the early experiences. I call them the 'movement words.' I also introduce the quarter rest early in their experience but it is important to make a difference between ♩ and 𝄽 . If you sing or play an example on the recorder, I believe you can be more certain that the class will hear the difference than if you play it on the piano. Here are two possible examples of twelve beats which use quarters, quarter rests and half notes.

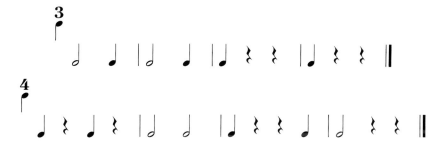

When the children are ready to work with the familiar rhythms in the triple-beat family, packets can be made which include: ♩., ♫♫, ♩♪, and later, ♪♩ and ♩.♫♫.

Note cards are helpful in the beginning stages of note reading and writing. The separate card for each beat helps to visually present each beat as a unit and if the cards are 'played,' spoken and tapped in a steady tempo, the rhythms on the cards are performed precisely on the beat. Children enjoy creating phrases of rhythm for their classmates to perform. Once basic rhythms are learned, the children will be ready for variations using rests, sixteenths, ties and syncopation. At that point it becomes impractical to continue using the cards.

A Duple Beat Versus a Triple Beat

This section may challenge your thinking about the teaching of meter, especially meter that is commonly called compound. I have explored the idea of teaching a duple beat (♩) versus a triple beat (♩.) to students of all ages, from kindergarten to college age, and the results – in listening, performing, creating, and reading and writing music – have been rewarding. (Of course, with the young children, it is merely the sound and movement of both beat families.) I am convinced of its validity in the teaching of music. The concept has been realized as a direct result of eurhythmics experiences. It is based on the idea that a person's instinctive response to music is movement that is close to the tempo of one's heartbeat.

Before offering specific eurhythmics experiences with duple and triple beats, I should like to explain these ideas in some detail and suggest ways to begin with your children.

It is best to begin with familiar songs. Your children probably know 'Yankee Doodle' and 'Row, Row, Row Your Boat.' Lead them in singing the songs and then discovering answers to the questions that follow.

Yankee Doodle

1. Fath'r and I went down to camp A - long with Cap - tain Good - in, And
2. Yan - kee Doo - dle went to town. A - rid - ing on a po - ny, He

there we saw the men and boys As thick as ha - sty pud - din'.
stuck a feath - er in his cap And called it mac - a - ro - ni.

Yan - kee Doo - dle keep it up. Yan - kee Doo - dle dan - dy.

Mind the mu - sic   and   the   step   and   with   the   girls   be   hand - y.

Row, Row, Row Your Boat

Traditional round

Row,   row,   row   your   boat   gent - ly   down   the   stream.

Mer - ri - ly, mer - ri - ly,   mer - ri - ly, mer - ri - ly,   Life   is   but   a   dream.

- ■ As you sing 'Yankee Doodle', find a way to show the beat.
- ■ If you can discover the accented beats, show them with a different movement.

Yan-kee Doo-dle went to town

- ■ How many beats are in a measure, in this song? *(Two)*
- ■ Now, sing 'Row, Row, Row Your Boat' and show the accented and unaccented beats in this song.

Row, row, row your boat

- ■ How many beats are in a measure in this song? *(Two)*

The children should respond quite naturally to the beat in both songs and their movement may be similar. If you look closely at these two songs, both with two beats per measure, the meter signature for 'Yankee Doodle' is $\frac{2}{4}$, two quarter notes per measure, but the meter signature for 'Row, Row, Row Your Boat' is $\frac{2}{4\cdot}$, two dotted quarter notes per measure. This is often shown as $\frac{6}{8}$ and students learn to count six eighth notes in each measure. We have already encountered meter signatures which identify note values used as the beat in earlier eurhythmics games:

The $\frac{6}{8}$ meter signature is so widely in print in scores and the tradition of counting it '1 2 3 4 5 6' is so ingrained in the teaching of music that it is difficult for teachers to consider using another approach. Yet, for most songs that have a written signature of $\frac{6}{8}$ or $\frac{6}{\flat}$, the music should be felt in $\frac{2}{\flat\cdot}$, or two-dotted-quarter meter.

Music educators have taught meter by the 'rule' of the meter signature:

■ **The top number tells us how many beats are in a measure and the bottom number tells us what kind of a note gets one beat.**

That rule is rehearsed over and over but unfortunately it doesn't always result in a genuinely musical response. When students look at music that has a meter signature of $\frac{6}{8}$ or $\frac{6}{\flat}$ they often plod through their counting of six equal beats and the natural grouping of $\sqrt{}\sqrt{}$ is lost. This procedure has always troubled me because when we hear, clap along, sing and dance examples of music with a meter signature of $\frac{6}{\flat}$, we feel a strong movement sense of swaying from side to side (on the dotted-quarter grouping). Unless it is quite slow, we rarely hear or feel it as a distinct expression of six beats per measure. There is a subtle difference between seeing and performing:

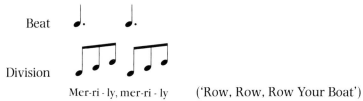

Du du du du du du   and   Du na nee Du na nee

Clap and speak each of these a few times.

I have found that a simple and basic beginning to all of this is the realization that there are duple beats and there are triple beats. When a beat has a natural division of three, it is a triple beat.

Beat

Division

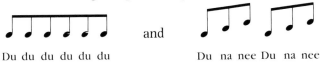

Mer-ri - ly, mer-ri - ly   ('Row, Row, Row Your Boat')

When a beat has a natural division of two, it is a duple beat.

Beat

Division

Yan-kee Doo-dle   ('Yankee Doodle')

If children can listen for the beat and then can hear a hint of either 'Yan-kee' or 'mer-ri-ly,' they can identify the beat as being duple or triple. We need to provide children with many experiences to hear, feel and compare the difference between duple and triple beats and then to understand the concept and apply it to unfamiliar music which they are learning. When they have sufficient skill and understanding of the duple versus the triple beat, the $\frac{6}{\flat}$ meter signature can be explained and understood. Since I write all the meter signatures with the note values on the bottom, it is not strange for the children to see $\frac{2}{}$ as well as $\frac{2}{}$, $\frac{3}{}$, or $\frac{4}{}$.

Children are experiencing a repertoire of duple-beat and triple-beat songs from the beginning of their lives. They hear 'Rock-a-bye-Baby' when they are in the crib. Then, throughout their pre-school years they may hear, sing and dance many more songs with a triple-beat feeling, such as,

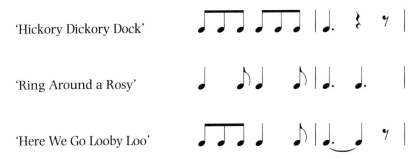

At the same time, they are responding to songs with a duple-beat feeling, such as,

During the primary grades, singing, moving and playing experiences should bring focus to the beat and its basic division of two or three sounds. Aural and visual experiences, no matter how simple, are also important in this (or any) musical development. For example, a few children can play 'mer-ri-ly' as an accompaniment to the song 'Row, Row Your Boat' by gently striking a maraca against the palm of the hand. Show them the rhythm on a card (♫). When that same pattern is played in a slightly different way on another song, the children can transfer the sound of 'mer-ri-ly' in their minds to the new music.

One of the most valuable ways to experience the difference between the duple and triple beat is for the children to decide on specific movements which best identify each beat. Some suggestions for the duple beat are a push–pull or down–up motion. A swinging or swaying from side to side is often used to illustrate triple beat. In my classes, when the children first found the beat to 'Yankee Doodle,' they marched or moved their arms like soldiers and they rowed a boat on 'Row, Row, Row Your Boat.' Two other songs which are good for comparing duple and triple beats – are 'Jingle Bells' and 'Over the River and Through the Woods.'

♫ = jin-gle *(Feel the trotting horse and say the word.)*

♫♫ = grand-mo-ther *(Feel the galloping horse and say the word.)*

Jingle Bells

Over the River and Through the Wood

Traditional Melody
Words: Lydia Maria Childs

1. O-ver the riv-er and through the wood, To grand-moth-er's house we go:___ The
2. O-ver the riv-er and through the wood, Trot fast___ my dap-ple gray!___ Spring

horse knows the way to car-ry the sleigh Through the white and drift-ed snow.___
o - ver the ground like a hunt-ing hound.___ For this is Thanks-giv-ing day!_

O-ver the riv-er and through the wood, Oh, how the wind does blow!___ It
O-ver the riv-er and through the wood, Now grand-moth-er's face I spy!___ Hur -

stings the toes and bites the nose As o-ver the ground we go.___
- rah for the fun! Is the pud-ding done? Hur-rah for the pump-kin pie!___

Here are five eurhythmics exercises to further develop this concept of a duple-beat 'family' versus a triple-beat 'family' in music.

1   *Determining the basic division of a beat in two or three.*

For this exercise the children should be able to move freely in an open space; however, the same exercise can be experienced by sitting and clapping. In the open space, they will feel a more natural physical relationship of ♫ to ♩ and ♫♫ to ♩.·.

■ **I will play a short example. As soon as you can, step the beat and if you hear a hint of 'Yankee' (♪♪) or 'merrily' (♪♪♪), show it with the wrist–tip motion. If I say 'change,' step what your hands were doing, either ♪♪ or ♪♪♪ .**

(If the children are sitting, they can sway from side to side on the beat and then add the hand motion on the beat division.)

Play very simple examples using a quarter-note beat for some and a dotted-quarter beat for the others. Here are some sample improvisations which you can try. Notice the purposeful simplicity of the left hand; you don't need to play any more than the beat. You will, however, have to repeat or expand the example. Remember, your music must convey a sense of movement and a definite hint at the division of the beat. To achieve more variety in your examples, use different tempos, dynamics, registers, and articulations.

2 Seeing and feeling a beat and its divisions.

Ask the children to sit facing a partner. Chairs or the floor are less restricting than a student's desk. Use the same examples of music as in Exercise 1 or play familiar songs. Partner A will clap the beat as if tossing it to partner B who will listen for the division of the beat and then pat it on thighs, either left–right for ♫ , or left–right–right for ♫♪. Not only will they feel what they are hearing, but they also will 'see' it.

3 Improvising with a duple or triple beat.

Ask individuals to sing or play a second phrase to one that you create. Here are examples of first phrases for you to play on a rhythm instrument, piano or recorder:

4 Introducing uneven divisions of the triple beat.

Soon you will want to teach other common patterns in triple meter. When it is appropriate, begin to highlight a new pattern by calling attention to it in familiar songs. The ♩♪ pattern in $\frac{2}{4}$ meter always sounds like 'gen-tly' as in:

Gen - tly down   the   stream   ('Row, Row, Row Your Boat')

Let the children create their own motion for the pattern or simply clap it when they hear it. For a quick-reaction exercise, ask them to clap dotted quarters until you signal

■ Change!

Then they should change their response to ♩♪ until you signal another change. Use this pattern on cards or charts for reading and playing. Add it to a list of rhythms that are familiar to the class. All of these activities can be used when any new pattern is being learned. The more common even and uneven divisions of the duple beat are: ♫, ♫♫, ♩♪. The more common even and uneven divisions of the triple beat are: ♫♫, ♩♪, ♪♩.

104

5 *Reading and performing notation in duple- and triple-beat families.*

Use extra moments in a lesson to have the class speak, sing and/or clap as you point to four or more rhythms or patterns notated on the chalkboard. These can be any patterns which you feel need to be practiced, especially those that should be compared to other patterns. Either point or improvise a simple accompaniment and call out the number of the example to be performed. If each example is repeated twice, the result is a more confident and correct response. Examples to be practiced:

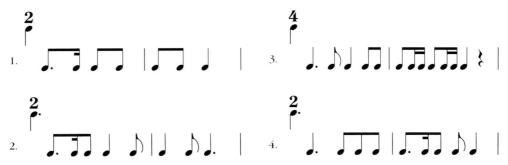

Children should be discovering these rhythms or patterns in songs that they see in their music books. Be sure that the example of a rhythm in the song is as clear as the one they have been seeing on the chalkboard or a card. For example, if you have been working with these two rhythms: ♫♩ and ♩♪, don't confuse the children by expecting them to sort out the two rhythms in this example:

These complications can be explained at a later time.

In summary, it is important to explore the difference in both sound and feeling of duple and triple beats. Let the children discover the beat and basic divisions of the beat in familiar and unfamiliar songs and recordings. Use movement to highlight the feeling of each experience. Show the notation of duple- and triple-beat rhythms whenever possible. Rewrite songs that are in ⅜ meter, in a ⅖. meter, and later, compare the two notated versions. When children are successful in recognizing by ear and eye and can perform music that has a duple or a triple beat, you can begin to introduce other possibilities. For instance:

= triple beats grouped in a meter of three.

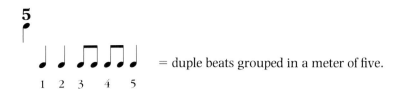

= duple beats grouped in a meter of five.

You will note that the triplet is absent in these experiences. I teach it at a later time to avoid confusing the issue when teaching the difference between the duple and triple beat. The triplet was previously highlighted with the song, 'Wally-a-cha.' When I am certain that the children are ready, we explore the fact that a duple beat can be divided in threes but that division is 'borrowed' from the triple beat and so must be marked ⌐⌐⌐.

You may also be wondering about songs that have a meter signature of ³. Most of the songs that we see notated in ³ are performed with a ² feeling and could easily be notated that way. 'Take Me Out to the Ballgame' can be notated either,

'Chim Chim Cheree' can be notated either,

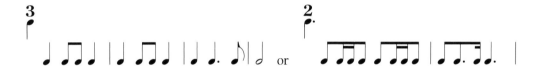

Suggested Music for Hearing Duple and Triple Beats.

Here are a few examples of songs and recorded music to which the children can listen and move to express the beat feeling. Let them be creative but their movement should show a distinct difference between duple and triple beats.

A suggestion might be:

■ **When you hear a triple beat, put your hands behind your back and imagine yourself ice skating to the music, gliding from the left to the right. When you hear a duple beat, imagine yourself pulling up a stage curtain or pulling a rope. Pull with your left hand, right, left, right.**

Duple

- 'Troika,' from *Lieutenant Kije Suite* by Prokofiev. (C)[2]
- 'Minka,' a Russian folk song. (B)
- 'Simple Gifts,' a Shaker folk song. (C)
- 'March of the Siamese Children,' from *The King and I*, by Richard Rodgers. (A)
- 'Bourrée,' from *Music for the Royal Fireworks Suite* by Handel. (E)

- 'Chim Chim Cheree,' from *Mary Poppins*, by Richard and Robert Sherman. (B)
- 'Skye Boat Song,' by Annie MacLeod. (E)
- 'Morning,' from *Peer Gynt*, Suite No. 1, by Grieg. (F)
- 'Gigue' from Suite for Strings, by Corelli–Pinelli (originally from Sonata No. 1 Op. 5 No. 9 for Violin and Piano, by Corelli.) (B)

The next two suggestions are traditionally notated with a $\frac{3}{8}$ meter signature but the beat is certainly felt as a triple beat. If you use 'Take Me Out to the Ballgame' let the children explore the beat, meter and rhythm in movement before seeing how it is usually notated. It would be my choice to notate it in $\frac{2}{4}$. meter. Here is the first phrase:

'Take Me Out to the Ballgame,' by Albert Von Tilzer. (D)
'Circus Music,' from *The Red Pony* by Aaron Copland. (D)

Anacrusis or Pick-up

One of the important rhythmic aspects of music is the anacrusis, sometimes called a pick-up. Musicians are conscious of the timing, energy and character of an anacrusis in music that leads towards a crusis (an accent).[3] Musical phrases either begin with an anacrusis (1) or a crusis (2).

One other related aspect of phrasing is the metacrusis – the relaxation or 'falling away' from the crusis ('-day' in the first example and '-dy Land' in the second example). The anacrusis, crusis or metacrusis in a musical phrase relates to the subtleties of timing, energy, weight and dynamics that are given to each note in performance. These three aspects of phrasing in music can become a very extensive study for performing musicians but children unconsciously develop a sensitivity to these aspects of performance by simply imitating your sound or responding to your facial expressions or arm gestures.

Children enjoy knowing and using 'important' terms, like 'crusis' and 'anacrusis.' When they have some understanding of the terms they will begin to perform a musical phrase with more expression and innate feeling for the music. Here are a few simple exercises to help children become aware of the anacrusis and crusis in music.

1   *Exploring stressed and unstressed syllables in names.*

With this simple activity, children can begin to develop an awareness of anacrusis and crusis in music. Children love to explore the sounds of their names. Which ones begin with a stressed sound and which ones begin with an unstressed sound? This activity might have been used in language arts or music in the primary grades to find the number of syllables in a word or the accentuation. Now it can be reviewed with some creative movement to show the anacrusis and crusis. Besides the names of classmates, try some of these:

John *Tho*-mas Sa-*man*-tha *Jer*-e-my E-*liz*-a-beth Eu-*gene*
Lou-*ise* Su-*zan*-na *Jane* Re-*bec*-ca Chris-*tine* *Ti*-mo-thy

2 *Throwing a ball to feel an anacrusis.*

Let the children experience an anacrusis by pretending to wind up their arm to throw an imaginary ball to a friend across the room. This is a very structured exercise in which the wind-up is progressively longer. First it is one circle of the arm into a throw (♩. | ♩.). Then, the wind-up is two circles and a throw (♩. ♩. | ♩.), then three (♩. ♩. ♩. | ♩.), and so on (I wouldn't go any higher than six wind-ups). Try the exercise at slightly different tempos and notice how the size of the arm movement for the wind-up will change. Instead of improvising music for this exercise, use your voice to reinforce the rhythm of the wind-ups. Don't hurry the movement, especially through the throws and getting back to start the next wind-up. When the class understands what they are going to do, you can begin to vocalize the movement:

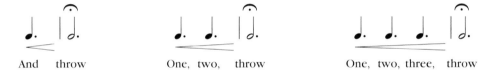

And   throw   One, two,   throw   One, two, three,   throw

3 *Feeling the crusis in a phrase.*

The following simple phrases can be put on the chalkboard to be read by the class. At first, establish a moderate tempo of beats in a meter of four. Ask the children to keep a silent steady beat across their desk as you read the phrases aloud. Read them again as the children clap the word 'cats' everytime they hear it. Show them how to clap as though they are tossing the clap across the room. The movement is more circular and the sound is more alive as though it is being 'sent' to someone rather than being 'dropped' in someone's lap. Try this with the children reading and clapping the phrases together.

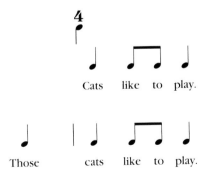

Cats   like   to   play.

Those   cats   like   to   play.

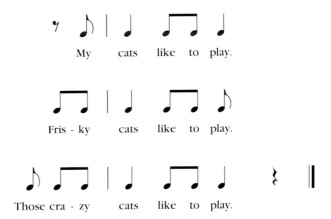

My   cats   like   to   play.

Fris - ky   cats   like   to   play.

Those cra - zy   cats   like   to   play.

4   Feeling the anacrusis and crusis of a phrase.

Ask the children to tap all the sounds that come before 'cats,' with their fingers on their thighs then clap the accent. That way, they will be tapping the anacrusis into the crusis (or the pick-up into the downbeat). If you are speaking the phrases, finish speaking each line softly. If the children are reading these phrases from the chalkboard or a transparency, they can think the rest of each line, so that the timing and rhythm remain in place.

Whenever you clap a phrase with an anacrusis, show the movement of the sounds leading into the crusis with a slight exaggeration, especially in the primary grades. If the children mirror your movement, they will be experiencing the sense of a musical line.

5   Tracing the phrase movement of a song.

Most of your children know the song 'Happy Birthday.' Have them sing it and show the phrases by drawing an arc from left to right in the air on each phrase.

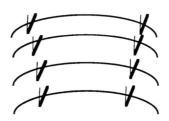

While one child traces the arcs at the chalkboard, invite the class to sing the song again and clap the crusis of each phrase. See if the child who is tracing the arcs at the board can put a mark with the side of the chalk where the crusis falls in each phrase (see illustration above). Then put a bar-line before each crusis.

It is possible that the children will hear another crusis at the end of each phrase, on the word 'you.' Now is a good time to talk about whole phrases in terms of anacrusis and crusis. Yes, wherever there is an accent, it is a crusis. Ask one child to bounce a ball so that it hits the floor on each crusis while the rest of the class claps the rhythm of 'Happy

Birthday.' The clapping should reflect the same arc movement seen in bouncing the ball. The first phrase will look like this:

(Prepare   bounce   catch   prepare bounce – catch)

Explore other words to describe a birthday besides 'happy.' You may even get some surprise suggestions such as 'rainy birthday' or 'sad birthday.' Write them on the board and let the children decide on a rhythm for each one. Choose four from the list, put them in an order, and sing the song by substituting the new words. Here is an example:

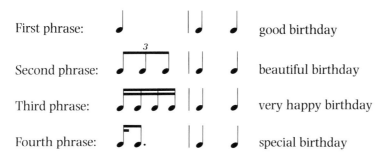

Another possible suggestion would be to notate the rhythm of the new words on the arcs.

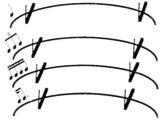

Movement as a Preparation for Music Literacy

A Hungarian Folk Song

110

This delightful Hungarian folk tune can be used to highlight certain aspects of music through eurhythmics. The following sequential plan guides the children to discover the rhythm pattern ♫♩ , find it in the music and decide where it fits into the meter, phrasing and plan (or form) of the composition. It is a very common pattern; one that children learn to recognize and call the 'short–short–long' pattern or the 'run-ning walk' pattern. Notice how easily the movement can be translated into a picture of the notation: ▬ ▬ ▬▬ or ♪♪♩ . Each of the following five eurhythmics experiences should be done in sequence as each is related to the previous one. They do not all have to be done in one lesson; you will probably want to spread them out over several lessons.

1   Highlighting a particular rhythm pattern.

In order to become familiar with the music, the children need repeated hearings, so ask them to listen and respond in the following ways:

- **Listen to the music that I will play and count how many times you hear the pattern,** ♫♩. *(Eight times)*
- **This time, clap the pattern each time it appears.**
- **Stand up and step the pattern but clap everything else.**

If the children have begun to creatively use the limited space beside their desks or chairs, they can step the rhythm forward, backward, or sideways. This is better than just stepping the rhythm in one spot.

2   Determining how many phrases there are in a song.

- **Take a partner.**
- **Decide who will be 'A' and who will be 'B.' You must listen for the phrases in the song. Partner 'A' will clap the beat of the first phrase to partner 'B.'** *(Demonstrate as if tossing the clap to a partner.)* **Then partner 'B' will clap the beat of the second phrase to 'A.' Keep alternating the phrases until the end.**
- **How many phrases are there in this whole song?** *(Four phrases)*

3   Determining the length of a phrase by counting the beats.

Ask the children to check their answer as they repeat the song. (Eight beats in a phrase.) If the children are at their desks, they can 'walk' their fingers across the desk to count the beats.

4   Establishing the placement of beats in a phrase.

Put eight circles, large enough to contain notes, on the chalkboard. Try to draw them in a steady tempo.

- **If I put this:** ♩ **in each circle, have I notated the rhythm of the first phrase?** *(No, the beats are there but not the rhythm.)*

As one child points to the circles on the chalkboard, assign half the class to clap the beats while the other half of the class sings the melody with 'loo' and taps the rhythm of the first phrase.

■ **Can you fill in any of the beats with rhythm?**
■ **Where does the ♫♩ pattern fit?** *(On beats one and two, and beats three and four.)*

Let individual children come up to the front and try to fill in the circles. If the time is limited, you may only be able to notate one line of rhythm; but the students should sing through the whole song to locate the phrase which begins with a different rhythm pattern. (The answer to the question is: none.)

I have found this technique of using circles ◯ or footballs ◯ to frame beats very helpful especially when focusing on a particular rhythm. It helps to isolate the picture of the sound (visual) and to connect it with all other experiences, that is, aural, kinesthetic, oral (speaking and singing).

5   *Demonstrating knowledge about a composition through movement or dance.*

In groups of four or five, ask the children to plan a movement sequence (dance) which illustrates the rhythm, the melody, and the phrasing of the Hungarian folk song they have been hearing. Encourage the children to determine in what way the melody is repeated or contrasted.

● The rhythm is repeated in each line.
● The melody (pitch) is repeated in lines one and four, and two and three.
● Each phrase of melody is the same length.
● (For more advanced classes) Lines one and four are in minor and two and three are in major.

The movement or dance sequence can illustrate a good example of ABBA form.

More Songs to Invite Movement

Here are three more songs which clearly demonstrate how easily eurhythmics experiences grow out of basic song material that we use everyday. These songs and activities are not sequenced nor do they focus on any one learning; they are included simply as additional examples of eurhythmics experiences. The song invites natural movements and you must challenge the ears of your students to hear specifics in the music. As the children refine their performance of the song, a link is made between the ear, the mind and the body. This is the outcome of eurhythmics.

The first two songs could be called play party games or singing games. They are excellent eurhythmics experiences in themselves; they call for a sequence of movement in a structured plan and they must be performed with correct timing, in an ensemble situation. In fact, the success of the activity is determined by everyone's sense of timing and beat. Usually the sequence of movement is dictated by the repetition or contrast of phrasing. In the song 'Circle Left,' the words dictate the movement.

Circle Left

Alabama singing game

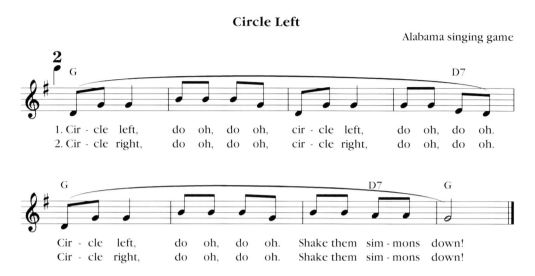

Teach the song with movement and then try these ear-training and eurhythmics experiences to focus on some aspects of pitch and rhythm.

1   *Highlighting basic tonal patterns.*

This is an excellent song to use for introducing children to syllables. If they have not had much experience with tonal patterns or syllables, you may want to sing the song for them and substitute the syllables *mi–mi–re–re–do* on the last phrase as you shake your hands downward ('shake them 'simmons down'). If they are already familiar with this tonal pattern, put it on the chalkboard:

m   *m*
     r   *r*
          d

Ask them to find it in the song and substitute the syllables for the words. This is another variation of the *mi–re–do* pattern studied before. The children can sing the song but substitute syllables and use hand levels to show the pitch direction on this phrase.

Another basic pitch pattern, *so,–do–do*, can be taught the same way. The hand motions that I use for this pattern are similar to the Curwen hand signs. Slap the side of your thighs on the low *so,*, then bring the hands up and bump them together with closed fists on *do*. For another musical example, this rhythmic gesture of slapping the thighs can be used for an anacrusis – for instance, the song 'Happy Birthday' ♫ | ♩♩. In all these motions with hand levels or signs, be sure that your movement illustrates the direction and the approximate size of the intervals in the pattern. The children should be encouraged to show this in

114

their movements. They will then see and feel the size of the intervals and the direction of the tonal pattern as they perform the movement.

2 *A challenge: listening and performing an assigned part.*

Divide the class into three groups and challenge them to perform the song in the following manner:

Group One: sing and motion only the *mi–mi–re–re–do* pattern.
Group Two: sing and motion only the *so,–do–do* pattern.
Group Three: sing the remaining part of the song with words.

3 *Creating new words to highlight a pattern.*

We usually expect children to use the same movement on repeated phrases in the music. Ask them to find repeated parts in the music. They will identify the first two measures of each line as being sung twice and the *so,–do–do* pattern being repeated three times. Challenge the children to think of other ways of moving besides 'circle left' and 'circle right.' When I challenged a class, they decided that some ways of moving could be varied and thus delineate the three repeats of the pattern. Here were their creations:

Walk forward,	do, oh, do, oh.	Reach in,	do, oh, do, oh.
Walk backwards,	do, oh, do, oh.	Reach out,	do, oh, do, oh.
Walk around,	do, oh, do, oh.	Reach up,	do, oh, do, oh.
Shake them 'simmons down!		Shake them 'simmons down!	

The Steamboat

Julia Schnebly-Black

I'm on a steam boat, Float-in' down the Mis - sis - sip - pi.

Not a sin - gle thing to do to - day.

Push pull push pull.

Ding, ding, ding, ding, ding, ding, ding, ding, ding, ding, ding, ding, bell!

1 Expressing note values in the motions of a song.

This song and the movement that accompanies it can be taught at the same time. It is important that the movement be precise so that the children experience the timing of the note values as well as the meter and phrasing. From the beginning, they will need help singing the second line. Once they can hear and sing the first two pitches of that line (*la*, and *la*), the rest of the line is easy. Note that three simple patterns are linked together to create the phrase.

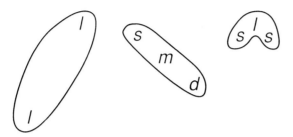

Line One: Strut on the deck of the steamboat with a strong and energetic quarter-note movement.

Line Two: Stop strutting; reach one hand slowly out to the side with the palm up as if to say 'Look, nothing to do!' Then the other hand reaches to the other side. Each motion lasts the duration of two measures or four beats.

Line Three: Push arms straight out and pull in, in the timing of half notes. This motion imitates the movement of the shafts on steamboat wheels.

Line Four: Using one hand held high, pretend to ring the ship's bell in the tempo of the eighth notes. Give the bell an extra strong pull on the last note.

2 Performing a round in movement.

It is important that the children can sing the song as well as they do the movement. Don't let the movement interfere with good singing. The song can be sung in a four-part round. Can they then do the movement sequence in a round, without music? Their success, both in singing and moving in a round will help them understand the meaning of ensemble in musical performance.

3 Experiencing duration with tennis balls.

This activity can be done either sitting or standing. Each child has a tennis ball to use on the following sequence. If there aren't enough balls for everyone, a few children at a time can do the activity.

Phrase One: Bounce–catch the ball on quarter notes.

Phrase Two: Carry the ball in a wide, high arc across the body to the other hand which returns it. Each arc is made in two measures or four beats.

Phrase Three: On a surface (floor or desk), roll the ball from one hand to the other on half notes. In my classes, if the children were standing they leaned down to roll the ball on the floor.

Phrase Four: Juggle the ball from hand to hand on eighth notes.

4 Recognizing familiar tonal patterns in the song.

There are several common tonal patterns in this song which children should be able to discover and substitute syllable names for the words. Place these patterns on colorful cards scattered around the room. You have probably noticed that in the early stages of note reading, I believe in writing the tonal patterns to show the direction of the sound.

$$d\ ^r\ m\ ^{f\ S} \qquad \text{instead of} \qquad d\ r\ m\ f\ s$$

That way, each representation of the pattern – body movement, hand levels, and notation – matches the direction of the sound. Notice how easily the pattern, written in the direction of sound, can be translated onto a staff.

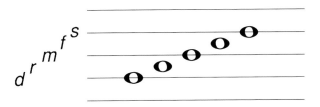

See if the children can find the following patterns, or similar ones, in the song. 'Similar' is important because once they have learned one pattern, it will appear in many different guises. For instance, s–m may become s–s–m–m, or as in 'The Steamboat,' s–s–s–s s–s–s–s s–s–s–s–m.

$$s\ ^{\prime}\ s \quad\Big|\quad d\ ^{m\ S} \quad\Big|\quad m\ _d \quad\Big|\quad ^{S}m\ _d m \quad\Big|\quad ^{S}m \quad\Big|\quad m\ ^{S}m\ _d$$

1   2   3   4   5   6

117

Chumbara

A French-Canadian Folk Song

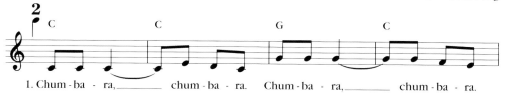

1. Chum - ba - ra,_____ chum - ba - ra. Chum - ba - ra,_____ chum - ba - ra.

Chum-ba - ra,_____ chum-ba - ra. Chum, chum, chum, chum, chum, chum, chum, chum.

Chum - ba - ra,_____ chum - ba - ra. Chum - ba - ra,_____ chum - ba - ra.

Chum - ba - ra,_____ chum - ba - ra, chum, chum, chum!

Here are a variety of activities involving children in the rhythm and pitch of this delightful song. Because there is only one word to sing (and it is a fun word), more attention can be given to the characteristic details of pitch and rhythm in the song.

1 Listening for a rhythm pattern.

Ask the children to echo the patterns you are going to clap: 1 ♫♩. 2 ♩♫ . Because the pattern is so short and so similar, perform each one twice and accent the first beat.

- ■ If you were to speak the words 'long and short,' how would you speak this pattern? *(Clap one of the patterns for them to listen.)*
- ■ How would you speak the other pattern?
- ■ Listen. *(The first is short, short, long and the second is long, short, short.)*
- ■ Sing the song and decide which pattern you hear. Put one finger on your desk if you hear pattern #1 and two fingers on the desk if you hear pattern #2. *(Only the first pattern appears in the song.)*
- ■ Sing the song again and every time that pattern appears, draw it with a finger on your desk.

118

2 Tracing the melodic rhythm.

■ **On your desk, tap out the song as you sing it. Begin over on your left each time you sing the short–short–long pattern.**

■ **Sing it again and tap only the short–short–long patterns. Let your finger slide through all the long sounds.**

Help the children learn how to 'jump' their eye and finger from the right back to the left to begin a new phrase or line. After their first try, you may want to signal them with the word 'back' or 'left' to tell them when to start the new phrase. A difficult place is after the descending scale. Be sure that they continue to sing the song as they do this activity. They can imagine that they are drawing the rhythm of the song with a magic marker. In fact, they could use a marker on sheets of newsprint. Their drawings should be an extension of their singing. Don't expect them to be precise or neat.

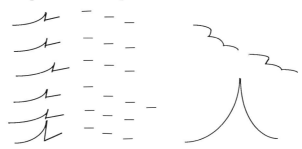

If they do this with a marker, the children should be encouraged to retrace the song from their drawing. Finding the long notes in their drawing will help them become more aware of the duration of long notes in music. They might also find and circle all the short–short–long patterns.

3 Listening for pitch direction.

Use your hand to illustrate the pitch direction of certain passages in the song.

■ **Find this in the song.**   *(Show with your hand)*

■ **Now, think the song, but sing this part on 'du'.**

■ **Do the same for this part.** *(Motion the last three notes of the song:*)

Ask the class to think the song and sing only that part. You can use other short patterns from the song, also. When the syllables are learned, the children should sing the same patterns with syllables.

119

4   Singing the descending scale with syllables.

This song can be of help in teaching the scale syllables in descending order: *do ti la so fa mi re do*. As an introductory step, ask children to sing the song with words. When you raise your hand, they should stop singing and listen to your words – the syllables in descending order. Notice that in the song, the scale ends on *re* and then begins the familiar first pattern: *do do do*. Do this several times and eventually ask them to try to join in. They will have trouble! It is difficult, but important for them to try this a few times without your help.

   I used a fun activity to teach my classes to speak and sing the syllables in descending order. Use speaking first and ask them to echo whatever you say. Speak short patterns of syllables in scale order, with dramatic inflections which express feelings and moods such as humor, anger, excitement, doubt and joy. If you use lots of facial gymnastics, they will mirror and copy you and with the exaggerated enunciation, they will remember the syllables. Here are a few examples of patterns to use:

   Speak the examples first so as to concentrate on the clarity of enunciation but then be sure to echo-sing the examples so the children will connect the correct syllables with the pitch patterns.

5   Drawing a 'sound picture' of the music.

As you sing this song during the year, all the learnings can be used as bits and pieces of a 'sound picture.' From the previous experiences, the children should be able to draw these aspects of the music:

(*a*)   the descending scale;
(*b*)   the last three pitches;
(*c*)   the short–short–long patterns.

The sound picture would look something like this:

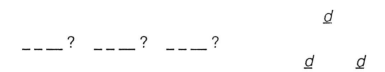

Remember these are drawn as movement extensions and therefore are not exact representations of the sound. Later, you can add the direction of the rhythm patterns and the other pitch patterns. The completed sound picture would look something like this:

6   *Reading and performing the sound picture.*

Let groups of children try to play the sound picture with rhythm sticks and pitched mallet instruments. Depending on the experience and understanding your children have, it might be helpful to stand the pitched instruments on end in a vertical rather than horizontal position so that they see, hear and move their arms in the direction of the pitch. Many teachers in the primary grades use this technique for the same reason – to connect the sound of pitch going up and down with the motion of the playing hand. It will also help in the intermediate grades.

It is not difficult to make a scale frame for resonator bells from a solid piece of styrofoam. There are directions for one in Appendix B.

An Ensemble Experience

Much of the time in a eurhythmics lesson is spent on exercises or on a sequence of experiences to develop skill and understanding along a particular line. On the other hand, it is very rewarding to guide a class through a series of experiences with a piece of music in which they discover the inner workings of that composition. By the time they explore various aspects of it through listening, moving and singing, they are ready to enjoy performing it in an ensemble experience. The Hungarian folk song 'Night Time' which has been arranged for an ensemble performance with Orff instruments lends itself well to this kind of exploration and discovery. If Orff instruments are not available, children could play individual parts on the piano, resonator bells and recorder. Here are other possibilities for you to consider:

Part Two: Recorder or solo voices on 'loo.'
Part Three: A high pitch, B, played on the piano.
Part Four: Piano.
Part Five: Two students playing resonator bells.
Part Six: A low pitch, E, played on the piano or plucked on the cello or autoharp.

121

Night Time

Hungarian
arr. Maria Foustalieraki

122

1	V		and the stars are watch-ing while the world is dream - ing.
2	R or AG 1		
3	⓪		
4	BM1		
5	BM2		
6	BASS		

(From *The Kodaly Method* by Lois Choksy) Reproduced by kind permission of Prentice Hall Inc.

Because 'Night Time' is slow and sustained, it would require an advanced group to accomplish all the steps including the ensemble performance at the end. Most of the steps are valuable ear-training lessons in themselves whether or not the ensemble experience is ever completed. Besides singing the song and playing the accompaniment, the children can express each line in movement. The experiences described below emphasize ear training and give the child an opportunity to improvise a movement interpretation of the music. The experiences do not have to be done exactly in the order given.

1   *Highlighting a particular rhythm pattern.*

■   **I am going to play something very simple; listen closely.** *(Play line four on the piano or on an Orff instrument)*

■   **Using your hands on your lap, imagine yourself stepping this.**

You could also ask a few children to step it while the rest of the class 'walk' their hands on their laps. After they do this, ask them to describe the music. They may not mention all of the following points but they enjoy being able to point out even the most obvious things in the music.

●   The tempo is slow.

●   The rhythm may be entirely half notes.

●   The same two pitches are repeated over and over except for two places where the pitch stays the same.

●   The music seems to be measured in two.

●   There are eight measures in all.

123

2 *Reading and singing tonal patterns to establish the mode.*

Put the following two patterns on the chalkboard and ask the children to echo each one several times so as to establish the sound of the minor mode in their ear.

1   2

‖: do ti la do mi do la :‖   ‖: la ti do re mi re do ti :‖ (la)

Then ask them to keep repeating the second example while you play line four again. This should set the mood and the sound of minor in their ears and mind.

3 *Discovering the order of phrases in a song.*

Put the following patterns from the song on the chalkboard, either with syllables and rhythm, as I have done here, or on a staff, depending on how much notation your children can read. Without the staff, these patterns can be written either in straight line (*l,t,drm*) or to show the direction of the pitch, as in the previous exercise. I usually show the direction of the pitch until students can read syllables and recall the correct pitch patterns simultaneously.

(a) l, m m m r   (d) l, t, d d r d t, d

(b) t, t, t, t,   (e) m d d t, l,

(c) l, l, l, l,

Practice singing these with syllables and then on 'loo.' Mix up the order and then play the melody of line one straight through and have them decide the order in which you sing the melody. They will need to hear it several times. The order of phrases is:

                    A   E   A   E
                    D   B   D   C

This would be a good time to introduce the text and learn to sing it. Encourage them to sing the song with expression, as if they are painting a picture with the song.

4 *Singing a melody while hearing something else.*

Ask the class to sing the melody on 'loo' as you play lines four and six. Repeat this, but as they sing, let half of the class gesture the movement of line four with their arms and the other half gesture the movement of line six. If this is successful, let them explore the possibilities of combining the movement of lines four and six with a partner as they continue to sing the melody.

5 *Expressing a melody in movement.*

Invite the children to step the melody as they sing it on 'loo.' Challenge them find another way to express it in movement. They might 'paint' it in the air, showing rhythm and pitch, or they might gesture the phrases with a partner, or combine stepping and gesturing.

I would like to give you a note of caution here. The song is notated with a meter signature of $\frac{4}{4}$. However, when the song is finally performed, it should be felt in $\frac{2}{2}$, with the half note as the beat. A comparison of the two meter signatures might be explored at a later time: $\frac{4}{4}$ and $\frac{2}{2}$. In the first experience with this song when you are playing line four – all half notes – the children will probably identify this as two slow beats in a measure. The pitch reinforces the feeling of two beats (E F♯ E F♯). In the other experiences, they will see measures of quarters and eighths and you may find yourself counting beats. Eventually you may want to talk about the meter of the song. That is why, in the first experience, I said, 'The music seems to be measured in two.'

6 *Performing in an ensemble experience.*

Have the children listen and express line five in movement. Then, in groups of three children, two can move line five and the third child can step the melody. If the children are sensitive to each other's performance in these experiences of singing and moving, suggest that they be more creative in ways of moving, perhaps stretching into interesting shapes on the long notes. Encourage them to imagine that they are creating a design which illustrates the music.

There are other possibilities for experiencing this music but it is important for you to realize that it is not necessary to try to complete all of these. Sometimes a class is particularly responsive to a song or to a situation where they are responding in ensemble with each other and with the music. If your children are still enjoying the song and movement, here are a few more ideas:

Lines two and three are wonderful compliments to the other lines but especially to each other. Partners could create hand motions to show how the two lines move in response to each other. It is important that they hear, feel and show the duration of the long notes. Suggest that on the long notes they imagine that they are pulling on a piece of elastic, and then on the eighth notes at the end of the measures, shake out the hand ready to pull again on the next measure. If you can play line two on the recorder, you can create the intensity on the long notes as they pull the elastic. A simple way to teach line three would be to establish the tempo of the half note (as practiced for lines four and five) and then ask the class to touch their knees gently on the rest and play an imaginary finger cymbal on the notes. They can follow this simplified picture of the line. (R = rest; P = play.)

R P R P R P R P
R R R P R R R P

With advanced classes, the notation with half- and whole-note rests could be put on the chalkboard and practiced.

Finally, if some of these experiences continue to be successful, assign certain lines of movement to small groups and perform them together. Don't 'rehearse' it; keep the creativity and spontaneity alive. Encourage them always to be refining what they are doing and move as a team. Discuss the meaning of the word 'ensemble.'

A final possibility would be to have each individual in a group of five or six choose a line which they would express in movement. As singers and instrumentalists perform the song, this movement group would perform the accompaniment in movement.

6. Experiences in the Upper Grades

In the upper grades, the objectives for eurhythmics experiences should be aimed at developing the students' independence in listening, performing and creating. The emphasis on independence in participation allows students to respond with understanding and confidence, thus discovering a lasting joy in music. Those children who pursue music in the future, as amateurs or serious students, will have developed basic skills and understandings which they will use the rest of their lives.

If we teachers are to develop this independence in students, it is necessary for us to design experiences which provide challenges yet assure progress for those with ability as well as provide successful experiences for those less talented or less interested. They will develop independence if they are given opportunities to initiate and lead, analyze what they are hearing and doing, and make decisions and critical judgments on what is happening musically. In this chapter, I often use the word 'leader' instead of 'you' (the teacher) or 'student' to indicate that directions may be initiated by either.

To begin the chapter, I offer a few suggestions for stimulating movement that reflects the expressive qualities of music. These will be helpful to those teachers whose classes have not had eurhythmics experiences in the earlier grades. Much of what has been encountered and studied in the intermediate grades will be reviewed and then explored further in music that is more challenging, especially in rhythm. Familiar and unfamiliar examples of music will be explored and enjoyed in various ensemble experiences. Instrumental, keyboard, vocal and movement improvisation will be continued as an opportunity for the students to express their musical ideas and try out new skills.

Encouraging Pre-teens to Express Music in Movement

If students have experienced eurhythmics throughout the elementary grades, they are comfortable being asked to express music in movement as pre-teens. They respond appropriately and creatively to various aspects in music and to the challenge,

- ■ **Can you find another way to show it?**

At the approach of the pre-teen years, some students may need to be encouraged and reminded that moving to music in a school classroom is a perfectly acceptable, enjoyable and worthwhile experience. Students who have not been exposed to eurhythmics will benefit from the games and exercises described for the earlier grades, but the music chosen will have to be appropriate to their age level.

The dynamics, energy, and character of all our music can be realized in our everyday expressions of movement and physical and vocal gestures, for instance,

■ **Oh, no!**

or

■ **Please, please, come here!**

Sometimes we can help students realize what is happening in the music by calling their attention to these common expressions. Consider the variations in tempo and character of your walk with two or three examples of music that you enjoy. The following experiences, designed to encourage movement, can later be used for vocal, keyboard or instrumental improvisation.

1   *Expressing an idea in movement.*

Divide the class into groups of four or five students. In a given amount of time, perhaps eight minutes, each group must choose one of the following words or phrases and design a movement sequence which expresses the phrase. The movement should be done without sound; it alone expresses the idea. Adding vocal or instrumental sound to the movement sequence is a worthwhile step to extend the experience. Take a little time to discuss the dynamics, energy and characteristics of each group's effort. Later, some of the same characteristics of movement may be compared to characteristics of sound in musical examples.

● Togetherness
● Outer Space
● Variation
● Contrast versus repetition
● Even versus uneven movement
● Competition at the last game

2   *Showing the character of a walk.*

As small groups of students 'take a walk,' their movement can change when you suggest an attitude or feeling, for instance: angry, scared, thrilled, moody, limping, confident, rushed, lighthearted, on ice, through deep snow, through water.

3   *Demonstrating gradual changes in the qualities of movement.*

Divide the class into small groups; each group chooses a pair of movement qualities from column A or B and its opposite in the other column.

A	B
firm, powerful	gentle, delicate
rapid, anxious	leisurely, sustained
direct, straightforward	flexible, elastic
free, uninhibited	restrained, controlled

Students plan a way to express the gradual change from one pair of movement qualities to their opposite. The change should happen within a count of ten. For instance, one group might choose to move from leisurely and sustained to rapid and anxious.

128

4   *Creating a group composition in movement.*

The following list contains common words which we sometimes use to describe music.

rising	sharp	soft
smooth	long	low
uneven	fast	repeating
loud	even	slow
falling	contrasting	high

In small groups, students should explore ways of expressing some of these words. Then, each group can plan a composition in movement which uses three or four of the words selected. The words may be used singly or in combination. The groups are free to plan the composition any way they wish. Give them about ten minutes to plan and rehearse. Students like to show the result of their efforts and when they are in groups – or at least in pairs – final results can be shared within a manageable time framework. Encourage quick planning because the real value of this experience comes when the class can identify the descriptive words used, the order in which they were used, and the effectiveness of the movement composition. Later, the same list can provide inspiration for simple keyboard, vocal or instrumental improvisations.

Continuing Basic Eurhythmics Experiences

Some of the experiences included in this chapter will be a review of the content and skills studied in previous chapters but they all develop the learning further with opportunities for the children

- to read and write notation;
- to improvise or create compositions;
- to lead or conduct the activity or performance; and
- to become familiar with examples of classic music.

1   *Responding to precise changes in rhythmic movement.*

Have students practice the following five actions which illustrate duple-beat rhythms. Using music that is spirited, but not too fast, ask them to perform whichever one of these five actions is signalled.

1   Clap the beat of the music: ♩ ♩.

2   Pat thighs, both hands together: ♫ ♫.

3   Same rhythm, but separate hands, left–right: ♪ ♪ ♪ ♪.

4   Slide both hands down the thighs on the dotted quarter and tap the eighth note with fingertips: ♩. ♪.

           slide tip.

5   Toss one clap up and around in a big circle: ♩.

Check the tempo of the music you choose to be sure that each of these can be performed comfortably. A leader will signal one of the numbered actions to begin and then changes should be made by phrases. The signal for a quick-reaction change must be given clearly and on the beat just before a phrase begins. Remind the students to listen for subtle changes in tempo. Some suggestions of music to use are:

● 'The Entertainer' by Scott Joplin
● 'Alley Cat' by Frank Bjorn
● 'March,' from *The Comedians*, by Dimitri Kabalevsky

The same exercise can be used with triple-beat rhythms and music but the rhythms will change as follows:

Suggestions of music to use for the triple-beat exercise are:

● 'My Favorite Things,' from *The Sound of Music*, by Richard Rodgers
● 'Morning' from *Peer Gynt*, by Grieg
● 'Chim Chim Cheree' from *Mary Poppins*, by Richard and Robert Sherman

2   Creating and reading a two-measure rhythm pattern.

Using football shapes helps to guide inexperienced eyes in reading music. Draw eight footballs on the chalkboard to represent two measures of four (duple) beats each. Place a half note at the end of the two measures so there is a sense of phrase ending. The tie shows that the note is held for two beats.

Choose individual students to fill in one or two beats with note values (see example). When the example is complete, the students can speak and clap the two-measure rhythm. You might suggest that they add some of the same movements experienced in the previous exercise. Students might like to improvise a melody for this rhythm using the pitches D E F♯ A B D. They can sing it or play it on a melody instrument.

3   Reading longer phrases of rhythm.

Opportunities must be provided for students to practice reading long lines of notes from left to right without getting lost. We teachers often notate only one measure or two on the chalkboard, or we provide a simple list of patterns. Instead, try putting individual patterns on large cards to stand on a ledge or be attached in a way that they can be moved around in a different order. That way the students can read the complete phrase on a line from left to right. A leader points to each beat with a steady sense of timing.

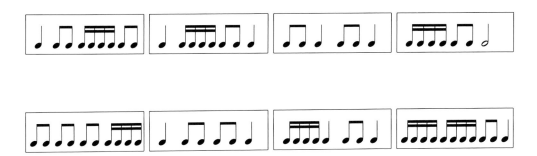

More Challenging Games with Tennis Balls

In the upper grades, some teachers use gym balls for more challenging games with tempo, accent, meter and beat. Other teachers have collected used tennis balls; these successfully allow students at this age to become more sensitive to the impulse and energy of the thrust when they bounce, toss, roll or catch the ball. If there are not enough balls for each student, use the trick described in Chapter Three,

■   **When you hear this signal, try to give your tennis ball to someone else.**

1   *Responding to subtleties of tempo.*

For this exercise, which involves the whole body in the tempo of music, students should be able to bounce–catch the ball and walk the beat at the same time. As they stand poised to begin moving, they should listen to a musical example, determine the tempo of the beat, and on a signal such as 'and' (spoken as an anacrusis), they begin. When the music stops they stop, listen for the next example, determine the tempo of that selection, and begin again on a signal. Since it is important to keep directions for a eurhythmics experience simple, you may want to explain this one step at a time.

It is best if you improvise music for this experience. The meter should be in two or four beats unless the students have discovered a way to bounce–catch a ball in a meter of three – something that can easily be done (bounce, catch, hold). The tempo is of utmost importance. Each example must be played at a comfortable tempo, for the students will be performing two tasks simultaneously: bouncing and catching the ball and stepping the beat. The tempo can change from one example to the next but you should consider each one carefully. The examples should be at least four measures, probably eight. Here are two examples that should be played with a well-articulated beat and tempo.

Another possibility for musical accompaniment is to select two or three songs that you can play easily in any tempo. You may choose duple or triple beat, but the meter should be in two so that the students feel a strong sense of bounce–catch. For instance:

2   *Distinguishing between the duple and the triple beat.*

Although it is more difficult to toss–catch a ball and step the beat at the same time, students will try because they enjoy the challenge. If they don't discover how to do this for themselves, suggest that the ball doesn't need to be tossed very high. Just a slight lift at the beginning will get them started. If they can bounce–catch and toss–catch, ask them to listen and decide whether the beat of the music is a duple or a triple beat. On the duple beat, they will bounce–catch; on the triple beat, they will toss–catch. Their decision will be based on what they hear in the music, either

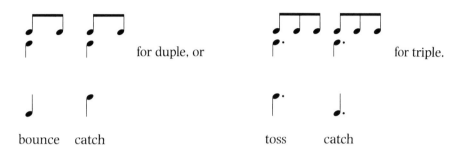

3   *Distinguishing between duple and triple beats when there is little space for movement.*

While students remain in their seats they can listen for the beat and either pat knees and clap the duple beats ♩♩ or, on the triple beats, clap as though tossing the beat across the room and then clap as though catching another one ♩. ♩..

4   *Responding to tempo changes while singing.*

Ask two or three students to each bounce–catch a ball at the front of the room. The students on one side of the room can sing the scale with syllables on each bounce. Those on the other side of the room can sing high *do* on each catch. Encourage everyone singing to conduct at the same time. Their conducting should mirror the movement of the ball (down–up). One side will sing the notes with stems going down and the other side will sing the notes with the stems going up.

For variety, on a signal everyone sings a descending scale on the off-beat (the 'catch' in bounce–catch). If they are conducting at the same time, they will be moving, performing and hearing a syncopated rhythm against the bouncing sound of the ball.

133

Expressive Conducting

Tempo could be an important emphasis in any of the experiences in this book. Students at all levels might be challenged to keep the tempo steady, determine the most appropriate tempo, change the response to fit the tempo of the music, or change the tempo gradually. In the upper grades students are ready to respond to more subtleties in tempo. As they perform in ensemble with others they should become more aware of their responsibility in keeping the tempo; as they learn to respond to each other with some musical sensitivity they can assume the role of conductor or leader. It is not so important for students in the elementary grades to learn the traditional skills of conducting, yet they enjoy this mastery. Conducting does, however, provide access to students' musical comprehension. For example, it can be a good indication of how they are perceiving the music and how well they understand when asked to respond a certain way. Conducting develops a strong sense of an inner beat – a crucial aspect of musical development. Whenever space is limited for movement, conducting provides an excellent means for physical involvement in the music.

Students should have a strong feel for a meter in two. Many of their previous eurhythmics experiences will have developed this skill. They should also know how to conduct in three and four. Hopefully the students have had opportunities to lead or conduct a small group ensemble in singing or playing. They may also have had a chance to establish a tempo for movement or singing. Whenever possible, listening lessons should include the challenge of conducting what is being heard. When students conduct they will begin to experience subtle changes in the music, not only tempo, but also such aspects as dynamics, articulation, accentuation and phrasing. The following list of compositions contains excellent examples to use for conducting.

- 'March of the Siamese Children,' from *The King and I*, by Richard Rodgers.
- 'Arabian Dance,' from *The Nutcracker*, by Tchaikovsky.
- 'Variations on a Theme by Haydn,' by Brahms (theme).
- 'Overture,' from *Music for the Royal Fireworks* suite, by Handel (a slow duple beat; notice the ♩♪ pattern).
- 'Alla Siciliana' from *Music for the Royal Fireworks*.
- 'Minuet' from *Music for the Royal Fireworks* (a stately meter of three).
- 'Hungarian Dance' No. 5 by Brahms (extreme changes in tempo).
- 'A Slovak Dance Tune'

This last piece can be sung in two parts. It is often begun at a very slow tempo and then gradually accelerates. Here is the score:

Slovak Dance Tune

La   La   etc....

Duple-Beat Rhythms

Practicing a vocabulary of rhythms develops skill needed to perform and read music. Exercises can be designed for quick recall with isolated rhythms and combinations of rhythms. I have found that a trip to the 'pie shop' is worthwhile and enjoyable. Your students may have progressed beyond this type of activity but many have not; it's hard to imagine that we can ever include too much practice seeing, reading and performing common rhythm and tonal patterns in music. Several exercises can be devised after one trip to the shop. You should realize that the names of the pies can be recited in two or three different rhythms; for instance,

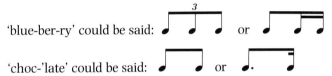

I chose one rhythm for each example in this exercise and if you choose to use another, you should be consistent whenever the word appears in these exercises again. Here is a further suggestion. Whenever it is appropriate, repeat each rhythm in an exercise, because the response will tend to be more accurate and confident when it is repeated.

The Pie Shop

135

1 Echoing duple-beat rhythms in movement and speech.

Ask the students to echo what you do and say. As you speak the rhythm of the pies (shown above) vary the usual clapping response this way: clap the word 'pie' into the palm of the hand, but pat the name of the pie down the arm, from the elbow to the wrist. For 'ap-ple,' pat at the elbow then at the wrist; for 'blue-ber-ry,' pat at the elbow, halfway between, and at the wrist (in three places for the three syllables). Divide the space on the arm to show the division of the beat. This illustration may help:

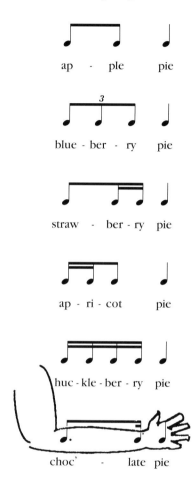

At first, don't describe what you are doing; just proceed and the students will follow you. If they don't begin to imitate you, stop and explain.

2 Reading sixteenth-note rhythms.

Notate each of the above two-beat rhythms on a card which can be held by a student or propped up to be easily seen by the whole class. Space the notes on the cards carefully so that the students can see the two beats and what sounds on each beat. It is important for young music readers and performers to see phrases of rhythm in which the spacing of individual notes indicates, or at least implies, where they fall in relation to the beat. On the reverse side of the card, notate the same rhythm with flags instead of beams.

While it is important for students to see both ways of notating the rhythms, this need not be an initial experience. Use the reverse side at a later date and even mix them up. Include an additional card which looks like this:

pics,   pies

Line the cards up and have your students speak the rhythms with 'pie' words and later a neutral syllable such as 'da.' At the same time, they should tap the beats on their desks. Encourage them to tap each beat in its proper place:

One   Two
Left   Right

Mix the cards up to form another line of rhythm. Instead of tapping the beats, challenge the students to conduct as they read the line of rhythm. Another time, use cards that show three beats on them by adding a quarter note to each of the 'pie' rhythms.

ap - ple pie   pie

3   *Singing sixteenth-note patterns.*

Write the letters of the scale syllables in a line going up the chalkboard. This could be written horizontally on the chalkboard, but reading and singing an ascending and descending scale may help some children to make the connection between what they are seeing and what they are hearing and singing. We know that it is true that many untrained singers say they read music by following whether the notes go up or down. Now, beside each syllable write the notation for one of the pies. For the eighth degree of the scale, repeat one of the other rhythms. Notice that these are two-beat rhythms. Practice singing the scale with these rhythms and then try the variations suggested.

(a) Add a quarter for a three-beat meter.

(b) Erase the quarter notes and sing one beat on each pitch.

(*c*) Choose a meter and as a leader points to one syllable for each measure, your students can sing the given rhythm on that pitch.

4   *Playing a game with duple rhythms.*

Individual students can notate a measure on a piece of scratch paper as a memory aid, and then speak and/or clap it for the class to echo and notate. Let the class speak it back in the 'pie shop' rhythms. Start the game with this pattern:

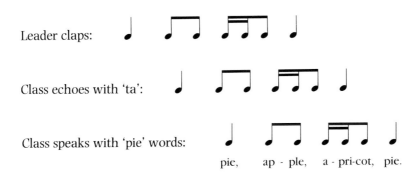

One student notates the pattern on the chalkboard. When it is time to check it, the whole class can read what is written to test whether it matches what was spoken.

Triple-Beat Rhythms

Most of the games and exercises designed to teach duple-beat divisions can be adapted to a continued study of triple-beat rhythms. The following two activities are particularly helpful in developing a feel for the most common triple-beat rhythms: ♩., ♩♪ and ♩♫ .

1   *Adding hand movements with a triple-beat song.*

Simple hand movements can help students feel the swinging quality of the meter as well as the individual rhythms in the song.

Noah's Ark

Black American spiritual

Verse

1. Old Noah built himself an ark, one more river to cross, And built it all of hickory bark, one more river to cross.

2. The animals came two by two, one more river to cross, The elephant and kangoroo, one more river to cross.

Refrain

One more river, And that's the river of Jordan;
One more river, There's one more river to cross.

3. The animals came three by three, one more river to cross.
   The baboon and the chimpanzee, one more river to cross. *Refrain*

4. The animals came four by four, one more river to cross.
   Old Noah got mad and hollered for more, one more river to cross. *Refrain*

5. The animals came five by five, one more river to cross.
   The bees came swarming from the hive, one more river to cross. *Refrain*

6. The animals came six by six, one more river to cross.
   The lion laughed at the monkey's tricks, one more river to cross. *Refrain*

7. When Noah found he had no sail, one more river to cross.
   He just ran up his old coat tail, one more river to cross. *Refrain*

8. Before the voyage did begin, one more river to cross.
   Old Noah pulled the gangplank in, one more river to cross. *Refrain*

9. They never knew where they were at, one more river to cross.
   'Til the old ark bumped on Ararat, one more river to cross. *Refrain*

Students can either perform the motions by themselves or find a way to do them with a partner. Be sure that as they sing and move, they are experiencing a strong sense of beat in the whole body.

Movement Code

T = Touch fingertips lightly on the anacrusis.
P = Pat thighs.
C = Clap hands.
W = Bump hands at the wrist (in readiness for the wrist–fingertip movement described before).
W T T = Wrist–tip–tip (♫).
L = Clap to the left.
R = Clap to the right.
S = Snap fingers.

Verse:

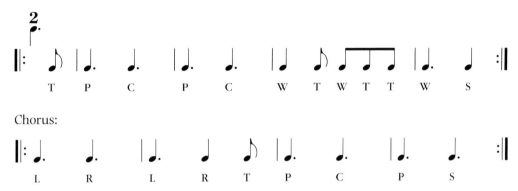

Chorus:

Here are two other songs with the familiar triple-beat rhythms. The same hand motions can be adapted to these two songs also.

We're all Together

We're all to-ge-ther a - gain, we're here, we're here!_ We're all to-ge-ther a - gain, we're here, we're here!_ Who knows when we'll be all to-ge-ther a - gain, Sing - ing all to-ge-ther a - gain, we're here, we're here.__

Paddy Works on the Railway

Irish-American Railroad Song

1. In eight-een hun-dred and for - ty-one I put my cor-du-roy breech-es on. I

put my cor-du-roy breech-es on to work up-on the rail - way.

Refrain

Fil - li - mee-oo - ree - oo - ree-ay. Fil - li - mee-oo - ree - oo - ree-ay.

Fil - li - mee-oo - ree - oo - ree-ay. To work up-on the rail - way.

2. In eighteen hundred and forty-two
   I left the old world for the new,
   Oh, spare me the luck that brought me through
   To work upon the railway. *(Refrain)*

3. It's 'Pat, to this' and 'Pat, do that.'
   Without a stocking or cravat.
   And nothing but an old straw hat.
   While working on the railway. *(Refrain)*

2   *Verbalizing the more difficult triple-beat rhythms.*

When students are practicing speaking triple-beat rhythms which include sixteenth notes, the 'te' sounds should be lightly articulated; they are always on the weakest part of the beat. Here is a suggestion for verbalizing triple-beat rhythms.

du du   du na nee du na nee du te nee du   du nee du nee te du te na te nee te du na te nee

The patterns with sixteenths are difficult for young musicians to hear or perform correctly, and stepping and clapping them is not always successful. Because these patterns do not make frequent appearances in songs that students sing or play, I prefer to spend time developing skills to hear, speak, perform, read and write the more common rhythms.

Is It a Meter in Three or a Triple Beat?

There are many pieces of music which we would call triple which make us want to sway from side to side in a rocking motion. Some of it is written in $\frac{3}{\rho}$ meter ♩. | ♩♩♩| and some is written in $\frac{2}{\rho}$ ♩. ♩.. It is often difficult to tell the difference when you are listening to the music. Compare the following examples and notice what a subtle difference the meter makes.

As I explained in Chapter Five, I refrain from counting six eighth notes when the meter is $\frac{6}{\rho}$ unless the tempo is quite slow. Experience has taught me that students automatically sway or gesture two strong beats (triple beats) in most music that is marked $\frac{6}{\rho}$ or $\frac{2}{\rho}$. For example, I once wanted to use an Israeli dance for some creative movement in my classes. I didn't have the music so I notated it from a recording. The instinctive movement that my students and I felt with this music was swinging arms from side to side. I notated it in $\frac{2}{\rho}$ meter. Much later, I found a score for the music notated in $\frac{3}{\rho}$ meter. I felt that something was certainly lost in that $\frac{3}{\rho}$ version. Compare these two examples and notice that if there is a difference, it is subtle. Imagine yourself moving to each of these.

1

Will children become confused by any of this when they start sight-reading music in a slow $\frac{2}{2}$ meter? Also, what about the meter signature of $\frac{6}{4}$ or $\frac{6}{8}$ which is used in much music? I believe that children who have experienced the duple- and triple-beat feeling in different tempos and in singing, moving, playing, reading and writing will have the tools necessary to understand and solve problems dealing with the notation. After all, the sound of music should be the primary aim in any listening or performing experience. The sound should bring to mind a kinesthetic and visual image of what is being heard. Likewise, a movement or visual image (notation) should bring to mind sound. When children hear ♩ ♩ they instinctively swing or sway; if they begin to swing or sway they instinctively hum: ♩ ♩.

A Slow Triple Beat

Review some of the quick-reaction exercises which involve children in such various ways as hearing, recognizing and performing triple-beat rhythms at a slow tempo.

1   *Practicing an unfamiliar rhythm.*

This exercise focuses on the rhythm ♩ ♫ ♩ as it appears in 'Silent Night.' Write an eight-measure phrase of rhythm on the chalkboard and number the measures.

Using any two measures from the phrase on the board, improvise a simple example in a slow $\frac{2}{4}$ meter. As the students clap the dotted-quarter beat, invite them to study the example on the board and find the two measures you have been playing. Once they can distinguish the two measures aurally and visually, have them practice speaking and clapping the rhythms as you play. Challenge them to speak and clap the same two measures but in reverse order. For instance, if you improvise on measures five and four

♩ ♪♫♫ | ♫♩♩. , they must concentrate and clap the measures in the opposite order, four and five ♫♩♩. | ♩ ♪♫♫ . As they perform this, they will be watching the notation intently and becoming aware of the sound of the one rhythm against the other.

For a variation on this exercise, let the class select any two measures from the original example on the board. As you improvise an accompaniment which has a strong beat feeling, ask the students to clap and speak their selected two-measure phrase. When you signal 'change,' they should clap measure four twice, and then resume their two-measure phrase. For example, suppose that the class chose measures six and eight.

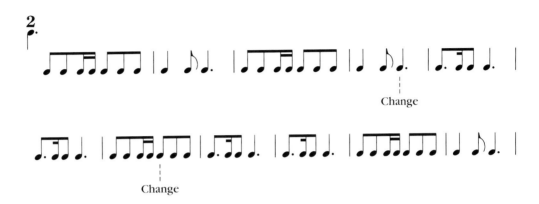

Any rhythm pattern can be practiced this way; seeing, hearing and performing it in the context of familiar patterns. It would be a good idea for the students to perform the above exercise on rhythm or melody instruments in addition to clapping and speaking.

2   *Reviewing triple-beat rhythmic notation.*

Ask the students to find a space where they can swing their arms from side to side on the beat. Improvise a simple musical example using only measure two as they put the beat in their hands. As soon as they feel this tempo correctly, ask them to

■   **Clap the rhythm using the wrist–tip motion.**

With this motion they will feel the elasticity of the beat from side to side when they bump hands at the wrist.

■   **Which measure am I playing?** *(Number two.)*

Try this activity, using each of the measures, until the students have a good feel for them and can easily identify the one you are playing. Practice speaking the rhythms, using whatever verbalization you choose or my suggestions, as follows:

145

du   du   du na nee du   du   nee du   nee   du   te nee du

du   nee du na nee   du na nee te du na nee   du   te nee du   te nee   du   nee du.

3 Practicing phrases of rhythm in various types of activities.

Continue to practice the different measures in the example until the students can perform them in any order as a leader points. Continue to try various ways to perform the example:

- Use the first two measures as an ostinato while the class performs the whole example.
- Perform it in a round, one measure late.
- Invite students to mix up the measures or create their own musical example of eight measures.

For instance:

4 Performing a song in a slow triple-beat rhythm.

The beautiful song 'Snow' appears to have three verses, each with a different melody. It can be sung as a unison song with any or all of the three endings. The three parts can also be sung simultaneously. If you want to use this for sight-reading, prepare the students for the ties, but otherwise, the rhythm is easy. For preparation, they might walk the ♩. beat and make a circle of eight on its side with one arm ∞ as they sing these two measures, alternately:

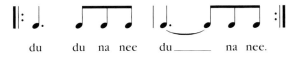

du   du na nee   du_____   na nee.

146

Snow

1. Snow, the blan-ket of snow, co-vers the world with a fresh coat of soft - ness.

2. Snow,___ fal - ling snow,___ fal - ling snow___ cool and white.

3. Snow-flakes so fra-gile come tumb-l-ing down, touch-ing the ground so gent - ly.

Snow.___

Snow

Words and Music: Doug Nichol

1. Snow, the blan - ket of snow, co - vers the world with a fresh coat of soft - - ness.

2. Snow,_____ fal - ling snow,_____ fal - ling snow_____ cool and white.

3. Snow - flakes so fra - gile come tumb - l - ing down, touch - ing the ground so gent - - ly.

Ending only: use any of the three. They may be sung simultaneously.

Snow.

Snow, the blan - ket of snow, blan - ket of

Snow, fall - ing snow, fall - ing

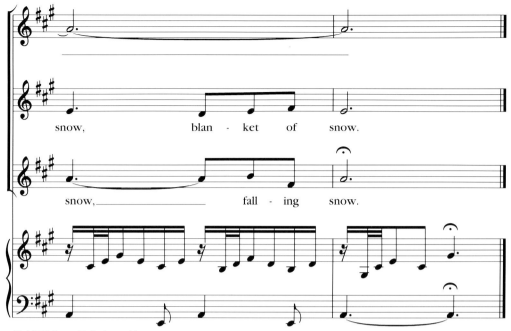

The Rhythm-Phone

This is a variation of the telephone game. Students should sit comfortably or stand in a circle with hands up, palms facing out to the side ready to receive and then tap a rhythm around the circle like a message traveling along a telephone wire. Everyone should continually tap a silent beat so that when the rhythm is sent around it is harder for the students to see exactly where and what the rhythm is. A leader taps a four-beat pattern into the hand of the student on the right; that student taps the same pattern into the hand of the next person, and so on, until the pattern travels all the way around the circle. The last person breaks the chain by clapping and speaking the pattern that was received. It is fun to see whether the pattern has been changed. You should probably be the leader while the game is being learned. Here are some patterns to initiate the game:

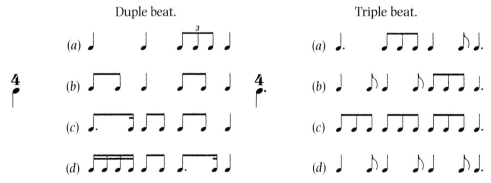

It is a good idea to use duple-beat patterns one day and triple-beat patterns another.

150

Dotted Rhythms

The most common dotted rhythms ♫, ♩♪ and ♫ add interest, energy and spirit to music. Can you imagine some well-known music without the dotted rhythms. Think of:

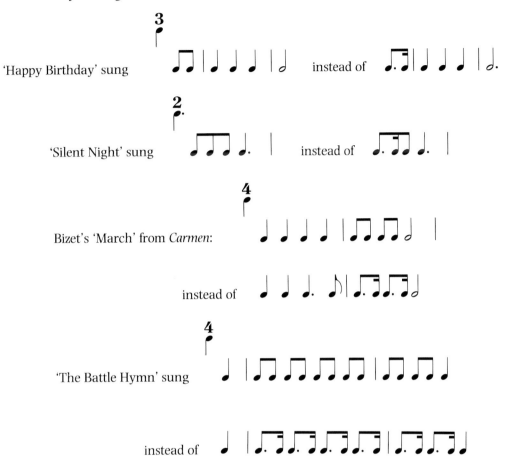

'Happy Birthday' sung

'Silent Night' sung

Bizet's 'March' from *Carmen*:

'The Battle Hymn' sung

Students of all ages often stumble over these rhythms when reading and performing music, and yet we have heard, sung, and played and danced to music which featured these rhythms from the time we were very young – from 'Rock-A-Bye Baby' to 'I've Been Workin' on the Railroad,' to 'Do-re-mi'

The following eurhythmics exercises look, at first glance, like repeats from Chapter Four and Five but they are extensions of previous work. As is the case with all skill development, the learning continually needs to be refined and extended. The first experience is a quick-reaction exercise using the four rhythms which were emphasized in the primary grades.

1 *Reviewing four basic rhythms.*

Write the four rhythms on the chalkboard. Establish a tempo for the quarter note in a meter of $\frac{4}{4}$.
As you call out each letter, the students step that rhythm until another one is signaled. Continue each rhythm for at least eight beats.

This exercise should be experienced in other meters also. You can either accompany this on a drum or improvise at the piano. In the beginning, play exactly what your students are stepping, then later enhance their listening by playing another rhythm as an accompaniment to their response. For those of you who are not comfortable improvising freely, choose a familiar song and accompaniment that you can play by ear and play in many different rhythms. The 'Keyboard Improvisation' discussion in Appendix A may help you.

2 *Performing measures of the* ♩♩ *rhythm in a longer phrase.*

Ask students to clap the following phrase, lightly.

Be sure that the rhythm is correct; ♩♩ should not sound like ♩♪. As soon as students have read and clapped it, ask some of them to step the phrase. It takes energy and precision to step the dotted rhythms correctly but students will enjoy being challenged to try.

The same phrase should be performed in a meter of two and also four.

Advanced students who can step the rhythm correctly and with ease can try to conduct the beat as they step the rhythm.

3   *Reading and performing the 'pizza pie' rhythm.*

The dotted eighth and sixteenth alone is not heard in isolation, nor can it be studied or performed that way. I have used the following exercise to help students read and perform the rhythm more precisely. The words 'pizza pie' are appealing and can be spoken and experienced with the same nuances that are required for performance. (I was surprised that it even worked with an adult bell choir.) The sixteenth note moves energetically into the next beat. When students are responding to this rhythm as in the first two experiences described in this section, you must complete the phrase with quarters or half notes. 'Piz-za pie' may seem too unsophisticated an approach to learning music in the upper grades, but this works easily for me. You must be sure to speak it with the correct timing,

piz - za pie.

The students should imagine the desk in front of them is divided into two sections representing two beats. Have them tap the beats (♩) and echo the following phrases as you speak them:

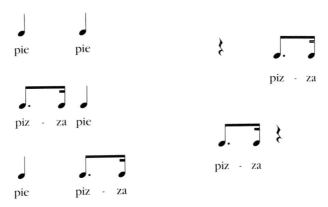

Repeat each phrase several times so that the students realize by touching, seeing, speaking and hearing, where the two beats fall. When you can see that they are tapping the beats and speaking correctly, ask them to tap the rhythm of each pattern. Be sure that they tap the dotted rhythm on one side of their desks and the quarter on the other.

Because it is important to work with phrases of music instead of isolated measures, try putting the two-beat measures into a long phrase. This would be a good opportunity to use the dotted rhythm as an anacrusis. For example:

Piz-za pie, pie pie piz-za pie, pie, piz-za pie   piz-za pie piz-za piz-za pie pie pie.

4   *Sight-reading the rhythm of a song that includes many ♩♪ rhythms.*

The song 'I Love the Mountains' is an excellent song for this activity.

I Love the Mountains

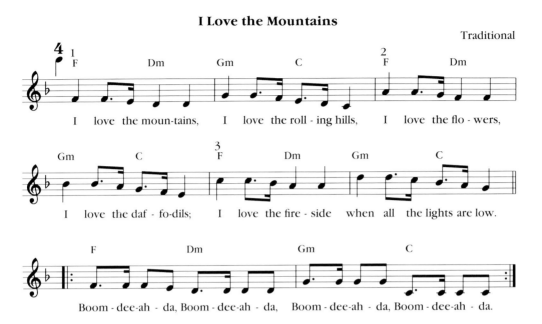

If students already know the song, the activity will be somewhat less challenging, but still worth doing. Students can of course use any verbalization for speaking the rhythm, but I asked a class to substitute the words 'pie,' 'piz-za' and 'eat-ing' for the corresponding rhythms in the song. Here is their solution:

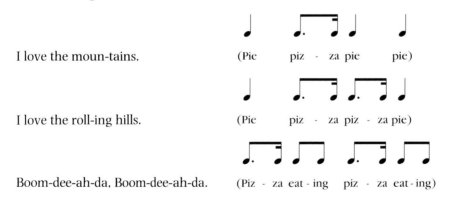

5   *Solving a notation puzzle with the fun song 'Three Craw.'*

If you want your students to try to notate this rhythm, teach the song by rote. It is important that they articulate the words with energy so that they hear the rhythm correctly and don't miss the spirit or fun of the song. The movement sequence, to be performed with a partner, will reinforce the strong sense of beat. It would be best to teach the song first, then the movement, and try the notation puzzle last.

154

Three Craw

Scottish folk song

1. Three craw sat up-on a wa', Sat up-on a wa', Sat up-on a wa'; Three craw sat up-on a wa', On a cold and fros-ty morn - ing.

2. The first craw couldna find his maw,
   Couldna find his maw,
   Couldna find his maw,
   The first craw couldna find his maw,
   On a cold and frosty morning.

3. The second craw couldna find his paw,...

4. The third craw ate the other twa,...

5. The fourth craw warna there at aw,...

6. And that's aw I hear about the craw,...

Movement Code

P = Pat knees.

C = Clap hands.

R = With hands outstretched – left palm up and right palm down. Partners stand facing each other, so their right hand can pat partner's left hand.

L = Quickly turn hands over so the left hands can pat partner's right hand.

S = Pat own shoulders.

s = Cross arms and pat opposite shoulders.

X = With both hands, slap partner's hands in the air.

The movement is performed in a quarter-note rhythm except for the last two X's, which are half notes.

```
P   P   C   C   R   R   L   L
            R   R   L   L
            R   R   L   L   L   L
P   P   C   C   R   R   L   L
S   S   s   s   X       X
```

Before you begin to play the notation game, ask the students to determine what rhythms are in the song. (♩ ♩ ♩♩) Divide the class into groups of four or five students. Each group should find an area, possibly on the floor, where they can line up 3 × 5″ index cards, on which these rhythms appear, to notate the song. Give each group an envelope of 26 cards which show the following distribution of rhythms:

eight = ♩   nine = ♩   nine = ♩. ♩

Each group lays down a half-note card – the first note in the song – and then individuals in each group take turns solving the rest of the notation puzzle by thinking through the song and adding a card or two to those already on the floor. If the students in each group number off, you can signal them, one at a time, to take turns completing the song.

Since the phrasing in this song is unusual, I found that it helped students to complete the task when they saw the text written to illustrate the irregular lengths of phrases and similarities in word rhythm.

Three craw sat upon a wa'

sat upon a wa'

sat upon a wa',...

Three craw sat upon a wa'

On a cold and frosty morning.

They should continue going around the group until the song is completed. The last student should be thinking through the whole song and checking for errors. Give each group some colored straws or small sticks to see if they can determine where the bar-lines should be placed. One very gratifying part of this for me has been to see how the students silently sing the song over and over to decide on the correct rhythm.

In the study of the dotted-quarter–eighth rhythm, our aim in eurhythmics is to guide students to feel the wonderful extension or elasticity of sound and the gentle burst of energy (an anacrusis) moving into the next beat. For those who merely teach this pattern by counting eighth notes ♪ ♪ ♪ ♪ ♪ ♪ (1 and 2 and 3 and) the suggestions here are going to seem quite unorthodox and difficult to believe unless they realize the importance of the physical sensation of movement in learning music.

The following is a sequence of steps to develop skill and understanding of this rhythm pattern. These early steps are very important and must not be overlooked.

A Guide the students to feel physically the elasticity of sound when a beat is extended.
B Guide the students to feel the eighth as an anacrusis or a 'lift' into the next beat.
C Guide the students to feel an inner sensation of the beat that is represented by the dot.
D Guide the students to see and understand how to perform the rhythm pattern correctly.

Since there are many songs that students know which feature the ♩. ♪ rhythm, it would be wise to review some of these and begin to highlight the pattern.

156

'Hey Ho'

'Make New Friends'

'Music Alone Shall Live'

Here are some eurhythmics experiences to help students focus on the ♩. ♪ pattern.

6   *Gesturing the ♩. ♪ pattern in arm movements.*

Select one of the above songs and with the students standing, ask them to imagine that they are painting something in the rhythm of the song. Encourage them not to 'lift their brushes' until the beginning of a new phrase. When you demonstrate the activity, show a good extension of movement through the dotted quarter note.

7   *Experiencing the ♩. ♪ pattern by tossing and catching a tennis ball.*

This experience may initially seem like fun for the students, rather than a deliberate step to teach the ♩. ♪ rhythm. They will need to use tennis balls and should have some skill in tossing and catching the ball (T–C) as well as bouncing and catching it (B–C). There are several steps to this experience; be sure that the students are successful with each one before you continue.

A   Children, standing in one place, should practice tossing and catching a ball:

a   ♩   ♩   ♩   ♩
   Toss C   T   C

B   Change to: toss catch bounce catch   and speak it.

b   ♩   ♩   ♩   ♩
    T   C   Bounce C

C   Continue B but add 'and.' Exaggerate the steady beat feeling:

c   ♫   ♫   ♫   ♫
   T & C & B & C &

157

D   Change the speaking to counting:

d

1   and   2   and   3   and   4   and

E   Alternate the speaking between B, C and D.

F   Introduce notation for speech patterns in B, C and D.

G   ■   **If I tie these sounds together, can you toss on 'one,' then catch on the 'and' of 'two'?**

g

1   and   2   and   3   and   4   and

T   C   B   C

H   Rewrite the tied notes; continue speaking but now simply clap the rhythm;

h

1   and   3   4

Encourage the students to talk about the difference in notation between ♪♪♪ and ♩.♪. Let them find examples of either pattern in their music books and see if they can use the other notation to rewrite the example. You can follow the same steps and substitute the rhythm on other beats in the measure. This whole experience is difficult to explain but the physical feel of the toss–catch, bounce–catch in this rhythm is worth the effort.

8   *Comparing four patterns in movement.*

You will be using four patterns in this exercise and eventually notating them on the chalkboard but to begin, ask the students to listen and then step what you are playing. Play one pattern until they are comfortable stepping it. Play with a good sense of arrival on that first beat so that their movement is rhythmical and precise. Ask them to put a click or a clap on the first beat of each measure.

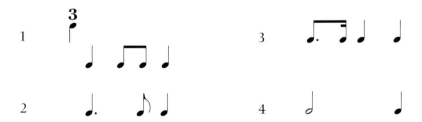

As soon as they are responding well to one pattern, change to another. After they have heard and responded to all four patterns, see if they can remember and notate any of them.

9   *Creating music which highlights specific rhythms.*

Using any melody instruments available (Orff instruments, recorders, the piano and resonator bells), establish the Dorian mode (D–E–F–G–A–B–C–D). Invite pairs of students to
create two-measure questions and answers using the rhythms in either experience no. 3 or
8. Here is an example.

Question: Answer:

Augmentation and Diminution

Augmentation and diminution are common, and interesting, compositional devices.
Sometimes a musical idea is stated in augmentation – that is, twice as slow as the original;
or it is stated in diminution – that is, twice as fast, or 'double time.' It is possible for a theme
to be augmented three times slower or diminished three times faster, but this chapter will
consider only twice as slow or fast.

In the earlier chapters, there were many opportunities for students to recognize and
respond to quarters, eighths and half notes. They experienced the relationship of these
three note values, but a keener awareness of this relationship can develop in the upper
grades. Some of the eurhythmics experiences for younger grades asked the students to
move at a given tempo, then twice as fast ('double time') or twice as slow. You probably
helped them feel the change with music that conveyed a precise relationship between the
note values. The students were experiencing diminution and augmentation and now they
can recognize these devices in music and learn the terms.

Several eurhythmics experiences follow, but first of all, a reminder. In many compositions, you may determine what you would identify as the obvious beat but then realize that
there is a faster or slower pulse which is also easily discernible. It is possible that some
students may perceive the beat as being faster or slower than the one you have in mind. I
wouldn't say that they are wrong, but for the experience you have planned, you may have
to say,

■   **Some of you are hearing a beat that is faster or slower than others are hearing; for this
exercise, let's use this as the tempo of the beat.** *(Demonstrate the tempo)*

1 Identifying three different walking tempos with one musical example.

Choose a sprightly recorded selection in a duple meter. It must be one that invites a hale and hearty walk. There are many suggestions from which to choose, but here are two.

'The Spanish Flea,' by Herb Alpert and the Tijuana Brass

'Pop Corn,' Kingsley

■ **Find a comfortable beat in this music and take a walk. If I say 'fast,' walk twice as fast, or 'double time.' If I say 'back,' change back to the original tempo. If I say 'slow,' walk twice as slow, or in slow motion.**

Give your signals just before the start of a new phrase. Don't expect students to change from one tempo to another in the middle of a phrase. It is best to let them discover the changes themselves, but if they seem puzzled or their movement is inaccurate or unsure, then step in and move with them to show them an example.

If there is little space for movement, a few students can walk around the room while others pat lightly on their desks or thighs, using both hands as if walking – left, right. Their arms should show the size of the steps they would be taking (slow tempo = large movements; fast tempo = small movements) so they will see the relationship of time (tempo) and space in their movement as they change from ♩ to ♫ to ♩ to 𝅗𝅥.

2 Dramatizing movement in augmentation and diminution.

Nat King Cole's 'Lazy, Hazy, Crazy Days of Summer' lends itself beautifully to moving in augmentation and diminution. Set the scene: small groups of people are sitting on the porch on a hot summer's day, doing everything possible to keep cool. Each group should follow a leader who improvises movements (a phrase or two at a time) to keep cool – fanning him or herself, waving to neighbors, mopping his brows, shaking her shirt to cool off, and even rocking forward and back all in time with the music. The leader of each group can change the timing of the movement at will, from an original tempo to twice as fast or twice as slow. Encourage them to keep returning to the original tempo often. They can probably create other 'play' actions for sitting on a porch on a hot summer's day.

This idea may also be used for walking in the three tempo on a summer's day. In this case, let the students change from one tempo to another at will. Their changes should come with the beginning of a phrase and be clean and confident. Encourage them to think and feel the change before making it.

3 Singing a song in augmentation and diminution.

Before attempting these devices with a song, students should practice singing the scale, ascending and descending, in a moderate tempo and then twice as fast and twice as slow. It is important that they keep a constant beat in both arms and even in their feet (by walking) if possible. Ask them to clap a *silent* quarter-note beat throughout.

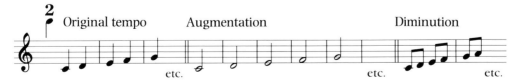

160

See if your students can sight-read the short song 'Feel the Beat.' It uses only the tonic chord and can easily be sung with syllables. Invite the students to imaginatively express the meaning of the text in movement.

Feel the Beat

We take great care to real-ly feel the beat.

While the students are learning the song and expressing the text in movement, see if they can do their movement twice as fast and twice as slow (diminution and augmentation). Let them sing it in diminution and augmentation.

These three versions of the song can be combined into a five-part composition; the meter and beat remain constant.

(a) Original; Sing the song at a moderate tempo.
(b) Diminution: Sing the song twice as fast. Sing it two times to complete four measures.
(c) Original: Repeat the song at the original tempo.
(d) Augmentation: Sing the song twice as slow.
(e) Original: Repeat the song at the original tempo.

4 *Rearranging a song with augmentation and diminution.*

Using a familiar song, 'Frère Jacques,' test the students' ability to change quickly from one tempo to another. Write these three terms across the chalkboard:

Diminution   Original   Augmentation

Be sure to write the word 'original' in the middle; it is wise to return to the original tempo often and before going to the opposite one (diminution or augmentation). Practice singing

'Frère Jacques' in each of the three tempos. The students should be able to do this by ear. It is important for them to continue to gesture a quarter-note beat throughout the song.

Frère Jacques

When you think the students are ready for some quick-reaction changes, begin the song at a moderate tempo and then on the repeat of each phrase, point to either diminution or augmentation. Always repeat any phrase sung in diminution. There are many possibilities for combining these ideas, but here is one suggestion.

Frère Jacques

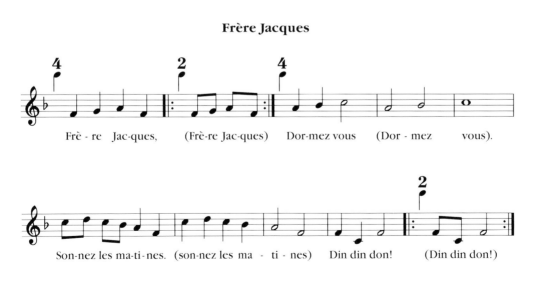

5   *Singing 'Ghost of Tom' in augmentation and diminution.*

This well-known song is often sung as a round but it can also be performed quite easily in augmentation and diminution. It is shown here in the three versions.

Original

Ghost of Tom

Diminution

Augmentation

Experiences with Syncopation

By the time our students are ready to concentrate on a more in-depth understanding of syncopation, it is a familiar part in their everyday music experiences. They can learn to identify certain aural examples of syncopation but they need other kinds of experiences in order for understanding to develop. In this section three examples of syncopation will be explored:

● an unexpected accent written in the score as a sforzando sf or an accent mark >;

● a rest on a strong beat or a note on a strong beat that is tied over from a weak beat;

● a long note (on a weak beat) which is preceded by a short note.

Here are several examples of syncopation; the beat is marked under the pattern and the syncopated note is circled.

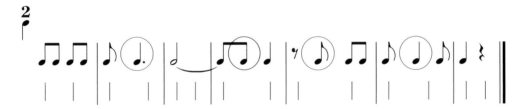

The following exercises are designed to help students hear, see and perform examples of syncopation.

1   *Echoing measures of beats with unexpected accents.*

For this experience, students should sit so they can pat the beat on their thighs. Play or improvise a march mostly in quarter notes.

■   **Tap the steady beat with your fingertips on your thighs. Move your hands forward to show that you are patting measures of four beats.**

When your students are comfortable with the tempo, put an accent on one of the beats other than the first. They should repeat your example, on the next measure. Try having them pat the accented beat with flat palms. If you accented the second beat, their response, a measure later, would be:

tap   pat   tap   tap

164

Continue the exercise as in an interrupted canon. For instance:

Discuss the surprise element in this kind of syncopation. Encourage them to think of everyday situations in which something catches them off guard or by surprise: riding a bicycle and hitting a tree root; meandering through a crowded mall and unexpectedly seeing an old friend. A good example of misplaced accents is in an early scene of Stravinsky's *Rite of Spring*, 'Augurs of Spring.' You might show them a short example of the notation before you play it for the class on a small drum.

Help the students learn to clap this example accurately by performing it as an interrupted canon, one measure at a time.

These written accent markings, > or *sf*, become more interesting and 'ear grabbing' when the tempo is faster or when they appear on a weak part of the beat or the 'off beat.' Try the following example as an interrupted canon.

2   Comparing syncopated and unsyncopated music.

Syncopated music is so common today that its effect is much less surprising than we thought years ago. However, when you compare music that is not syncopated with a syncopated version of the same thing, it becomes clear that something is disrupting the

165

feeling of a steady beat. Compare these two ways of singing the first phrase of 'He's Got the Whole World in His Hands.'

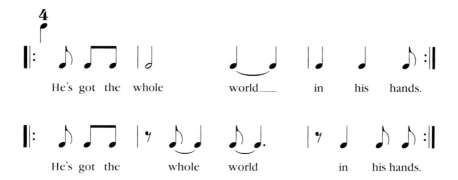

Write the following word phrases and rhythms either on a transparency or on the chalkboard. It would be helpful to use two transparencies. On one notate the rhythm and on the other write the words, lining them up carefully so that when one is placed over the other the students can read the words and rhythm together. That way you can eventually remove the words and the students can read the rhythm with 'ta' or another neutral syllable.

After the students have read the phrases several times, ask questions about the rhythm. For instance:

- **Are all these rhythms syncopated?**
- **Who can point to one rhythm that is syncopated and explain why?**
- **Can anyone rewrite an example so that it is not syncopated?**
- **Is there another way to write one of the syncopated rhythms and have it sound the same?**

3   *Learning to read syncopated patterns.*

Careful planning is required to help students read syncopated patterns. I believe in beginning with examples which use ties:

The following sequence of notated patterns is my way of 'taking it slowly' in guiding students to read syncopation. This sequence, which can be used for echo response (clapping and speaking), proceeds from the most obvious beat pattern to the more difficult written notation.

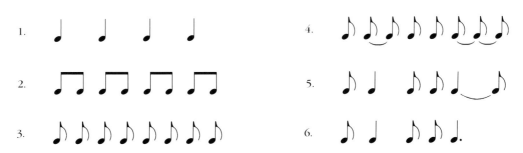

Advanced students need to be able to simplify a complicated rhythmic example to its underlying beat. They will understand this if you reverse the order of the patterns. For instance, if they see a pattern that they can't read, help them to simplify it by 'reducing' each note value to the lowest common denominator and then add ties where needed. Students should practice each step several times.

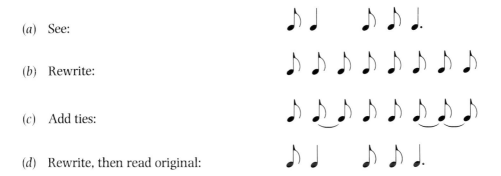

(a)   See:

(b)   Rewrite:

(c)   Add ties:

(d)   Rewrite, then read original:

4   *Discovering how syncopation is notated.*

Here is a very simple song which students can sight-read from the chalkboard or a transparency – the rhythm first, followed by the pitches with syllables. Be sure that they conduct or gesture the beat while they are sight-reading. After they have successfully sung the song, have them sing it with the words.

We've All Got Rhythm

Now, lay a blank transparency over the original and sing the following version for them.

Challenge the students to find and circle the words or places in the music which are now syncopated. Here are the places they should circle.

Invite the students to solve the problem of how to notate the new version. It may help if they mark where the strong and secondary accents fall.

For fun, add some syncopated rhythms for an accompaniment and sing the song as a canon, each part beginning one measure later.

168

Reviewing Previous Learning

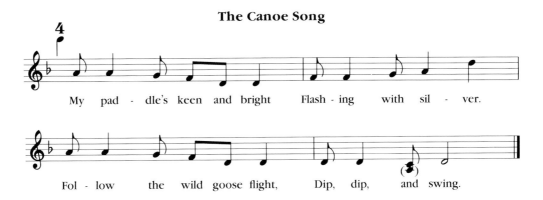

The Canoe Song

Like many simple rounds, 'The Canoe Song' can be performed as a beautiful ensemble piece with singing, moving and playing. As students are learning to perform the music, they can also be reviewing previous learnings. The movement suggested with this song (as is the case with much of the movement in this book) was designed for students to kinesthetically experience certain specifics in the music and connect what the ear hears, the eye sees and the body feels with a mental understanding of the concept. The rhythmic notation for each line of movement is given and should be performed exactly.

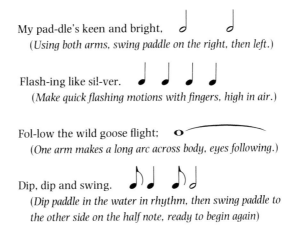

My pad-dle's keen and bright,
(Using both arms, swing paddle on the right, then left.)

Flash-ing like sil-ver.
(Make quick flashing motions with fingers, high in air.)

Fol-low the wild goose flight;
(One arm makes a long arc across body, eyes following.)

Dip, dip and swing.
(Dip paddle in the water in rhythm, then swing paddle to the other side on the half note, ready to begin again)

Either teach the whole song with the movement sequence at the outset, or let the students simply pretend to paddle a boat in half notes (♩♩), first on the left and then on the right. When you teach the movements described above, try to connect one line to the next so that the movement flows throughout the song. Although the movement of the last phrase isn't the way one paddles a canoe, it expresses the syncopated rhythm. The length of the half note is felt as the arms swing up and around to the other side of the body to begin the song again.

There are two versions for singing the last phrase. It may depend on the vocal range of the students. I tend to use the lowered seventh instead of the low dominant pitch.

169

There are many ways to further develop performing skills and an understanding of musical concepts with a song. In the following experiences students will be able to review syncopation, minor tonal patterns, how to recognize the minor mode aurally and visually, and how to create an arrangement of a song for performance.

1   *Experiencing the composite of a syncopated rhythm and a steady beat.*

Notate the rhythm of the song on the chalkboard with each phrase lined up carefully to show beat placement and similarities in the patterns (a).

- **What can you tell me about the rhythm of this song?**

- The rhythm is syncopated. The syncopated pattern is eight–quarter–eighth and it is repeated at the beginning of each line.
- Lines one and three are exactly alike.
- There are four beats in each measure.

- **What is the meter of the song? ($\frac{4}{4}$)**
- **Can someone draw a dotted line down through the lines to show where the beats are? (Example (b)).**
- **Stand up with a partner; face each other ready to clap your partner's hands.**

I usually demonstrate this by putting my hands up, with palms facing forward and just say,

- **Hands up.**

As the students sing the song, partner A, using one hand, claps the beat into one of B's hands, and partner B, with the free hand, claps the rhythm into A's free hand.

2   *Responding to gradual or quick changes in music.*

Continue the first exercise but now you will be playing the song on the piano. Can the partners change roles on a quick signal from you? Can they continue to perform the

170

movements (the beat versus the rhythm) as you make quick or gradual changes in tempo, dynamics and articulation of the musical accompaniment?

3   *Recognizing common minor tonal patterns by hearing and by sight.*

The same techniques that you have used to develop the students' skill in hearing, singing, and reading major tonal patterns can be used with minor patterns. Students should have practice echoing the following patterns, singing them from your hand signs, or sight-reading them from notation.

d r m r d	*d t, l, t, d*	*l, d m d l,*
m r d t, l,	*d t, l, d m*	*m r d l, l,*
d l, l, s, l,		*d r m l l,*

Other ways for students to practice these patterns are:

● Sing them in a scrambled order determined by a leader.
● Echo them in various rhythms, for instance, *m–r–d–t,–l,* could be sung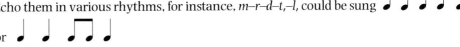

or

● A few students can sing an ostinato while the others sing the patterns in order. An example might be:

●   Sing the patterns as questions and answers. A leader can sing any pattern as a question and someone can sing another pattern as the answer.

The students might suggest other creative ways to practice the patterns.

A few words need to be said about minor. With the limited time that we have for music instruction in the elementary school, I am pleased if the students can sight-read a few common tonal patterns in major and recognize them in the keys of C, F, G and D. Also, if the chords are given and the name of the last chord in the song is the same as the name of the last note, students can assume that the song is in that key. For instance, here are the first and last measures of the song 'America.' The last note is G and the last chord is G major and so it can be assumed that probably the key is G major. I realize that this is risky, but there are so many valuable musical experiences which the general population of elementary school children should have that I believe in giving them that simple and accessible way to discover the key. This is not true, however, when a song is in minor.

The sounds of major or minor should be learned in the primary grades and reviewed in the intermediate grades. Upper elementary students can learn to use two other clues as to whether a song is in major or minor. Besides listening to the sound of the tonal patterns used, students can look at the score.

- **Look at the key signature; what major scale does it represent? Does the song end on the syllable,** *la* **in that scale?** If so, students can assume that the song is in minor.
- **If you look at the music, do the tonal patterns center around** *do–mi–so,* **as in major, or** *do–ti,–la,* **and** *la,–do–mi,* **as in minor?**

With that much knowledge your students can at least discuss whether the song seems to be in major or minor and why.

4   *Experimenting and making decisions on arranging a song.*

Plan an opportunity for small groups of students to explore ways of creating an accompaniment for 'The Canoe Song.' Give them some guidelines:

- **Create an introduction and coda to be performed with the song. They do not need to be the same.**
- **What instruments should play these parts?**
- **Create a simple melodic ostinato which can be played as an accompaniment to the song. Decide what instrument should play the ostinato.**
- **Is there a characteristic rhythm pattern in the song which could be used as an accompaniment throughout the song? What percussion instrument would be best for this accompaniment?**
- **Decide on the plan for performing the song. How many times will it be sung, and how – in a round, in unison, or what? Will all the accompaniment parts be performed throughout, or at a particular time?**

Students in each group can discuss, experiment, and then practice their arrangement and perform it for the class. In the end, let the whole class decide on a final form for 'The Canoe Song.' Here is one possibility:

Introduction:	Two measures on an instrument, then two measures with vocal introduction added.
Song:	Sung in unison with movement and accompaniment.
Song:	Sung in a canon with movement, no instruments;
Interlude:	Instrumental accompaniment and movement (without singing) performed in a canon.
Song:	All! Song sung in a round with movement and accompaniment.
Coda:	Two measures sung and played, then two measures instrument alone.

The Canadian folk song 'Land of the Silver Birch' and 'The Canoe Song' can be performed as partner songs. It is possible to incorporate the teaching ideas from the one song to the other. If and when you decide to combine the two performances, be careful because you will have more ostinatos and accompaniment patterns than singers, and it will be far less than satisfying. When I did it, I simply used the second song as a countermelody to 'The Canoe Song.' The words of the 'Land of the Silver Birch' are beautiful.

172

Land of the Silver Birch

Canadian Folk Song

1. Land of the sil - ver birch, home of the bea - ver,
2. Down in the for - est, deep in the low - lands,
3. High on a rock - y ledge, I'll build a wig - wam,

Where still the might - y moose wan - ders at will,
My heart cries out for thee, hills of the north.
Close by the wa - ter's edge, si - lent and still.

Refrain

Blue lake and rock - y shore, I will re - turn once more. Boom de de boom boom,

Boom de de boom boom, Boom de de boom boom, Boom___ boom boom.___

Rests Are Silent Sounds

Until we highlight those magical moments of silence in music called 'rests,' they probably don't even exist in students' minds. They probably think of them as 'zero sound.' One of the times that they are sure to pay attention to a rest in music is in the jingle,

Shave and a hair-cut, two bits

We know the importance of rests in music as something that encircles sound or frames the sound. It is a moment of attending to what is coming or what has just happened. I like to think of a rest as an anacrusis to sound, or a metacrusis after sound. We need to help

173

students discover the 'sound of silence.' There are three common examples of rests in music which are easy to recognize. They are:

1   The rest which acts as a surprise. It happens when sound is expected but is not there and results in syncopation. This is obvious in the example above. Another very obvious, but more sophisticated example, is at the end of Handel's 'Hallelujah Chorus' (from *Messiah*), just before the last 'Hallelujah.'

2   Rests at the ends of phrases or beats seem insignificant. At the end of a phrase, a rest is often thought of as a sign to breathe, and within a beat, for instance, it happens so fast that it is practically ignored. These rests should be experienced as active silences which connect with what is to follow. With students in the upper grades these rests can be highlighted with a slight movement and therefore be given the importance they deserve at the moment. A very simple way that I have found to direct students' attention to rests in music is to use the Israeli folk song 'Debka hora.' As I sing it, they are to find places in the song where they can insert a silent clap. Another way for them to actually feel the silence is to suggest that they clap the melodic rhythm of the song but clap the air on the rests. I found one other idea by chance. If they tap their temples on rests, they can hear as well as feel them physically. Try this idea.

Debka hora

Israeli folk song

3   The third example of rests in music is a string of rests in which children must feel the movement and timing of the beats as they wait and count for their part to begin again. For an example of this, divide the class so that they can perform the following two-part rhythm.

Experiment with two different sounds, for instance, clapping and tapping of pencils, or combinations of something hitting wood versus something hitting metal. When this is performed well, these two parts work in harmony with each other. For a greater challenge, let your students try it with partners or by themselves, using both hands.

Quick-reaction exercises in which students substitute movement for rests are a good place to begin. Here are some eurhythmics exercises to try.

1   *Feeling the hesitation and silence of rests.*

Ask students to walk with the music and stop on the rests. This is challenging because it is impossible for them to know when rests will appear in your music. However, the exercise sharpens their hearing and prepares them for the next exercise.

2   *Feeling and counting a specific number of rests.*

When the students are responding with precision, ask them to walk at a given tempo and rest for a certain number of beats.

■   **When I call out a number** (*between two and ten*), **freeze for that many counts, with your arms out to help hold your balance, and then continue walking.**

When students first try this exercise, I sometimes ask them to count very softly so that they help each other to keep a steady tempo. They can also touch their temples to feel the steady beat of the rests. As soon as possible they should rest without any outward showing of the tempo or counting. Practice the exercise yourself before you try it with children. It is tricky to call out the number at the right moment for them to hold back their forward motion.

3   *Experiencing an active rest.*

A fun activity is to have the students stand with a partner and as you play 'Shave and a haircut, two bits' in an exaggerated variety of tempos, dynamics registers, and moods, have them perform the following actions:

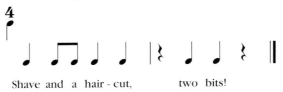

Shave   and   a   hair - cut,   two   bits!

■   **Clap the first measure to yourself.**
■   **Slap your thighs on the rest.**
■   **Clap your partner's hands on 'two bits' and put a finger snap on the final rest.**

This should give the students a good feel for the function of the two rests; the one on the first beat of the measure is given a strong, downbeat movement, and the second rest at the end is given a less dynamic snap, because it is what we would call metacrusic since it is rebounding from the crusis or accent.

■   **Now try the same actions but do not make a sound on the rests, only a motion.**

175

4 *Learning to read rests.*

This experience uses a familiar musical example, one that was introduced earlier in the chapter.

Feel the Beat

We take great care to   real - ly feel the beat.

With this short song, there are many possibilities for substituting rests or delaying sounds because of rests. You may not want to present all the following variations of the rhythm at one time, but each one is worth trying. Students should be able to sing the example before trying the variations. Here is the rhythm of the song and five variations which use rests. Each variation has one or two changes from the previous rhythm.

Take one variation at a time and ask your students to study it and see if they can speak the phrase in the new rhythm pattern. Sometimes a word or words may have to be omitted or moved, but the general meaning of the phrase remains the same.

Here are other ways to use the song 'Feel the Beat' or the rhythmic variations.

● Have the class read all the patterns with a neutral syllable.
● Choose one pattern for half the class to clap while the other half of the class sings another familiar song – for instance, the fourth pattern above, as an ostinato with 'I've Been Workin' on the Railroad.' The first line of the song is given here with the ostinato notated above the melody.

I've   been work-in' on the rail - road,   All   the live-long   day.

● Sing 'Feel the Beat' twice as fast and twice as slow. Here is the notation for each example.

● Sing the song as a four-part round with each voice entering two beats late.

5   *Challenging students to read rests.*

This experience is difficult and should be tried only with an advanced group. Show your students the following notation which is the solo clarinet part for the composition 'The Cuckoo in the Deep Woods,' from *Carnival of the Animals* by Saint-Saëns. Ask the students whether they could play this solo part with an orchestra.

The Cuckoo in the Deep Woods

177

The students will have to know the difference between the half- and whole-note rests and be able to count them. Have them read part of the score without the orchestra part to let them see how challenging it is and important for a musician to be able to read and count rests.

After they have begun to count and clap or tap the part accurately, start back at the beginning with the recording and go through the whole piece. Notice how the clarinet enters on different beats of the measure. Notice also that the last entry is an augmentation of the motive.

The Cuckoo in the Deep Woods
(Le coucou au fond des bois)

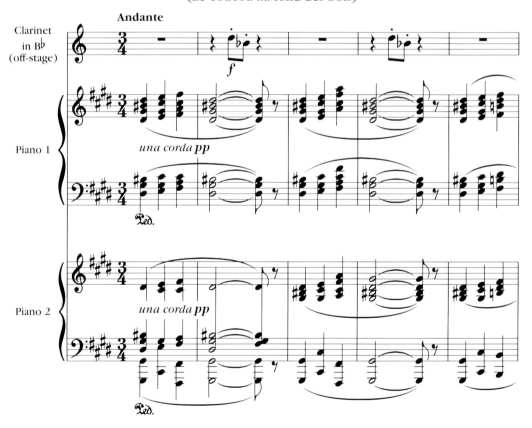

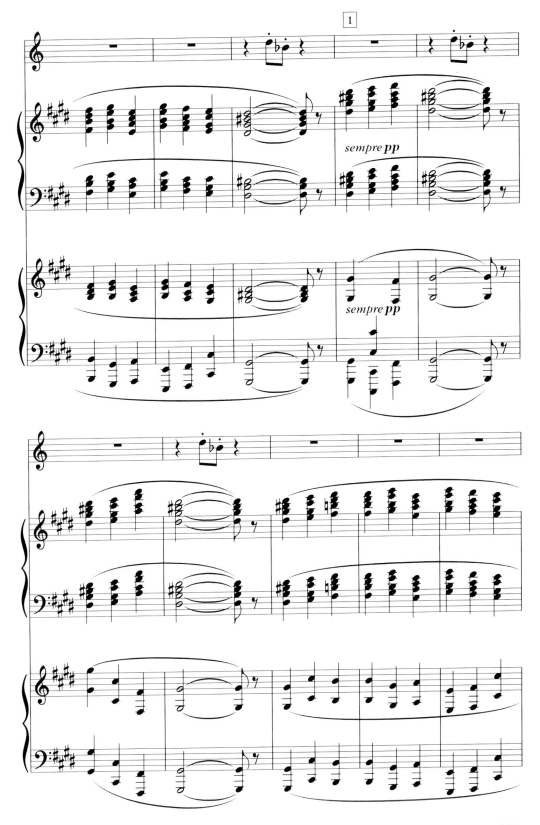

180

Changing Meter

Meter changes in music can create interesting shifts in accents and groupings and they really aren't too difficult for students in the elementary grades to perform well. The American folk song 'Shenandoah' is an interesting example of a song that changes meter.

Shenandoah

Oh, She-nan-doah,__ I long to hear you, A - way, you roll-ing ri - ver, Oh She-nan-doah,__ I long to hear you, A - way, I'm bound to go, Cross the wide Mis - sou - ri.

When preparing students to perform and recognize music that changes meter, it is important that they feel a strong impulse on the change – the first beat of each measure – as well as feel the duration of the measure. Try these eurhythmics exercises or games in your classes:

1 *Playing ball to feel changing meter.*

Prior to this experience the students should be able to manipulate a ball in several creative ways to show meter in two, three, four, five and six. For example, in a meter of five, bounce the ball on the first beat of the measure, catch it on two and roll it from hand to hand on other beats in the measure.

5 = bounce, catch, roll, roll, roll.

A leader can signal a change of meter from time to time.

2 *Feeling the steady beat even though meters are changing.*

Ask students to mentally divide their desks into a measure of two beats and lightly tap the beats in a given tempo. Do the same thing for a measure of three beats, four, and even five. The duration or timing of the beat must not change from one meter to another.

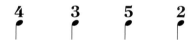

Write a sequence of duple meter signatures on the chalkboard, for example:

After the students have practiced this sequence of meters, let each of them choose a way to perform it four times as if it were a composition. They can either choose to clap it, move it, or play it on an instrument. Be sure that they experience a slight accent on the first beat of each measure. The phrase will sound like this:

They should also vocalize the phrase by singing and holding each word for the duration of the measure. Syllables are given for a suggested melody.

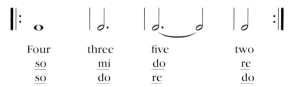

183

3   Playing the 'Game of Five.'

These directions are for circles of six or eight students but this can be done in lines where there is space to move forward and backward. At a tempo established by a leader, the students step into the circle with five steps (clicking fingers on 'one'). They turn and step out four counts, in three, out two and in one.

> Step in five,
> out four
> in three
> out two
> in one

Variation 1: Immediately, after that last count on 'one,' students can turn and reverse the first part, continuing clicks.

> out two
> in three
> out four
> in five.

Variation 2: Students count off with letters A and B and perform the above in canon. The A's begin and the B's start when A's begin their second measure (four counts). They must feel comfortable doing it in unison before this variation is tried. Be sure they continue the clicking of fingers on every first beat.

Variation 3: This variation looks more difficult than it is. Have the A's face out from the circle and the B's face in. The A's begin the sequence by moving out from the circle first and the B's move in towards the center, like an accordion. They begin at the same time.

Variation 4: Repeat Variation 3 but give percussion instruments to a few students in the A group and to a few in the B group. Perform the sequence with the instruments playing the first beat of each measure as the rest of the class steps. Eventually, have both groups try to perform only the instrumental part, thinking the silent beats.

Variation 5: This variation takes a great deal of concentration and is difficult. The whole exercise is performed in a two-part canon, but only the first beat of each 'measure' (set) is sounded. If each group has a distinct sound to make for their part, the resulting rhythm of the canon is interesting and fun to hear.

4   Exploring the meter and rhythm of a new song with eurhythmics.

Here is a delightful song, 'Finale,' which changes meter often and yet is very easy to learn. It is from a group of five songs by Keith Bissell called 'Children's Games.' Although I have included his complete arrangement for chorus and Orff instruments, the experiences described below are sequenced and pertain only to teaching the rhythm.

184

Finale

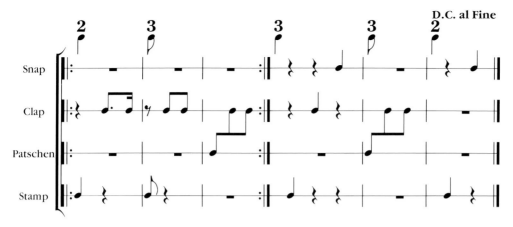

(from *Songs for Singing and Playing*)

A   Establish a quarter-note tempo and have the students step until you say 'Change,' when they will change to stepping eighth notes. At the signal 'Back,' they should return to quarter notes. Their response must be accurate and precise.

B   Using the same exercise, signal the class to step so many eighth notes (between two and six) and then return to quarters. Signal the number three often so that the students begin to feel comfortable stepping a measure of $\frac{3}{8}$ in the middle of a string of quarters.

C   Put on the chalkboard:

The students should practice stepping exactly what the meter signatures say – the 'skeleton' of the rhythm, which is the meter.

Repeat this several times with a clap on the beginning of each measure. Try another phrase below the first one.

Ask a student to notate the measures. Now practice the whole song – three phrases, the first one is repeated.

D   Have the students experiment with ways to conduct this song. Since it is to be sung 'lively,' the measures in three should probably be conducted as one beat (𝅗𝅥.). While they are exploring the conducting, play the melody of the song for them.

E   Having heard the melody, can they sing it on 'loo' as they practice the conducting? Next, challenge them to clap the rhythm of the song and step it. Be sure that you play

186

the dotted pattern so that they step it with an energetic and lively skip. Invite them to put a finger snap on the last beat.

F   The instrumental parts of this song can also be explored in movement. The rhythm of all the xylophone parts is particularly interesting in movement. Let the students hear these by ear and then translate what they hear into movement.

G   This song, with instrumental accompaniment and movement, could be a good finale for a program with these various activities sequenced into a composition. I would like to suggest a second verse to include the words 'end of our clapping,' 'end of our moving,' 'end of our fun.' My students created a simple movement sequence by stepping in a circle to the left on the first phrase, to the right on the second, and on the last phrase, they stepped three quarters into the center, back out on the eighths, stamped the last note and threw the final snap over their heads.

Unusual Meters – Unequal Beats

In the song 'Finale,' the meter changed almost every measure. The overall sequence was:

When students perform this song, they experience the change in beat feeling from quarters to dotted quarters when the meter changes. They should realize that the inner pulse of the eighth note remains constant. One experience that might be added to the ones previously described is to use the wrist–tip motion on all eighths as the song is sung. The students should recognize that the eighths (*a*) are constant, or equal, but the beat (*b*) changes from quarter notes to dotted quarters. Because the change happens between measures, it is called changing meter.

   When duple and triple beats are combined in the same measure, the meter can be called unusual. Here are a few examples from familiar music showing meters in which duple and triple beats have been combined. Usually it is possible to discern whether the beats are duple or triple by the way the notes are grouped or by the melody. Try these yourself so that you have a good feel for unequal beats before you lead the following exercises.

Tchaikovsky, Symphony No. 6, 2nd movement:

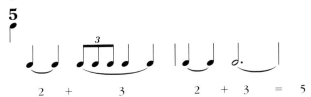

Holst, 'Mars' from *The Planets*:

$$3 \quad + \quad 2 \quad = \quad 5$$

Dave Brubeck, 'Unsquare Dance':

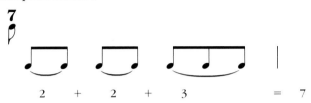

$$2 \quad + \quad 2 \quad + \quad 3 \quad = \quad 7$$

If you think back to Chapter Five, when experiences with duple beats (♩ = ♫) and triple beats (♩. = ♫♫) were described, attention was given to the sound of 'yankee' in 'Yankee Doodle' as a duple division of the quarter-note beat and the sound of 'merrily' in 'Row, Row, Row Your Boat' as a triple division of the dotted quarter-note beat. I like to continue using the same clues as yardsticks or guidelines to help students further their knowledge and understanding. They need consistency in procedure, activities and vocabulary to assure carry-over from one lesson to another and from year to year.

Suppose you combined 'yankee' and 'merrily' into measures. As students speak the following exercise, be sure that each syllable is of the same duration. 'Merrily' must not sound like a triplet. Put a slight accent on the beginning of each word (the beat) and it will be easy to hear and feel the unequal beats.

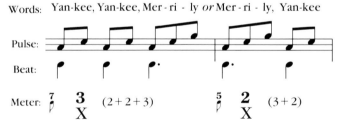

There are several ways to notate an unusual meter. In the first example shown above, there are three prominent beats in the measure, ♩♩♩ but because they are of unequal length an 'X' is used in the meter signature instead of a given note value. In Bartók's music, an indication of the duple/triple meter is given in parentheses as you see above. I feel that if a performer is directed to think only eighth notes, as in ⁷⁄₈ , the performance has a tendency to plod along and is unmusical. Here are some meter signatures and their more common arrangement of unequal beats:

In each case, students should be aware of an inner pulse which is constant and the more prominent, or larger-beat feeling which will be a combination of duple and triple beats.

The following exercises can be used to develop students' awareness and feel for music with unequal beats.

1   *Feeling the grouping of pulses and the unequal beats.*

■   **Listen to this music; find the beat and pat it on your knees.**

(I have included three examples below.) Be sure that the music you play encourages students to hear the groupings of the pulse. The accents should not be too obvious, but think of each grouping as a gesture in motion or speech. For example:

= *Have*-n't you *seen* it?

■   **Can you detect the inner pulse of the beats?**
■   **Can you tell whether the beats are duple or triple?**
■   **Pat the accent on one knee and fill in the steady pulses on the other knee.**

Notice that I have not mentioned quarters or eighths; the sounds are all relative and the students are not looking at notation.

■   **Take away the pulse; pat only the beat.**

If they have learned to show the length of a beat by the size of their movement, they will see, as well as feel the unequal beats.

189

2 *Swinging on triple beats and push–pulling on duple beats.*

Asking students to show the difference between triple and duple beats with these motions has proven helpful. It does not work with every example of music that has unequal beats, but it is included here as another option for movement. With a partner, students touch hands or at least mirror each others' motions and swing their arms from side to side on triple beats or push–pull on duple beats. Even without music, you could speak,

mer - ri - ly,   mer - ri - ly,   yan - kee,   yan - kee,   yan - kee
(swing   swing   push   pull   push)

3 *Singing the scale with unequal beats.*

Put the syllable letters on the chalkboard with quarter notes above each.

d   r   m   f   s   l   t   d

As the class sings the scale up and down, have them use one of the 'measuring sticks' to feel the eighth notes within each quarter, either the wrist–tip motion, or one hand patting the beat and the other, the pulse.

    Next, change one of the quarters to a dotted quarter and repeat the same exercise. The students will enjoy adding more dotted quarters themselves. Here is one possibility:

You might want to show the eighths below the scale as I have done above.

4 *Changing the meter of a familiar song.*

In this exercise, students will change the meter of 'Are You Sleeping?' from $\frac{4}{4}$ to $\frac{4}{x}$ (or $\frac{9}{8}$). The simple rhythm of this song makes it particularly easy and adaptable for this experience; it also seems more exact when sung in English rather than French. Notate the four measures of rhythm from the song on a transparency. Although the measures are repeated, they don't need to be notated here. Ask your students to sing 'Are You Sleeping?' and at the same time, use one of the motions in the previous exercise to 'measure' the beats (either duple or triple).

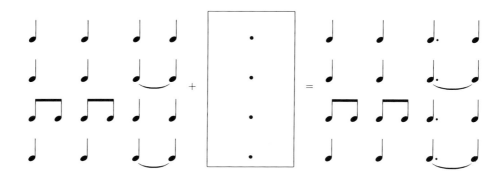

On another half sheet of transparency, put four dots in place so that when they are lined up on top of the original rhythm, one beat will become a dotted quarter. Line it up, at first, after the third beat of each measure. Ask the students to 'read' the revised notation (shown above, on the right) and sing the song again. If they 'measure' the beats with their hands, they will see and experience the dotted quarter on the third beat.

The meter signature for the song will now be $\frac{4}{x}$ meaning that the beats are not all equal. It is possible to place the dots on the first, second or fourth beats but the song is more difficult to sing that way. Try this with other familiar songs.

5   *Creating a composition in unusual meters.*

Give the students suggestions of unusual meters which they will use for a composition, or simple improvisation. For instance:

A. $\frac{7}{p}$ (3 + 2 + 2)

B. $\frac{4}{x}$ (2 + 2 + 2 + 3)

The students should work in groups and design a composition either in movement, singing or playing instruments, or a combination of any of those. They might determine their own choice of meter as well.

191

6 Practicing a two-part rhythm in a meter of five.

Put the following rhythmic example on a transparency and number the measures.

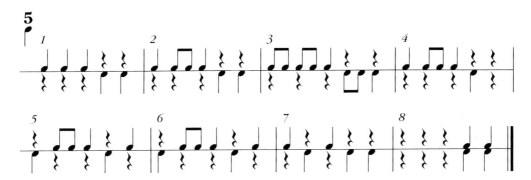

Half of the class can perform the rhythm with the stems going up and the others, the stems going down. You may want to use the quick-reaction technique and call out measures they need to correct or repeat for clarity. For instance, if they are having trouble with measure three, call out 'three' on the last beat of the previous measure so they have a chance to correct their error. You can keep returning to measure three until they seem to be comfortable with it. Encourage the students to clap to a partner as though they are conversing. I realize that at first their eyes will be on the notation and not on their partner, but later, they may be able to follow the same 'metric skeleton' (3 + 2) and improvise with a partner.

7 Performing a song with a meter of five.

'This tune' by Clark Bell has been a favorite of mine to help students feel a meter in five.

This Tune

Words and Music: Clark Bell
Verse 3: Mead

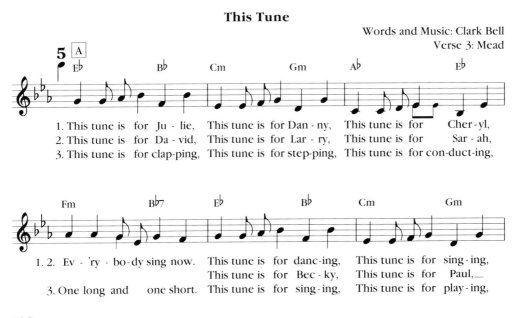

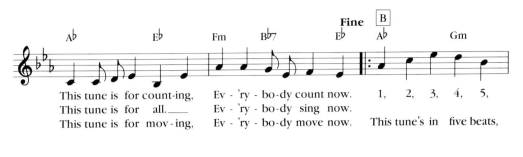

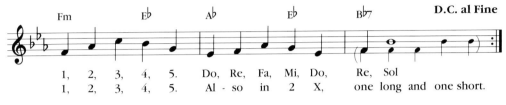

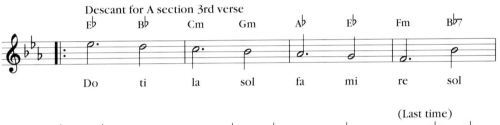

(from *Mixed Metres for Minors*, Book and LP Record)
Copyright 1975: Clark Bell Productions
P.O. Box 1237 Boca Raton, Fl 33432 USA

The song is notated here in the original version but verse three evolved out of eurhythmics experiences I designed to teach the song. If the students have completed the previous experiences with unequal beats, they should be able to sight-read the rhythm of the whole song and sing the descant with solfège. The scale study in No. 3 above can be notated with half and dotted half notes.

Many of the previously described activities can be explored with this song but here are a few which I urge you to do.

● Clark Bell suggests that students translate the 3 + 2 pulse to stepping. It looks and feels like a peg-leg walk.

Left right right left right

193

- Students who perform this song and rhythm well can easily improvise in five meter on a percussion instrument.
- After working on this song for a while, hide the score and see whether your class can notate the whole song.

Musical Expression

Last, but not least, is the important task of teaching musical expression or developing musicality. Although there are many things that influence the way we express a musical phrase, this section will focus on rhythm which is the energy and life of a phrase moving through time. In our teaching we spend a great deal of time on individual aspects of rhythm such as beat, accent, meter and patterns but little time on how to express something musically. From the beginning of students' music education, we should expose them to experiences which are of the highest degree of musical expressiveness. Whether we sing 'Happy Birthday' for the thousandth time, or play the melody of a Chopin mazurka to illustrate a musical concept, we should strive to perform the music with a sensitivity to all the nuances of expressiveness such as dynamics, accentuation, tempo and articulation.

Musical expression is the result of connecting sequential sounds in a meaningful way so that each is an important part of a larger idea. One of the most natural ways to realize this is to sense a continuing line through a phrase. How do you do this? Anyone who has studied Dalcroze eurhythmics knows how vivid the sensation of 'line' can be when a musical idea is stepped or moved in space. This is, for me, the essence of eurhythmics. How many times have we heard a private teacher, a choral director or orchestral conductor ask for 'more line' in the performance? As we experience the connecting of sounds in a musical line, our attention is drawn to how and when the energy of the phrase is expended. The nuances of dynamics, accentuation, tempo and articulation work together with the natural flow of energy to create expression in the music.

How can we teach musical expression? Very young children will instinctively imitate our subtleties of expression when we sing or play for them and this is the way to begin. We should encourage students to translate the unique characteristics of the music into any movement response, for instance, duration, intensity and articulation. As they become older, we need to encourage expressiveness in every musical response; we need to talk about it and help them become aware of what it is that makes something expressive.

There are several ways to help students become aware of musical expression. These first few exercises are to be done without music so that students can imagine and sense, kinesthetically, the continuum of sound in a musical phrase or line. More sophisticated eurhythmics experiences will follow.

1   *'Threading' a line of beats.*

Ask the students to imagine that they are moving a garden hose on a lawn. They will need to walk then pull or stretch the hose.

- **Walk four beats, then pull four beats;**
- **Walk four, then pull five;**

194

- **Walk four, pull six, etc.**
- **Continue until you are stretching a long measure of eight beats.**
- **Put a finger snap on the first beat of each measure.**

The pulling sensation will help them experience a slight resistance as their body measures a certain number of beats.

Here is a variation on that exercise. It is virtually the same idea but the students will have to be even more imaginative. Standing and facing a partner, they should imagine that they have a magnet and they can pull their partner towards them – by an arm, a shoulder, a foot or the nose. Establish a tempo for counting beats but do not use music. They will alternate 'measures,' beginning with four beats, then five, six, seven, eight; then reverse the counting – seven, six, and so on.

2 *Clapping a message or phrase around a circle.*

Students group themselves in circles of three or six and choose someone in their circle to begin the exercise. Each person will clap one word or syllable of a phrase as it travels around the circle several times. Try these two phrases, or something similar.

Tick   tack   toe.   What 'cha know, Joe?

Notice that with the first phrase, there will be three claps (three sounds) and the same student will always begin the phrase. For the second phrase, there will be four claps (four sounds) and therefore a different student will start the phrase each time.

Here are a few ways that you can help students experience that sense of line in their response which can be transferred to a musical response later.

- Suggest that they imagine the clapping to be 'speaking the phrase.'
- Remind them (if necessary) that some words sound longer than others and the movement should continue through the words.
- Encourage them to speak and clap the phrase as though they are sending it around the circle.

Now, we should look more closely into ways of helping students perform music with a sense of line and with attention to how much or how little energy flows from one beat to the next.

3 *Experiencing subtleties of expression in speaking.*

This activity, which will focus on expression in speech, is closely related to the flow of energy and breath in singing and playing music. The same nuances which we use in speech can be used in musical expression and should be explored by students. Write the following word phrases on the chalkboard.

Rain!	I like the rain.	Rain on the grass.
A wonderful rain.		It's raining all around the town.
My, it's nice!		The rain fell softly all night long.
Have you ever seen so much rain?		I'd rather have snow!

Ask individual students to read these aloud, with expression. Encourage them to gesture the important words with their hands at the same time as they are expressing each phrase with their voices. Let them try different ways of saying the same phrase. Guide them to analyze how and why a phrase is spoken with expression. Encourage them to use some of the same terms that we use with any sounds or with music: accent, dynamics, tempo, articulation, pitch, for example. Translate the descriptive words that the students use into musical terms whenever it is appropriate.

4   *Feeling the movement of beats in time and space.*

For this simple exercise the students will clap measures of $\frac{4}{\bullet}$ meter from left to right so as to feel the timing and energy of the beats in space. Suggest that they are communicating or 'giving' these measures to someone. Your aim should be for them to experience the flow of energy as it travels in a line, though the crusis (or accent) of the first beat, on through the second and third beats to the fourth-beat anacrusis (or preparation) for the next measure. Continue this at one tempo until you can see that the students are experiencing the function of each beat in the measure. Try the same exercise in different tempos. You will probably notice a change in the spacing of their claps.

The next step is to substitute a rhythm for one of the beats, for instance,

■   **Change the fourth beat to two eighths.**

Once they begin to clap measures of rhythm, they may lose the sense of a continuing line in their clapping, so don't add too much, too soon. Immediately, invite them to talk about this experience and see if they can transfer what they are experiencing to singing a familiar song or to playing instruments.

5   *Exploring how the phenomenon of line and the extent of energy expended in a musical example can determine expression.*

'Tzena, Tzena' is an exciting song in which the overall movement of energy and built-in accentuation can invite students to perform with all the nuances of musical expression.

Tzena, Tzena

Words: Mitchell Parish
Music: Issachor Miron and Julius Grossman

Teach this song to your students and let them experience performing it in a variety of ways: singing and conducting, clapping the rhythm, walking the beat and singing, stepping the rhythm. Lead them in a discussion of the unique aspects of the music and guide them in determining how to express it musically. Often, it is the text that determines the nuances of expression but with this song, the music itself gives us clues. Guide the students to realize that, as with instrumental music, these determinations can be made from the music alone. You want to help them to understand that it is more than text that determines musical expression.

Here are two aspects of the song 'Tzena, Tzena' which help determine how we perform it.

A   The dotted rhythm on the first beat of some measures is particularly crusic and propels the music forward. It is natural to express these accents at the beginning of the measures and then on the last beat of the measure crescendo slightly in preparation for the next crusis.

197

B   The crusis at the beginning of other measures is the result of an intensity of energy on elongated and higher pitches. In both instances, it is natural to accent the pitch and then let the breath 'spin out' through the measure.

It is not enough to say simply 'accent that word,' or 'that note.' The accent will tend to be isolated; only one word or note will be given attention. Singing or playing a musical line means giving attention to each note in the phrase and being aware of its place in the whole phrase or composition. Each crusic point has a slightly different quality. Let your students use their imaginations to compare the impulse of a water sprinkler, flicking a mosquito off the arm, hitting a golf ball, tossing a balloon, corn popping. Each of these has a different quality of movement just as the crusic accents in the song are different in character.

All of these ideas about the rhythm are best realized and understood through movement of the whole body, as in eurhythmics. When this is not possible, clapping will have to take the place of the locomotor movement. This is why clapping must express all the nuances which are naturally found in the music.

6   *Planning the musical expression of a song.*

'Ifca's Castle' can be performed in a round. An interesting accompaniment can be achieved by having eight students sing the refrain continually, each entering two measures later.

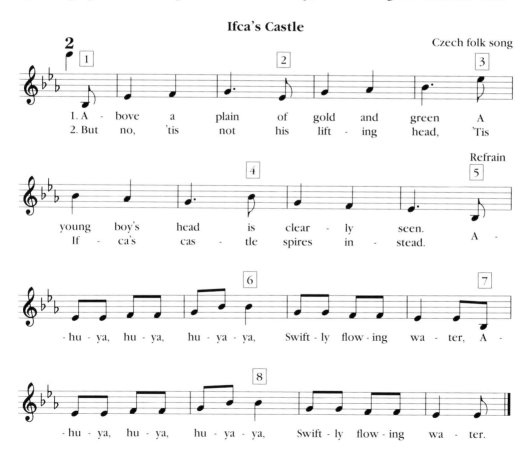

Ifca's Castle

Czech folk song

1. A - bove a plain of gold and green A
2. But no, 'tis not his lift - ing head, 'Tis

young boy's head is clear - ly seen.
If - ca's cas - tle spires in - stead. A -

Refrain

-hu - ya, hu - ya, hu - ya - ya, Swift - ly flow - ing wa - ter, A -

-hu - ya, hu - ya, hu - ya - ya, Swift - ly flow - ing wa - ter.

198

After you have taught the song, divide the class into small groups to plan how this song should be sung with expression. The groups can share their ideas and then decide how the whole class will express the song. Hopefully, they will notice the rise and fall of the melody. As an accompaniment to the singing, invite the groups to create movement to illustrate this melodic characteristic. Dynamics usually are a natural outgrowth of this experience. When it is all performed as a round, the movement and the singing together give the effect of waves of water rising and falling. It is quite a beautiful picture to see and hear.

It is possible that your students will become more sensitive to expression in music as they compare one song with another and plan and perform their own arrangement of songs. The more they are involved in the discussion, experimenting and planning, the more they will be motivated to perform musically.

Conclusion

It has been a most gratifying experience for me to have finally written down so many of my strong beliefs, ideas, teaching techniques and a few tricks that I discovered by chance along the way – all deeply influenced by the Dalcroze approach. I can only hope that what I have learned will help you, as well. This book is really just a beginning. You will be modifying these ideas and techniques in ways that best suit your students, your individual situation, and your own teaching style. The same ideas can be used in various contexts and repeated many times with variations in the exercises and with new musical examples.

Experiences with eurhythmics can continue to influence one's musical development throughout life, especially as one develops a keener awareness of the connection between the ear hearing music, the body feeling it through movement, and the mind thinking and acting upon what was heard.

In the first part of the book, you were introduced to the man Emile Jaques-Dalcroze, his inspiring professional career, and the observations and beliefs which led him to develop his approach to teaching music. A description of the approach, its three components – eurhythmics, solfege and improvisation – and the relationship between them was given. I related my own understanding of the Dalcroze approach and shared the reasons why I believe it should be at the core of all music teaching as well as a prominent part in the sequence of any music learning. In the third chapter I explained some techniques which have been particularly successful or effective in my classes and which, over the years, I have revised and elaborated in my own way. Some of those techniques and guidelines are appropriate to many music teaching situations. I have tried, in several instances, to speak of the possibility of adapting Dalcroze techniques to the elementary music classroom where classes are large and space and time are limited.

Part Two was divided into experiences for primary, intermediate and upper grades. In the Dalcroze approach, many of the experiences are variations of basic games or exercises with further development of skills and understanding. If you have read the chapters for all three levels, you will have discovered that you can adapt experiences given for one grade level to another. Many of these experiences can be adapted for the beginner as well as the very advanced student.

While reading this book, you may have felt that the same experiences were being repeated over and over and that the same skills and understandings were being developed at all levels. That is not exactly true. Any kinesthetic development must be repeated many times in order to be learned. Think of the athlete, the dancer, the instrumentalist; it takes countless hours to train the muscles. As we have seen, the basis of eurhythmics is the development of a kinesthetic awareness of the properties of sound. The awareness is then manifested in a physical response or an internalizing of the sound property. Because eurhythmics is rarely at the core of music teaching in the schools (though I believe it should be), it remains a unique music education approach for all students. Therefore, the most basic experiences must be repeated over and over.

In conclusion, I want to close with a few important reminders for any movement and music experience that you plan for your classes. These are based on the suggestions and guidelines presented in this book.

1   Let the music do the teaching whenever possible. Step away and allow the children to truly have an experience with the music. Allow them opportunities to assume some responsibility for their own listening and response. In other words, give them some freedom to imagine, to create ways to show the music in movement or to discuss among themselves what they hear.

2   Focus the initial response to listening on a natural or instinctive physical movement, probably to some aspect of the timing or energy in the music.

3   Express the duration and dynamics of sound in movement responses in the same way as you would any singing or playing response. Other elements and nuances heard in the music will eventually be expressed in movement; when this happens they should be acknowledged and encouraged. These elements include: accentuation, articulation, melody direction, harmonic change, and so on.

4   Demonstrate visually with movement what is experienced aurally and physically and enjoyed emotionally. Use every opportunity possible to 'draw' (in the air, on the arm, with a finger on the floor or table, on large newsprint) what the movement represents. If planned and sequenced well, this can result in writing and reading notation.

5   Adapt many eurhythmics exercises to singing and improvising experiences which will further allow the children to internalize the music and use what they have felt in movement.

6   Be inventive and resourceful when you are faced with space limitations. Don't be intimidated in your planning or in your efforts to use eurhythmics in the classroom. Sometimes children will arrive at unique solutions to the problem of lack of space. Start with the children seated; next, let them stand; finally, then pose the problem of

■   **Can you find a spot on the floor where you can ...**

Encourage them to use the space available as freely and creatively as possible. When asked to do something with a partner, or a small group, the children usually can find some space in a corner or a path in which to move.

7   Relate movement experiences to natural everyday gestures. If you think about the various ways we gesture with our hands or use body language to express an idea, a musical line should also be expressed with meaning. If you set an example, the children will imitate you. I have always defined clapping in one spot as applause and that's not why we are clapping in eurhythmics. It is the same with stepping; children can learn to step a

phrase or rhythm as a musical line – imagining that it is leading towards something or away from something.

8 Listen carefully to your musical example and be sure that it truly expresses what you want the children to hear and then to feel in movement.

Your understanding and awareness of the value of these ideas will be further realized only when you are able to experience eurhythmics at your own level. Eurhythmics is something that you can hardly read about and then expect to know or understand how vividly it awakens the whole body to the totality of the musical experience. You must experience it for yourself.

How can you learn more about the Dalcroze approach? There are workshops and conferences offered throughout the United States as well as Europe, Asia and Australia. These provide an opportunity for active participation to anyone interested. The Dalcroze Society of America sponsors a biennial national conference with regional conferences in the intervening years. There are local chapters of the Dalcroze Society: the Tristate Chapter in and around New York City, chapters in Los Angeles, Seattle, Boston and a Great Lakes Chapter with members from Illinois, Wisconsin and Michigan. A number of Schools of Music offer courses in Dalcroze work, some of which carry credit toward certification. The following schools are authorized to grant certification:

Carnegie Mellon University
Department of Music
Pittsburgh, PA 15213

Longy School of Music
One Follen Street
Cambridge, MA 02138

Dalcroze School of Music
161 East 73rd Street
New York, NY 10021

Manhattan School of Music
120 Claremont Avenue
New York, NY 10027

You are welcome to become a member of the Dalcroze Society of America. Members receive the *American Dalcroze Journal* which is published three times a year and which contains articles, teaching ideas and news and information about courses, workshops and conferences. For more information, write to:

Dalcroze Society of America,
613 Putnam Drive,
Eau Claire, WI 54701.

Appendix A

Keyboard Improvisation

How often do you get in your car, start the motor and drive down the street without thinking? How often do you fix your breakfast while still half asleep? What we do regularly becomes a habit; we are comfortable doing it and we don't have to plan the next step. How often do you decorate your living room? How often do you improvise at the piano? For most people, the answer is rarely, if ever. How can you expect to be comfortable and sure of yourself doing something only once in a while?

The following guidelines and suggestions for practicing improvisation have been gleaned from many sources, friends and colleagues. It would be impossible to determine the source of each idea but hopefully collecting and printing them will inspire some systematic practice on your part. An art teacher once said, 'If you are serious about learning to draw, you should do at least one sketch a day.' Might this also hold true if you want to learn to improvise? You must improvise!

Why improvise? First of all, it can be important for your own enjoyment of creating and expressing musical thoughts, or, for exploring such elements as colors, textures, and dynamics in music. Dalcroze maintained that with just two pitches you can express a musical idea that implies a melody, rhythm and harmony. Improvising can further develop your musicianship. Since it is your own creation, your ear pays close attention to what is happening. Your musical imagination and knowledge come to the foreground of your thought as you explore the keyboard. You discover new sounds and new ways of expressing them. Improvising is an opportunity to develop freedom and facility to create simple musical examples for teaching at any level, in any situation. A musician–teacher will find it beneficial to improvise a musical example to clarify a point or to design an on-the-spot ear-training game. A licensed Dalcroze teacher must be able to improvise, yet that is the part of the training that frightens so many people. Dalcroze believed that with improvised music for eurhythmics and solfège experiences, we can develop more attentive and responsive listeners. Improvised music is not always predictable, which means the teacher can, at an appropriate moment, change the mode, tempo, meter or dynamics for instance. In addition, by improvising musical examples, a teacher has more capability and freedom to respond appropriately to changes and subtle nuances in the students' movement.

Since there are often negative feelings expressed about improvising, here are some tips for a helpful, healthy attitude or frame of mind in which to begin. The following suggestions are meant for beginners or those persons who lack confidence and don't have much incentive to practice or even try.

1 In the early stages of practice, it is the doing that counts, not the finished product.

2 Have a musical idea (a rhythm, a melodic gesture, a muscular sensation of timing and energy) before you start. Feel it in your arms, hands and in your whole body. Hear it in your

'thinking ear.' Prepare to play by moving, gesturing or playing in the air to realize the physical feel and expression of what you are imagining. This seems like a long process, but it really isn't. Within a second or two, you will 'hear' an idea with your fingers.

3   Always play what you hear (in your mind or inner ear), and hear what you play (with your expressive fingers). What you play should be an extension of your 'thinking voice.' Mentally sing it!

4   Once you begin, follow it, possessively, with your ear. It's yours! Keep going. Don't give up in disappointment or frustration. It is too easy to stop and decide that it's time for a cup of coffee! Don't! Insist that you always find an ending or a satisfying cadence.

5   In the beginning, do not evaluate; just listen and assume a receptive attitude – one of curiosity and interest in what you are hearing. It is so easy to compare your initial efforts with the memory of someone else's improvisation. If you are receptive to what you are playing, it is natural that you will try to make it more interesting.

6   One usually uses too much material; your earliest efforts should be simple. Try to remember what you have played, repeat it with a sense of purpose as though meaning to do so. Then let it develop, remembering that a returning idea (a recapitulation) is satisfying.

7   It is also important to have contrasting material or contrasting sections. When you are improvising, there are many possibilities for contrast in meter, dynamics, tonality, and so on. Another suggestion is to think 'the opposite.' Explore possibilities by playing a short motive with one hand and immediately try to play the opposite – direction of melody, tempo, articulation, note values – in the other hand.

8   Think of your beginning idea as the seed of an idea and let it grow. Embellish it, repeat it, vary it, mirror it. For practice, play a sort of 'follow the leader' game with another person at the same piano. Whatever the first person plays, the second person either plays a repetition of the idea, a contrasting idea, or a variation.

9   If you hear something that you think sounds wrong, or that you just don't like, try repeating it as though you meant it. Make it important and let it resolve naturally.

10   Use silence to highlight something. Let your music breathe. Allow tense, dissonant, 'wrong' places to resolve naturally.

11   As you begin to feel more comfortable improvising, concentrate on creating an interesting melody or on a sense of phrasing in the music. Let the music sing; sing silently along with it.

12   When you begin to improvise, think shape, line, gesture, emotion, dynamics, expression, rather than scale, key, chords, pitch, rhythm pattern.

And now for some specific ideas and models for you to try. For some of the following, you will simply be listening and creating line, melody, timing, harmony and resolution. Other suggestions may give you more freedom to explore and develop facility at the keyboard. Some ideas are good listening or ear-training exercises as you explore combinations of pitches in a slow, calm tempo. Still other ideas may give specific improvisation ideas for use in teaching.

1   Begin with one pitch. Repeat it over and over as though singing a song or dancing a dance. Listen and then let it change gradually or suddenly in duration, dynamics, or articulation. Try exploring that one pitch in a different register; you will find it interesting to combine registers.

2   Have a musical conversation with someone else at the same piano or playing another instrument. To begin, each person can play in the other person's silences. As the conversation develops let the voices overlap and the conversation become heated, then let it calm down and resolve to an end.

3   There are various musical materials and elements that can be explored in improvisation. Some are listed here. You should eventually combine two or three of them. For instance, with a black-key ostinato in one hand, and a black-key pentatonic scale in the other hand, improvise music that uses staccato and legato articulation.

black keys   articulation
clusters   tempo
octaves   dynamics
ostinatos   register
triads   texture (thick or thin)
intervals   harmonic progression
scales/modes

4   If you are going to practice improvising you need to set some limitations. Here is a very simple idea which can also be used for a group to explore movement.
Play eight steady counts (not divisions of the beat or a rhythm). For instance: eight quarter notes or eight half notes. Play single pitches, a harmonic progression, clusters – any musical idea of eight steady counts. Here are three examples:

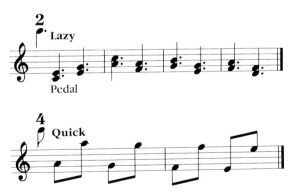

Ask someone to echo what they heard in movement. You will be able to see how effectively you have communicated a musical phrase as you watch them recreate your example in movement. Immediately, without missing a beat, play another phrase of eight counts using different musical material, articulation, or tempo. Don't delay the beginning of each eight-count phrase. It will be a continual pattern of the following:

Player: Improvise eight counts (or equal sounds).

Movers: Echo what was heard, but in movement.

Player: Improvise the next phrase of eight counts.

Movers: Echo that new phrase.

When trying this at home, children can be movers. Let them count out loud so that they keep the tempo steady.

5   Choose three pitches and design a melodic and rhythmic motive to be used to create a composition. Begin by repeating the motive several times and then changing and developing it further. An ostinato can be created as an accompaniment. In the following example, the motive is: D A C.

6   Choose two commands to be used as the nucleus for an improvisation either played by yourself or with another person. For example:

206

Using this pair of greetings, improvise a composition similar to the following.

Try to have a logical and satisfying end. Explore changes in inflection and energy through melody, dynamics, timing and many other aspects of the music. Another example of commands to use:

Get off the grass!   Who said so?

7   Choose an interval. Explore it melodically and harmonically and then choose two or three ideas from your exploration to improvise a short composition. Notice that an interval can be turned upside down, thus creating a new interval. In the example below, the interval is a major second. It is played harmonically on the first beat and then, immediately, as a melody, the interval becomes a minor seventh (D to C). Remember, once you have established an idea, you should let it develop freely; in other words, an improvisation on a major second does not only include major seconds.

8 Choose a work or play movement such as walk, run, skip, swing, jump rope, chop wood, swim, paint. Stand up and actually go through the action. Try to capture the physical feeling in your arms, hands and fingers. Sit down at the piano and play that feeling.

9 Create an ostinato for one hand. Using intervals, triads or clusters in the other hand, improvise a composition.

10 Just as a thread weaves itself through a piece of fabric, a musical thread can be woven through an improvisation. Establish a musical thread to be played continually as you improvise (embellish or fill in the sound) around it. It may sound like an ostinato but it can be very subtle in its simple transparent nature. Here is one idea:

11 Create a chord with any three pitches, close together or wide apart, and at a slow tempo. Play this chord for three or four beats. Listen carefully to the chord. Don't be concerned if it is discordant; let it register in your ear. On the next measure, move one of the voices up or down a half or whole step. You can make your own rules.

Continue, changing one voice on each new measure. Soon you will begin to anticipate which voice you want to change. Delight in any surprises. Allow the dynamics to change naturally as dissonances are created and resolved.

If you listen carefully during this exercise your ear will soon tell you which voice you want to change. The same exercise can be used with students in the upper elementary grades and above to identify which of the three voices have moved and whether they have moved up or down.

12 Improvise on a predetermined rhythm pattern, either using one or two hands. Improvise on this pattern in a scale from D to A.

208

13 Create an ostinato in the left hand, using E♭, B♭ and F. With the right hand improvise a black-key melody. Remember to improvise in different meters, tempos, moods, with different rhythms, etc. Here are four different possibilities for the ostinato:

14 Using a black-key ostinato in one hand, improvise with white-key triads in the other hand.

15 Choose a simple folk song that you can play well from memory, even with your eyes closed. Play it everywhere on the piano, in every key, in different meters, disguising it as much as possible and yet using it as the basis for an improvisation. Try this with several folk songs for practice.

16 Create from a model. Find a book of very simple piano music – something a beginning piano student might use. Read and play the first two measures of a composition, look away and improvise the remainder of the piece.

17 Improvising in modes or other scale arrangements is a wonderful way to open ears, or perhaps clear the ears of the hierarchy of tonic–subdominant–dominant harmony which we all learned so thoroughly in college. The simplest way to begin exploring the modes is to play only on the white keys of the piano. Later, you can transpose the modes to other pitches on the keyboard. To improvise in the Dorian mode, use the white-key scale (no accidentals), but center around D. To improvise in the Phrygian mode, play a white-key scale from E to E. F to F is the Lydian mode, G to G is the Mixolydian and A to A (the natural minor scale) is the Aeolian mode. The Locrian mode, B to B, is rarely used, but the Ionian mode, C to C, is the major scale.

Use a simple ostinato in the left hand and concentrate on a pleasing melody in the right hand. Stay away from any hint of tonic, subdominant or dominant harmony in the melody although an ostinato on I and V in the mode is the easiest to perform.

Other scales to explore are the pentatonic, whole tone, and one simple version of the blues scale:

C   D   E♭   F   F♯   G   B♭   C

An easy way to begin improvising in the whole-tone scale is to establish a mind set which tells you that the only keys on the piano are:

C   D   E   and   F♯   G♯   A♯

Concentrate on seeing only those keys. Explore possibilities for using them in clusters, melodies and arpeggios.

18   Recite a poem in a very rhythmic and expressive way. A nursery rhyme works well. For example:

> Jack and Jill went up the hill
> To fetch a pail of water.
> Jack fell down and broke his crown
> And Jill came tumbling after.

Say it several times and 'play' it with your fingers on your lap or on a hard surface, using both hands with lots of finger action. Continue speaking the rhyme and 'play it' on the wood above the piano keyboard. Next, drop your fingers onto the black keys of the piano and play the rhyme. It should be very rhythmic and alive.

Now it is up to you – you should try to improvise something every day. For a while, simply explore, enjoy and create with sounds at the piano, but always begin with a sound that you can hear or imagine in your inner ear and that you can sense kinesthetically.

(This is a revised version of an article that first appeared in the *American Dalcroze Society Journal*, Fall, 1990)

Appendix B

Directions for Properties

Kites

For each kite, cut two diamond-shaped pieces of colored paper, about the size of a child's hand. Connect the two pieces with a strip of paper, about an inch wide, attached at the center of each kite, so that the child can slide it between two fingers. One kite will cover the palm of the hand and the other one will cover the back of the hand. Tape or staple colored twisted crepe paper streamers to the end of one kite for a tail.

Small Rhythm Sticks

Buy 36″ dowel sticks, $\frac{1}{4}$ inch in diameter. Cut them in four equal lengths; sand the ends; then brush them with polyurethane.

Step Bell Ladder

Measure, then cut with a dull knife, a solid piece of styrofoam (even an odd piece used for packing). The measurements are: Width, $3\frac{1}{2}″$; Length, 16″; Height, 11″.
The other measurements are shown on this diagram.
Note: the half steps between
mi and *fa*, *ti* and *do* are 1″ high.

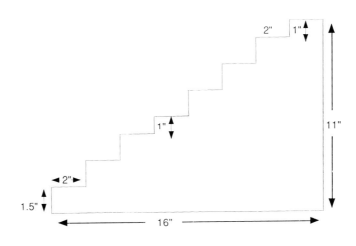

Yarn Balls

Use rug yarn. The heavier the yarn, the firmer the ball will be. Prepare two cardboard disks with holes in the center. The diameter of the disks determines the size of the ball. These are bound together by winding the yarn through the hole in the center and around the doughnut shape. Either use small balls of yarn to force it through the hole or you can cut a slit in the disks to slip the yarn through. Be careful, however, because eventually you want to cover the whole circle. When the surface is covered and the center hole has almost disappeared, insert scissors between the discs around the outer edge so that you can cut the yarn. Cut all around the outer edge; pull the discs slightly apart and wind a piece of string (not yarn) tightly, around the center to hold the yarn in place. Secure it with a tight knot and trim the ends. Either slit the disks to remove them or gently pull them away. Puff up the ball and trim, if necessary.

Note Cards

The cards can either be $3 \times 5''$ or $4 \times 5\frac{1}{2}''$ index cards. If you make the $4 \times 5\frac{1}{2}''$ cards, you can put several on a full sheet of card stock and make copies before you cut them and have them laminated. If you choose to use packages of $3 \times 5''$ cards, you will have to draw the notes on each individual card. The $3 \times 5''$ cards take up less room when they are laid out in a line for notating a phrase of rhythm.

Appendix C

Eurhythmics Experiences in Chapter Four

Exploring movement

1 Experiencing different ways of walking.
2 Imagining movement in pictures.
3 Telling a story in movement.
4 Expressing music with fingers, hands and arms.

Sound and silence: beginning and ending

1 Drawing sound in the air.
2 Moving like parts of a machine; starting and stopping.
3 Listening and anticipating sound and silence in music.
4 Listening and anticipating the length of a song.
5 Singing, moving, and responding to signals – all at the same time.

Timing, beat and tempo

1 Watching the movement of a pendulum.
2 Creating a swinging pendulum with a partner.
3 Responding to the timing in a singing game.
4 Watching and imitating the timing of a bouncing ball.
5 Accompanying songs with work and play rhythms.
6 Using small rhythm sticks to feel a steady beat.
7 Feeling a steady beat twice as fast and twice as slow.
8 Playing a game of timing and energy.
9 Passing a ball to develop a sense of timing and beat.

Hearing and singing pitch

1 Hearing and responding to high and low pitches.
2 Singing the direction of a bouncing ball.
3 Gesturing the direction of pitch in a simple song.

Solfège games

1 Hearing and singing the tonal pattern *so–mi*.

2   Showing the placement of *mi–re–do* in space.
3   Playing solfège games to practice one tonal pattern.
4   Recognizing variations of a familiar pattern.
5   Listening for familiar tonal patterns in a new song.
6   Listening for melody direction.
7   Listening for the direction of melody in a more challenging example.

Duration and rhythm

1   Responding to four basic note values in a story.
2   A Halloween game with quarters, eighths and half notes.
3   Creating machine-like movements for certain note values.
4   Feeling the rhythm of a song in arm and hand gestures.
5   Notating rhythm with a finger or rhythm sticks.
6   Physically feeling the relationship between quarters and eighths.
7   Notating simple rhythmic examples.
8   Listening for specific rhythm patterns.

Accents

1   Using hand motions on accented and unaccented syllables.
2   Bouncing a ball on accented syllables of words.
3   Listening and bouncing a ball on metric accents in music.
4   Finding accents other than the first beat of the measure.
5   Expressing accents, meter and rhythm in creative movement.

Rests

1   Hearing and responding to silence in music.
2   Feeling rests on different beats of the measure.
3   Reading rhythms which include quarter-note rests.
4   Recognizing rests in a fun song.

Listening perceptively; moving expressively

Musical examples

Go Round and Round the Village	Climbing Up the Elevator
Mighty Pretty Motion	Love Somebody
Hickory Dickory Dock	Shoemaker's Song
Sing, Sing Together	Minka
Rig-a-Jig-Jig	Gavotte (Gossec)
Hot Cross Buns	Jeering Song (Bartók)
Sandy Land	Skinnamarink
Clap, Clap, Clap Your hands	There and Back (Finney)

Appendix D

Eurhythmics Experiences in Chapter Five

Exploring movement

1   Feeling the duration of four beats.
2   Changing back and forth from quarters to eighths.
3   Timing movement precisely.

Further response to timing in music

1   Tossing and catching an imaginary ball.
2   Passing the ball.
3   Keeping a steady beat.
4   Passing the ball and counting in a steady tempo.

Meter and measure in music

1   Organizing beats into measures by means of accents.
2   Bouncing a ball on the accent to feel meter.
3   Measuring the meter in familiar music.
4   Understanding the terms and symbols for meter.
5   Picturing the grouping of beats in a measure.
6   Reading beats and bar-lines.
7   Singing in meters.
8   Improvising music in a meter.

Hearing, recognizing and reading divisions of the beat

1   Feeling the beat and its simple divisions.
2   Stepping a division on one beat.
3   Hearing, then echoing divisions of the beat.
4   Differentiating between divisions of the beat in a song.
5   Practicing reading rhythm with beat divisions.
6   Practicing reading pitch and rhythm with beat divisions.
7   Creating music that uses beat and simple beat divisions.

Longer than a beat

1   Creating a long note with a tie.

2 Practicing reading and performing ties.
3 Substituting a dot for a tied note.
4 'Solving' the rhythm of an unfamiliar song.

Using note cards to develop music reading and writing

1 Measuring beats in a meter.
2 Substituting two eighth notes for a quarter-note beat.

A duple beat versus a triple beat

1 Determining the basic division of a beat in two or three.
2 Seeing and feeling a beat and its divisions.
3 Improvising with a duple or triple beat.
4 Introducing uneven divisions of the triple beat.
5 Reading and performing notation in duple- and triple-beat families.

Suggested music for hearing duple- and triple-beats

Anacrusis or pick-up

1 Exploring stressed and unstressed syllables in names.
2 Throwing a ball to feel an anacrusis.
3 Feeling the crusis in a phrase.
4 Feeling the anacrusis and crusis of a phrase.
5 Tracing the phrase movement of a song.

Movement as a preparation for music literacy

1 Highlighting a particular rhythm pattern.
2 Determining how many phrases there are in a song.
3 Determining the length of a phrase by counting the beats.
4 Establishing the placement of beats in a phrase.

More songs to invite movement

'Circle Left'
1 Highlighting basic tonal patterns.
2 A challenge: listening to and performing an assigned part.
3 Creating new words to highlight a pattern.

'The Steamboat'
1 Expressing note values in the motions of a song.
2 Performing a round in movement.
3 Experiencing duration with tennis balls.

4 Recognizing familiar tonal patterns in the song.

'Chumbara'

1 Listening for a rhythm pattern.
2 Tracing the melodic rhythm.
3 Listening for pitch direction.
4 Singing the descending scale with syllables.
5 Drawing a 'sound picture' of the music.
6 Reading and performing a sound picture.

An ensemble experience

1 Highlighting a particular rhythm pattern.
2 Reading and singing tonal patterns to establish the mode.
3 Discovering the order of phrases in a song.
4 Singing a melody while hearing something else.
5 Expressing a melody in movement.
6 Performing in an ensemble experience.

Musical examples

Wally-ach-a

Michael, Row the Boat Ashore

The Boatmen's Dance

Chairs to Mend

Early to Bed

Yankee Doodle

Row, Row, Row Your Boat

Jingle Bells

Over the River, Through the Wood

A Hungarian Folk Song

Circle Left

The Steamboat

Chumbara

Night Time

Appendix E

Eurhythmics Experiences in Chapter Six

Encouraging pre-teens to express music in movement

1   Expressing an idea in movement.
2   Showing the character of a walk.
3   Demonstrating gradual changes in the qualities of movement.
4   Creating a group composition in movement.

Continuing basic eurhythmics experiences

1   Responding to precise changes in rhythmic movement.
2   Creating and reading a two-measure rhythm pattern.
3   Reading longer phrases of rhythm.

More challenging games with tennis balls

1   Responding to subtleties in tempo.
2   Distinguishing between the duple and the triple beat.
3   Distinguishing between duple and triple beats when there is little space for movement.
4   Responding to tempo changes while singing.

Expressive conducting

Duple-beat rhythms

1   Echoing duple-beat rhythms in movement and speech.
2   Reading sixteenth-note rhythms.
3   Singing sixteenth-note patterns.
4   Playing a game with duple rhythms.

Triple-beat rhythms

1   Adding hand movements with triple-beat songs.
2   Speaking triple-beat rhythms.

Is it a meter in three or a triple beat?

A slow triple beat

1 Practicing an unfamiliar rhythm.
2 Reviewing triple-beat rhythmic notation.
3 Practicing phrases of rhythm in various types of activity.

The rhythm-phone

Dotted rhythms

1 Reviewing four basic rhythms.
2 Performing measures of the ♩♪ rhythm in a more musical setting.
3 Reading and performing the 'pizza pie' rhythm.
4 Sight-reading the rhythm of a song that includes many ♩♪ rhythms.
5 Solving a notation puzzle with the fun song 'Three Craw.'
6 Gesturing the ♩. ♪ pattern in arm movements.
7 Experiencing the ♩. ♪ pattern by tossing and catching a tennis ball.
8 Comparing four patterns in movement.
9 Creating music which highlights specific rhythms.

Augmentation and diminution

1 Identifying three different walking tempos with one musical example.
2 Dramatizing movement in augmentation and diminution.
3 Singing a song in augmentation and diminution.
4 Rearranging a song with augmentation and diminution.
5 Singing 'Ghost of Tom' in augmentation and diminution.

Experiences with syncopation

1 Echoing measures of beats with unexpected accents.
2 Comparing syncopated and unsyncopated music.
3 Learning to read syncopated patterns.
4 Discovering how syncopation is notated.

Reviewing previous learnings

1 Experiencing the composite of a syncopated rhythm and a steady beat.
2 Responding to gradual or quick changes in music.
3 Recognizing common minor tonal patterns by hearing and by sight.
4 Experimenting and making decisions on arranging a song.

Rests are silent sounds

1 Feeling the hesitation and silence of rests.
2 Feeling and counting a specific number of rests.
3 Experiencing an active rest.
4 Learning to read rests.
5 Challenging students to read rests.

Changing meter

1 Playing ball to feel changing meter.
2 Feeling the steady beat even though meters are changing.
3 Playing the 'Game of Five.'
4 Exploring the meter and rhythm of a new song with eurhythmics.

Unusual meters – unequal beats

1 Feeling the grouping of pulses and the unequal beats.
2 Swinging on triple beats and push–pulling on duple beats.
3 Singing the scale with unequal beats.
4 Changing the meter of a familiar song.
5 Creating a composition in unusual meters.
6 Practicing a two-part rhythm in a meter of five.
7 Performing a song in a meter of five.

Musical expression

1 'Threading' a line of beats.
2 Clapping a message or phrase around a circle.
3 Experiencing subtleties of expression in speaking.
4 Feeling the movement of beats in time and space.
5 Exploring how the phenomenon of musical line and the energy expended in its performance can determine expression.
6 Planning the musical expression of a song.

Musical examples

A Slovak Dance Tune	We've All Got Rhythm
Noah's Ark	The Canoe Song
We're All Together Again	Land of the Silver Birch
Paddy Works on the Railroad	Debka Hora
Snow	The Cuckoo in the Deep Woods (Saint-Saëns)
I Love the Mountains	Shenandoah
Three Craw	Finale
Feel the Beat	This Tune
Frère Jacques	Tzena, Tzena
Ghost of Tom	Ifca's Castle

A Select Bibliography

Books

ABRAMSON, ROBERT M., *Rhythm Games for Perception and Cognition*. Music Movement Press. 1973.

Two 60 min. cassette tapes of piano improvisation, performed by Abramson, are available for use with the text.

ARONOFF, FRANCES W., *Move with the Music*. Turning Wheel Press. Washington Square Village, NY, 1982.

——*Music and the young child*. Turning Wheel Press. Washington Square Village, NY, 1979.

CHOKSY, LOIS, ROBERT ABRAMSON, and AVON GILLESPIE, *Teaching Music in the Twentieth Century*. Prentice-Hall. 1985.

A comparison of four well-known music methodologies: Kodály, Dalcroze, Orff and Comprehensive Musicianship.

DRIVER, ETHEL, *A Pathway to Dalcroze Eurhythmics*. Thomas Nelson and Sons, London, 1951 (reprint).

DUTOIT, CLAIR-LISE, *Music Movement Therapy*. Dalcroze Society Publication, England, 1965.

FINDLAY, ELSA, *Rhythm and Movement; Applications of Dalcroze Eurhythmics*. Summy-Birchard, 1971.

GELL, HEATHER, *Music, Movement and the Young Child*. Australasian Publishing Co., 1949, 1973.

JAQUES-DALCROZE, EMILE, *Rhythm, Music and Education*. Dalcroze Society Publication, 1921, 1967.

LANDIS, BETH and POLLY CARDER, *The Eclectic Curriculum in American Music Education: Contributions of Dalcroze, Kodály and Orff*. Music Educators National Conference, 1972, 1990.

MACK, GLENN, *Adventures in Improvisation at the Keyboard*. Summy-Birchard, 1970.

NOONA, WALTER AND CAROL, *The Contemporary Performer*. Mainstreams Piano Method 3. The Heritage Music Press, 1975.

ROSENSTRAUCH, HENRIETTA, *Essays on Rhythm, Music, Movement*. Volkwein Bros., 1973.

VANDERSPAR, ELIZABETH, *Dalcroze Handbook*. Principles and Guidelines for Teaching Eurhythmics.

Order from Musik Innovations, 9600 Perry Highway, Pittsburgh, PA 15237. (Tel.: 412–366–3631)

Articles and Studies

ABRAMSON, ROBERT, 'Dalcroze-Based Improvisation.' *Music Educators Journal*. January, 1980.

ARONOFF, FRANCES W., 'Games Teachers Play: Dalcroze Eurhythmics.' *Music Educators Journal*. February, 1971.

BECKNELL, ARTHUR F., 'A History of the Development of Dalcroze Eurhythmics in the United States and Its Influence on the Public School Music Program.' Doctoral diss., University of Michigan, 1970.

FARBER, ANNE, 'Speaking the Musical Language.' *Music Educators Journal*. December, 1991.

FARBER, ANNE and LISA PARKER, 'Discovering Music Through Dalcroze Eurhythmics.' *Music Educators Journal*. November, 1987.

JOSEPH, ANNABELLE S., 'A Dalcroze Approach to Music Learning in Kindergarten.' Doctoral diss., Carnegie Mellon University, 1982.

MEAD, VIRGINIA, 'Keyboard Improvisation.' *American Dalcroze Journal*, Fall, 1990.

——'More Than Mere Movement: Dalcroze Eurhythmics.' *Music Educators Journal*. February, 1986.

Footnotes

Chapter Two

[1] Emile Jaques-Dalcroze, *Rhythm, Music and Education*, Dalcroze Society Publication, Woking 1921, 1967, p. 4.

[2] Emile Jaques-Dalcroze, *Eurhythmics, Art and Education*, New York, Benjamin Blom, N.Y. Inc. 1972, p. 140.

Chapter Four

[1] From Béla Bartók, *For Children*, Vol. 1

[2] From Ross Lee Finney, *25 Inventions*.

Chapter Five

[1] This section refers to a quarter-note beat. However, the same ideas and eurhythmics experiences may be applied to any note value which serves as the beat: ♩. ♪, ♩, ♩ and so on.

[2] Letters refer to the following sources:
Barbara Staton, Merrill Staton and others, *Music and You*, New York, Macmillan, 1988.
Macmillan, 1988.
(A)   Grade Two
(B)   Grade Three
(C)   Grade Five
Jane Beethoven, Jennifer Davidson and Catherine Nadon-Jabzion, World of Music, Morristown, Silver Burdett & Ginn, 1988
(D)   Grade Three
(E)   Grade Four
(F)   Bowmar Orchestral Library. Series 1 *Legends* No. 59, California, Bowmar Records, Inc.

[3] The terms 'anacrusis' and 'crusis' are used in the Dalcroze approach instead of 'pick-up' and 'downbeat.' By the time my students have an understanding of accented and unaccented sounds in music I introduce these terms, but at the same time I might describe something as a 'pick-up into the downbeat of the phrase.' Those two words describe what is happening in the music when there is an anacrusis moving towards a crusis.